THE STATE OF THE WORLD'S REFUGEES

2012

IN SEARCH OF SOLIDARITY

UNHCR

OXFORD
UNIVERSITY PRESS

OXFORD
UNIVERSITY PRESS

Great Clarendon Street, Oxford OX2 6DP
United Kingdom

Oxford University Press is a department of the University of Oxford.
It furthers the University's objective of excellence in research, scholarship,
and education by publishing worldwide. Oxford is a registered trade mark of
Oxford University Press in the UK and in certain other countries.

© UNHCR 2012

This publication seeks to contribute to reflections on forced displacement in the 21st century.
However, the views expressed in this book do not necessarily
represent official statements of UNHCR or United Nations policy.

The maps in this volume do not imply the expression of any opinion on the part of UNHCR
or the United Nations concerning the legal status of any country, territory, city
or area or the delimitation of frontiers or boundaries nor are they warranted to be error-free.

Unless otherwise specified, all maps are produced by the UNHCR Field Information and
Coordination Section of the Division of Programme Support and Management.

Unless otherwise stated, the book does not refer to events occurring after 31 December 2011.

Unless otherwise stated, all statistics are as of 1 January 2011.

Links to third party websites are provided by UNHCR and Oxford in good faith and
for information only. UNHCR and Oxford disclaim any responsibility for the materials
contained in any third party website referenced in this book.

British Library Cataloguing in Publication Data

Data available

Library of Congress Cataloging in Publication Data

Data available

ISBN 978-0-19-965474-1
ISBN 978-0-19-965475-8 (pbk.)

Printed in Barcelona, Spain on acid-free paper by Grafos S.A.
Design by Vincent Winter Associates (VWA), Paris, France
Cover photograph: Spontaneous settlement of Somali refugees on the outskirts
of Dagahaley and Ifo camps, Kenya, October 2011 (UNHCR/ IOM /B. Bannon)

Editorial Team

Editor in chief	JUDITH KUMIN
Associate editor	ANDREW LAWDAY
Advisors	JEFF CRISP, ERIKA FELLER, VOLKER TÜRK
Statistician	TAREK ABOU CHABAKE
Cartographer	YVON ORAND
Graphic artists	FRANÇOISE JACCOUD, STÉPHANIE GOMEZ DE LA TORRE, JULIE SCHNEIDER
Editorial assistant	STÉPHANIE DE HEMPTINNE

External Contributors

ELIZABETH G. FERRIS, SUSAN FORBES MARTIN, WALTER KÄLIN, ANNA LINDLEY, KATY LONG, MAUREEN LYNCH, ERIN MOONEY, NICHOLAS MORRIS, TIMOTHY MORRIS, NIR ROSEN, NINA SCHREPFER AND JOANNE VAN SELM.

Acknowledgements

The editorial team wishes to thank all UNHCR staff who contributed to the preparation of this book, including: Allehone Abebe, Mirna Adjami, Guido Ambroso, Geraldine Ang, Areti Sianni, Christoph Bierwirth, Jorunn Brandvoll, Vincent Cochetel, Peter Deck, Julie Dunphy, Alice Edwards, Leigh Foster, Bilqees Esmail, Montserrat Feixas Vihé, Madeline Garlick, Radha Govil, Karen Gulick, Andrew Harper, Katherine Harris, Susan Hopper, Arjun Jain, Arafat Jamal, Stéphane Jaquemet, Anne Kellner, Andreas Kiaby, Anja Klug, Maja Lazic, Ewen Macleod, Mark Manly, Ann Maymann, Jozef Merckx, Juan Carlos Murillo, Shigeko Nambu, Kai Nielsen, Mildred Ouma, Andrew Painter, Matthias Reuss, Natalia Prokopchuk, Marc Rapoport, José Riera, Kimberly Roberson, Roland Schoenbauer, Paul Spiegel, Elizabeth Tan, Blanche Tax, Gisela Thater, Vicky Tennant, Brinda Wachs, Alia Al-Khatar Williams, Kees Wouters, Kylie Alcoba Wright, Josep Zapater.

CONTENTS

Contents

by the United Nations Secretary-General

FOR 60 YEARS, THE UNITED NATIONS HIGH COMMISSIONER FOR REFUGEES (UNHCR) has been at the forefront of international efforts to protect refugees and to find lasting solutions to their plight. When the first UN High Commissioner for Refugees took office in 1951, a handful of staff occupied four small rooms in the Palais des Nations in Geneva. Today, UNHCR is a global organization, with more than 7,000 staff working in over 120 countries to safeguard the rights and well-being of tens of millions of refugees, internally displaced and stateless people.

In December 2011, 155 Governments met in Geneva to commemorate the anniversaries of the 1951 Refugee Convention and the 1961 Convention on the Reduction of Statelessness. They confirmed the enduring value and relevance of these instruments.

Despite the hope that the end of the Cold War would bring an end to refugee flows, war and persecution continue to compel people to flee their homes. Global forced displacement reached a 16-year high in 2011 and has become more complex than ever before.

Today, conflict and human rights abuses—the traditional drivers of displacement—are increasingly intertwined with and compounded by other factors, such as population pressure, food insecurity and water scarcity. Many of these factors are in turn related to the relentless advance of climate change. Growing numbers of people are being uprooted by natural disasters.

This edition of *The State of the World's Refugees*, covering the period 2006-2011, provides a detailed analysis of contemporary forced displacement, including insights from UNHCR's field experience. I have met many displaced persons in my travels. I have heard their painful testimony about enforced flight—but also their gratitude at receiving international assistance. Their experiences reinforce my determination to ensure that the United Nations effectively serves the world's powerless and most vulnerable people.

This publication is a tribute to the resilience of refugees and displaced people the world over, and to those who come to their aid. I commend it to all who care about the state of the world's refugees.

BAN KI-MOON

by the United Nations High Commissioner for Refugees

WHEN WE EXAMINE THE STATE OF THE WORLD'S REFUGEES, IT IS EASY TO become disheartened. Armed conflicts and ethnic clashes. Human rights abuses. Border closures and expulsions. Racist discrimination and xenophobic violence.

Every day, hundreds of people—often the poorest and most vulnerable members of society—are forced to abandon their homes and to flee elsewhere in order to survive.

But they have no guarantee of finding safety. Whether they escape to another country or remain within their homeland, refugees and displaced people are invariably confronted with extremely hazardous journeys. And those who succeed in reaching their intended destination are likely to be faced with new threats and dangers.

Many are obliged to live in overcrowded camps, where basic needs such as food and water are in limited supply and where security is fragile. A growing number choose to take up residence in run-down urban neighbourhoods and squalid shanty towns, eking out a living by means of dangerous, degrading and exploitative work.

But there is another and more positive side to the refugee story—one which is to be found in the solidarity that individuals, communities, countries and humanitarian organizations in every part of the world continue to extend to those who have been uprooted.

We should remember that many countries, especially the poorest nations of the developing world, keep their borders open to refugees and allow exiled populations to remain on their territory, often for long periods of time and despite the fact that they are struggling to meet the needs of their own citizens. It is time to give greater recognition and support to those states that host the vast majority of the world's refugees.

At the local level, we continue to witness acts of extraordinary generosity by the host populations that are most directly affected by the arrival of refugees and displaced people. Local communities often demonstrate a remarkable willingness to share their land, water, forest resources, as well as their health and education services with strangers who have fled from man-made and natural disasters.

Another positive feature of the refugee story is to be found in the very substantial resources that continue to be mobilized for humanitarian action, even at a time when the global economic recession is threatening national economies and creating real hardship for millions of people.

When disaster strikes, members of the public invariably dig deep into their pockets to support the work of aid agencies. A growing number of states around the world are contributing to the welfare of refugees and displaced people through the provision of funding, relief items, logistical support and expertise. Private sector companies are also increasingly willing to share their resources and know-how with UNHCR and its humanitarian partners.

Every year, many thousands of asylum seekers are granted refugee status and given the opportunity to become full members of the society that has recognized their need for protection. The number of states that receive resettled refugees from countries of first asylum is steadily increasing, and now includes several which in the relatively recent past produced refugees themselves.

Another area where solidarity has not only been sustained, but has also been substantially strengthened, concerns the plight of stateless people. Many non-governmental and civil society organizations have taken up the cause of people who lack an effective nationality and who are thus deprived of the right to have rights. A growing number of states have acknowledged their obligations towards stateless people, ratifying relevant international conventions and amending their domestic legislation to address this previously neglected issue.

Finally, I am constantly struck by the solidarity that exists among our partners in the humanitarian community. That community is an extraordinarily diverse one, consisting of local, national and international organizations with varying mandates, motivations and funding sources. And yet even in the heat of the most intense emergencies, such agencies are able to work together in a spirit of cooperation.

Looking to the future, it will be essential to sustain and strengthen these different forms of solidarity. The world is currently affected by a number of disturbing global trends: human rights violations, armed conflict, rapid urbanization, volatile energy and commodity prices. And the process of climate change, coupled with the degradation of the environment, is exacerbating these trends, reinforcing their interaction and intensifying competition for scarce resources.

As a result, millions more people seem certain to be displaced or to abandon their own community, country and continent. Protecting their rights, meeting their essential needs and finding sustainable solutions for them will be one of the international community's major challenges in the years to come. But how might that be done?

When the UN Refugee Convention was adopted in 1951, the world recognized that the refugee problem was international in scope and nature and that effective responses to the issue could only be achieved on the basis of international cooperation.

As demonstrated in the following pages, the turbulent nature of the contemporary world is placing this principle under pressure. Individuals and societies are becoming increasingly anxious, prompting them to defend their immediate interests and to lose sight of the values and aspirations that we all share.

Let us resist this dangerous tendency, building upon the many forms of cooperation that we continue to witness in the domain of refugee protection and humanitarian action. If we are to strengthen solidarity, then we must actively celebrate it.

ANTÓNIO GUTERRES

Current Trends in Forced Displacement

THE REFUGEE PROTECTION SYSTEM, DEVELOPED IN THE AFTERMATH OF THE Second World War along with the creation of the Office of the United Nations High Commissioner for Refugees (UNHCR) in 1951, was designed to provide an effective response to the potentially destabilizing effects of population movements. It was also intended as an expression of international solidarity to uphold the rights of refugees and support the countries which host them.[1]

'Nothing great and good can be furthered in the world without cooperation', said Fridtjof Nansen, the first High Commissioner for Refugees under the League of Nations.[2]

Today, in difficult economic times and when security concerns are heightened, states understandably tend to focus on the well-being of their own populations. Yet global challenges call for more, not less, international cooperation and solidarity. This is particularly the case with respect to forced displacement, as this sixth edition of *The State of the World's Refugees* demonstrates.

Current trends in forced displacement are testing the international humanitarian system to an unprecedented extent. UNHCR, the agency mandated to lead and coordinate international action to protect refugees and resolve refugee problems worldwide, is now called upon to work with new populations and in new ways.

While the number of 'people of concern' to UNHCR increased from 19.2 million in 2005 to 33.9 million at the start of 2011, the proportion of refugees among them decreased from 48 per cent to 29 per cent—and these figures do not include the millions of displaced Palestinians who come under the mandate of the United Nations Relief and Works Agency for Palestine Refugees in the Near East (UNRWA). UNHCR has adapted its operations to respond to the needs of large numbers of internally displaced and stateless people around the globe; it can no longer be seen as only a 'refugee' agency.

| FIGURE 0·1 | **Total population of concern to UNHCR by region and by category** | 1.1.2011 |

COUNTRY/TERRITORY OF ASYLUM	REFUGEES	ASYLUM SEEKERS [1]	RETURNED REFUGEES	IDPS [2]	RETURNED IDPS	STATELESS PERSONS	OTHERS [3]	TOTAL POPULATION OF CONCERN
UN major regions [4]								
Africa	2,408,676	329,608	43,466	6,230,071	979,370	21,119	164,113	10,176,423
Asia	5,715,818	72,410	152,287	4,376,376	1,940,865	2,853,245	1,001,715	16,112,716
Europe	1,587,387	302,791	1,815	419,303	2,998	588,689	89,751	2,992,734
Latin America and the Caribbean	373,867	71,373	58	3,672,054	-	17	-	4,117,369
Northern America	430,123	57,310	-	-	-	-	-	487,433
Oceania	33,815	3,986	-	-	-	-	-	37,801
TOTAL	10,549,686	837,478	197,626	14,697,804	2,923,233	3,463,070	1,255,579	33,924,476

SOURCES: GOVERNMENTS; UNHCR

(1) Persons whose application for asylum or refugee status is pending at any stage in the asylum procedure.
(2) IDPs protected/assisted by UNHCR. It includes persons in IDP-like situations.
(3) Individuals who do not necessarily fall directly into any of the other groups but to whom UNHCR may extend its protection and/or assistance services.
(4) The regional classification used here is that of the UN Population Division, UN Statistics Division, New York.

Global trends suggest that displacement will not only continue in the future but will take different forms. The world's population is expected to grow from today's 7 billion people to 10.1 billion by 2100,[3] and most of this increase will occur in Africa and Asia. Confronted with rising poverty and food insecurity, young people will continue to head from rural to urban areas where housing and jobs are already in short supply.

This situation is likely to be exacerbated by climate change. Experts predict that natural disasters, which are already displacing millions of people every year, will increase in number and intensity.[4] As droughts and unpredictable rainfall patterns continue, even more rural inhabitants can be expected to move to urban areas. Climate change is also expected to reduce agricultural output in Africa and Asia–raising already-high food prices.[5] Another likely consequence of climate change is increased conflict over scarce resources, which could lead to larger internal displacement and refugee flows. Finally, some long-term effects of climate change may make whole areas uninhabitable, so that populations will have to be relocated.

Over the past six years, since publication of the last edition of *The State of the World's Refugees*, trends in forced displacement and developments in the international system have significantly affected UNHCR's work. As a consequence of humanitarian reforms initiated by the United Nations in 2005, international humanitarian action has become more efficient, accountable, and predictable. UNHCR has increasingly engaged with internally displaced persons (IDPs), undertaken new efforts on behalf of stateless people, and responded to populations affected by major natural disasters. It has paid growing attention to the particular needs of people displaced in urban areas, and urgently sought solutions to protracted displacement. Meanwhile, UNHCR has responded to new emergencies in places such as Libya and Côte d'Ivoire, even as it continued to address long-standing–but no less dramatic—displacement in and from countries such as Afghanistan, Colombia, the Democratic Republic of the Congo, Iraq, Somalia, and Sudan.

UNHCR's work has been bolstered by international efforts to improve the protection of basic human rights, particularly in situations of armed conflict, including through endorsement by the UN Security Council of the 'Responsibility to Protect' doctrine and a new emphasis on the protection of civilians in peacekeeping operations. Accountability efforts have been reinforced through the International Criminal Court, and through mechanisms at national and regional levels.

UNHCR's mandate for refugee protection sets it apart from other humanitarian actors. That mandate is based on the understanding that refugees do not enjoy the protection of their governments and hence need international protection—a task entrusted by the international community to UNHCR. However, the need to ensure the protection of IDPs and others affected by conflict is now widely accepted, and a broad definition of protection has been affirmed by the UN-led Inter-Agency Standing Committee (IASC) as encompassing '[A]ll activities aimed at obtaining full respect for the rights of the individual in accordance with the letter and spirit of the relevant bodies of law, namely human rights law, international humanitarian law and refugee law.'[6]

A further development of the past six years has been the recognition that UNHCR's principal accountability—indeed, that of all humanitarian actors—is to the people they serve. Refugees, IDPs, and stateless people are far from homogeneous; they include women, men, children, elderly

▼ **Young migrants** and asylum seekers in a crowded detention centre, on the Greek island of Lesvos.

UNHCR/L. BOLDRINI/2009

persons, all of whom have specific needs and capabilities that must be taken into account.

Recognizing and responding to diversity in displacement is central to UNHCR's ability to carry out its mandate, and the agency has taken important initiatives to ensure that its programmes are tailored to meet these different needs. UNHCR's Age, Gender and Diversity Policy sets out the organization's continued commitment to ensuring that its operations deliver equitable outcomes.[7]

Recognizing diversity

Diversity can be defined in many ways and has many dimensions. In UNHCR, it is understood in a broad sense as encompassing not only age, gender, race, ethnicity and religion but also a person's values, attitudes and cultural perspectives; sexual orientation and gender identity; health and social status; education, skills and a multitude of other personal characteristics.

Diversity affects people's opportunities, capacities, needs and vulnerabilities. In the many contexts in which UNHCR works—with refugees, internally displaced and stateless people—it must recognize and understand diversity and translate this understanding into effective actions to meet their needs and protect their rights.

In 2011, UNHCR released its updated **Age, Gender and Diversity Policy**, as well as its 2011–2015 Age, Gender and Diversity Forward Plan. These set out the organization's commitment to making sure that all of its operations are based on a solid understanding of the people it serves. The pillars of UNHCR's **Age, Gender and Diversity approach** are set out below:

1) **Working in partnership** with persons of concern means involving refugees, internally displaced and stateless persons in the planning and implementation of UNHCR programmes;

2) **Accountability** means that everyone—from the most junior to the most senior staff—is responsible for making sure that his or her work respects the diversity of the people UNHCR serves;

3) **Results-based management** means that the organization's focus is on the equitable impact of its work, not only on the activities;

4) **Capacity development** means that UNHCR must provide guidance and learning opportunities to enable all staff to understand what diversity means in practice;

5) **Sufficient human and financial resources** need to be available to ensure that age, gender and diversity mainstreaming achieves the desired results;

6) **Oversight** in the form of monitoring, evaluation, audit and reporting is needed to keep track of UNHCR's performance with respect to age, gender and diversity mainstreaming. ◆

UNHCR is a multilateral agency whose work to help individuals is rooted in the notion of international solidarity. Its core engagement with refugees is based on the recognition that, when people are forced to flee across borders, international cooperation and support are needed to complement the efforts of the host country, which bears the primary responsibility for meeting the needs of refugees. Solidarity takes different forms when it comes to helping people who are displaced within their own country or people who lack citizenship; in those cases, UNHCR endeavours to help—and sometimes to challenge—governments to live up to their human rights obligations.

When awarding the Nobel Peace Prize to UNHCR in 1981, the chairman of the Norwegian Nobel Committee predicted that forced displacement would continue and would take on new and unpredictable forms. However, he found encouragement in mankind's 'fundamental ideas on human rights and a sense of fellow feeling that goes beyond countries and continents, religions, cultures and racial borders.' He found such fellowship expressed in UNHCR's work.[8] Indeed, solidarity is often defined as a fellowship of responsibilities and interests.

This sixth edition of *The State of the World's Refugees: In Search of Solidarity* provides an overview of key developments relating to forced displacement from 2006 through 2011, a period which corresponds roughly to the first five-year term of António Guterres as UN High Commissioner for Refugees (mid-2005 to June 2010) and the start of his second term. Produced by UNHCR with input from independent experts, the book is divided into eight chapters, each focusing on a particular theme. Boxes in each chapter give examples from UNHCR's field experience.

Chapter 1 focuses on the context in which many UNHCR operations now take place, one of armed conflict. It looks at the impact on humanitarian action of the changing nature of conflict. Agents of violence have become more diverse, and include insurgents, armed groups, criminal gangs and an assortment of paramilitary forces. Distinctions between combatants and civilians have become less clear, and displacement is a deliberate strategy of many armed groups. As it is working increasingly with IDPs, UNHCR finds itself operating more and more often in active conflict zones, where security and access to the displaced are constant challenges. Humanitarian principles of impartiality, neutrality, and independence are under pressure, and space for humanitarian action is limited. Today's fragile environments make refugees, returnees, and internally displaced people more vulnerable, present operational challenges for UNHCR, and threaten both the institution of asylum and the achievement of durable solutions.

Chapter 2 looks at trends in asylum, 60 years after adoption of the 1951 Refugee Convention, and at the changed environment for refugee protection. Approaches to asylum remain inconsistent around the globe, with high levels of legal protection for refugees in some regions and virtually none in others. Understandings of protection needs are evolving, and controversies have arisen concerning the scope and interpretation of the refugee definition. Irregular migration has become globalized, requiring a 'protection-sensitive' approach to migration management. Governance systems for asylum and refugees are in a state of flux. In this context, UNHCR's role, and its ability to bring countries from all regions together to address asylum issues, remains critically important.

The search for durable solutions, the theme of **chapter 3**, also faces new constraints. While voluntary repatriation has long been considered the preferred solution for refugees, the number of returns has decreased sharply over the last six years. The line between conflict and post-conflict situations is often blurred, causing difficulties for refugees who go back home. UNHCR remains convinced that in many settings, integration in the first country of asylum would be the most appropriate solution, but some host governments have been reluctant to support the local integration of refugees, citing economic, social and security concerns. The number of states which implement annual resettlement programmes has grown, but resettlement places are still available for only a small percentage of the world's refugees. New and more comprehensive approaches are needed, including recognition that refugee mobility may be part of the solution, and that

BOX **0·2**

Somalia: the state of the world's refugees in microcosm

The complex crisis in Somalia illustrates nearly all of the topics examined in this edition of *The State of the World's Refugees*. The vicious and unpredictable nature of the conflict has dramatically limited space for humanitarian action, even as internal displacement has reached alarming proportions. The conflict, coupled with a drought the UN called the worst in 60 years, led in 2011 to a sharp upsurge in the exodus to neighbouring countries, with nearly 300,000 Somalis fleeing to Kenya, Ethiopia, Yemen and Djibouti during that year. The capa-city of these host countries has been severely strained, regardless of whether the refugees stay in camps or in urban areas, and there are few durable solutions for Somali refugees at the present time. In this difficult environment, solidarity and responsibility-sharing must be sustained.

Somalia has been in upheaval since the outbreak of civil war in 1991, with dramatic humanitarian consequences. Clan warfare, political conflict and military activity have taken a heavy toll. There have been more than a dozen failed peace initiatives, periodic external interventions, several deployments of UN forces and most recently, the creation of the African Union Mission in Somalia (AMISOM) in 2007. While the self-declared Republic of Somaliland in the northwest and the semi-autonomous region of Puntland in the northeast have achieved some degree of stability, central and southern Somalia have been plagued by almost continuous—but constantly changing—conflict.

By late 2011, the insurgent group Al-Shabaab (the name means 'the youth') controlled large swathes of the southern part of the country. It had earlier controlled, and then withdrawn from the capital, Mogadishu. The group is engaged in combat against Somalia's Transitional Federal Government, which is supported by AMISOM forces, as well as against other foreign and domestic groups. Civilians continue to face acute risks as a result of ongoing conflict in Mogadishu and other regions.

No one knows how many civilian casualties there have been over the past 20 years, how many people are still living in Somalia, nor how many have left the country. There has not been a census in Somalia since 1975, when the population was reported at 3.3 million. In 2011, official estimates put the population at 7.5 million. Even tallying up the number of people who have fled is complicated, as not all register with UNHCR or the authorities in the countries where they seek refuge.

At the end of 2011, there were nearly one million Somali refugees registered in countries in the region, including in Kenya (520,000), Yemen (202,000), Ethiopia (186,000) and Djibouti (18,700). Within Somalia itself, it was estimated that 1.4 million people were internally displaced.

Expanding internal displacement and shrinking humanitarian space

The UN High Commissioner for Refugees visited Mogadishu in August 2011 to highlight civilian suffering there and to call for more international solidarity. 'We should not aim at emptying Somalia', he said, 'but rather at making every effort to provide aid inside.' [i] But UN and other humanitarian actors have struggled to operate within the country and can meet only a fraction of the people's needs.

Somalia is without doubt one of the worst places in the world to be displaced. IDPs face constant threats to their physical security. They are the group most affected by the food crisis caused by the combination of drought and conflict. Hardly any displaced children attend school. Gender-based violence is widespread in IDP settlements. Overcrowded living conditions, the lack of clean water and absence of sanitation create major health risks. IDPs have limited, if any, livelihood possibilities.

Just keeping track of internal displacement is a challenge. UNHCR supported the development of a Population Movement Tracking System which gathers all available information on IDP movements, and maintains an information portal on the displacement crisis, which is widely used by aid agencies.

The ability of UNHCR and other UN agencies to operate in central and southern Somalia has been severely constrained by the nature of the conflict. Finding ways to deliver humanitarian assistance in Somalia has remained a top UN priority, and was highlighted by UN Secretary-General Ban Ki-moon when he travelled to Somalia in December 2011. At the peak of the emergency in 2011 UNHCR was able to launch three airlifts to Mogadishu, the first such UN operation in many years, and emergency relief items were distributed to nearly 400,000 people as a result. UNHCR has consistently tried to expand assistance into drought-stricken southern Somalia by working with partners. Humanitarian action in 2011 contributed to a drop in the mortality rate and to reducing the incidence of acute malnutrition, but reaching people in need remained an uphill battle.

Humanitarian workers are constantly at risk, and aid agencies struggle to balance the imperatives of staff security, the dramatic needs of the population, and to maintain operational independence from AMISOM, which engages in humanitarian action alongside its military operation. Throughout Somalia, local partners are vital actors in the delivery of aid. Yet they, too, are under threat from armed militants. The situation was further complicated late in 2011 when Al-Shabaab banned 16 aid agencies, including UN agencies and NGOs, from operating in areas it controls. The independent *2011 Aid Worker Security Report* points out that if Somalia appears as only the third most dangerous place for humanitarian workers (after Afghanistan and Sudan) when judged by the number of casualties, this is because many expatriate staff have been withdrawn. [ii]

Safeguarding asylum

Already in October 2010, the High Commissioner told his Executive Committee that Somalis had become a 'quasi-permanent refugee population', seeking asylum everywhere from Costa Rica to Nepal. In the absence of a political breakthrough, he said, Somalis would 'continue to wander the world in search of safety and a chance to rebuild their lives.' [iii] There has not been a political breakthrough, and the exodus has continued. Neighbouring countries have shown remarkable solidarity with Somali refugees, allowing them to enter in large numbers and opening new refugee camps. But insecurity in border areas and in and around refugee camps has remained a concern. UNHCR has provided support to governments to establish reception arrangements, to implement screening processes during registration, to maintain the civilian nature of refugee camps and to enforce law and order in the camps. At the end of 2011, the Dadaab refugee camp in northeastern Kenya had become the world's largest, in effect a medium-sized city with a population of nearly half a million. During the year, new Somali refugee sites were opened at Dollo Ado in the remote Ogaden desert in Ethiopia. By year-end the new sites hosted over 140,000 refugees.

Somali refugees have continued to cross the Gulf of Aden to Yemen, despite the risks involved and the political turmoil in Yemen. Many lost their lives in the process; 25,000 arrived on Yemen's shores in 2011. In addition, thousands of Somalis who had fled over the years into Libya stayed put there despite the violence, desperately trying to survive, while others crossed the border into Tunisia or Egypt, looking for safety and hoping for resettlement elsewhere.

Although it is difficult for Somalis to travel beyond their immediate region, UNHCR statistics show that around half a million have applied for asylum on an individual basis in the industrialized world over the past two decades. In recent years, large numbers have also sought and received protection in South Africa. Transit and destination countries grapple with mixed migratory flows, with many people from central and southern Somalia travelling alongside others who are on the move for non-protection related reasons. Asylum authorities and courts in Europe have taken varying approaches to applications for protection from Somalis, in some

cases finding them not eligible for refugee status under the 1951 Convention because they had fled generalized rather than individually targeted violence.

Throughout 2011, UNHCR maintained its position that people fleeing from central and southern Somalia need international protection. Within Africa, they are generally considered as refugees in the context of the extended refugee definition contained in the 1969 Convention Governing the Specific Aspects of Refugee Problems in Africa, and are often recognized as such on a *prima facie* basis, although many also satisfy the 1951 Convention's refugee definition. UNHCR urged governments to respect its guidance on the protection needs of Somalis and to refrain from sending anyone back to central or southern Somalia against his or her will.

Finding durable solutions

The return of refugees and IDPs to their home areas will not be possible unless there is peace and stability. To the extent possible, displaced families within Somalia should be helped through the provision of cash, seeds and fertilizers, to enable them to build resilience and achieve some degree of self-reliance. The capacity of authorities and communities in Somalia to absorb and use international assistance needs to be improved to help farmers, fishermen and pastoralists to strengthen their coping mechanisms to withstand environmental stresses associated with climate change (*see box 7.2*).

Somali refugees in countries in the region are for the most part confined to camps, where they are dependent on humanitarian aid. Although some—for instance, the large Somali community in Nairobi—have made their way to urban areas and become self-sufficient, local integration is not a solution which is officially open to them, even if it is the one which many would prefer. UNHCR continues to call on governments in the region to allow Somali refugees to exercise freedom of movement and to have access to employment and livelihood opportunities.

In 2011, UNHCR was seeking resettlement places for some 35,000 Somali refugees to ensure their protection or to enable them to reunite their splintered families. However, resettlement countries remained reluctant significantly to increase resettlement opportunities for Somalis, citing security concerns and integration challenges. Yet there is a very strong Somali diaspora in Europe, North America and elsewhere, willing and able to support resettlement of their countrymen. UNHCR statistics show that 90,000 Somali refugees were resettled during the period 1991–2010, primarily to the United States of America, to Canada, and to Nordic countries.

In search of solidarity

Neighbouring countries have borne a disproportionate burden in coping with the continuous influx of Somali refugees. They have kept their borders open and shared scarce resources with the refugees.

Over many years, the international community has mobilized enormous resources for humanitarian action in and around Somalia. Still, unmet needs remain immense, and a certain amount of 'donor fatigue' has set in. In 2011, UNHCR appealed for US$400 million to assist Somalis inside and outside their country. By year's end, around 70 per cent of that budget had been funded.

The UN's 2012 Somali Consolidated Appeal asked donors for $1.5 billion to address the Somalia emergency. In a difficult economic context, the humanitarian community needs to reach out to new donors. It is a positive sign that both the African Union and the Organization of Islamic Cooperation have organized pledging conferences for Somalia. The Gulf States and Turkey have emerged as major donors, and NGOs from these countries are increasingly active within Somalia. These new actors should be encouraged to participate in existing mechanisms for planning and consultation, in the interest of a coordinated response. ◆

i   UNHCR Press release, 'UNHCR Chief Calls for Scaled-up Aid Effort inside Somalia', 31 August 2011.
ii   A. Stoddard, A. Harmer and K. Haver, Humanitarian Outcomes, 'Aid Worker Security Report 2011: Spotlight on Security for National Aid Workers: Issues and Perspectives', August 2011.
iii A. Guterres, UN High Commissioner for Refugees, 'Opening Statement to the 61st Session of the Executive Committee of the High Commissioner's Programme', Geneva, 4 October 2010.

refugees themselves must be much more directly involved in discussions about solutions.

Statelessness, the theme of chapter 4, has been recognized as a problem for decades. A Convention relating to the Status of Stateless Persons was adopted in 1954, and followed by the Convention on the Reduction of Statelessness in 1961. The consequences of statelessness are devastating because recognition of nationality is central to the ability of individuals to exercise their rights to education, health care, employment and political participation, for example. UNHCR has intensified its efforts to address statelessness, clarifying the legal definition, encouraging law reform, providing states with technical assistance on issues such as birth registration, and developing ways of identifying and counting stateless persons. In 2011, it launched an energetic campaign to promote further accessions to the two international conventions on statelessness.

Chapter 5 looks at UNHCR's work with internally displaced persons—an area which has expanded greatly since the last edition of *The State of the World's Refugees*. At the start of 2005, UNHCR worked with 5.5 million IDPs; by 2011 that number had expanded to almost 15 million—higher than the number of refugees under the organization's mandate. In 2011, UNHCR was operationally engaged with IDPs in 27 countries, from the aftermath of communal violence in Kyrgyzstan to the humanitarian emergency in Somalia. UNHCR has taken on new responsibilities as lead (or co-lead) agency for protection, shelter, and camp coordination and management in the case of IDPs displaced by conflict. While by definition, refugees need international protection, it is the responsibility of national authorities to protect those displaced within their countries. UNHCR has played an important role in strengthening the normative framework applicable to internal displacement, for example by providing technical expertise to governments to develop relevant laws and policies and by supporting the new African Union Convention on Protection and Assistance of IDPs.

Chapter 6 examines the particular challenge of working in urban environments. Increasingly, refugees, asylum seekers, returnees, and the internally displaced do not live in camps, where UNHCR has long experience developing programmes to meet their needs, or even in rural areas, but in cities. Working in cities means engaging with many different actors, developing new partnerships, and managing a more complex environment. Simply identifying refugees is difficult when they are dispersed in urban neighborhoods, particularly if they are reluctant to be identified because of concerns about security or discrimination. Issues of data, documentation, shelter, livelihoods, and education cannot be addressed in the same way in cities as in camps. Relations with host communities require different working methods. In 2009, UNHCR re-focused its approach to urban contexts, releasing a new policy on Refugee Protection and Solutions in Urban Areas and devoting the High Commissioner's Annual Protection Dialogue to the topic.

A new theme for this edition of *The State of the World's Refugees* is displacement linked to climate change and natural disasters, the subject of chapter 7. As noted above, climate change is expected to increase displacement, directly impacting UNHCR's operations. While many are likely to be displaced internally (and thus will be the primary responsibility of their governments and fall under the UN Guiding Principles on Internal Displacement), there are no normative frameworks to address the situation of those who are externally displaced because of the effects of climate change. Moreover, the triggers of displacement are not always easy to identify, as climate change can lead to resource scarcity which may cause conflict. One of the most immediate consequences of climate change is the expected increase in sudden-onset natural disasters. Already in 2010, the number of those displaced by sudden-onset disasters was estimated to be over 40 million. While most of this displacement is short-term, it challenges the international humanitarian community to respond. In particular, UNHCR's protection expertise can be used to help those displaced by natural disasters.

Chapter 8 looks at the issue of solidarity—the theme of this volume—and makes the case that protection of refugees and displaced persons must be at the core of both national responsibility and international solidarity. There is a strong humanitarian argument in favour of increased international solidarity, in the sense of international cooperation to share burdens and responsibilities. The chapter looks at the ways in which solidarity manifests itself, including through hosting and resettling refugees; and through financial support to alleviate the strain on poorer host countries. The challenge of international solidarity is to ensure that arrangements for international cooperation expand and improve the protection space and do not constrain it. ■

CHAPTER 1

Conflict, Displacement, and Humanitarian Space

WHEN UNHCR MARKED ITS 60TH ANNIVERSARY IN 2011, the context in which it worked around the globe, more than ever before, was one of armed conflict. The majority of refugees under UNHCR's mandate had fled from conflict situations. Over 50 per cent were from just three countries: Afghanistan, Iraq and Somalia. Conflict had caused the internal displacement of more than 27 million internally displaced people (IDPs) worldwide,[1] and UNHCR was engaged in providing protection and assistance in many of these situations.

Displacement has long been a consequence—and on many occasions an aim—of war. UNHCR's presence in zones of conflict and insecurity is, however, relatively recent.[2] During the Cold War, humanitarian organizations, with the important exception of the International Committee of the Red Cross (ICRC), generally did not operate in areas of active conflict. UNHCR worked in neighbouring countries where refugees were received, and where the conflict sometimes crossed borders, as with attacks on refugee camps during the liberation struggles in southern Africa, but generally had very few staff stationed outside capital cities, and only deployed into countries or zones that had suffered conflict after a political settlement had been reached.

◀ **A woman at the ruins of her house in Osh,** Kyrgyzstan following a wave of ethnic violence in June 2010.

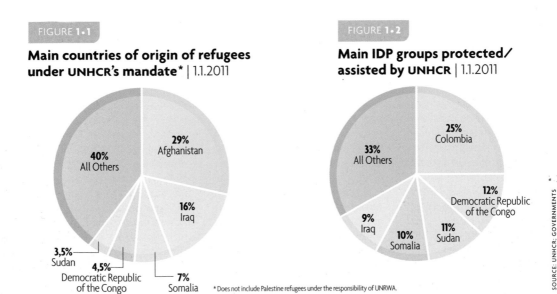

FIGURE **1·1**

Main countries of origin of refugees under UNHCR's mandate* | 1.1.2011

40% All Others
29% Afghanistan
16% Iraq
3,5% Sudan
4,5% Democratic Republic of the Congo
7% Somalia

FIGURE **1·2**

Main IDP groups protected/ assisted by UNHCR | 1.1.2011

33% All Others
25% Colombia
12% Democratic Republic of the Congo
11% Sudan
10% Somalia
9% Iraq

* Does not include Palestine refugees under the responsibility of UNRWA.

UNHCR / S. SCHULMAN

SOURCE: UNHCR; GOVERNMENTS

This changed sharply in the 1990s. UNHCR's first significant engagement in ongoing conflict was in the Balkans in 1991–1995.[3] This was followed by operations in what was then Zaire, in the aftermath of the 1994 genocide in Rwanda, in an environment that was highly insecure. More operations in countries affected by conflict followed rapidly, in Afghanistan, Colombia, Iraq, Somalia and elsewhere. Many of the challenges encountered in the Balkans and in the Great Lakes region of Africa found parallels in later operations. Today, UNHCR is involved in the UN system's response to almost all complex emergencies.

This intensified engagement in conflict situations is a direct consequence of UNHCR's expanded role with regard to IDPs. In late 2005, UNHCR was designated the lead UN agency for the protection of IDPs displaced by conflict, as discussed in chapter 5. It also reflects UNHCR's efforts to support the reintegration of former refugees. In some cases they are returning to countries where old conflicts have not been definitively resolved, or where new conflicts are erupting, such as Afghanistan and South Sudan.

Timely and effective humanitarian action requires an environment where people in need can have safe access to protection and assistance, and those who deliver aid are able to do so without obstruction. In conflict situations, it requires respect by all parties for humanitarian principles, a condition which is not always met.

BOX **1•1**

Understanding humanitarian principles

Humanitarian principles provide the moral foundation for international humanitarian action. In 1991, the UN General Assembly in Resolution 46/182 endorsed **three core principles** governing humanitarian action: *humanity, impartiality, and neutrality*.

These principles derive from the tenets of the International Committee of the Red Cross (ICRC) and from international humanitarian law (IHL). The 1949 Geneva Conventions and their Additional Protocols on the laws of war established the principle of aid to all victims of war without discrimination.

Humanity characterizes the motivation of the action: to address human suffering wherever it is found. Impartiality means that aid is provided purely on the basis of need, without discrimination between or within affected populations. Neutrality requires humanitarian actors not to take sides in an armed conflict or other dispute.

A fourth principle is frequently included: *independence* means that humanitarian actors should not be subject to control by non-humanitarian actors, nor subordinate to political, economic, military, or other objectives.

Observers have frequently pointed out that UN agencies cannot be entirely independent of decisions made by the political organs of the United Nations. In 2004, the UN General Assembly adopted Resolution 58/114, recognizing *independence* as an additional 'guiding principle' for humanitarian action. It was defined as: 'the autonomy of humanitarian objectives from the political, economic, military or other objectives that any actor may hold with regard to areas where humanitarian action is being implemented (...).' The UN's Office for Coordination of Humanitarian Affairs (OCHA) refers to this as 'operational independence'.

In a renowned commentary on 'The Fundamental Principles of the Red Cross' written in 1979, Jean Pictet asserted that humanity and impartiality are 'substantive' principles concerned with objectives, while neutrality and independence are 'derivative' principles concerned with ways and means. He stressed that humanity holds a special primary place, as the 'essential' principle from which all the others flow.

Today, most humanitarian organizations have explicitly committed to observing these principles, even if understandings of the import of each, and in particular of neutrality and independence, may differ in relation to each organization's mandate and institutional links. ◆

Humanitarian action is also more visible than ever before.[4] Greatly increased media attention to the impact of conflict has generated the expectation that there will be a swift international humanitarian response, and the use of social media has produced greater demands for accountability from humanitarian actors, whose successes and failures can be tracked and monitored minute-by-minute.

This chapter looks at how conflict and insecurity affect forced displacement and humanitarian responses.[5] It examines key humanitarian dilemmas, from the changing nature of conflict, to the limited space available to humanitarian actors, to the complexities arising from integrated missions and stabilization approaches. It concludes with a description of the operational responses adopted by UNHCR and its partners, including the 'risk management' approach, and an outline of future challenges in responding to humanitarian needs in situations of violent conflict.

The changing nature of conflict

WHEN UNHCR WAS ESTABLISHED IN 1951, in the aftermath of the Second World War, large-scale conflict was still thought of in terms of wars between states. Episodes of civil war and liberation struggles followed, as did other internal conflicts, pitting rebels and insurgents against a government they hoped to replace. Many of the parties to these conflicts were identified with, and often supported by, one or the other side of the Cold War.

The global systems established after the Second World War were designed to address conflicts that were expected to have a clear resolution, as well as clearly defined combatants. As already noted, there was limited scope for humanitarian action until such resolution took place.

Inter-state wars remain a threat, though the incidence of such wars has declined over the last quarter-century. UNHCR has increasingly had to operate in other types of conflict, which frequently have their roots in ethnic or religious strife, or where political, ethnic and criminal violence are interlinked.[6] Political movements may obtain funding from violent criminal activities, and criminal gangs may support political violence. Violence may appear to be indiscriminate and generalized, but, upon closer analysis, it can in fact involve the deliberate targeting of certain groups of civilians.

Sexual and gender-based violence (SGBV), particularly but not only directed against women, is widely encountered as a weapon in conflict. It has, for example, become a dramatic and defining feature of the conflict in the Democratic Republic of the Congo (DRC). There is evidence from the North and South Kivu provinces that systematic rape has been used by armed groups as part of their military strategy. UNHCR's protection monitoring across the eastern DRC shows that sexual violence is one of the most recurrent human rights violations reported by the civilian population in conflict-affected areas, and reveals a direct link between forced displacement and sexual violence. SGBV is also

BOX 1•2

Ethnic violence in Kyrgyzstan

A wave of ethnic violence swept southern Kyrgyzstan over several days in June 2010, forcing some 375,000 people to flee their homes. About 75,000 of them, mostly women and children, crossed into neighbouring Uzbekistan, where they were accommodated in public buildings and temporary camps. Smaller numbers sought safety in Russia, Turkey and elsewhere in Europe. By 27 June, when a referendum was held in Kyrgyzstan on the country's interim Presidency and constitutional future, almost all of the refugees who had fled to Uzbekistan had returned.

The violence erupted early on 10 June in the southern city of Osh, and spread rapidly across the provinces of Osh and Jalalabad. Clashes between ethnic Uzbeks and ethnic Kyrgyz left hundreds dead and displaced almost 20 per cent of the population of the two provinces. Thousands more were affected but not displaced. The violence destroyed over 2,000 buildings, mostly homes, deepened the gulf between the ethnic communities, and resulted in loss of property, as well as of identity documents and land titles. Instances of arbitrary detention, disappearances, sexual and gender-based violence, intimidation and extortion were all reported.

UNHCR immediately launched an emergency operation in both Kyrgyzstan and Uzbekistan. Prior to the events, UNHCR had a small presence in Kyrgyzstan, including in the town of Osh. However, UNHCR had been asked to leave Uzbekistan five years earlier, following the serious violence in Andijan in May 2005.

In Kyrgyzstan, the emergency operation got off to a slow start because of restrictions imposed by the UN's Department of Safety and Security. Only on 21 June could UNHCR receive UN security clearance to open an office in Jalalabad, and only on 24 June could it re-open its office in Osh.

Thus during the first two weeks of the crisis, UNHCR concentrated on supporting existing local and international partners to start protection monitoring and interventions and to deliver assistance. The first two UNHCR consignments of aid brought in by air were transferred to the International Committee of the Red Cross for distribution. UNHCR was able to relocate non-Kyrgyz refugees and asylum seekers out of conflict areas, thanks to its strong local partnerships in Osh.

At the same time, UNHCR provided help to Uzbekistan. The government, which coped efficiently with the sudden influx of refugees, accepted a UNHCR emergency team and the delivery of humanitarian supplies. UNHCR dispatched six airlifts to Uzbekistan carrying 200 tons of tents and non-food items over three days, 16–18 June. The first arrived within 72 hours of the government's appeal for assistance.

Challenges remained for UNHCR to carry out its international protection function in Uzbekistan, the only Central Asian country which has not ratified the 1951 Refugee Convention and 1967 Protocol, and where the agency no longer had an established presence. Access to the refugees was limited, the refugees had no freedom of movement, and it was not clear whether they had sufficient information about what was happening at home. For these reasons, but also because Kyrgyz government officials visited the camps to encourage refugees to return before the referendum, many observers raised questions about whether the sudden repatriation met international standards of voluntariness. As the refugees returned home within weeks, UNHCR concentrated on protection interventions and providing emergency aid as well as transitional shelter to returnees and IDPs in the south of Kyrgyzstan.

A Rapid Protection Assessment was undertaken at an early stage by the agencies participating in the Protection Cluster led by UNHCR. This was a 'light and quick' exercise to set priorities for protection actions and avoid duplicative assessments. In another innovation, following a model that the agency had successfully employed before the conflict in the context of its activities to prevent and reduce statelessness in rural areas of Kyrgyzstan, UNHCR supported the deployment of joint mobile teams. These teams, made up of representatives of the authorities, NGO and UNHCR staff, visited conflict-affected neighbourhoods to replace lost or destroyed personal documents. This was important as many victims of the conflict were afraid to leave their communities. It also helped the authorities to re-establish a relationship of trust with people affected by the conflict.

Still, winter loomed large after the widespread destruction of property. A shelter assessment revealed that many of the 2,000 houses which had been damaged would need complete reconstruction. As co-ordinator of the Shelter Cluster, UNHCR, with its partners and the Kyrgyz government, developed a strategy which involved emergency aid (tents and other items), the construction of emergency shelter, and support to displaced people living with host families. UNHCR funded much of the shelter construction programme, which was implemented by NGOs. By the end of November this rapid action had put a roof over the heads of 13,400 former refugees and displaced people, helped to restore a sense of community in destroyed neighbourhoods, and demonstrated to those who had returned from Uzbekistan, as well as to the IDPs, that their plight had not been forgotten.

In this fast-paced operation, the challenge for UNHCR was to deploy the right people to the right place at the right time. When the emergency began on 10 June, the agency had no presence at all in Uzbekistan, and just three expatriate staff in Kyrgyzstan. By the end of June, UNHCR offices in Bishkek, Osh, and Jalalabad had 24 international staff (including 21 on emergency deployment), 35 national employees and 20 additional personnel on service contracts. Deployment of a critical mass of Russian-speaking staff members to the region was of key importance.

The operation enjoyed a very high level of donor support. By 22 September 2010, over 93 per cent of the organization's US$27.5 million appeal had been funded, with the largest contributions coming from the United States of America, Japan and the UN's Central Emergency Response Fund (CERF). ◆

endemic in many refugee situations. For example, in Chad, UNHCR documented over 1,000 cases of such violence affecting refugees in 2010 alone.[7] Reports from the Somali refugee camps in Kenya have also highlighted the prevalence of SGBV in the country of origin, during flight and after arrival in the camps.

In contemporary contexts, the distinction between armed conflict and violence used as a means of securing or reinforcing social or economic power is often blurred. Some countries that did negotiate an end to violent political conflict, and to which many refugees returned (such as Guatemala and El Salvador) are wracked by high levels of violent crime. Other conflicts do not have a clear end but are ongoing or repeated, and occur in countries with weak governance and chronic instability. This is reflected in the number of protracted refugee and IDP situations around the globe and creates tremendous challenges in terms of securing durable solutions (*see chapter 3*).

The World Bank's *World Development Report 2011* provides a detailed examination of the changing nature of violence and its impact. It notes that '90 per cent of the last decade's civil wars occurred in countries that had already had civil war in the last 30 years' and that 'the large majority of countries currently facing violence face it in multiple forms'. The report stresses that no country or region can afford to ignore areas that suffer repeated cycles of violence, and that unemployment, corruption, and exclusion increase the risk of violence.[8]

The picture is not uniformly bleak, however, as there are also some positive developments. The decline of superpower rivalry has meant fewer proxy wars and less destabilization. The demands of a globalized economy and the advantages of membership in good standing of influential regional organizations may act as a restraint on governments. More generally, there is increased recognition of the need to adapt global conflict prevention and resolution mechanisms to meet the challenges of contemporary violence.

AGENTS OF VIOLENCE

The agents of violence have multiplied, from uniformed forces to non-state actors who often exercise *de facto* control over territory and people, and develop some sense of responsibility towards them, to a myriad of private actors with no such sense.[9] Forced recruitment, including of children, and extreme pressure on civilians are characteristic of some conflicts.

In some contexts, violent criminal organizations may also be involved, not only in trafficking drugs, arms and people, but also in the control of land and territory for economic purposes. Some are transnational criminal enterprises. Many operate outside formal command structures and are dispersed and opportunistic, although they may also have links to elites and local authorities. Their activities are likely to be concentrated in border areas or where the civilian state presence is weak, but there is also a spill-over effect into urban areas, with intra-urban violence increasing, resulting in further displacement.

Agents of violence include international ideological movements, whose aim may not involve control of territory, but who ally with local movements and exploit local grievances as well as committing or sponsoring acts of terrorism. Such movements have themselves at times been supported by states.

As a result of this plethora, the distinction between combatant and civilian—the cornerstone of international humanitarian law—has become blurred. When violence in a given area is perpetrated by actors with different and sometimes incompatible motivations and aims, with unclear chains of command, political resolution and (in the meantime) negotiation of humanitarian access present particularly acute challenges.

TERRORISM AND HUMANITARIAN ACTION

Terrorism has on occasion directly threatened UN humanitarian action. The nature of this threat, which may not be geographically circumscribed, is not easily countered by the classical responses to insecurity. The security measures that have had to be adopted have been a significant inhibiting factor in some operations, yet have not always been able to shield humanitarian workers from harm, as attacks on UN and other aid agencies in Afghanistan, Algeria, Iraq, Nigeria, and elsewhere have demonstrated.

Over the last decade, the response to global terrorism has also challenged humanitarian principles and in some cases has affected the ability of humanitarian organizations to help those in need. For instance, legal sanctions have been introduced that risk equating humanitarian action in certain particularly challenging contexts with providing material support to terrorists. This may have a chilling effect on funding and even expose humanitarian workers to the risk of criminal prosecution. Donor conditionality has curtailed operations in areas controlled by designated individuals or groups, and has complicated relations between humanitarian organizations and local communities and partners.

One recent study found that 'the stated or implied policy of some governments and inter-governmental organisations to ban all contact with entities designated as "terrorist" has severely undermined opportunities for humanitarian actors to negotiate access for aid to civilians'.[10] Another concluded that 'over-zealous application of counter-terrorism laws to humanitarian action (...) could become an additional factor in the unravelling of the legitimacy and acceptance of humanitarian response in many of the world's worst humanitarian crises.'[11]

THE IMPACT OF CONTEMPORARY CONFLICTS ON CIVILIANS

At the global level, the number of internally displaced persons (IDPs) who had fled violence and armed conflict (some 27.5 million) was double the number of refugees under UNHCR's mandate (10.5 million) at the start of 2011. Although 2011 and early 2012 saw new refugee outflows—notably from Côte d'Ivoire, Libya, Mali, Syria and above all from Somalia—the global trend seemed to be one of internal displacement characterized by tremendous fluidity, often in response to rapidly shifting patterns of conflict and territorial control. And displacement statistics, by definition, do not reveal the impact of violence and insecurity on those who do not or cannot flee, but who may be even more vulnerable than those who do.

BOX 1•3

The Lord's Resistance Army: a transnational threat

The Lord's Resistance Army (LRA) has attacked civilians across the Great Lakes and Central Africa regions for decades, depopulating entire areas and hindering humanitarian access to affected populations. In 2011, the international community and the African Union (AU) showed new resolve to put an end to this enterprise of crime and terror. But questions remain as to whether the initiative will succeed.

Once a Ugandan rebel group, the LRA now seems to lack any objective other than sustaining its top leadership and perpetrating atrocities against civilians. Following a Ugandan military campaign in late 2008 and early 2009, and inconclusive peace negotiations between the government of Uganda and the LRA before that, the LRA moved out of Uganda. Yet it proceeded to intensify its attacks across three neighbouring countries.

Between 2006 and 2011, its fighters, thought to number no more than 500, are believed to have murdered 2,000 people, abducted 2,600, and displaced over 400,000 across the Central African Republic (CAR), the Democratic Republic of the Congo (DRC), and South Sudan. However, 'copycat' attacks by other armed elements made it difficult to determine responsibility.

In Uganda and neighbouring countries, LRA fighters have committed acts of extreme violence against civilians, including indiscriminate killings, kidnapping of children, rape and mutilation, looting, burning and destruction of property. Terrified villagers have fled *en masse*. Most often, the LRA has attacked remote areas where infrastructure and communications were minimal at best. When state military forces did react, the LRA systematically retaliated against civilians.

Most of those affected were small-scale farmers whose livelihoods were ruined. Afraid to return to their remote communities, they fled to other villages, heaping pressure on schools, health centres, police and civil administrations whose capacities were already weak.

The LRA has continued its terror year after year with staggering impunity, even though the International Criminal Court (ICC) indicted the LRA leadership in 2005. While humanitarian actors, including UNHCR, have tried to assist affected communities, many attacks took place in areas with limited road networks and plagued by other conflicts and banditry.

Despite the LRA's deadly toll across four countries, governments have not yet succeeded in addressing the LRA threat as a common priority. Uganda, with support from the United States, has committed the greatest capacity to fighting the LRA. The overstretched armed forces of the DRC and CAR have been able to dedicate fewer resources to tackling the LRA, and South Sudan's authorities have been focused on building their new state.

By 2011, a more coherent approach to the problem had started to emerge. In June 2010, an International Working Group was formed to exchange information and coordinate responses to the LRA; the group includes the AU and the European Union, the UN, the US and several European countries. In May 2011, a UN interagency evaluation conducted across the four affected countries called for a common policy approach, greater efforts by military actors to protect civilians, and a strengthened humanitarian response. In November 2011, the UN's Special Representative for the Central African Region briefed the UN Security Council on the LRA threat. That same month, the UN Secretary-General issued a report on the LRA-affected areas, including evolving international attempts to address the threat.

At the regional level, the AU has taken the lead in coordinating efforts against the LRA by the affected states. After an AU summit in Bangui in July 2010, the four states developed plans for an AU-authorized mission to eliminate the LRA threat. The plans provided for the appointment of a special envoy, the establishment of a joint operations centre, and the deployment of a Regional Task Force (RTF) with a 5,000-strong military component. The initiative received support from the international community, with American and European officials calling for protection of civilians to be included among its strategic objectives. In October 2011, the United States announced the deployment of military advisers to help regional forces combat the LRA.

UNHCR cautiously welcomed the AU initiative, also stressing that the Task Force should ensure protection of civilians, prevent displacement, facilitate humanitarian access, and create conditions for displaced people to return home in safety. Along with other humanitarian actors, UNHCR has advocated for extending the mandates of UN peacekeeping forces, including MONUSCO in DRC and UNMISS in South Sudan, to include a clear responsibility for protection of civilians.

As a humanitarian agency, UNHCR needs to maintain its operational independence from the AU military force. However, if access can be improved, and if donors provide the necessary resources, UNHCR and other agencies will be able to offer more help to the affected civilian populations, including psychosocial support for victims. UNHCR is also keen to relocate displaced people away from border areas, which would help to maintain the civilian nature of camps.

Finally, UNHCR recognizes that development interventions are essential to enhance the safety and security of rural populations and their livelihoods. This would require governments and donors to strengthen civil administration, police, and law enforcement capacities in the isolated communities upon which the LRA preys. ◆

A myriad of negative factors often accompany or combine with conflict. Government dysfunction, the loss of livelihoods, shortages of basic necessities, natural disasters, climate change, and demographic pressures all contribute to insecurity and displacement, and increase the vulnerability of those already displaced.

The number of civilians killed in wars is often reported to have decreased since the end of the Cold War. However, the exposure and vulnerability of civilians to of violence appears to have increased, particularly where failing states are unable to provide even minimal security for their citizens, as in the case of Somalia. People are likely to prioritize security over any other need, and insecurity is the determining factor for the great majority of those who flee.

The impact of contemporary conflict on civilians is far-reaching. Provision of basic services and essential supplies becomes more difficult, and shortages increase tensions. Ordinary citizens may be at risk from military action but also from suicide attacks and improvised explosive devices. Forced recruitment is a danger, both before and during flight. In fragile states, law and order and the justice system itself may break down. Weak administrations become even weaker and less able to protect refugees, displaced people, minorities and others. Leaders who seek to protect the rights of their communities may be at particular risk, as in Colombia. Individuals who are vulnerable under normal situations, such as children, persons with disabilities, or the elderly, face heightened risk.

The displacement caused by conventional wars and even by large-scale human rights abuses such as those of the Khmer Rouge in Cambodia in the 1970s generally took place in relatively well-defined and limited areas. Contemporary forms of violence force people to flee their homes to destinations that are less predictable, less circumscribed, and often themselves also insecure. Growing numbers of refugees and displaced persons are fleeing both to urban areas (*see chapter 6*) and much further afield. In 2011, for example, Somali refugees and asylum seekers could be found in nearly three dozen countries across six continents. The same was true for refugees and asylum seekers from Afghanistan.

In response to new patterns of forced displacement as well as to security concerns, many governments in both the global North and South have moved to restrict access to their territories and to their asylum procedures, and are taking a strict approach to eligibility for refugee status or complementary forms of protection, as discussed in chapter 2. Security concerns have also reduced resettlement opportunities, and resettlement processing in certain countries of first asylum has been delayed because of limitations on access of receiving country officials.

Protracted conflict and insecurity translates into seemingly permanent displacement, often in dire conditions, and dependency on outside aid. Two-thirds of the refugees of concern to UNHCR are living in long-term exile. Many Somalis have been refugees for over 20 years and many Afghans for over 30 years. Continuing or cyclical violence in a country of origin has an obvious adverse effect on the prospects for voluntary repatriation and the sustainability of return. Moreover, refugees may find themselves caught up in conflict or violence in countries where they had sought protection, as has recently been the case in Côte d'Ivoire, Libya and Yemen, for example.

Significantly fewer refugees were able to return home in 2010 than in previous years: 200,000 as compared to over a million five years earlier. Afghanistan is a case in point. The number of refugees returning dropped by half in 2011, with 68,000 repatriating compared to 118,000 in 2010. Insecurity was the reason cited most often for not going back.

Shrinking humanitarian space?

THE CHANGING NATURE OF CONFLICT AND VIOLENCE has left tens of millions of civilians internally displaced and in need of protection. Ironically, they are in many cases more accessible to humanitarian organizations, albeit not without risks, than was the case during the Cold War, when access to certain areas was restricted. The international community has encouraged humanitarian action in conflict zones and donor states have provided significant financial support for it. Where external military intervention has occurred, humanitarian action has sometimes been promoted in support of political objectives.

The increase in humanitarian operations in conflict zones has focused attention on the conditions for their success. The term 'humanitarian space' is widely used to describe those conditions.[12] Although understandings of this term differ, safeguarding humanitarian space has become a key objective. What unites the varying interpretations is a consensus that humanitarian space is not an end in itself, but is necessary to enable people in need to have access to protection and assistance, and to enable humanitarian actors to respond.

For UNHCR, the term 'humanitarian space' refers to the conditions necessary for effective and principled humanitarian action, whether for the benefit of refugees, internally displaced persons, returnees or others who have not been able to flee. In a narrower sense, it refers to the conditions that allow the full and unimpeded discharge of UNHCR's core mandate to provide international protection to refugees and to assist governments in finding durable solutions to refugee problems.

Humanitarian space is widely held to be shrinking but the concept does not lend itself to precise measurement, as it is highly context-specific.[13] Nonetheless it is clear that there are major challenges to humanitarian action today, and that these are most acute in situations where the causes of displacement and serious abuses of human rights have not yet been tackled effectively. The challenges grow with the passage of time without a political solution to the conflict. The difficulties faced by humanitarian organizations are compounded where the violence is uncontrolled and indiscriminate. There are new patterns to some conflicts, and new types of actors. All of this translates into a changing context for UNHCR field operations in countries as diverse as Afghanistan, Côte d'Ivoire, the Democratic Republic of the Congo, Libya and Yemen (*see box 1.5*), to cite only some of the more recent examples.

BOX 1•4

Humanitarian response to the Libya crisis

In 2011, UNHCR was caught up in the turbulent Arab Spring. In Libya, human displacement on a massive scale emerged as a tragic accompaniment to the unfolding political drama which erupted in February.

External displacement

The Libyan conflict generated a huge exodus, with around a million people leaving the country in a matter of months, crossing mainly into Tunisia and Egypt but also into other neighbouring countries. Most were migrant workers who had found employment in Libya, but over 100,000 were Libyans seeking protection outside their country. Still others were refugees from places such as Eritrea and Somalia who had sought refuge in Libya over many years. More than 20,000 people, mostly sub-Saharan Africans, took to boats in an effort to reach Italy or Malta. The number who perished at sea remains unknown.

In Tunisia and Egypt, UNHCR and the International Organization for Migration (IOM) launched a joint humanitarian evacuation operation, to help the migrant workers to return to their countries by air and by sea. This initiative, together with evacuations organized by many individual governments, relieved the dramatic overcrowding at the borders. By late summer, when the joint operation ended, more than 144,000 people had been repatriated by UNHCR and the IOM, while hundreds of thousands more had returned home with the help of their governments.

UNHCR devoted particular attention to ensuring protection for the refugees within the massive flow of people, and sought urgent resettlement places for several thousand of them, including a number of unaccompanied children, who were stranded in Tunisia and Egypt.

Humanitarian action within Libya

Within Libya, the situation was volatile, with violent conflict, a revolution in progress, and few trusted sources of information. The country was deeply divided and had to confront the legacy of decades of autocratic rule funded by oil wealth. Early on, UNHCR defined its goals inside Libya as the following: to protect the refugee population in the country; to deliver aassistance to displaced Libyans; to lead the UN's Protection Cluster; and to cultivate partnerships for the future.

During the conflict, UNHCR staff found themselves very close to acts of violence, including the Tibesti Hotel bombing in Benghazi, shelling of a humanitarian ship in Misrata harbour, and air raids in Tripoli. Haunted by the deaths of UN staff in previous attacks around the world, the UN imposed strict security measures with staff ceilings and movement restrictions intended to protect staff, but which necessarily also limited their ability to operate.

Determined not to compromise on either safety or reach, UNHCR complied with the requirements (for example, by airlifting armoured vehicles and deploying seasoned security officers, both of which served as assets for the UN team as a whole) and made the best of the restrictions. It deployed small, versatile teams, and relied heavily on 'remote' management of operations and deliveries. Despite security requirements, the agency managed to operate, in multiple locations, almost throughout the conflict.

CHALLENGES TO HUMANITARIAN PRINCIPLES

As indicated earlier, humanitarian action is predicated on and defined by respect of its principles: humanity, impartiality, and, neutrality. A fourth important principle, independence, characterizes the standing of the action, meaning that it is not subordinate to or subject to control by others. Important as they are in their own right, these principles are a means to an end: the delivery of protection and assistance to civilians caught up in conflict. For UNHCR, the principles are understood within the framework of the agency's Statute, which states unequivocally that UNHCR's work shall be of an entirely non-political, humanitarian character.

The oldest humanitarian institution, the International Committee of the Red Cross, is recognized as the 'guardian' of humanitarian principles, and has the longest and most extensive experience of humanitarian action in situations of conflict. As UNHCR's engagement in conflict situations has increased, so its relationship with the ICRC has deepened.

The principles are of critical importance to humanitarian organizations operating in

Maintaining neutrality

Working in an environment characterized by internal conflict and NATO air strikes put pressure on humanitarian actors to ensure that they were perceived as neutral and impartial. With the country divided, the humanitarian team had to ensure a balanced engagement. In both Benghazi and Tripoli, the UN could not avoid dealing with entities affiliated with the respective sides, but these actors could not always be relied upon to deliver assistance impartially. There was also the phenomenon of 'revolutionary' NGOs—openly partisan groups working under a humanitarian identity. Finally, the political arm of the UN, and the prospect of an integrated mission, had to be taken into account.

A particular effort had to be made to ensure that communication with both sides was transparent, and that they were kept informed of activities and partners on each side. This transparency, coupled with explanations of humanitarian principles to inexperienced parties, was well received. In spite of the fighting, Libyans were concerned about the plight of their fellow citizens, and supported purely humanitarian work wherever it was undertaken.

Credibility and relevance

Libya is a wealthy country, whose citizens were accustomed to a certain quality of life, and humanitarian actors needed to take this into account. Humanitarian minimum standards, such as the Sphere standards, and many of the usual relief items, were of little relevance in the Libyan context. A number of traditional humanitarian actors were disturbed by this. Some new actors, such as those from Gulf countries, understood the context better, and established aid programmes better suited to local needs. UNHCR was able to benefit from the fact that its teams were staffed by personnel who had worked in other middle-income, urban, Middle Eastern operations.

Libya was not only embroiled in violent conflict, but was also—along with other countries in the region—in the midst of a political transformation. Whereas in the past UNHCR had a very tenuous status in Libya, it now had the opportunity to make a difference, and its large-scale operations in Tunisia and Egypt helped to reinforce its relevance for the future.

Inside Libya, UNHCR realized that it needed to engage in issues concerning justice and the rule of law. Libya had a cadre of very well educated people, but they had little experience with refugee and human rights law. For this reason, UNHCR took the decision—in the middle of an active conflict—to conduct training in human rights, gender, and refugee protection for a range of professionals: lawyers, judges, doctors, and professors. The process was electrifying, with youthful groups of trainees filling lecture halls, eager to learn, to challenge and to be challenged.

UNHCR also tackled sensitive issues, such as that of rape. For years this was an entirely taboo topic in Libya, but this began to change as public allegations of mass rape emerged.

Unpopular causes needed to be addressed by UNHCR, in particular the intense persecution suffered by dark-skinned people, both foreigners and Libyans. This was especially sensitive, as prejudice combined easily with accusations of collaboration.

The Libya operation was a new arena for humanitarian engagement, in the wider context of the Arab Spring. UNHCR and other agencies were able make a positive impact, both inside Libya and in the neighbouring countries which bore the brunt of the population movements. As events in the region continue to unfold, the UN has a stronger base, and a stronger image, from which to proceed. By the end of 2011, the UN team in Tripoli had agreed to phase out its humanitarian 'cluster' system and to work with the new Libyan government to support the country's recovery process. ◆

insecure environments, for only those organizations that respect them are entitled to the protection of humanitarian action that should be afforded under international law. Operating in line with the principles is also critical to acceptance of humanitarian action by the parties to a conflict and by affected communities. In many situations there are constraints on full respect that are outside the control of humanitarian organizations, but in others a lack of full respect has been a matter of choice.[14] If respect of the principles by humanitarian organizations is a necessary condition, it is clearly not sufficient: the parties to a conflict must also respect them.

Humanitarian principles have been flouted in countless situations, and they appear to be under particular threat in the context of contemporary violence. The parties to a conflict (or other agents of violence) may not accept or even understand them. States may subordinate them to political imperatives and to their own security concerns. When the principles are not fully respected yet action to meet vital needs still appears possible, humanitarian organizations may have to choose between bad and still worse options.

For those who can facilitate or obstruct humanitarian action, the perception of that action and its impact on their objectives will be determining. Where civilians are targets of violence, and their displacement an objective, humanitarian action that seeks to protect and assist civilians will not be seen as neutral, whatever its intent. In conflict-torn Somalia, for instance, rebel groups have sought to limit humanitarian assistance in areas under their control, considering it contrary to their interests. Humanitarian access has also been restricted in Yemen.

BOX **1•5**

Yemen: a complex environment

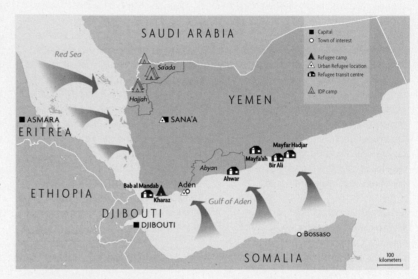

In Yemen, UNHCR and its partners have faced many obstacles to their operations, including widespread political unrest in 2011. Yet the agencies have found innovative ways to remain in the country, and to assist large numbers of refugees and IDPs.

Yemen is the only state on the Arabian Peninsula to have ratified the 1951 Refugee Convention. UNHCR first established a presence there in 1992, in response to the Somali exodus that has continued unabated ever since. At the end of 2011 there were more than 200,000 Somali refugees registered in Yemen, of whom 25,000 arrived in 2011 alone. Yemen remains one of the world's poorest countries, ranking 136 out of 170 on the 2011 Human Development Index.

In recent years, the challenges faced by UNHCR and other humanitarian actors in Yemen have multiplied. Besides a continued influx of refugees and asylum seekers from Somalia, Ethiopia, and Eritrea, a massive internal displacement crisis was generated over seven years of conflict between the government and the Al-Houthi movement in the north of the country. That conflict, along with new disturbances and displacement in the south, the fight against terrorism, and the outbreak of political violence in 2011 created formidable obstacles to humanitarian work.

From 2004 until 2010, fighting in northern Yemen killed thousands of civilians, displaced an estimated 350,000 people, and affected more than 800,000 in five governorates. The conflict's intensity increased

over six successive rounds of fighting, with reports of violations of humanitarian and human rights law, including aerial bombardments, shelling of civilians, and use of cluster munitions.

In 2011, almost 90 per cent of IDPs in the north lived in spontaneous settlements, with the remaining 10 per cent living in camps in Hajjah and Sa'ada. Most had been forced to abandon their cattle—often their primary source of income. Alternative livelihood opportunities for them were very scarce. The needs of IDPs and their host communities were extensive, but security concerns made it difficult for UNHCR and others to assess these needs in a comprehensive way. In spite of a ceasefire reached in February 2010,

sporadic clashes continued.

Access to affected populations remained limited. The Al-Houthi movement maintained control over vast areas of Sa'ada governorate, and access by humanitarian agencies to the country's northernmost province was sporadic. In June 2010 the parties agreed to reinforce the ceasefire and enable IDP returns, but few returns took place. By March 2011, the Al-Houthi movement had taken over Sa'ada City, signifying *de facto* control of the whole governorate. UNHCR, with the rest of the humanitarian community, worked toward a common understanding with the *de facto* authorities to facilitate humanitarian activities and enable them

Integrated UN missions and stabilization approaches

NOTWITHSTANDING THE EFFORTS OF UNHCR TO BE STRICTLY NON-POLITICAL, AID itself can be highly political. The risk of politicization of aid is heightened where humanitarian action is closely associated with political action. This explains the concern many humanitarian actors have expressed about what the UN terms 'integrated missions'.

Where multidimensional UN peacekeeping or political missions are deployed,

to reach displaced persons and affected communities.

The government, UNHCR, and other agencies sought to coordinate relief activities. In 2009, the government had established a High-Level Inter-Ministerial Committee for Relief Operations, headed by the Minister of Health. At the operational level, it established an Executive Unit for IDPs, which was to coordinate the humanitarian response, facilitate access, and appeal for resources. To strengthen institutional capacities, UNHCR supported an IDP Strategy Task Force, composed of government, UN and civil society representatives. A National Strategy on Internal Displacement Due to Natural Disasters, Conflict and Other Causes was completed at the end of 2010.

However, the strategy could not be implemented because of Yemen's political unrest in 2011, and it quickly became redundant. The unrest led to new displacement , particularly in the southern governorate of Abyan, where during the summer months clashes between pro-government factions and militants displaced tens of thousands. Fighting resulting in displacement also occured in other governorates—including the capital Sana'a. At the end of 2011, Yemen had over 450,000 registered IDPs.

Humanitarian space continued to shrink, with the spread of political unrest. Humanitarian agencies had to scale up their responses to assist the large numbers of people fleeing fighting in southern Yemen; many arrived without assets in neighbouring districts where public services were disrupted. At the same time the insecurity resulted in the killing of civilians, multiple constraints and disruptions to the delivery of aid, and the evacuation of aid workers.

Alongside the massive internal displacement, migrants and refugees continued to arrive in Yemen from across the Gulf of Aden and the Red Sea, mainly Somalis, Ethiopians and Eritreans. Between 2008 and 2011, some 265,000 people reached Yemeni shores in search of protection, better opportunities, or transit before continuing north into Saudi Arabia and beyond. Yemen has long maintained the practice of considering all Somalis *prima facie* as refugees while other nationalities undergo refugee status determination by UNHCR. Only some 20 per cent of the Ethiopian new arrivals seek asylum, while nearly all Eritreans do.

During 2011, refugee communities in urban areas were beset by fear, in the face of armed conflict which was waged intensively at times. More than 80 per cent of refugees live in Yemen's urban areas, particularly Sana'a, where fighting broke out on at least three occasions in 2011. Unlike Yemeni city-dwellers, the refugees do not have a village in which to seek safety in case of extended violence in the city.

Overall, humanitarian operations in Yemen—both for refugees and IDPs—were challenged by the government's limited ability to provide basic services to its own citizens, and by the capacity of UNHCR's national partners, which is still modest in many instances. National partners were needed more than ever as insecurity became a growing constraint on international presence. In the context of fighting in the North, various terrorist incidents, counter-terrorism operations, and kidnappings of humanitarian workers, the UN put strict limits on the number of international staff allowed to work in the country at any one time.

Access to populations in need has remained sporadic. The provision of humanitarian assistance has been restricted by tribes in various governorates, as well as by government and rebel forces in connection with the civil unrest. Aid deliveries have been disrupted by ambushes and checkpoints aimed at claiming a share of the assistance intended for IDPs. The difficult operating environment has been compounded by a certain hesitation on the part of donors to fund humanitarian operations in Yemen.

UNHCR's operations, like those of others, have been disrupted by the unrest. The UNHCR office, located in Sana'a, had to close 18 times in 2011 due to insecurity, including when mortars hit the office premises. In the second half of 2011, the office had only 30 per cent of its international staff in the country, while the others were evacuated waiting for the situation to stabilize. As of late 2011, a back-up operation was being set up outside Yemen to provide 'remote support'.

In this extremely delicate context, UNHCR used a combination of approaches to continue providing assistance to the IDPs in northern and southern Yemen, as well as to the refugees in urban areas, the Kharaz camp in southern Yemen, and coastal reception centres. The agency aimed to reduce its exposure to the most serious risks, while seeking all available opportunities to meet needs.

UNHCR also invested in building 'acceptance' of its activities by both the central and local authorities. In situations of civil conflict, any perceived lack of neutrality can generate additional risks. ◆

the UN presence is organized around the principle of 'integration', meaning that the objectives and actions of all UN agencies and forces present in the country are channelled coherently toward the same goal: to resolve conflict and assist in the recovery of affected states. In a 2006 Guidance Note, the (then) UN Secretary-General Kofi Annan explained that an integrated mission 'is based on a common strategic plan and a shared understanding of the priorities and types of programme interventions that need to be undertaken at various stages of the recovery process.'[15] The integrated mission concept is the translation of the 'whole of government' approach increasingly adopted by individual countries. While the rational use of resources is one objective, one authoritative review noted that 'integration is seen as a prerequisite for tackling a set of peacebuilding challenges that are themselves narrowly intertwined.'[16]

It is undisputed that security, human rights and development challenges are inextricably linked but it is important not to lose sight of the very specific mandates and responsibilities of different parts of the United Nations. Humanitarian agencies have raised concerns about the impact of integration on the space for neutral, independent humanitarian action. It is argued that humanitarian action requires impartiality, whereas supporting a political transition process by definition demands a degree of partiality. This is evident, for instance, where UN peacekeeping forces are engaged in enforcement action. Others maintain that by ensuring that humanitarian action is an integral part of a wider UN mission, humanitarian space will ultimately be safeguarded and strengthened.

Those who believe that integrated missions complicate humanitarian action argue that where there is tension between humanitarian and political imperatives, the latter will prevail. They fear that integration contributes to a blurring of distinctions between political and peacekeeping actors on the one hand and humanitarian actors on the other. Integration may not present a problem when the mission is implementing a political resolution that has the broad support of all parties. But when the conflict is ongoing, or where a political settlement remains elusive, the various actors may not make a distinction between a mission's political and military components, on the one hand and its humanitarian objectives on the other. If the political strategy pursued by a mission is perceived as running counter to the interests of a particular political or military group, the ability of the UN's humanitarian agencies to operate may be affected.

UNHCR's experience has been that whilst integration can bring real benefits in countries which have already moved solidly into the peacebuilding phase, in situations where conflict is ongoing or the peace process has not yet taken root, it is crucial that humanitarian actors not be perceived as aligned with political or security agendas.[17] For this reason, the humanitarian community opposed proposals for a rigid form of structural integration in Somalia, arguing that the Humanitarian Coordinator, supported by the UN's Office for the Coordination of Humanitarian Affairs (OCHA), should remain outside the mission structure.

The 'stabilization' approaches adopted by NATO members and others in failed or conflict-affected states raise many of the same issues, as they similarly seek to combine a range of foreign policy, military, and assistance tools, with the stated aim of enhancing human secrity as well as state security. Even more than in the case of UN integrated missions, this approach poses fundamental challenges for humanitarian actors concerned by the growing involvement of the military in the humanitarian sphere. Military and civilian assistance programmes have been presented as humanitarian when that is not their primary motivation, they are not undertaken without discrimination, and they may be conditional. Some humanitarian actors are concerned that political advantage has been sought from their engagement, or that they have effectively been required to be supporters of political and military actions. All of this can have a negative impact on 'humanitarian space', undermine efforts to promote acceptance of humanitarian action, and put staff at risk.

Where humanitarian action is not perceived to be neutral, the humanitarian actors may become targets, as has been tragically evident in numerous instances. In the last decade, UN humanitarian action in Iraq and Afghanistan has been seen (or represented) by armed opponents of the foreign military presence there as part of that presence.[18] The blurring of lines has also occurred elsewhere, including in the context of regional interventions, as for example in Somalia and Sudan. A continuing effort to maintain the distinct character of humanitarian action is necessary.

Operational challenges and responses

THE MOST SIGNIFICANT IMPACT ON HUMANITARIAN OPERATIONS OF THE CHANGING environment has been on staff security and access to potential beneficiaries. Recent years have been dangerous not only for civilians caught up in conflict but also for the staff of humanitarian organizations. According to an independent report on aid worker security, the largest number of attacks on aid workers in the period 2005–2010 took place in Afghanistan, Sudan, and Somalia, followed by Sri Lanka, Pakistan, the Democratic Republic of the Congo, Iraq, and the occupied Palestinian territory. During the period 2000 to 2010 there were 986 incidents, including kidnappings, injuries and 781 deaths. The number of major attacks on aid workers has increased dramatically. The annual average over the period 2000–2005 was 49 per year; this rose to an average of 124 attacks per year in 2006–2010.[19]

The reasons for attacks on humanitarian action are varied, from deliberate targeting to opportunistic criminal activity, and some are unknown. A 2009 analysis of the attacks showed that the percentage considered to be politically motivated increased each year from 2005 to 2008.[20]

Operating in an environment of uncontrolled violence is inherently risky. Conflict creates or exacerbates shortages of essential supplies, and humanitarian relief may have political as well as material value. In some insecure locations, humanitarian organizations have felt constrained to adopt measures that distance the operation from those it should serve, such as resorting to armed escorts and closer cooperation with military forces, whether national, regional, or those of the UN. Such measures are likely to increase local perceptions that the humanitarian organizations are not acting independently, can widen the distance between humanitarian actors and the communities they serve, and lead

BOX 1•6

Working alongside the military

The humanitarian principles of neutrality, impartiality, and independence demand that a clear distinction be made between humanitarian action and military activity. Failure to do so can place persons of concern and humanitarian staff at risk.

Maintaining distinct roles

In recent years, it has become more difficult to maintain this distinction, as the international community has increasingly engaged its military capacities—whether UN peacekeeping forces, NATO, African Union or EU deployments—in complex emergencies, sometimes with tasks that include the facilitation of humanitarian aid and the protection of civilians. This new reality has required both humanitarian and military actors to reassess their relationship.

In responding to natural disasters such as earthquakes or floods, in many cases, it is the military and civil defence—whether of the affected country or from other countries—that can provide the necessary logistical capacity. The interaction between humanitarian and military actors is less complicated in the context of disaster relief than in conflict situations, but can still affect perceptions of independence and neutrality, depending on the political environment.

The UN Office for the Coordination of Humanitarian Affairs (OCHA) has issued 'Guidelines on the Use of Foreign Military and Civil Defence Assets in Disaster Relief' (known as the 'Oslo Guidelines'). This document stresses the need to retain 'a clear distinction between the normal functions and roles of military and humanitarian stakeholders', although it does not address the issue of cooperation with the military of the affected country.[i]

When the situation is one of armed conflict, international humanitarian law (IHL) obliges the parties to facilitate the passage of humanitarian aid. IHL does not prohibit the military from supplying aid itself, but the military cannot present itself as a civilian actor. Humanitarian actors have expressed concern about the blurring of the lines, for instance when military actors use humanitarian action to 'win hearts and minds' of people in conflict zones.

This concern has given rise to a multiplicity of guidelines issued by the UN, the Red Cross and NGOs, on how the humanitarian sector should work with the military. Some are of a general nature, others are specific to situations such as Afghanistan and Iraq. The UN has issued 'Guidelines on the Use of Military and Civil Defence Assets to Support United Nations Humanitarian Activities in Complex Emergencies', known as the 'MCDA Guidelines', but these pertain only to military resources deployed at the request of the UN.[ii] Like the Oslo Guidelines, the MCDA Guidelines do not cover relations with the military of the host country.

A document which is relevant to contexts where humanitarian actors find themselves operating alongside the military is the UN Inter-Agency Standing Committee's Reference Paper on the Civil–Military Relationship in Complex Emergencies.[iii] That paper recommends a clear distinction between security-related and humanitarian tasks. It discourages military forces from taking on the role of provider of humanitarian aid, while stressing that the military has an important role in creating a secure operating environment that makes civilian humanitarian action possible. The paper does not deal with issues which have emerged more recently with respect to non-state armed groups or private security companies.

Within the UN, OCHA is the focal point for civil–military coordination, including for the development and dissemination of guidelines, training and support to military simulation exercises.

Experience from integrated missions

UNHCR recognizes that integrated UN missions can present risks but also opportunities to improve humanitarian outcomes. Participants in a UNHCR workshop on integrated missions in November 2008 distinguished between situations of ongoing conflict, where they felt that the UN's humanitarian coordination should be separate from the broader UN mission, and post-conflict situations, where integration was seen as offering significant opportunities to support the return and reintegration of refugees and IDPs, by linking this issue to broader conflict resolution and peacebuilding processes. Participants also saw a role for integrated missions with respect to the protection of civilians and the security of IDP and refugee camps.

In the crisis that engulfed Côte d'Ivoire after disputed presidential elections in November 2010, leading to the displacement of over one million Ivorians, UNHCR worked in the context of the integrated UN mission in Côte d'Ivoire (ONUCI). ONUCI had over 9,000 uniformed personnel and over 1,300 civilians deployed across the country, and UNHCR benefited from its security-related information. But after the UN certified the provisional election results, ONUCI became the target of attacks by militias, and anti-UN propaganda that affected perceptions of the UN as a whole, with significant implications for the security, movement and response capacity of all international humanitarian agencies. Uncertainties over security restrictions also delayed the deployment of additional UNHCR staff until January and February 2011.

In January 2011, the UN's OCHA, the Department for Political Affairs (DPA) and the Department for Peacekeeping Operations (DPKO) commissioned a study aimed at assessing the impact of integrated missions. Published in December 2011, the study found that the debate remained highly polarized, and that more needed to be done to build confidence among the political, peacekeeping, and humanitarian communities.[iv] It found evidence that UN integration arrangements have both positive and negative impacts on humanitarian space, and pointed to further opportunities for UN integration arrangements to support aid worker security, humanitarian access, engagement with non-state actors and humanitarian advocacy.

UN/B. ZOMA

In Afghanistan, for instance, UN humanitarian actions are integrated under the UN political mission (UNAMA), which is mandated to support the Afghan government and works closely with the NATO-led International Security Assistance Force (ISAF). The study found that threats to the UN mission, including its humanitarian components, appear to stem from non-state actors' negative perceptions of UNAMA's association with ISAF. As a result, some NGOs have withdrawn from UN-led humanitarian coordination mechanisms, as a risk mitigation measure.

In the Democratic Republic of the Congo (DRC), where the UN peacekeeping operation MONUSCO (formerly MONUC) is authorized to 'use all necessary means' to protect civilians, including humanitarian personnel, and to support the government in its stabilization and peace consolidation efforts, the study found a similarly mixed picture. While MONUSCO's security rules may have contributed to restricting humanitarian access, in other cases, its air assets increased access, and through their engagement with MONUSCO, humanitarian actors were able to influence the force's prioritization of protection of civilians. The report touches on an issue which has been of concern to humanitarian actors, namely MONUSCO 's support of DRC armed forces, some of which had been accused of human rights violations. This issue ultimately led to the development of the UN's 'human rights due diligence' policy.

The report found the most difficult situation in Somalia, where the African Union leads a peace-support mission (AMISOM). The study highlighted that proposals for the structural integration of UN humanitarian agencies within the UN's Political Office for Somalia (UNPOS)

▲ **UN troops deliver water** to villagers in Côte d'Ivoire.

were resisted by the humanitarian actors, due to concerns that they would then be perceived as having forfeited their neutrality. Given the operating context in Somalia, many humanitarian groups feared that any perception that they were not strictly neutral could lead to targeting of their staff and/or even greater restrictions on access to persons in need. NGOs warned that they would have to curtail their engagement with UN humanitarian agencies, if such structural integration were to occur. The process of establishing an integrated *strategic* framework was better accepted, in particular as a way of bringing UN humanitarian, political and peacekeeping actors together.

These and many other examples illustrate the challenges which UNHCR and other humanitarian agencies will continue to face when working alongside the military. They will need to find ways to maximize opportunities for fulfilling humanitarian tasks, while minimizing risks for humanitarian space. It will remain a difficult balancing act. ◆

i   UN Office for the Coordination of Humanitarian Affairs (OCHA), Guidelines on the Use of Foreign Military and Civil Defence Assets in Disaster Relief ('Oslo Guidelines'), November 2007, para 32 (iv).

ii UN Office for the Coordination of Humanitarian Affairs (OCHA), Guidelines on the Use of Military and Civil Defence Assets to Support United Nations Humanitarian Activities in Complex Emergencies, March 2003.

iii Inter-Agency Standing Committee, Civil–Military Relationship in Complex Emergencies: An IASC Reference Paper, 28 June 2004.

iv V. Metcalfe, A. Giffen and S. Elhawary, 'UN Integration and Humanitarian Space: An Independent Study Commissioned by the UN Integration Steering Group', Overseas Development Institute (Humanitarian Policy Group) and the Stimson Center, London and Washington DC, December 2011.

to the humanitarian action being seen by a community as contrary to its interests.

Some challenges are specific to refugee operations, as opposed to those affecting internally displaced people. As non-nationals, refugees are particularly vulnerable when law and order break down, and are likely to have even less protection than nationals in situations of generalized violence. With state institutions and services under pressure, refugees may become scapegoats for failings of the authorities, or be used to advance local political and economic objectives. Worse, they may be seen as allied with one of the parties to the conflict, and targeted because of this perception.

This was the case in 2011 during the post-election crisis in Côte d'Ivoire, when Liberian refugees were confronted with allegations that they were mercenaries fighting for ex-President Laurent Gbagbo. Many sought safety at UNHCR's compound in Abidjan. Later in 2011, sub-Saharan Africans in Libya were severely victimized in the face of similar allegations of mercenary activity.

UNHCR's responsibility for refugees and, since 2005, for leading the response to the protection needs of internally displaced people, gives it a necessarily high profile in insecure environments and can place it in direct opposition to those whose actions are directed against or threaten refugees and displaced people. Promoting and assisting voluntary repatriation has on occasion placed UNHCR staff at risk from those using violent means to oppose it, as was fatally the case in West Timor in September 2000. Defending the rights of the internally displaced can also draw hostile reactions from some parts of the government or from non-state elements. Hostile perceptions of UNHCR can affect security in many contexts, and these can persist long after the operation in which they were formed.[21]

PREVENTION

Humanitarian action cannot remove the causes of displacement, but it can and should mitigate the consequences. It is widely accepted that strengthening legitimate institutions and governance in order to provide citizens with security, justice and jobs is crucial to break cycles of violence.[22] The core element of the 'Responsibility to Protect' doctrine endorsed at the World Summit in 2005 is not the provision for military intervention to stop human rights abuses, however vital this may be. It is rather the emphasis on the responsibility of each state to protect its population and prevent abuses, and on other states to assist them, as appropriate, to discharge this responsibility.[23]

Where national justice systems are unable or unwilling to bring to account those who commit large-scale abuses against civilians, international justice mechanisms must. The ending of impunity, including for those who attack or hinder humanitarian assistance, also has a preventive effect.

WHAT LIMITS?

UNHCR—and humanitarian organizations in general—have no control or leverage over violent operating environments. In situations of protracted conflict, humanitarian assistance

▲ **Fighting in 2008** forced civilians to flee to this makeshift camp in eastern DRC.

can become part of the fabric of war, and governments may impose restrictions which compromise the independence of humanitarian action.

When humanitarian principles are in jeopardy and/or the environment is highly insecure, humanitarian action may not be possible without compromises that undermine its standing. Some argue that it should then be suspended. This issue arose in early 2009, when the government of Sri Lanka constructed the Menik Farm Welfare Centre to accommodate more than a quarter of a million IDPs who fled during the final months of the conflict. The international community criticized conditions in the camp and limitations imposed by the government on freedom of movement during the initial stages of displacement. Several agencies decided to suspend operations until conditions improved. However, UNHCR continued to work in the camp, carrying out emergency shelter activities, providing relief items and conducting protection monitoring for the benefit of persons of concern to the organization. Since the end of the conflict in May 2009, nearly all of the IDPs have left Menik Farm either to return to their homes or to stay with friends and relatives. Less than two per cent of the initial population remained at the end of 2011.

The reality is that it is often where needs are the greatest that the risks are also greatest. As a result, humanitarian organizations have often been ready to continue operations even in conditions that, as a matter of general policy, they would not accept. There are few recent examples of organizations suspending their operations because their principles could not be respected. Most suspensions are in response to specific security considerations, often in the aftermath of deadly attacks, and are short-lived.

One recent study notes that in Somalia the NGO consortium operating there identified 'red lines', and affirmed that any 'threat or compulsion to cross a "red line" would (in theory) result in the suspension or closure of a programme'. But the study observes that 'many more examples exist in Somalia and Sudan where red lines have been drawn and redrawn time and again to accommodate the increasing threats agencies face on the ground'.[24]

It is very difficult to identify the point at which the problems faced outweigh the benefits delivered, and humanitarian organizations are understandably reluctant to make this determination. If humanitarian action continues whatever the circumstances, it may forfeit the protection accorded to it under international law. Some fear that it may also come to be counted on as a substitute for essential but difficult political action.[25] Even compromised assistance can be life-sustaining, and the pressures of the media, public opinion and donors are likely to argue against suspending aid. The reasons for continuing will be obvious and the case for a principled suspension much more difficult to communicate. These are dilemmas that require the most careful consideration, and UNHCR and its partners have to keep such issues under constant review.

Risk management

THE GREATEST DIRECT CHALLENGE FACING UNHCR AND OTHER HUMANITARIAN organizations today is insecurity, and considerable attention has therefore been devoted to finding ways to operate safely in high-risk environments. UNHCR's responsibilities are such that risk cannot be eliminated. Moreover, UNHCR does not operate in an institutional vacuum, but in the context of a common approach to security led by the UN's Department of Safety and Security (UNDSS). Within the UN, there has been a shift in focus from risk avoidance ('when to leave') to risk management ('how to stay'), as outlined in the 2011 study entitled 'To Stay and Deliver', commissioned by the UN Office for the Co-ordination of Humanitarian Affairs.[26]

A risk management approach includes several important elements. First, it entails a careful appreciation of the threats in the operating environment, at the earliest stages of programme planning, to determine the likelihood of dangerous events and their possible impacts. In the context of UNHCR's work, this process means considering risks both to staff and to persons of concern, including where threats may come from within that population.

Risk assessment also requires weighing risks against the importance of the humanitarian action. There is no simple formula to capture the many factors involved; it may be very difficult to assign a relative importance to objectives as varied as assessing emergency needs, preventing rights abuses and establishing conditions for safe return.

Finally, risk management calls for measures to reduce the likelihood or impact of threats to humanitarian work. The 'Stay and Deliver' study explored a range of good practices. The first step is invariably to encourage and support actions by the authorities to uphold their responsibility for the safety of humanitarian staff. Where risks remain, other measures may be necessary; in recent years the UN has developed clear guidelines called Minimum Operational Safety Standards (MOSS) to articulate, and regularly to review, the security requirements of each duty station.

PROMOTING ACCEPTANCE

For UNHCR, it is vital to ensure that all concerned, and particularly the local communities, understand and accept the aim of its work. The fact that UNHCR's work is of an entirely non-political character and is underpinned by international refugee and human rights law provides a solid foundation on which to explain the agency's action. UNHCR's 'people orientation' is perhaps the most important element in promoting its acceptance by beneficiaries and local communities.

The local media play an important role. UNHCR has sought to deliver, through the media, a consistent message that its assistance is impartial and needs-based. Yet the strategy of promoting acceptance cannot eliminate all risks. The volatility of the environments in which UNHCR works was underscored by an attack on the UNHCR office in Kandahar (Afghanistan) in October 2011 which killed five people, including three UNHCR staff members. Following the attack, High Commissioner Guterres reiterated that

UNHCR would continue to 'reach out to the population (...) to show that we are fully committed to humanitarian principles.'[27]

Where the threat is not local in nature, but comes for instance from wider extremist movements, local acceptance of a humanitarian presence may not be sufficient to ensure its security. Difficult operating environments have forced humanitarian responders to re-evaluate traditional ways of delivering services and develop new models.

NATIONAL STAFF AND PARTNERSHIPS

Working in insecure environments requires an in-depth understanding of the conflict and the dynamics at play. Local actors have a comparative advantage because of their knowledge of the environment. UNHCR has therefore sought to empower its national staff and to build effective local partnerships. Sustained investment in training and mentoring national staff and partners can yield important dividends.

Ethical considerations demand conscientious review to ensure that risk is not simply transferred from international to national personnel. A decision to send a national staff member to a location to which an international staff member could not go must be founded on an assessment that the risk is lower to the national staff, due to local knowledge or the fact that he or she is less likely to attract attention.

Any decision to transfer implementation of programmes to local partners has implications for operational and financial accountability that require careful attention. Increases in insecurity and lack of access make it more difficult not only to deliver aid but also to monitor the protection needs of refugees, internally displaced people and returnees. This has prompted the development of new mechanisms to track programme delivery (*see box 1.7*).

PROTECTIVE MEASURES

In some environments, the strategy of promoting acceptance must be complemented by protective measures to reduce staff exposure to risk. Such measures may range from simply avoiding insecure locations, to physical barriers to protect offices from vehicle bombs, to the use of armed guards outside premises, and armoured vehicles or police or military escort when travelling. Such measures have been the source of considerable controversy over questions of principle and with respect to their effectiveness.

Where protective measures are necessary, the first recourse is normally for these to be provided by the host government. UN or other foreign military forces may be mandated to provide a safe and secure environment for humanitarian action. While cooperation with such forces can give rise to significant problems, it may be the only option if humanitarian action is to continue.

The requirement for armed escorts for humanitarian action can introduce other complications. Government officials who control clearance for movement and provide escorts can influence what aid goes where, citing security considerations that aid agencies

BOX **1•7**

Monitoring aid amid insecurity[i]

Humanitarian agencies operating in insecure situations face a major problem: lack of regular access to refugees and displaced people, owing to a high level of security risk. Where insecurity limits the possibility to monitor operations on a regular basis, humanitarian actors are often faced with a choice between reducing their activities or accepting the consequences of minimal oversight.

In Iraq, UNHCR developed a system designed to enable it to continue to operate in remote and insecure locations, but to reduce the amount of time that national and international staff would need to spend in high-risk locations. It also wanted a system which would help to raise awareness of the needs of displaced people in locations which were rarely visited by donors or the media; to improve planning, targeting, and coordination of its interventions; and to address donors' and auditors' requirements with respect to monitoring and evaluation. The result was the development of a 'live' project management tool.

The software for this innovative tool was developed within UNHCR, mainly by Iraqi colleagues, some of whom were themselves IDPs. Aside from the software development, the total cost was less than US$50,000, and most of this was for purchasing computers, digital cameras, and other hardware.

The system established a database for recording everything from the initial needs assessment of groups of concern, justification for a proposed action, the cost and expected time-frame for the intervention, through to evidence of completion of the project in the form of photographs with the Global Positioning System (GPS) location of the action. The system contained a wealth of information and data and provided a user-friendly platform where partners and staff could view the status of an activity. In other words, staff and partners could provide 'evidence' of their achievements even in the most challenging locations. Donors and other stakeholders were able to access the database as well and did not have to visit the project on location.

Since much of the work was undertaken in areas that remained extremely insecure but where humanitarian needs were great, the system was intended to enable UNHCR to demonstrate that a commissioned activity had been carried out. It registered data on each intervention made by UNHCR staff and partners—whether the construction of houses, the delivery of blankets, or the clearing of rubbish. Unless GPS-encrypted photos of the intervention were uploaded, it was assumed the activity did not occur as planned.

Staff and partners had an incentive to upload new data quickly, both to demonstrate their achievements and to facilitate the release of payments. The provision of location-tagged photos enabled recognition of the achievements of agencies in difficult-to-access locations but also reduced the potential for inflated claims in relation to the status or delivery time-line for an activity. Stakeholders could verify the GPS coordinates embedded in the photos against the location agreed for the activity, and the date encrypted on the photo should be consistent with the agreed time-frame for implementation.

As soon as photos and related information were uploaded, the database extracted the GPS coordinates, registering these against each shelter, IDP camp, or other location with a Google Earth interface. UNHCR provided GPS-enabled camera phones to partners—although sometimes the technology proved insufficiently robust for conditions in Iraq, and in some areas, GPS simply did not work well enough. As data was uploaded, the database automatically generated Google Earth views, summary reports with demographic and geographic breakdowns, average prices based on the Bill of Quantities, and more. Maps could also be generated, using almost any number of variables.

The tracking system supplemented—but did not replace UNHCR monitoring and evaluation procedures. Its roll-out across Iraq enabled UNHCR to have a high level of confidence in the location, time, date, and cost, of almost all activities undertaken, and reduced the need for multiple monitoring missions.

Providing a visual image of humanitarian needs—such as those in IDP camps—and linking it to Google Earth allows stakeholders to review key information and determine priorities and responsibilities accordingly. A visual review via Google Earth of where agencies are working can also help to illustrate programming gaps.

Perhaps most importantly, by providing a comprehensive overview of all the displaced sites including geo-tagged photographs, the system helps to reduce the anonymity of human suffering. Similarly, the ready availability of evidence and data supports advocacy with donors, other agencies, and concerned authorities. Based on visual evidence of conditions, such advocacy has led to increased support for the displaced, and in a number of cases, has prevented the eviction of vulnerable populations. ◆

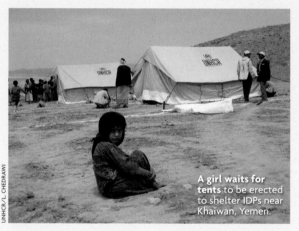

UNHCR/L. CHEDRAWI

A girl waits for tents to be erected to shelter IDPs near Khaiwan, Yemen.

---

i   Some of this text appeared previously in *Forced Migration Review* 38 (November 2011) and is reproduced with appreciation.

cannot assess independently. Depending on the context, where humanitarian actors need armed escorts in order to operate safely, it may be better accepted if such escorts come from local rather than foreign forces. In some cases, the provision of area security may be preferable to armed escorts.

The UN and other actors may also provide assistance to strengthen local capacities to maintain the rule of law, including in camps for refugees and the internally displaced, and in host communities. In 2011, the UN Secretary-General issued a policy on UN support to non-UN security forces entitled the 'Human Rights Due Diligence Policy'.[28] That policy sets out standards to ensure that support to non-UN security forces is always consistent with the UN Charter and international law.

One of the most important factors determining UNHCR's ability to operate effectively is the training of its staff. This has four key dimensions. First, UNHCR invests heavily in training managers in security risk management policy and practices, as their decisions will impact the staff at large. Secondly, training focuses on UNHCR's professional field security staff, whose day-to-day recommendations affect all staff in high-risk locations. Thirdly, training is provided to staff serving in high risk areas, with a focus on guards and drivers, the two categories facing the greatest risk. And finally, training is aimed at UNHCR staff at large, as all need to understand how to avoid and manage risk.

The road ahead

TODAY'S CONFLICTS POSE MANY CHALLENGES FOR HUMANITARIAN organizations. The operating environment is highly political, not only from a national perspective but also in the international context. Humanitarian action is affected by many factors over which humanitarian organizations have little if any control.

Some challenges are specific to UNHCR and result from its unique responsibility for non-nationals. As the examples in this chapter show, despite the many constraints, in recent years UNHCR and its partners have been able to continue operating in many complex and insecure environments. The trends of forced displacement suggest that there will be a continuing, and probably increasing, need to do so. To 'stay and deliver' in such contexts requires innovation, discipline and principles. It also requires realism, for however strong UNHCR's response capacity, there will be limits to its ability to influence its operating environment and therefore to meet its protection objectives.

The most effective humanitarian action can only be palliative: addressing root causes of forced displacement requires other tools. In the absence of action to tackle these causes, greater international solidarity with refugees, internally displaced people and their host states and communities must be achieved. Today's fragile environments not only make refugees and other forcibly displaced people more vulnerable and challenge UNHCR operationally, but also, as explored in the next two chapters, threaten the institution of asylum and the achievement of durable solutions. ■

CHAPTER 2

Keeping Asylum Meaningful

I N 2011, A EUROPEAN DAILY NEWSPAPER CARRIED A STORY about a group of Somalis whose applications for asylum had been denied and who had been detained. A government spokesman was quoted as saying: 'That is the procedure, they are illegals. We are going to verify their identity and arrange to return them to their country'. Just days earlier, UNHCR's spokesperson had briefed journalists about the humanitarian emergency in Somalia, which an authoritative report had labelled 'the world's most dangerous country'.[1] Countries in the region—Kenya, Yemen, Ethiopia and Djibouti—hosted nearly one million Somali refugees, and the High Commissioner had consistently appealed to governments to refrain from deporting people to Somalia.

This example—one of many which could have been cited—illustrates a core problem facing the international refugee regime today. For the most part, it is countries in the developing world that are confronted with mass influxes of refugees fleeing conflict. Unlike countries that are geographically removed from crisis zones, neighbouring states face an immediate, and often very visible, humanitarian challenge at their borders. These countries, by-and-large, grant admission and protection on a *prima facie* or group basis. Refugees are thus protected from *refoulement*, but in many of these contexts, their rights are very limited and they are frequently confined to camps. In such situations, host states assume that the refugees' stay will be temporary and that they will return home in the near future, but the number of protracted refugee situations around the globe shows that this assumption is frequently incorrect.

Wealthier countries, on the other hand, are usually far removed from countries in crisis, and have put in place, with varying degrees of success, an array of measures to deter and prevent the arrival of asylum seekers and refugees. The behaviour of these states is incongruent, as one author has noted, insofar as 'great importance is attached to the principle of asylum but enormous efforts are made to ensure that refugees (and others with less pressing claims) never reach the territory of the state where they could receive its protection'.[2]

Young refugees from Côte d'Ivoire have arrived in Liberia after the disputed election at the end of 2010.

It has been suggested that there are two parallel systems in operation: the asylum regime (in the global North) and the refugee regime (in the global South).[3] Without going that far, it is clear that there are divergent practices as well as different understandings about who deserves protection, what the content of that protection should be, and where protection should be provided.

For more than six decades, UNHCR has been tasked with ensuring international protection in cooperation with states, with the 1951 Convention relating to the Status of Refugees and its 1967 Protocol as the cornerstone of this effort.[4] This chapter looks at how UNHCR can take this responsibility forward in today's complex protection environment. The chapter begins with an overview of the international legal framework for refugee protection and the contemporary asylum landscape. It then sets out the need, in an increasingly globalized world, for greater consistency in the practice of asylum, and to address mixed migration in a way that ensures access to asylum. Finally, the chapter suggests that the institutional and political 'governance' of asylum should be strengthened to preserve the integrity of the institution of asylum and to keep asylum meaningful.

The international legal framework

WHEN THE 1951 CONVENTION WAS WRITTEN, THE WORLD WAS STILL IN SHOCK after acts that had outraged the conscience of humanity. Its authors were determined to contribute to building a world in which human beings could find safety from persecution and enjoy freedom from fear. Their belief in fundamental rights helped to anchor the concept of refugee protection in the international legal system.

The Convention they conceived is a human rights instrument, non-discriminatory in its application and (today) global in scope. At its core is the principle of *non-refoulement*, signifying that no refugee may be returned to danger. Article 1 of the Convention sets out the definition of a refugee as a person who is outside his or her country of origin and unable or unwilling to return owing to a well-founded fear of being persecuted there. The fear may be based on five grounds: race, religion, nationality, membership of a particular social group, or political opinion. The Convention also enumerates the rights to which refugees are entitled in their countries of asylum, and their duties and obligations. Initially, the Convention applied only to persons who became refugees as a result of events occurring before 1951. Signatories had the option of further limiting its application to persons who became refugees as a result of events in Europe. Developments in different parts of the world soon made it clear that both limitations needed to be removed. This was achieved by the 1967 Protocol, which has been accepted by almost all Convention signatory states.

Over the past 60 years, the Refugee Convention has proved both resilient and adaptable. The Convention can be applied to mass influx situations as well as to individual arrivals. It is sensitive to the security concerns of states and the protection needs of individuals. Although the Convention encourages the integration of refugees in their country of asylum followed by naturalization, it also sets out the conditions under which refugee status can come to an end. However, the Convention has notable gaps: it does not set out an explicit framework for responsibility-sharing and is limited in the extent to which it addresses solutions to refugee problems. Importantly, the Convention is not an instrument to manage migration.

In December 2011, UN member states reaffirmed that the 1951 Convention and its 1967 Protocol are the 'foundation of the international refugee protection regime' and have 'enduring value and relevance.' They recognized the importance of respecting and upholding the principles and values that underlie these instruments.[5]

The benefit of such a multilateral treaty is its ability to generate mutual understanding of rights and obligations; refugee protection practised in a consistent manner is in the interest of all. By contrast, when states do not accede to the Refugee Convention, fail to live up to their obligations under it, or enter reservations to the text, the potential for a system of mutual understanding and collaboration is weakened. For this reason, UNHCR continues to work toward universal accession to the 1951 Convention and the 1967 Protocol.

There are various reasons why countries remain reluctant to accede to the Refugee Convention. They may be apprehensive about multilateral engagement, loss of flexibility, costs or the potential for abuse. They may see the Convention as representing 'Western' standards of treatment that some cannot provide, or as concerned only with 'political' refugees when most of today's refugees flee from conflict situations. Some worry that recognizing refugee status under the 1951 Convention could affect their relations with other states. Middle Eastern states tend to see refugee matters primarily in terms of the unresolved Palestinian refugee question.

Some countries point out that they have protected refugees for decades even without acceding to the 1951 Convention—a fact which UNHCR acknowledges, while continuing to advocate for accession. In 2000, when Mexico ratified the Convention, the then High Commissioner Sadako Ogata noted: 'Mexico has had a long tradition of asylum (...). Its accession to these universal instruments reflects this generous tradition and further strengthens the international refugee protection regime'.[6]

Accession to the 1951 Convention is one factor by which the safety of refugees can be measured, but accession alone is not sufficient; contracting states must also establish national laws and procedures reflecting their Convention obligations. After Italy returned migrants and asylum seekers to Libya in 2009, UNHCR stressed that 'the establishment of an effective protection system in Libya would require, among other steps, its accession to the 1951 Convention and the adoption of appropriate asylum legislation'.[7]

In the case of a proposed agreement between Australia (a signatory to the 1951 Convention) and Malaysia (a non-signatory) for the transfer to Malaysia of 800 non-Malaysian asylum seekers, the High Court of Australia noted *inter alia* that being a party to the Convention made it more likely that a country's laws would provide for recognition and protection of refugees, although it was not necessary for a state to be a party to provide such recognition and protection. The High Court barred the transfer.[8]

The 1951 Convention has been complemented by regional instruments in Africa, Latin America, and the European Union (EU). Given UNHCR's statutory responsibility for the progressive development of international refugee law and standards, the Office has been closely involved in the elaboration of these instruments.

The 1969 Convention Governing the Specific Aspects of Refugee Problems in Africa (the OAU Convention) translated the 1951 Convention into the African context at the time.

MAP **2•1**   **States bound by international and regional refugee instruments** |31.12.2011

This map does not imply the expression of any opinion on the part of UNHCR or the United Nations concerning the legal status of any country or territory, or the delimitation of frontiers or boundaries, nor is it warranted to be error-free.

Parties to the 1951 Refugee Convention and the 1967 Protocol

Parties to the 1951 Refugee Convention only

Parties to the 1967 Protocol only

Not parties to either the 1951 Refugee Convention or the 1967 Protocol

Parties to the 1969 Convention governing the Specific Aspects of Refugee Problems in Africa

States bound by EU asylum Directives

Denmark has opted out of the EU asylum Directives; Ireland has opted out of one; the UK has maintained the option to opt out.

BOX **2·1**

Building the Common European Asylum System

The European Union (EU)'s effort to align the laws, policies and practices of its Member States in the sensitive area of asylum is an unprecedented undertaking.

In 1999, when EU leaders pledged to establish a Common European Asylum System (CEAS), the Union had just 15 Member States. By 2011, membership had expanded to 27 countries, with Croatia to become the 28th. Most new members had little experience with asylum, and when they joined, their systems had to be strengthened substantially to comply with EU standards.

The Treaty on the European Union, as amended by the Treaty of Amsterdam (which entered into force in 1999), required the adoption of EU laws that set common minimum standards on asylum. The requirement was ambitious, given the challenge of defining agreed standards for such a large and diverse group of states.

The first phase of work toward the CEAS focused on the legislative foundation of the

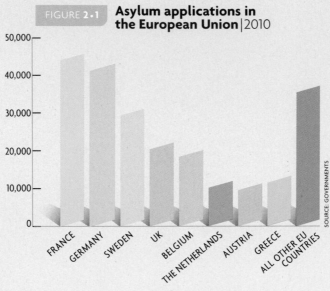

FIGURE **2·1** **Asylum applications in the European Union** | 2010

SOURCE: GOVERNMENTS

system. By 2005, four Directives had entered into force. One establishes a temporary protection status to be applied in situations of mass influx, although it has not been utilized to date.[i] Another stipulates how asylum seekers are to be treated.[ii] The third gives greater concrete content to the notion of asylum, *inter alia* by establishing 'subsidiary protection' for persons who do not meet the

refugee definition but nonetheless face a serious risk in their country of origin. It also enumerates the rights to which refugees and subsidiary protection beneficiaries are entitled, and obliges states to grant status if the criteria are fulfilled.[iii] The final Directive, the one on which agreement was most difficult to reach, sets out standards for asylum procedures.[iv]

In addition, the 'Dublin II Regulation' was enacted, setting out criteria for determining which EU country—or other European state taking part in the arrangement—is responsible for examining an asylum application (*see box 8.4*).

In a second phase, the European Commission proposed to amend these initial instruments to fill identified gaps, achieve a higher common standard of protection and greater equality of treatment, and to reinforce solidarity among the Member States.

In response to large-scale refugee flows which then resulted mainly from Africa's wars of independence, it stipulated that the refugee definition also extended to people who flee events 'seriously disturbing public order'.[9] The OAU Convention provides that member states shall 'use their best efforts' to receive refugees and to 'secure the settlement' of those who are unable or unwilling to return home. It also provides for temporary residence pending resettlement elsewhere and sets out, for the first time, treaty standards for voluntary repatriation.[10] Burden-sharing is also a central aspect of the OAU Convention.

Latin American countries followed Africa's lead in adopting a framework designed to address refugee problems in their region. The 1984 Cartagena Declaration on Refugees encouraged all nations in Latin America to enlarge the concept of a refugee beyond the

Initially, the plan was to complete the common system by 2010; but the deadline was later extended to 2012.

This second phase proved difficult. Member States voiced concerns about raising standards as they feared this would lead to increased costs, attract asylum seekers, and invite abuse. Instead of more legislation, they wanted to focus on better implementation of existing legislation, more practical cooperation to align their asylum systems, and energetic efforts to control access to the EU territory. Two new agencies were created which reflect these priorities.

The first was the European Agency for the Management of Operational Coordination at the External Borders of the Member States of the European Union (Frontex). Established in October 2005, Frontex's initial annual budget was US$9 million. This grew to over US$120 million in 2011, by which time the agency had 289 staff.

In June 2008, UNHCR concluded a cooperation agreement with Frontex. UNHCR was keen to make sure that border control arrangements included safeguards enabling asylum seekers to have access to EU territory and asylum procedures. Frontex has consistently affirmed its commitment to the full respect of human rights, including access to asylum, although questions have arisen in about its role with regard to interception at sea, involuntary returns, and detention—particularly in Greece.

The second new body was the European Asylum Support Office (EASO). Set up in May 2010, its mandate is to strengthen practical cooperation on asylum among EU countries, to help those whose asylum systems come under particular pressure, and to enhance the implementation of the nascent Common European Asylum System. One of EASO's key concerns, shared by UNHCR, is to address the lack of consistency in asylum decision-making within the EU.

During 2007–2011, three separate UNHCR research reports revealed vast differences in how EU countries conduct asylum procedures and interpret legal concepts which are central to asylum decisions. They found that an individual's chances of receiving protection in the EU could range from near zero to well over 50 per cent, depending on the Member State in which he or she is able to seek asylum.

UNHCR has urged the EU to focus not merely on the consistency of asylum decisions, but also on their quality. This is critical in view of Article 18 of the Charter of Fundamental Rights of the European Union, which provides that 'the right to asylum shall be guaranteed, with due respect for the rules of the 1951 Convention.'

European courts will play an important role in the further evolution of the Common European Asylum System. The Court of Justice of the EU (CJEU) has jurisdiction to interpret the EU asylum instruments, and to rule on any alleged infringements by Member States. National courts at all levels in the Member States have power to refer questions of interpretation to the CJEU.

The European Court of Human Rights has also addressed questions arising from the EU instruments, although its responsibility is limited to enforcing the European Convention on Human Rights within the legal framework of the Council of Europe.

These courts will continue to be the source of rulings that shape the scope and limits of refugee rights and state protection obligations under European law. Given that their decisions bind states that are among the largest recipients of asylum applicants worldwide, these courts will have a very significant influence on the wider development of international refugee law. ◆

i   Council Directive 2001/55/EC of 20 July 2011 on minimum standards for giving temporary protection in the event of a mass influx of displaced persons and on measures promoting a balance of efforts between Member States in receiving such persons and bearing the consequences thereof, Official Journal of the European Union, L 212/12 of 07.08.2001.

ii   Council Directive 2003/9/EC of 27 January 2003 laying down minimum standards for the reception of asylum seekers, Official Journal of the European Union, L 31/18 of 06.02.2003.

iii   Council Directive 2004/83/EC of 29 April 2004 on minimum standards for the qualification and status of third country nationals or stateless persons as refugees or as persons who otherwise need international protection and the content of the protection granted, Official Journal of the European Union, L 304/12 of 30.09.2004.

iv   Council Directive 2005/85/EC of 1 December 2005 on minimum standards on procedures in Member States for granting and withdrawing refugee status, Official Journal of the European Union, L 326/13 of 13.12.2005.

definition contained in the 1951 Convention, to include persons who have fled because of 'generalized violence' or other circumstances which have 'seriously disturbed public order'.[11] Although the Cartagena Declaration is not binding law, most countries in the region have included this extended definition in their national legal frameworks.

The most far-reaching regional legal developments, for the breadth of issues covered, have come from the EU since its 1999 decision to create a Common European Asylum System based on the 'full and inclusive application of the Geneva Convention'.[12] Four Directives have been adopted, each adding content to refugee law in an area not addressed by the 1951 Convention (*see box 2.1*).

There are no corresponding binding instruments in Asia or the Middle East. The 1994 Arab Convention on Regulating Status of Refugees in the Arab Countries, adopted by the League of Arab States, has never been ratified.[13] Nonetheless, the Organization of Islamic Cooperation (OIC) has devoted increasing attention to the question of refugees, and a conference on refugees in the Muslim world is planned for 2012.[14] In 2001, Asian countries adopted the revised 'Bangkok Principles' on the status and treatment of refugees.[15] Both documents use the 'extended' refugee definition as contained in the 1969 OAU Convention; the Arab Convention extends it further to persons fleeing natural disasters or other grave events disrupting public order. These non-binding documents are important but have not achieved the same prominence and legal value as the instruments in other regions.

With the exception of legislative developments in the EU, international refugee law itself has evolved little over the past 40-plus years, since adoption of the 1967 Protocol and the 1969 OAU Convention. Despite this, very significant developments have emerged from the relationship between international refugee law and other bodies of international law, in particular international human rights law and international humanitarian and criminal law. The latter has had considerable influence on the understanding of who should be excluded from the scope of refugee protection.[16]

International human rights law contains principles relating to protection from *refoulement* which help to fill gaps and to ensure the enforcement of states' obligations. It also makes an important contribution to establishing a common understanding of what constitutes persecution. The Convention on the Elimination of all Forms of Discrimination against Women (CEDAW) and the Convention on the Rights of the Child (CRC), for example, are increasingly seen as relevant in the asylum context and are frequently cited in decisions on applications for refugee status or when assessing whether a planned action is in the best interest of a child refugee or asylum seeker (*see box 2.2*).

Regional human rights courts and bodies are playing a key role in interpreting and enforcing legal standards for the protection of refugees, in particular in Europe and in Latin America.[17] The Council of Europe and its Human Rights Court, the Court of Justice of the EU, and the Inter-American Commission on Human Rights are prime examples. There is also growing interest in asylum on the part of the African Human Rights Court and sub-regional courts in Africa, and the Association of Southeast Asian Nations' (ASEAN) Intergovernmental Commission on Human Rights. UNHCR interacts regularly with these institutions, in support of their standard-setting role, through seminars and training events, and by providing its views to the relevant regional, as well as national, courts.

The UN human rights treaty bodies also exercise a degree of oversight of the rights relevant to people of concern to UNHCR. These bodies systematically review the treatment of refugees and asylum seekers when examining state practice, and seek input from UNHCR and NGOs. The concluding observations of human rights treaty bodies in many cases emphasize the need for states party to cooperate and coordinate with UNHCR, thereby complementing UNHCR's supervisory role as set out in its Statute and in the 1951 Convention. Refugees and asylum seekers have also used these judicial and quasi-judicial avenues to assert their rights.

The practice of asylum: in search of consistency

THE ASYLUM LANDSCAPE IS FRAUGHT WITH INCONSISTENCIES. These concern how and where protection needs are determined, to whom international protection is extended, and the content of that protection. This state of affairs is complicated further by the many factors behind forced displacement today, and by the globalization of irregular migration.

By 2011, 148 countries had ratified the 1951 Convention and/or its 1967 Protocol, yet more than 40 per cent of refugees under UNHCR's mandate were hosted by states which had not acceded to either of these instruments. Even in signatory states, the number of refugees who enjoy Convention refugee status and the full set of rights it entails is a fraction of those who receive some form of protection, often limited to non-return.

HOW ARE PROTECTION NEEDS IDENTIFIED?

The 1951 Convention leaves it to each contracting state to establish the procedure it considers most appropriate for determining international protection needs.[18] This does not have to be through an individual procedure; status may be granted on a *prima facie* basis.[19] In 2010, eight out of ten refugees were hosted in countries of the developing world, mainly as a result of group or *prima facie* determinations of refugee status following large-scale influxes.

For many years it was mainly countries in Europe, North America and Australia that operated individual refugee status determination procedures. Today, asylum seeking is a global phenomenon. In 2010, 850,000 individual asylum applications were lodged in 167 countries or territories around the world, although the top ten countries accounted for 56 per cent of applications. South Africa received more asylum applications (180,600) than any other country, coming those to the number received by the 27 European Union Member States combined (235,900).

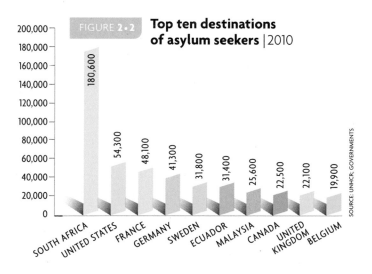

FIGURE **2·2** **Top ten destinations of asylum seekers** | 2010

SOUTH AFRICA 180,600
UNITED STATES 54,300
FRANCE 48,100
GERMANY 41,300
SWEDEN 31,800
ECUADOR 31,400
MALAYSIA 25,600
CANADA 22,500
UNITED KINGDOM 22,100
BELGIUM 19,900

SOURCE: UNHCR; GOVERNMENTS

By 2010, 100 countries had national refugee status determination procedures. In 46 countries that had not ratified the 1951 Convention or its 1967 Protocol, or where national asylum procedures were not fully functioning, UNHCR continued to determine refugee status under its mandate. Thus in 2010, UNHCR registered 89,000 new asylum claims and issued 61,000 substantive decisions—11 per cent of all individual asylum decisions worldwide, making the agency the second-largest asylum adjudicator after the Government of South Africa.

| FIGURE 2·3 | Individual decisions on applications for refugee status taken by states, by UNHCR, and jointly |

	2008	2009	2010
States	468,900	512,300	512,700
UNHCR	46,800	69,200	61,100
Jointly	31,200	21,000	5,200
Total	546,900	602,500	579,000
% UNHCR only	9%	11%	11%

SOURCE: UNHCR, GOVERNMENTS

Note: This table does not include cases which were closed for administrative reasons without a decision on the substance.

UNHCR encourages states to assume their responsibilities for refugees, including through the development of national legal frameworks and the establishment of refugee status determination procedures. The tendency of some countries to refrain from *refoulement* but otherwise to take little responsibility for identifying refugees on their territories or according them relevant rights remains a serious concern.[20] Building the protection capacity of national authorities is an essential part of UNHCR's global strategy, and in recent years, states as diverse as Burundi, Cambodia and Georgia have established and started to implement national status determination procedures.

Between 2001 and 2010, some 2.1 million people were found, through individual determinations, to be refugees under the terms of the 1951 Convention, or to be entitled to a complementary form of protection. In most cases this brought access to rights enabling them to integrate in their countries of asylum. During the same period, 2.7 million people were considered as refugees on a *prima facie* or group basis, mainly in countries

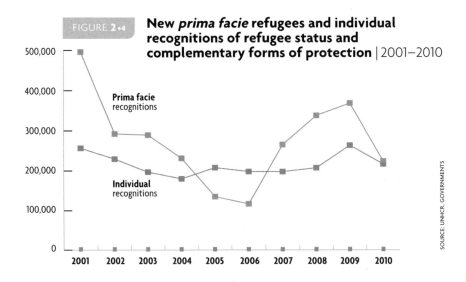

| FIGURE 2·4 | New *prima facie* refugees and individual recognitions of refugee status and complementary forms of protection | 2001–2010 |

SOURCE: UNHCR, GOVERNMENTS

neighbouring their own, frequently with limited access to rights. Of these 4.8 million people, most had fled conflict situations in their countries of origin, notably in Afghanistan, Iraq, and Somalia. In 2011, the deteriorating situation in Somalia produced a sharp increase in the numbers entering the *prima facie* system.

VICTIMS OF GENERALIZED VIOLENCE

There is a lack of coherence with regard to how states respond to people fleeing violence and conflict. This response is critically important, as such people today are the majority of those who seek international protection. Of the 10.5 million refugees under UNHCR's mandate at the start of 2011, more than two-thirds had fled from countries in conflict and 52 per cent were from just three countries: Afghanistan, Iraq, and Somalia.

UNHCR has sought to make clear that there is nothing in the 1951 Convention refugee definition which excludes its applicability to persons fleeing conflict (whether international or internal) or generalized violence. On the contrary, it is particularly relevant in the case of conflicts rooted in racial, ethnic, or religious animosity. In such contexts, individuals or whole communities may be threatened, attacked, uprooted, or exposed to danger for reasons which have a clear link to the 1951 Convention grounds.

While many states accept this understanding of the 1951 Convention, its application appears to present problems in practice. Where protection is granted using the refugee definition applied in Africa or in Latin America, the very fact of having fled a country in turmoil is the determining factor. Along with the compelling grounds that triggered the displacement in the first place, the sheer impossibility of conducting individual determinations results in protection being extended on a group basis. Conversely, in individual procedures where a specific link needs to be articulated between the harm feared and one or more of the Convention grounds, this may be hard for a claimant fleeing generalized violence to articulate or demonstrate.

In the EU, this has emerged as a particularly thorny issue. The 2004 'Qualification Directive' establishes subsidiary protection for civilians at real risk of serious harm owing *inter alia* to a 'serious and individual threat to a civilian's life or person by reason of indiscriminate violence in situations of international or internal armed conflict'.[21] Decision-makers have been particularly challenged by this convoluted language. To benefit from this provision, people seeking protection from armed conflict must overcome the multiple hurdles contained in this definition, or have fled a situation where the level of violence is so intense and extreme that no one should be returned to it.[22]

A UNHCR study of state practice in the EU, conducted in 2011, observed wide variations in the interpretation of this provision and the understanding of the applicability of the 1951 Convention to persons fleeing conflict situations. The study looked at the assessment of asylum applications lodged by Afghans, Iraqis, and Somalis in six EU Member States and found that outcomes differed significantly, with first instance protection rates for Afghans ranging from 9 to 62 per cent, for Iraqis from 10 to 78 per cent, and for Somalis from 34 to 89 per cent.[23]

BOX **2 • 2**

Children who seek asylum alone

Children, like adults, leave their countries for various reasons, including war, persecution, lack of opportunity, family pressure and other factors. The child rarely makes the decision to leave; parents or extended family usually are involved. The number of children on the move without parents or guardians is unknown, but those who register as asylum seekers are thought to constitute a fraction of the total.

Children who seek asylum alone are often described as 'unaccompanied'. It may be more accurate to call them 'unaccompanied or separated', since some are in fact accompanied, for instance by older youth or family friends, although they are separated from their parents or guardians. Sometimes children are escorted by smugglers who pose as family members.

Unaccompanied or separated children often lack accurate information about asylum procedures. They may have been told not to ask for asylum until they reach a particular destination, because there is a community of fellow nationals there or chances of securing permission to remain are thought to be higher there. Some children pass through several countries without being identified or assisted by authorities. Children who do not apply for asylum often receive no support, and are vulnerable to abuse and exploitation. Many are detained, sometimes in deplorable conditions, often with unrelated adults. Some experience traumatic events in the course of their journeys, such as the loss of siblings or friends during sea crossings.

Data collection

UNHCR has tried to collect statistics on children who seek asylum alone, and by 2010, 63 countries reported these data. For 2007–2010, UNHCR figures show that more than 62,000 unaccompanied or separated children applied for asylum. The real number is probably higher, given the difficulties in collecting data on this phenomenon. Some major asylum countries, such as Canada, the United States and South Africa, do not provide figures for applications by unaccompanied children, and the statistics obviously do not

capture the many young people on the move who remain below the radar. Still, certain trends can be observed.

The number of children who seek asylum alone fluctuates by year and country, but they have represented around four per cent of all asylum applicants each year since 2007. This is remarkably consistent with the estimated proportion of unaccompanied children in refugee camps. Most children who seek asylum alone are teen-aged boys, though there are smaller numbers of girls and younger children as well. The largest numbers come from countries in conflict.

Rights of the child

States generally recognize the applicability of the refugee law regime to unaccompanied children. However, they may be far less aware of their specific protection obligations with regard to all children, including non-national children whether or not they apply for asylum.

The Convention on the Rights of the Child (CRC), ratified by all but two countries, defines a child as a person below the age of 18. Asylum countries use various medical and other methods to assess biological age, but none is entirely accurate, and procedural safeguards are not always applied. Moreover, this approach tends to inflate the importance of biological age and as a result, asylum seeking children may experience completely different treatment before and after their eighteenth birthday. This sits uncomfortably with the CRC's concern to ensure treatment in accordance with a youngster's level of development and maturity.

Since 2006, several important policy documents have focused on asylum seeking children. In 2006, the UN Committee on the Rights

▲ **Afghan girls attend classes** at their school in a refugee camp in Islamabad.

of the Child issued General Comment 6 on the 'Treatment of unaccompanied and separated children outside their country of origin,' which made clear, in line with Article 3 of the CRC, that the child's best interest must be a primary consideration in all decisions concerning a child throughout the displacement cycle, including whether to send a child back to his or her country. Also in 2006, UNHCR published Guidelines on best interest determination, but these were mainly intended for use in host countries in the developing world. Few industrialized asylum countries carry out formal determinations; most maintain that their asylum procedures take the child's best interests into account.

Many wealthier countries have highly developed child protection systems, which are subject to judicial oversight. Reception centre staff, child welfare authorities, guardians, teachers, social workers and others may all play a role in ensuring that unaccompanied children are able to exercise their rights. However, cooperation between immigration and law enforcement officials on the one hand, and child welfare authorities on the other, is not always easy, and this can complicate the design and implementation of a process for identifying a durable solution that takes account of the child's best interest.

In some countries, unaccompanied children tend to be channelled into asylum procedures, possibly because other options are lacking. While many are found to need international protection, states often provide forms of protection other than refugee status. Some grant a humanitarian status based on a young person's need for protection as a minor. This can create a problem when the child turns 18, at which point he or she may—in theory at least—be compelled to return home. This prospect, known as 'ageing-out,' creates anxiety for many children and may discourage them from investing in their future.

UNHCR has expressed concern that states do not always take child-specific forms of persecution into account and in 2009, issued 'Guidelines on International Protection No. 8: Child Asylum Claims'. However, determining whether a child has a 'well-founded fear of persecution' according to the 1951 Convention may be difficult when a child left his or her country a long time ago, spent years on the move, or cannot clearly articulate his or her protection needs.

European countries report that numerous asylum seeking children disappear from reception facilities. Some may leave to try to reach a preferred destination, but other disap-pearances could be linked to child-trafficking. The trafficking risk has also led some authorities to argue that children should be detained for their own safety, although experience shows that intensive social work with children, along with close monitoring, can keep them safe without resorting to detention. The disappearance of asylum seeking children receives little attention, compared to the highly publicized alert systems activated when national children go missing.

Compulsory returns

In the European Union, discussions about durable solutions for unaccompanied children took a new turn with the entry into force of the EU's 'Returns Directive'.[i] This legislation allows states to send children whose asylum applications have been rejected, or who never claimed asylum, back to their country of origin or even to a third country, as long as 'adequate reception facilities' are available there.

Advocates for children's rights expressed alarm at this, particularly as the term 'adequate' was not defined. With the option of sending a child to an orphanage or other facility, one concern is that EU countries may not be inclined to pursue family tracing efforts before returning a child. Some authorities maintain that family tracing stands a better chance of success once the child is back in the country of origin. Other concerns relate to uncertain legal responsibility for children upon return, particularly in countries without functioning child protection systems.

The debate over compulsory return crystallized in 2009–2010, when large numbers of Afghan children applied for asylum in Europe, and security was reported to be deteriorating in Afghanistan. In 2010, UNHCR published an Aide-Mémoire outlining special measures which should apply to the return of unaccompanied children to Afghanistan.

Since the phenomenon of unaccompanied children on the move is unlikely to disappear in the near future, policy and operational responses for such children will need further development. To be effective, responses will have to be aligned and harmonized with broader child protection systems in countries of origin, transit, and destination.

The Conclusion on Children at Risk, adopted by UNHCR's Executive Committee in 2007, emphasized the importance of comprehensive child protection systems.[ii] Asylum, immigration, and enforcement officials need to work closely with child protection officials, social workers, educators, guardians, and others. Ministries of development and foreign affairs should coordinate with counterparts dealing with immigration and asylum, with respect to interventions in countries of origin and transit.

In addition, information gaps need to be addressed. All countries should collect statistics on unaccompanied or separated children who seek asylum, in a form that allows for disaggregation by age, gender, and nationality. Incidental information on children who are not formally registered could also be gathered and analysed more actively. Finally, there is a need for child-specific country of origin information to be readily available to decisionmakers, and for best interest determinations to be more systematically conducted.

Overall, important advances in law and policy have been made in recent years with regard to unaccompanied children on the move, but continued efforts are needed to make sure these children receive the protection and care to which they are entitled. ◆

i   Directive 2008/115/EC of the European Parliament and of the Council of 16 December 2008 on common standards and procedures in Member States for returning illegally-staying third country nationals, Official Journal of the European Union, L348/98 of 24.12.2008.
ii UNHCR Executive Committee Conclusion No. 107 (LVIII), 2007.

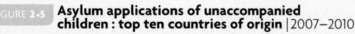

FIGURE 2•5 **Asylum applications of unaccompanied children : top ten countries of origin** | 2007–2010

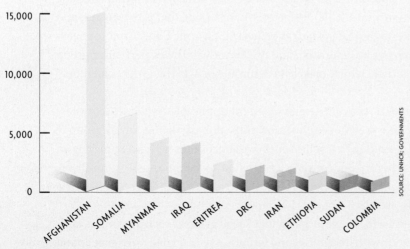

SOURCE: UNHCR; GOVERNMENTS

Note: This table reflects data provided by 63 asylum countries. However, reporting is not necessarily consistent from year to year and some major asylum countries do not report.

UNHCR has launched a number of research projects in other regions to learn more about how countries assess applications for protection presented by people fleeing conflict and generalized violence, in view of the importance of this subject, and intends to issue guidelines in an effort to encourage improved global coherence. Greater consistency in the approach to the protection of persons fleeing generalized violence would markedly contribute to ensuring meaningful asylum at the global level.

MEMBERSHIP OF A 'PARTICULAR SOCIAL GROUP'

A further area where the practice of states has varied widely is in the understanding of persecution linked to membership of a particular social group. A person who is persecuted for this reason is a refugee under the terms of the 1951 Refugee Convention and/or its 1967 Protocol. But what is a 'particular social group', and what constitutes 'membership'? With its lack of obvious 'ordinary meaning', this is arguably the most complex of the five Convention grounds, and the one with the most potential to respond to the changing ways in which persecution manifests itself, 60 years after the Convention was drafted. It has been of particular relevance to claims based on gender and sexual orientation.

The drafting history of the 1951 Convention sheds little light on what its authors intended with the last-minute insertion of the 'particular social group' ground in the refugee definition. The challenge in interpreting this ground is to do so in a way that is not so broad that it makes the other Convention grounds superfluous, and to remain consistent with the object and purpose of the Convention—namely that people at risk of persecution shall receive protection.

In 1979, when UNHCR issued its Handbook on Procedures and Criteria for Determining Refugee Status, it explained that a 'particular social group' normally 'comprises persons of similar background, habits or social status'. Since then, decision-makers have taken two approaches to interpreting this Convention ground. The first, known as the 'protected characteristics' approach, looks at whether a group is united by a characteristic which cannot be changed (an 'immutable' characteristic) or by one that is so fundamental to human dignity that a person should not be compelled to forsake it. The second approach is known as the 'social perception' approach, and examines whether a particular group shares a common characteristic which makes it cognizable or sets the group's members apart from society at large.

In 2002, in an effort to settle the controversy about the applicable standard, UNHCR issued Guidelines on the interpretation of 'membership of a particular social group'.[24] These Guidelines offer a definition that reflects the two approaches without requiring an applicant to satisfy both of them. They consider a particular social group as a group of persons who share 'a common characteristic other than their risk of being persecuted, *or* who are perceived as a group by society.'

States have recognized a wide range of 'particular social groups', such as women, children, families, tribes, persons with disabilities and lesbian, gay, bisexual, transgender and intersex (LGBTI) persons. Not all of these are uniformly accepted, and a number of states have objected to the notion of refugee status on account of on sexual orientation. Some states have also introduced explicit definitions of 'particular social group' in their national legislation, either by enumerating groups that may qualify, or by adding an additional ground for refugee status, such as gender or sexual orientation.

In recent years, however, the scope of the 'particular social group' ground has been narrowed in a number of jurisdictions in Europe and in the United States, by regarding protected characteristics and social perception as cumulative rather than alternative approaches. The EU's Qualification Directive appears to require the satisfaction of both tests, although state practice in the EU varies.[25] In transposing the Directive into national law, some EU countries have viewed the tests as alternatives, in line with the UNHCR Guidelines, while others have opted for the cumulative approach. In the US, UNHCR has intervened in numerous judicial proceedings to reiterate its view that a particular social group can be identified either by its 'protected characteristic' *or* by its social perception.

Claims based on gender and sexual orientation have been widely recognized using the protected characteristics approach, while states have been more reluctant to use this approach for groups based on occupation and class. On the other hand, the use of the social perception test has in some cases resulted in denial of claims based on membership of a particular social group, arguing the group is not 'sufficiently distinguishing',[26] lacks 'exterior manifestation'[27] or the necessary 'social visibility'[28] that would render its members readily identifiable. UNHCR has clarified in several judicial interventions that 'social perception' does not require that the common attribute be visible to the naked eye, nor even easily identified by the general public.[29] Moreover, UNHCR has underlined that people cannot be required to be 'discreet' to avoid persecution, for example, by concealing their identity or characteristics as members of a social group.

THE VARIABLE CONTENT OF ASYLUM

The problem of inconsistency arises not only with respect to determining who qualifies as a refugee, and how this determination is made, but also with respect to the rights enjoyed by refugees—the content of asylum. The term 'asylum' is widely used but has no universally determined meaning in international law. It does not appear in UNHCR's Statute, and is not defined in the 1951 Convention. As one scholar put it, 'the UN General Assembly urges the grant of asylum and observance of the principle of asylum, and states' constitutions and laws offer the promise of asylum, yet nowhere is this act of states defined'.[30]

Protection from return to danger is an essential component of asylum, but not a sufficient one. One of the central purposes of the 1951 Convention was to establish uniform standards for the treatment of refugees that go beyond protection from *refoulement*. The Convention sets out rights which contracting states are bound to guarantee to refugees within their territory, covering areas such as non-discrimination, personal status, access to employment, public education, and housing and relief. Asylum has come to be understood as a status which guarantees those rights.

Many signatory states scrupulously respect the requirements of the 1951 Convention and 1967 Protocol; others maintain legal reservations to key entitlements foreseen by these instruments; still others have not translated the Convention provisions into national law. Violations of the Convention range from denial or failure to uphold refugees' socio-economic rights to egregious acts of *refoulement*.

At the regional level, the 1969 OAU Convention reiterates the principles of *non-refoulement* and non-discrimination while citing the 1951 Convention as the core instrument, but does not otherwise enumerate the rights which refugees enjoy. However, both Conventions speak of solutions. The 1951 Convention (Article 34) encourages states to facilitate the 'assimilation and naturalization of refugees'. The OAU Convention requires states to use their 'best endeavours' to 'secure the settlement' of refugees who are unable or unwilling to return to their country of origin. The Common European Asylum System (*see box 2.1*) establishes a detailed legal framework regulating access to, and the content of, substantive rights, not only for refugees but also for asylum seekers.

There continue to be a number of problematic areas in the 'practice' of asylum, both in signatory and non-signatory states. One of the most consistently troubling is the detention of asylum seekers and refugees. Although detention is often intended as a signal to deter others from arriving, a UNHCR-commissioned study, released in 2011, stresses that there is no empirical evidence that detention deters irregular migration.[31]

Despite international law's prohibition on the penalization of refugees solely on account of illegal entry, and notwithstanding the high costs of detention, it remains the norm in many countries.[32] No comprehensive statistics are available, but it is clear that at any given time, on all continents, in both signatory and non-signatory states, thousands of refugees and asylum seekers are detained. UNHCR and the Office of the UN High Commissioner for Human Rights have worked to promote alternatives to detention.[33]

The practice of requiring refugees to live in camps or designated areas, albeit much less constraining than detention, is another way in which states limit refugees' freedom of movement. The establishment of refugee camps is often a rational response to a refugee emergency, in that it allows for the efficient delivery of life-saving assistance to a large number of new arrivals. However, over time and in the absence of viable alternatives or durable solutions, life in a refugee camp can be a grave affront to human dignity.

The refugee camp at Dadaab, established in 1991–1992 in a remote area of north eastern Kenya near the border with Somalia, illustrates the sheer magnitude—and longevity—of the challenges posed by large-scale refugee influxes. Two decades later, Dadaab is the world's largest refugee camp, with a population of around half a million Somali refugees, but lacking anything like the resources normally required to manage a 'city' of that size. Moreover, even if camps initially appear to address states' security concerns, they can also bring additional risks; maintaining the civilian nature of camps can be challenging, especially when they are established in close proximity to the border and to theatres of war.

In more recent mass influx situations, camps have been established as short-term options pending the possibility of return. During the 2010–2011 crisis in Côte d'Ivoire, resulting from the contested presidential elections, 200,000 refugees crossed into neighbouring states, with most going into Liberia (*see box 8.2*). In mid-December 2010, Liberia declared *prima facie* refugee status for those who had fled the violence in Côte d'Ivoire.[34] The refugees were initially received in nearly 100 villages in the border region.[35] UNHCR then set up refugee camps as well as an emergency registration operation. As the situation in Côte d'Ivoire began to stabilize, the refugees started to return.

In states that have not acceded to the 1951 Convention or its 1967 Protocol, the treatment of refugees varies widely. In some cases, refugees are considered as 'illegal' aliens, and may try to remain invisible to the authorities for fear of harassment, detention, or deportation. They may then be prone to abuse and exploitation, and have difficulty in obtaining basic services. Some non-signatory states leave it largely to UNHCR to handle refugee matters and to provide or arrange for basic services such as health care, housing, and even education.

In other contexts, however, states that are not parties to the 1951 Convention have taken in large numbers of refugees, allowed them to settle in both urban and rural areas, and given them access to state services, including education and medical care. Ensuring that refugees are able to exercise their rights when they live outside refugee camps requires coordinated efforts by many national and municipal authorities, as well as civil society entities.

In the face of the largest displacement crisis in the Middle East since 1948, the exodus of Iraqi refugees which started in 2003, two countries most affected—Syria and Jordan—did not establish refugee camps and allowed refugees to settle in urban areas. These host states were not parties to the 1951 Convention, and did not have specific legislation concerning asylum; their responses were based on core values and an Islamic tradition of hospitality.[36] While the delivery of protection and assistance to such large numbers of refugees mainly living in cities posed many challenges (*see chapter 6*), it enabled the majority of the refugee population to preserve a degree of normality and dignity during their long exile.

Mixed migration and access to asylum

TODAY'S ASYLUM CONTEXT IS INCREASINGLY TESTED BY MIXED POPULATION FLOWS. The essence of the 1951 Refugee Convention, to ensure that people can find safety, live a life of dignity, and not fear return to a situation of danger, is frequently overshadowed by the imperatives of border control.

Border control mechanisms and other strategies for dealing with irregular migration do not necessarily distinguish different categories of people on the move. In particular, they do not always identify—or even try to identify—people who seek protection. Border closures, push-backs and interception at sea are only the most visible ways in which access is denied. Visa requirements, carrier sanctions and offshore border controls all impede access to protection, if less visibly.

BOX 2•3

Asylum and mixed migration in southern Africa

Over the past decade, growing numbers of people have travelled from the Horn of Africa and the Great Lakes region of Africa towards the southern part of the continent, and in particular to South Africa , which now receives more asylum seekers than any other country in the world. This flow includes refugees, asylum seekers, people seeking work, education or family reunion, and many others.

The movement of people from the Horn of Africa comprises Somalis, Ethiopians and Eritreans who travel over a 4,500-kilometre route, mostly through Kenya and onward via Tanzania, Malawi, Mozambique, and Zimbabwe. For most Somalis, the initial trigger for leaving their country is to escape from violence, but in many cases economic, educational and family considerations propel them further south. Some lodge asylum applications in Malawi or Mozambique and stay in refugee centres there, before continuing to South Africa.

People on the move from the Great Lakes region are mostly from the Democratic Republic of the Congo (DRC). Since the 1990s, their number has grown steadily, and an estimated 30,000–40,000 Congolese now live in South Africa. Many are seeking better employment and educational opportunities, but a large portion of them—particularly those from eastern DRC—are also likely to have international protection needs.

A third flow originates within the southern Africa region itself. Zimbabweans have continued to flee economic, social and political upheaval in their country. Some commentators suggest that even if many may not meet the 1951 Convention definition of a refugee, they should be considered as a new category of forced 'survival' migrants.

These movements of people tend to be characterized by extreme hardship, rights violations, and unmet protection needs. Unaccompanied children, single women, the elderly and the infirm, as well as victims of trafficking, raise particular humanitarian and protection concerns, but others may also face abuses during their journey.

It is impossible to know exactly how many people have crossed into South Africa in recent years. In 2009 and 2010 combined, some 400,000 lodged asylum applications in the country—around 25 per cent of the worldwide total. The largest numbers were Zimbabweans, followed by Ethiopians, Congolese and Somalis.

The inflow has had a strong impact on the social and economic fabric of South Africa, which is already under strain from high levels of rural-to-urban migration and unemployment. In May 2008, the country was convulsed by outbreaks of xenophobic violence, which left dozens of foreigners dead and displaced an estimated 100,000 people. Sporadic xenophobic incidents have persisted.

In the face of such large movements of people, a major challenge is to make sure that those who are seeking protection have an effective opportunity to ask for asylum. This is complicated when asylum seekers and refugees travel alongside migrants, and when individuals have a mixture of motivations—political, environmental, economic and personal—for being on the move. Host states need fair and efficient mechanisms to identify individuals with protection needs, and the capacity to deliver protection, material assistance and vital services.

Increasing restrictions

Concerned to defend their sovereignty and security in the context of this influx, governments in southern Africa have taken steps to tighten border controls and prevent irregular arrivals. South Africa, Zimbabwe, Mozambique, Tanzania, Malawi, Zambia and Kenya discuss migration on a bilateral level. Current debates in southern Africa sound increasingly like those in Europe and other regions, including suggestions that refugees should seek protection in the first 'safe' country they reach.

South Africa's Department of Home Affairs (DHA) has stated that international law upholds the 'first country of asylum' principle. The Minister of Home Affairs indicated that his department was considering implementing that approach, or alternatively, the 'safe third country' concept, which would mean the return of asylum seekers and refugees to countries they had stayed in or passed through, such as Kenya, Zimbabwe or Mozambique. The Department has not confirmed implementation of either policy, but NGOs report that many Somalis and Ethiopians have been turned away at the border without assessment of their need for asylum.

In September 2011, South Africa began deporting Zimbabweans once again, and concerns were voiced that police were not checking for pending asylum applications. In April 2009, the South African government had put a moratorium on deportations of Zimbabweans and allowed a short period for those in the country to apply for regularization. During that time around 275,000 out of an estimated 1.5 million Zimbabweans in South Africa were able to apply.

South Africa's fledgling refugee protection system has come under very serious strain. The country first began accepting asylum applications in 1994; the asylum system established by the 1998 Refugee Act became operational in 2000. The state shouldered its responsibilities, granting asylum seekers and refugees freedom of movement and the opportunity to work, and investing considerable resources in the asylum system. But as the asylum channel became seen as the only way for many migrants to stay in the country, the volume of applications rapidly overwhelmed the capacity properly to assess claims.

The inflow also put pressure on South Africa's urban areas, where refugees have tended to stay and seek work as day labourers or in service industries. In Johannesburg, for example, access to public services is limited for refugees and asylum seekers, and only patchy support is available from civil society organizations. Many refugees live in substandard housing without reliable water, electricity and sanitation services.

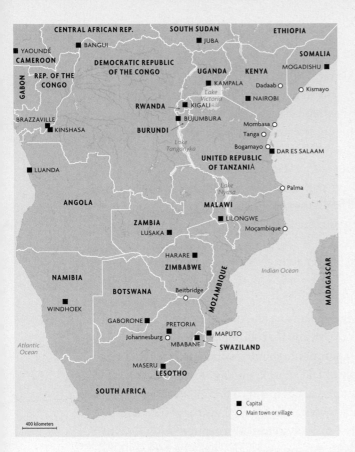

In response to widespread concerns about new arrivals, Malawi, Mozambique, Zambia and Zimbabwe have taken various approaches. These include: encampment policies; increased security and policing; interception, detention, and deportation; and roadblocks and border closures. There is a very real risk of chain deportation resulting in *refoulement*.

Among such responses, Mozambique has sent Somalis and Ethiopians back to Tanzania, where they are often detained. Others have been sent to Malawi, where most simply wait for a while and try to cross again. Malawi is considering barring migrants from using its territory for transit , though how this would be done in practice is not clear. Zambia is postponing refugee status decisions to test whether asylum seekers intend to remain. Zimbabwe has reportedly closed its northern border to undocumented arrivals, including asylum seekers. Malawi and Zimbabwe have transit centres at strategic border points, and in 2011, Mozambique was considering establishing one at its northern border.

Finding workable strategies

Restrictive measures may provide a temporary deterrent and allay public fears, but are unlikely to be an effective policy over the longer term. Given the 'push factors' in the Horn of Africa and the Great Lakes region, it is virtually impossible to contain people within those regions. A purely enforcement-oriented approach risks absorbing state resources without bringing a corresponding reduction in mixed migration—and without ensuring protection of fundamental rights. Efforts to confine refugees to camps and prevent their onward movement have also proved ineffective.

For these reasons, in South Africa, UNHCR has devoted much effort to building the country's capacity to undertake refugee status determinations, while also advocating for more effective migration management strategies that would remove people with weak claims from the asylum process. This would help to enable a higher standard of refugee status decisions to be made, and to accelerate the appeals process. The agency has advocated for maintaining the moratorium on deportation of Zimbabweans, and for allowing those who do not have a refugee claim to regularize their status by other means.

By focusing on effective outreach to refugees in urban areas, South Africa could set a powerful example in the region and beyond. A community-oriented approach, in liaison with police and local leaders, could strengthen early warning of xenophobic violence, and promote conflict resolution and peaceful coexistence. It could build on the successes of the inter-agency Protection Working Group formed during the 2008 violence by UNHCR, the Office of the United Nations High Commissioner for Human Rights and the national Consortium for Refugees. Third-country resettlement could continue to provide durable solutions for refugees with specific protection needs, including women at risk, survivors of torture, or victims of xenophobic violence.

Elsewhere in southern Africa, UNHCR has also worked to strengthen national asylum systems and improve refugees' living conditions. Countries are encouraged to reconsider encampment policies and to provide opportunities for refugees, especially those in urban areas, so that they will feel less compelled to move further south. For countries that maintain camps, the example of Maratane camp in Mozambique could be followed, where refugees are able to pursue *de facto* local integration.

At regional level, UNHCR and its partners have encouraged the development of coordinated strategies on mixed migration and refugee protection. In 2010, UNHCR and the International Organization for Migration (IOM) organized a conference on this subject, hosted by the government of Tanzania in Dar es Salaam. Participants from governments, civil society, and international and regional organizations called for more cooperation, including through regional bodies such as the Southern African Development Community (SADC) and the East African Community (EAC). They also pointed to the need for improved national policy and legal frameworks to address mixed migration; reiterated the importance of strengthening national capacity to respond in a human rights and protection-sensitive manner; and recognized that more accurate data, and improved analysis, were needed to ensure the development of evidence-based policies.

Authorities in the southern African region may be tempted by initiatives that appear to offer quick solutions. But restrictive measures rarely achieve the intended objectives, and can result in the creation of new clandestine routes, higher levels of bribery and corruption, as well as increased dangers for refugees, asylum seekers and migrants.

The experience in the southern African region mirrors that in other parts of the world grappling with the contemporary phenomenon of mixed migration. Continued international cooperation will be needed to strengthen the ability of states in the region to manage these complex migratory flows, and to preserve asylum space for persons in need of international protection. ◆

States have a sovereign right to manage immigration and to control the entry, stay and removal of foreigners, but they also have an obligation to respect international refugee and human rights law. Reconciling these objectives has become increasingly difficult with the dramatic increase in human mobility, including irregular migration, complex migratory flows, and security concerns in the environment following the events of 11 September 2001.

Today, people cross borders without prior authorization in a variety of circumstances, and for a variety of reasons: to seek safety from persecution or conflict; in the aftermath of natural disaster; to join family members; to find better opportunities; or simply to survive. In many cases, people are on the move for a combination of reasons. Many risk their lives in the process.

In 2006, UNHCR developed a 'Ten Point Plan on Refugee Protection and Mixed Migration', in an effort to encourage states and other actors to incorporate refugee protection considerations into broader migration policies.[37]

The Ten Point Plan is not a blueprint, but a planning and management tool to help to ensure that people who need protection receive it, and that all—whether in need of protection or not—are treated with dignity while appropriate solutions (including return home) are worked out. It is based on the principle of cooperation among interested states and other actors, and promotes comprehensive approaches to mixed migratory flows.

The ten areas covered by the Plan are: (i) cooperation among key partners; (ii) data collection and analysis; (iii) protection-sensitive entry systems; (iv) reception arrangements; (v) mechanisms for profiling and referral; (vi) differentiated processes and procedures; (vii) solutions for refugees; (viii) addressing secondary movements; (ix) return arrangements for non-refugees and alternative migration options; and (x) information strategies.

The motivations of people on the move cannot always be neatly divided into those who need protection and those who do not. Some people may prefer to remain 'under the radar', rather than risk being sent back to their countries of origin, but the Plan is predicated on the understanding that there are a range of needs that have to be addressed differentially.

Between 2008 and 2011, UNHCR led a process of regional consultations focusing on five situations of mixed migration: the movement of Somalis and Ethiopians across the Gulf of Aden; migration and displacement within West Africa; mixed movements in the Americas; in Central Asia; and in Southern Africa.[38] This consultative process, and the background research which preceded each consultation, helped to improve the empirical basis for policy development and to raise awareness of the protection-related aspects of mixed migratory flows. The process also sought to improve protection responses through better cooperation among key actors, including governments of countries of origin, transit and destination, and the development of comprehensive regional strategies.

The regional consultations heightened awareness that mixed migration is not only a South–North phenomenon. Indeed, the magnitude of South–South flows dwarfs that of movement from the developing to the developed world. The scale and nature of mixed flows toward South Africa (*box 2.3*) are illustrative of the challenges faced by countries in the global South.

HUMAN TRAFFICKING AND REFUGEE PROTECTION

Sensitization of governments and other partners to the potential protection needs of victims of trafficking has been a focus of UNHCR's work under the Ten Point Plan. Awareness of trafficking in persons has increased since adoption in 2000 of the UN Convention against Transnational Organized Crime and its Protocols on Smuggling and Trafficking.[39] As states intensify their efforts to control irregular migration, there is a risk that human trafficking may be addressed strictly from a law enforcement perspective, despite its protection dimensions, including both refugee protection and victim protection. Moreover, it is not always recognized that even if women and children are particularly vulnerable to trafficking, men are also victims.

UNHCR has advocated with other UN agencies for comprehensive strategies to respond to trafficking, and has strengthened its cooperation with the International Organization for Migration (IOM) in this respect. Standard Operating Procedures applied by both agencies have been developed to ensure that victims of trafficking receive the attention they deserve.

There is not always sufficient appreciation of the importance of assessing whether the harm an individual fears as a result of having been trafficked may amount to persecution. There is a need for particular attention to this since a number of 'safe country of origin lists' include countries or territories where trafficking is common—for instance, Moldova or Kosovo. Courts in a number of countries have found that victims of trafficking may be considered as 'members of a particular social group', depending on the risk upon return.[40]

In 2006, UNHCR issued Guidelines on the application of Article 1A(2) of the 1951 Convention to victims of trafficking.[41] The Guidelines highlight the importance of assessing the risk of reprisals, which a victim (or his or her family) may face for having cooperated with law enforcement officials investigating or prosecuting trafficking. In such contexts it will be particularly important for asylum authorities not to neglect the individual's fear of ostracism, discrimination, or punishment by family or community, as well as the risk of being trafficked again in the absence of state protection. In some cases the treatment experienced may be so atrocious as to amount to persecution in its own right and the trauma of returning too great.

RESPONDING TO SECURITY CONCERNS

Any discussion about the management of mixed migration must also take account of security concerns. Following the events of 11 September 2001, and other terrorist attacks, and with the steady increase in irregular migration, states have become increasingly cautious about who they let in and allow to remain. No state wants to take the risk of 'importing' a terrorist under the guise of a refugee or an asylum seeker. UNHCR also has to address this challenge when carrying out refugee status determinations under its mandate, when presenting refugees for resettlement, and when implementing its responsibility for supervising the application of the 1951 Convention.

BOX **2·4**

Crossing the Sinai

For several years, growing numbers of sub-Saharan Africans, including asylum seekers and refugees, have been smuggled and trafficked through Egypt's Sinai Peninsula into Israel. The majority are Eritrean and Sudanese. At the end of 2011, the Israeli authorities estimated that they numbered over 50,000.

A complex context

This mixed migration situation is one of the world's most complex. The Sinai border area is very sensitive from a political, strategic, and security perspective; it is also plagued by high levels of crime, including drug and arms smuggling, alongside human smuggling and trafficking. Egypt and Israel are the only countries in the Middle East—besides Yemen—to have ratified the 1951 Convention. Yet neither has incorporated its Convention obligations into domestic legislation, and incidents of forcible returns from both countries have periodically been reported.

For Eritreans, the route to Israel often starts in eastern Sudan, at the Shagarab refugee camp, close to the Eritrean border. Some have been registered as refugees by UNHCR in Sudan; others have just arrived from Eritrea or Ethiopia. When High Commissioner António Guterres visited Shagarab in January 2012, he called for reinforced international action against the criminal networks behind the movements. UNHCR and the International Organization for Migration are working

together to research the smuggling, trafficking, and kidnapping phenomenon, in order to improve security in the refugee camps and help the local authorities tackle the problem.

For Darfurians and South Sudanese, the route generally starts in Cairo. Again, some are registered with UNHCR, while others simply transit briefly in Egypt to connect with smugglers. Still others already link up in Sudan with smugglers who take them directly to the Sinai. The vast majority of people go voluntarily, but their journey soon becomes dangerous and sometimes deadly.

High levels of human suffering

The risks *en route* are many. Smugglers and traffickers perpetrate hostage-taking, extortion, imprisonment, torture, and sexual violence, and have even been accused of organ theft. An NGO report in late 2011 painted a horrific picture of ill-treatment allegedly inflicted by traffickers, and spoke of hundreds held hostage in the Sinai region.[i] Observers say that part of the problem is the impunity with which the Bedouin tribes in the Sinai Peninsula and the Rashaida tribes of eastern Sudan appear to act.[ii]

At the end of 2011, UNHCR estimated there were 600–700 individuals detained by the Egyptian authorities after being caught along the smuggling route that reaches from Aswan on the Sudan border all the way to Al-Arish at the border with Israel. Egypt routinely sends Eritreans to Ethiopia, and is reported to have

deported individuals directly to Eritrea.[iii] UNHCR is also concerned that Darfurians, many of whom might qualify for refugee status, may be sent back to Sudan.

The risk does not diminish once the smugglers and traffickers drop off their human cargo at the border between Egypt and Israel. In 2010 and 2011, there were reports of individuals being shot by the Egyptian military border patrol, following which the Egyptian authorities pledged to the High Commissioner that such incidents would not recur. There have also been protests in the past at Israel's 'hot returns' of asylum seekers to Egypt. Israel has stated that such returns no longer take place.

The need to reinforce protection

Efforts to protect refugees and uphold the rights of vulnerable migrants are complicated by national security concerns related to sensitive border areas, Nile Basin inter-governmental relations, Egyptian–Israeli relations, Eritrea–Ethiopia tensions, and the social and economic marginalization of the Bedouin and Rashaida tribes in Egypt and Sudan respectively. The loss of economic opportunity and remittances for hundreds of thousands of sub-Saharan Africans as a result of the Libya crisis has complicated the situation further.

In Israel, those who are confirmed as originating from Eritrea or Sudan are provided with a type of 'visa' allowing 'conditional release' from detention. People of other

In view of security concerns, and to maintain the integrity of the institution of asylum, in 2010 UNHCR set up a new unit devoted to issues of protection and national security. It thus cooperates with many stakeholders, including in the UN Inter-Agency Counter-Terrorism Framework. The Office has also led a project to ensure that Refugee Travel Documents issued by states in accordance with the 1951 Convention are compliant with the security requirements of the International Civil Aviation Administration (ICAO).[42]

Asylum systems are not immune to abuse, but individual asylum seekers undergo detailed scrutiny in the course of the examination of their claims. Asylum channels are

nationalities also receive this 'conditional release' document and are subject to an individual refugee status determination process. 'Conditional release' allows freedom of movement but does not give access to basic services, although emergency medical treatment is available. Many 'conditional release' holders find work on the informal labour market.

UNHCR and NGOs in Israel regularly identify new arrivals, both men and women, who have suffered severe abuse at the hands of traffickers in the Sinai. Their dramatic testimonies indicate that many need specialized help, including longer-term medical and psycho-social care. The identification of traumatized individuals should take place at the earliest possible stage, but this is difficult when they are held in detention. Procedural guidelines for the detention and release of new arrivals are in place, but are not systematically followed, and many individuals who do not have identity documents remain in detention for long periods pending determination of their nationality.

The medical and psychological treatment available to victims inside and outside of detention needs to be strengthened. In principle, victims of trafficking are entitled to rehabilitation in a shelter outside of detention; but this has been available only for a small number of people deemed to meet the strict definition of a victim of trafficking.

At the end of 2011, it was reported that migrants and asylum seekers continued to enter Israel at the rate of around 2,000 per month. Israel's national legal framework and Asylum Regulation remained limited, and only a handful of asylum seekers were recognized as refugees under the terms of the 1951 Convention. Meanwhile, the authorities were taking measures to deter new arrivals. An amendment to the Prevention of Infiltration Law adopted in early 2012 provides for longer-term detention, and construction of a large detention facility is planned. A fence along the southern border is also intended to have a deterrent effect.

UNHCR's goal remains to engage the affected states in a dialogue on humanitarian principles, recognizing the rights of people who seek asylum and of victims of human trafficking, as well as the legitimate interests of the governments. If it could be achieved, a comprehensive regional approach could curb some of the worst human rights violations faced by the Eritreans, Sudanese and others.

Such an approach would require raising awareness about the dangers posed by human smuggling and trafficking, and those associated with unauthorized border-crossing. All along the route through Ethiopia, Sudan, and Egypt, and within Israel, psycho-social and medical care for survivors of torture and trauma is needed.

There would also be a need for continued training and awareness-raising for state officials on refugee law, human smuggling and trafficking, and ways of addressing mixed migration, along with the development of relevant national legislation and administrative arrangements to identify persons in need of international protection. Reception facilities should be set up where assistance can be delivered and protection needs can be assessed; detention ought to be avoided.

Finally, a concerted effort is required to find durable solutions for the individuals concerned. Persons who are found to be refugees should have access to the rights set out in the 1951 Convention. There is a need for investment in sustainable refugee livelihoods in the host countries, for resettlement of those refugees for whom this presents the best solution, and support for voluntary return or readmission to countries in which individuals have previously stayed, if such return is feasible and safe. For persons who are not in need of international protection, states should be helped to arrange safe and dignified return to countries of origin.

A comprehensive approach would require strong political engagement on the part of countries along this route, and the support of other actors, including UN agencies and other international organizations. Without such a commitment, refugees, asylum seekers, and vulnerable migrants will continue to pay a high human price. ◆

i   Amnesty International, 'Broken Promises', 22 November 2011, 41 – 44; Physicians for Human Rights (Israel), 'Hundreds of Refugees held in Sinai Torture Camps need Rescuing', 30 November 2011; Human Rights Watch, 'Sinai Perils: Risks to Migants, Refugees and Asylum Seekers in Egypt and Israel', 12 November 2008.

ii I. Timberlake, 'People Traffickers Stalk Eritreans in Sudan Desert', Agence France Presse, 13 January 2012; S. Kirkpatrick, 'Smuggling in North Sinai Surges as the Police Vanish', *The New York Times*, 14 August 2011.

iii Human Rights Watch, 'Egypt: Don't Deport Eritreans', 15 November 2011.

among the most closely regulated of entry channels and are therefore less likely to be attractive to individuals who wish to avoid attention.

Moreover, the drafters of the 1951 Convention were already aware of states' security concerns, and they built a number of provisions into the Convention accordingly. Article 9 is designed to allow states to take provisional measures pending the examination of a claim, where essential to the country's national security in time of war or other grave and exceptional circumstances. Article 1F sets out the grounds under which exclusion from refugee status may take place: where a refugee has committed a war crime, crime against

UNHCR / J. OATWAY

▲ **A refugee woman** in the aftermath of xenophobic violence in South Africa.

humanity, or other serious offence before seeking protection.[43] Articles 32 and 33(2) allow states to expel refugees who are a threat to the community, public order, or national security, subject nonetheless to procedural safeguards. And Article 2 stipulates that refugees must respect the laws of their host country—they are not immune from prosecution. In short, the 1951 Convention was drafted in a way which enables the security concerns of states to be managed.

Strengthening the 'governance' of asylum

IN ORDER TO ADDRESS THE CHALLENGES identified in the preceding sections, including the wide variation in the practice of asylum, and to provide a more predictable framework for international protection, the international 'governance' of asylum needs to be strengthened. This task has both institutional and political dimensions, and work on both fronts is required to preserve the integrity of the institution of asylum and to keep asylum meaningful for individual refugees.

THE INSTITUTIONAL ASPECTS

As early as 1946, the General Assembly recognized that the refugee problem was international in scope and character.[44] As a result, the UN put in place various institutional arrangements, including the establishment of UNHCR.

UNHCR and its Executive Committee, composed of states, have long been key actors in the governance of asylum. As of 2011, the Executive Committee had 85 member states, having started its work (as the High Commissioner's Advisory Committee for Refugees) in December 1951 with just 15 members. This increased participation is a positive signal of the commitment of an ever-growing number of countries to the protection and well-being of refugees; but it has also brought increased polarization and corresponding difficulties in reaching decisions.

Since 1975, a principal contribution of the Executive Committee has been the adoption of Conclusions on international protection. The good faith engagement of states in this process has been an important means of maintaining a global consensus on the international protection regime and ensuring its further evolution.

In the early years, the Committee adopted four or five Conclusions annually, on key topics of relevance to refugee protection. In 2002 the Committee endorsed a far-reaching and comprehensive 'Agenda for Protection', which stemmed from the Global Consultations process, and was also welcomed by the General Assembly.[45] Although the Conclusions of the Executive Committee are not binding, they have made an important contribution to the development of the international protection regime. In recent years, however, it has become difficult to secure a consensus on proposed Conclusions on international protection. In 2011, for the first year since 1975, no Conclusion was adopted, and this triggered informal consultations within the Committee on how to revitalize this process.

In parallel with the growing membership of the Executive Committee, discussion of asylum has increasingly shifted to other groupings, notably those located at regional levels. This shift carries both opportunities and risks. Many regional organizations, including human rights bodies and regional courts, have helped to develop refugee protection standards, and play an important monitoring role.[46] However, there is also a risk of fragmentation of the international refugee regime, and some of the regional bodies are focused primarily on migration control rather than on refugee protection.

In light of these developments, the High Commissioner's annual Dialogues on Protection Challenges have become the principal forum for discussions at the global level on pressing contemporary protection issues, with follow-up activities ensuing from the deliberations in a spirit of international cooperation rather than on the basis of binding agreements. The first Dialogue took place in 2007 and addressed the connection between refugee protection and international migration. Subsequent meetings have looked at protracted refugee situations, refugees in urban environments, and protection gaps and responses.

At the same time, supervision of the application of the 1951 Convention remains a statutory responsibility for UNHCR, which is also set out in Article 35 of the 1951 Convention and Article II of the 1967 Protocol.[47] As with international law generally, it is not easy to hold states accountable for respecting their freely accepted obligations. UNHCR's role in operational responses to refugee emergencies and as the second-largest adjudicator of asylum claims in the world is well accepted, but its supervisory role meets with considerably more resistance in some quarters.

The lack of a supervisory mechanism for the 1951 Convention akin to the treaty bodies established for other UN human rights instruments has frequently been noted, along with the unwillingness of states to establish such a body. In the absence of a specific mechanism of this kind, UNHCR has developed a variety of other methods to carry out its supervisory role. These include issuing guidelines on international protection matters and on the eligibility of persons of specific nationalities for refugee status, supporting states in developing laws and policies relating to asylum, and working to enhance state capacity to conduct high-quality refugee status determinations. By way of example, the collaboration launched in 2004 between UNHCR and the United Kingdom on a 'Quality Initiative' became a model for numerous similar projects in Europe and in other regions.[48]

In recent years, one particular area of UNHCR supervisory activity has grown: making submissions to national or regional courts in the form of *amicus curiae* briefs, interventions or other submissions. UNHCR's active judicial engagement reflects the agency's search for more constancy in the practice of asylum, which the courts can help to provide.

BOX 2•5

Media and public opinion

More than six decades after the end of the Second World War, few people in the industrialized world have any personal experience of flight. Most people, including many opinion-shapers, do not have a refugee among their personal friends. What they know about war, persecution, and displacement comes mainly through the mass media, and perceptions of refugees and asylum seekers are shaped in large part by the language of journalists and politicians, and the images they create.

In his opening statement at the 2011 session of UNHCR's Executive Committee, High Commissioner António Guterres pointed out that racism and xenophobia are not the sole preserve of extremists. Similar sentiments, he said, are expressed by populist politicians and some elements of the media—sentiments which threaten asylum space and social cohesion and that are 'not always opposed with sufficient energy and courage by mainstream political and social movements'. In difficult economic times, migrants, asylum seekers and refugees are easy scapegoats, for a multitude of societal ills.

Populist politicians and journalists frequently depict migrants, asylum seekers and refugees as a threat to security and stability. Crucial distinctions between these categories are often overlooked. Researchers at the communications department of the University of Rome monitored over 5,600 television reports on immigration in the first six months of 2008 and found only 26 which did not make a link with security. In 2010, the Italian government put forward a package of legislative measures primarily pertaining to immigration which it called

the 'security package', a label which went unquestioned by the media.

It has been pointed out that journalists tend to mimic the language of politicians. Terms like 'illegal' and 'clandestine' are routinely used in connection with migratory flows, as well as vocabulary with warlike overtones, suggesting that a country is being 'invaded' or is 'under assault' by migrants or asylum seekers, especially when they arrive by sea. Yet experts at the EU Border Agency Frontex have made clear that the main source of irregular immigration is not in the media limelight at all, as '[t]he majority of the people apprehended within the Schengen Area who are staying illegally actually come in legally by plane, and then overstay their visas (...)'.[1] The same is true in other parts of the world.

In 2011, while Tunisia opened its border to nearly one million migrant workers and refugees fleeing conflict in Libya, Italian government ministers described the arrival by boat in southern Italy of 28,000 Tunisian migrants as a 'human tsunami'. Experts have deplored the consistent portrayal of boat arrivals in southern Italy as an emergency, noting there have been boat arrivals every summer for the past 15 years. But language is a political choice, one which can fuel racism, xenophobia, and social tensions, and discourage people from seeking to understand why others are on the move, and from supporting rational responses.

In many countries, the rhetoric of politicians and the media creates the perception that there are 'good' and 'bad' refugees. Reporting in the Western press about Somali refugees fleeing into Kenya, Ethiopia, and

In addressing the European Court of Human Rights in 2011, the High Commissioner underlined the importance of 'coherent legal interpretation and guidance from judicial bodies, whose role is to remain above the vagaries of public opinion, including in times of economic and social difficulty'.[49]

THE POLITICAL ASPECTS

Asylum cannot survive without a clear political commitment to the fundamental values of human rights and human dignity that underpin the institution of asylum. Although asylum is first and foremost a responsibility of states, it cannot be viewed solely through the lens of state responsibility. Politicians, community leaders, and the media have an important responsibility to contribute to a climate of tolerance in which asylum can be properly managed, and in which civil society can contribute by providing hands-on services and support.

In many countries, asylum and immigration debates are intertwined, and politicians have staked out anti-immigration positions. Populist politics, intolerance and xenophobia, and the 'scapegoating' of immigrants, refugees, and asylum seekers present a serious challenge to meaningful asylum. Portions of the population will always be susceptible to rhetoric that suggests reasons to fear newcomers, whether because of perceived threats to

Yemen has been uniformly compassionate. Yet when the same individuals reach Europe, North America, or Australia, and apply for asylum, they are often called 'queue jumpers', and chastised for coming in through the 'back door'.

One expert has pointed out that when 'viewed from a distance, displaced people are portrayed as helpless victims of circumstance, deserving of compassion and assistance. This imagery changes dramatically when refugees and asylum seekers make their way to the developed world to seek protection under the 1951 Convention (...)'.[ii] In other words, when refugees are transformed from 'passive objects of compassion' into actors in their own right, they provoke a sense of fear which can be exploited for political gains.

Asylum seekers are easy prey for those who pursue a populist agenda, and their demonization in the press is an ongoing problem. This has particularly been the case in the United Kingdom, where tabloid newspapers have run lurid headlines and repeatedly used the words 'asylum seeker' and 'refugee' in conjunction with words like 'terrorist', 'disease', 'fraud', and 'bogus', creating a distorted and negative image in the public's mind, and indirectly inciting hostility and resentment.

Because refugees and asylum seekers are not of a single race or religion, laws governing race relations and hate crimes are rarely invoked in reaction to this kind of reporting. The emergence of new social media platforms may make it even harder to combat hate speech, and quality journalism faces growing difficulties in reaching its audience owing to what has been called 'information clutter'.[iii]

The media can—and often does—promote an atmosphere conducive to refugee protection by reporting on the conditions which

force people to flee their homes and the contributions they make to their host societies. Racism and xenophobia can be reduced through accurate reporting and by presenting positive role models.

In a number of countries, UNHCR has taken steps to promote more accurate media coverage. In France, UNHCR and the daily newspaper *Le Monde* have established an annual competition that rewards objective reporting of refugee issues by journalism students. In Italy, UNHCR, together with the Journalists' Association and the Press Federation, developed a code of conduct for reporting on asylum and migration; known as the Rome Charter, it provides guidelines to ensure balanced and accurate information, and is now used in journalism schools. In Belgium, UNHCR and the Union of Journalists published a brochure providing guidance on terminology and advice on ethical approaches to interviewing and photographing asylum seekers and refugees. While fully respecting the freedom of the press, UNHCR encouraged such voluntary codes in its 2009 'Strategic Approach to combating racism, racial discrimination, xenophobia, and related intolerance'.

More such partnerships and constant vigilance are needed to avoid the stigmatization of asylum seekers and refugees, and to build environments conducive to refugee protection. ◆

i   Frontex Spokesperson Michal Parzyszek: 'Ties with Turkey, Border Control Investments Help Bulgaria Tackle Illegal Migration', Bulgarian Information Agency BGNES, 27 May 2011.

ii P. Mares, 'Distance Makes the Heart Grow Fonder: Media Images of Refugees and Asylum-seekers', in E. Newman and J. van Selm (eds.) *Refugees and Forced Displacement: International Security, Human Vulnerability, and the State*, Tokyo: United Nations University Press, 2003.

iii P. Meyer, *The Vanishing Newspaper: Saving Journalism in the Information Age*, Columbia and London: University of Missouri Press, 2004.

security, economic concerns (competition for jobs, downward pressure on wages, and the costs of receiving asylum seekers and refugees), or hostility to ethnic and cultural diversity.

The Council of Europe's High Commissioner for Human Rights has expressed concern about the support gained by political parties with xenophobic agendas, and has highlighted the risk of this trend continuing unless strong political action is taken to counter it. Europe, he has written, 'is not a racism-free zone. An intensified struggle against xenophobia and intolerance is acutely needed in most European countries.'[50] This is not only a northern phenomenon. In South Africa, xenophobic violence erupted in 2008, and has been periodically reported since then.[51]

Negative attitudes are easily fuelled by concern about the costs of maintaining asylum systems or providing asylum. These may be compounded by the belief that asylum systems are abused by non-refugees who seek access to labour markets or social welfare benefits.[52] Yet there has been relatively little investigation into the motives and situations of the large numbers of persons who are found not to be in need of international protection. More in-depth research in this area might help to reduce perceptions of abuse, and enable the development of alternative policy responses.

To build a climate conducive to asylum, three elements merit particular attention: first, explaining the asylum issue as distinct from immigration in general; second, focusing on education about global forced displacement, including through the media; and third, taking resolute steps to counter xenophobia and intolerance. In 2009, UNHCR issued a strategy on 'Combating Racism, Racial Discrimination, Xenophobia and Related Intolerance' primarily intended to help its Offices around the world to develop relevant actions. The document notes that negative public attitudes pose a considerable obstacle to refugee protection, and calls for cooperation with a broad range of partners, including police, government officials, and the media.[53] In 2011, UNHCR concluded a Memorandum of Understanding with the Organization for Security and Cooperation in Europe (OSCE), outlining a commitment to collaborate to address racism, discrimination, xenophobia, and related intolerance.[54]

REALIZING ASPIRATIONS

The 1951 Refugee Convention was designed to confer a right to international protection on persons who are at risk because they lack national protection. The Convention and its 1967 Protocol were designed to assure refugees the widest possible enjoyment of their rights. The universal and non-discriminatory character of this regime remains its strength.

The challenge of translating this aspiration into reality is ever-present. There is a need to ensure that all refugees are able to exercise their rights. The availability and scope of protection should not depend on where an individual is able to seek asylum or whether the need for protection is identified through a framework based on individual determination of eligibility for refugee, or through a group determination.

Maintaining the integrity of asylum requires building a better bridge between the approaches taken in different regions of the world, particularly in the context of people seeking protection from contemporary conflicts. It calls for a renewed effort to achieve consistency in the practice of asylum around the world. This will require a willingness to develop further the governance structure for asylum, both institutionally and politically, in order to resolve the many tensions that threaten asylum today. UNHCR will continue play its part as guardian of the international refugee protection regime, and to promote efforts by states and the international community as a whole to ensure that the institution of asylum delivers on its promise of providing freedom from fear. ■

CHAPTER 3

Durable Solutions:
Breaking the Stalemate

F OR MORE THAN 60 YEARS, UNHCR HAS WORKED TO HELP GOVERNMENTS find lasting solutions to refugee problems. In 2011, the High Commissioner expressed his concern that this is becoming increasingly difficult, as evidenced by the number of refugees under UNHCR's responsibility who remain trapped in protracted exile (7.2 million at the start of 2011).[1] The reality of today's global politics, the High Commissioner said, is that conflicts are becoming more complex, refugee crises are multiplying, and 'solutions are proving to be more and more elusive'.[2]

The ultimate aim of refugee protection is to secure lasting solutions to refugee problems. Refugees may return to their home country–'voluntary repatriation', settle permanently in the country where they have found protection–'local integration', or be relocated to a third country which offers them permanent residence 'resettlement'. Yet for many refugees, none of these solutions is available. International efforts often face an impasse whereby countries of origin, host countries, and donor nations are unable, and sometimes unwilling, to work together to achieve solutions.

In 2008, the High Commissioner launched an Initiative on Protracted Refugee Situations and devoted his annual Protection Dialogue to the topic, in an effort to draw attention to the problem and mobilize political will to address it.[3] The Initiative focused on five specific groups: Afghans in Pakistan and Iran, Muslim refugees from Myanmar's northern Rakhine State in Bangladesh, Eritreans in eastern Sudan, Croatians and Bosnians in Serbia, and Burundians in Tanzania. The case studies in this chapter present some of the main developments since that Initiative was launched.

The demand for durable solutions today challenges the expectations built into the refugee protection system 60 years ago. In the Cold War context in which UNHCR was established, it was assumed that if refugees could not safely return to their home countries, they would be settled permanently in their first countries of asylum, or resettled elsewhere. The emphasis in UNHCR's Statute on the 'assimilation' of refugees within new national communities reflects that expectation.[4]

◀ **Afghan returnees** building their houses near Jalalabad.

Today, donor countries tend to argue that solutions should be found as close as possible to a refugee's country of origin, while host countries in the developing world, where 80 per cent of the world's refugees are found, consider that they bear a disproportionate share of the responsibility, and are often reluctant to allow refugees to settle permanently on their territories. In the absence of reinforced solidarity, this results in a stalemate that leaves many refugees in a legal and socio-economic limbo for years.

Contemporary refugee crises are likely to involve mass outflows of people fleeing situations where conflict, human rights violations, poor governance and acute deprivation are intertwined, and resolving the underlying causes of forced displacement seems ever more difficult. In this environment, it is not surprising that voluntary repatriation has steadily declined. In addition, some host countries, as in the Great Lakes region and in the Horn of Africa, are themselves suffering crises of governance, adding to the challenge of promoting local integration.

Moreover, approaches to durable solutions have traditionally focused on refugees, people who are outside their country of origin. Recently, the international community has begun also to look at the question of solutions for internally displaced persons (IDPs), reflecting the rising number of IDPs. The focus of this chapter is on refugees but, as discussed in chapter 5, UNHCR's expanded engagement with internal displacement has also led to its involvement in helping states to find solutions for IDPs.

This chapter begins by reviewing the three durable solutions and the importance of integrating development and peacebuilding actions into efforts to make voluntary repatriation and local integration possible. It then considers the relevance of cessation of refugee status to the search for solutions, and looks at how refugees themselves consider that their situation can be resolved. The chapter concludes with suggested policy directions that could help to revitalize the search for solutions.

Established approaches

THE INTERNATIONAL COMMUNITY continues to pursue the well-established formula of three durable solutions: voluntary repatriation, local integration and resettlement. But in many cases, none of these options is available. The question therefore arises: can this framework be adjusted or reinforced in order to respond better to the needs of today's refugees?

UNHCR's work takes place in a broader geopolitical context that is not always conducive to solutions. Protracted conflict coupled with the complex politics of aid can make it hard to break cycles of displacement that have characterized some regions since the end of the Cold War. Refugee assistance programmes in Pakistan, for example, have continued for more than three decades. Finding sustainable solutions to on-going or cyclical displacement requires political will, strong leadership, robust burden-sharing, and a readiness to look beyond classical approaches.

VOLUNTARY REPATRIATION
While the 1990s are often celebrated as the 'decade of repatriation', thanks largely to post-Cold War circumstances that made repatriation feasible, in the first decade of the twenty-first century there was a sharp decline in overall return numbers.[5] In 2010, voluntary repatriation fell to its lowest level in 20 years.

Voluntary repatriation of refugees | 2001–2010

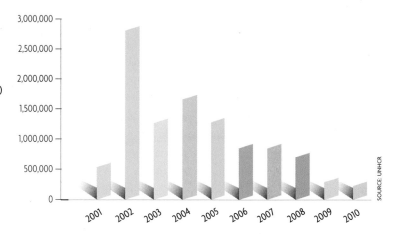

SOURCE: UNHCR

In many contexts, voluntary repatriation is clearly not possible because of continuing conflict in the country of origin. But in other situations, even when conflict has officially come to a halt, ending displacement remains a challenge. Localized violence may persist and conflicts reignite, reducing the attractiveness or the sustainability of returns. After prolonged conflict, infrastructure and markets are damaged or destroyed, constraining livelihoods and complicating access to basic services.

When conflict has involved inter-communal or sectarian violence, establishing mechanisms for transitional justice and ensuring viable community relations is often problematic, especially when disputes over land rights or reparations are involved. Above all, even when a state is *willing* to offer protection to its returning citizens, it may not be *able* to do so.

UNHCR's experience in Afghanistan, particularly since the deterioration of security as from late 2006, is evidence of how a fragile peace process can tip into reversal, making successful return and reintegration extremely difficult. Similarly, in South Sudan, both before and after the January 2011 referendum on independence, large-scale returns linked to the wider peace process continued alongside considerable new displacement. Both operations illustrate the complexities of trying to solve refugee problems amid unresolved political and governance crises.

Between 2002 and 2011, 5.7 million Afghan refugees returned, mostly from Pakistan and Iran. This voluntary repatriation was initially assessed in terms of numbers, and judged to be an 'overwhelming success'.[6] Yet from 2005 onwards, as security in Afghanistan deteriorated, the numbers declined. A UNHCR survey to assess reintegration after ten years noted that only a small proportion of returnees were in regular employment, and that the lack of livelihood opportunities, limited access to basic services and insecurity were preventing full reintegration.[7]

In 2011, more than 2.6 million Afghans were still registered as refugees outside the country: 1.7 million in Pakistan and 910,000 in Iran, most of them long-term exiles.[8] This has presented a new dilemma. While many Afghan refugees in the region–particularly those who fled the Soviet invasion over 30 years ago–may no longer be in need of international protection, the prospects for their sustainable return and reintegration are linked to the stability and development of Afghanistan and also depend on their continued access to labour and trade markets in neighbouring countries. In this context, and with both host states increasingly faced with asylum fatigue, UNHCR has sought to promote an innovative and comprehensive approach to solutions (*see box 3.5*).

The second major voluntary repatriation operation, to South Sudan, began after the signing of the Comprehensive Peace Agreement (CPA) between the government of Sudan and the Sudan People's Liberation Movement (SPLM) in January 2005. The CPA laid the groundwork for the voluntary repatriation of refugees from outside the country, and for the return of IDPs from northern Sudan, especially from Khartoum. Not only did the peace agreement signal a prospective end to violent conflict, but the future political ambitions of the SPLM also turned on ensuring a vote for independence in the January 2011 referendum. The SPLM was 'keen to see the repatriation of refugees from neighbouring countries, to demonstrate political legitimacy, capacity and to include in the April 2008 census as many of its constituents as possible'.[9]

Between the 2005 peace agreement and the referendum, more than 320,000 South Sudanese returned from exile in neighbouring countries and many more returned from the North. While return to South Sudan offered the prospect of a durable solution, the region continued to face massive development challenges and the risk of further conflict, particularly in border areas. In the first year of independence, South Sudan experienced considerable new internal displacement as well as movements from the states of Blue Nile and South Kordofan, and from the flashpoint of Abyei.

Sustainable voluntary repatriation requires long-term engagement in reintegration, reconciliation and reconstruction, and the involvement of many actors going well beyond UNHCR, as is highlighted in the Preliminary Framework on 'Ending Displacement in the Aftermath of Conflict' endorsed by the UN Secretary-General in October 2011.[10] Premature repatriation can exacerbate insecurity, and strain infrastructure, markets and services. Addressing the return of refugees in a broader context should allow donors, development actors, host communities and refugees themselves to plan and implement more sustainable repatriation programmes.

State fragility is not the only challenge. Countries of origin may refuse the return of ethnic minorities, or refuse to guarantee their rights upon return. Although the general consensus holds that refugee repatriation is an essential prerequisite for peace, experts suggest that the return of refugees—and IDPs—to areas where they form an ethnic minority may weaken rather than strengthen peace-making efforts.[11] This may especially be the case when minority return is framed as return to a previous place of residence, rather than the securing of citizenship within a wider state.

After the war in Bosnia and Herzegovina in the mid-1990s, the Dayton Peace Accords were intended to reverse 'ethnic cleansing' by guaranteeing the right to return to one's place of origin, but the success of minority returns has remained limited (*see box 3.1*).[12] In Iraq, displacement of specific groups has also been used as a means to secure political and territorial power. As of late 2011, UNHCR considered that the security situation in Iraq was not such that it could actively promote the return of refugees.

BOX **3•1**

Closing the displacement chapter in the Western Balkans

The violent break-up of the former Yugoslavia that began in 1991 led to a series of conflicts—first in Croatia and Bosnia and Herzegovina, and later in Kosovo—characterized by campaigns of 'ethnic cleansing' in which displacement was not just a side effect of the violence, but its central aim.

In all, more than 3.5 million people were uprooted, creating the largest population displacement in Europe since the Second World War. In Bosnia and Herzegovina, where conflict raged from 1992 to 1995, half of the country's population of 4.4 million was displaced. In Croatia, mainly during the initial phase of the fighting in 1991 and again in 1995, hundreds of thousands fled. In Kosovo, conflict in 1998–1999 first caused an exodus of more than 800,000 ethnic Albanians and, after their massive return, an outflow of more than 200,000 ethnic Serbs.

Beginning in 1991, UNHCR was assigned to lead the humanitarian response. In Bosnia and Herzegovina the agency mounted an operation that was unprecedented in scale, scope and complexity, and involved operating in an active war zone the first time. When the conflict ended in 1995, UNHCR was tasked by the Dayton Peace Agreement with developing a plan for the return of refugees and IDPs. In 1999, Annex 2 to UN Security Council Resolution 1244 set out principles on which agreement should be reached to resolve the Kosovo crisis, including the safe and free return of all refugees and displaced persons, under the supervision of UNHCR.

Twenty years on, some three-quarters of those displaced in the 1990s have returned home or found other solutions. In Bosnia and Herzegovina alone, more than a million refugees and IDPs have exercised their right to return. This achievement came in fits and starts. While the highest number of returns took place in the years immediately following the 1995 Peace Agreement, those were overwhelmingly 'majority' returns, with refugees and IDPs going back to areas where their ethnic group was in the majority and occupied key positions of authority. A significant breakthrough on 'minority' returns only came in 2000, following concerted international and national efforts in four key areas: facilitating freedom of movement; enhancing security; establishing an effective mechanism for property restitution; and reconstructing war-damaged homes. There have also been initiatives to facilitate minority returns in Croatia and in Kosovo, although efforts are still needed to support the sustainability of such returns, especially in terms of livelihoods and access to social protection, and to counteract discrimination.

By late 2011, the number of refugees remaining from the 1991–1995 conflicts in Croatia and Bosnia and Herzegovina had fallen to well below 100,000; most were refugees from Croatia living in Serbia. According to government statistics, there were 113,000 IDPs in Bosnia and Herzegovina. The number of persons still displaced from the Kosovo conflict was reported by the authorities to exceed 200,000, most of them living in Serbia, with smaller numbers displaced inside Kosovo itself and elsewhere in the region.

While these remaining refugees and IDPs are a fraction of the number at the height of the conflicts, they are often very vulnerable people for whom it is hard to find solutions. Many live in overcrowded collective centres which were only ever intended to provide temporary shelter. High unemployment, lack of documentation, war trauma, and unresolved claims to tenancy rights, property and pensions frustrate their ability and willingness either to return home or to integrate locally. Meanwhile, international attention and resources have largely moved on to other crises.

In 2010, the government of Bosnia and Herzegovina adopted a revised strategy for implementing Annex VII of the Dayton Peace Agreement, with a focus on supporting the sustainability of returns and on finding alternative solutions for vulnerable IDPs who cannot or do not wish to return. However, a comprehensive solution to the displacement legacy of the Balkans requires regional cooperation. The countries in the region acknowledged this in their Sarajevo Declaration of 2005, but in practice, progress lagged.

The plight of Croatian and Bosnian refugees in Serbia was identified as one of five priorities for the High Commissioner's Special Initiative on Protracted Refugee Situations announced in 2008. In March 2010, the governments of Bosnia and Herzegovina, Croatia, Montenegro and Serbia pledged to cooperate to put an end to this longstanding refugee problem, with strong backing from UNHCR, the EU, the OSCE, and others. Intense efforts, spearheaded by a newly-appointed personal envoy of the High Commissioner, culminated in November 2011 with the four countries signing a Ministerial Declaration on Resolving the Refugee Situation in the Western Balkans. The Declaration contains firm commitments to ending displacement from the 1991–1995 conflicts, and UNHCR hailed it as showing 'courage and wisdom'.

The four countries recognize that addressing the legacy of displacement is an important benchmark for their accession to the EU, along with the development of national refugee protection systems. Already, countries in the region are changing from being the source of displacement to becoming countries of asylum. Ongoing work is needed to build effective asylum systems, and in particular, refugee status determination processes, in line with international and European standards. Moreover, continued efforts will be needed to reduce the risk of statelessness, especially among the Roma minority, including by ensuring that they have personal documentation and secure residency rights.

Two decades after conflict and ethnic cleansing consumed the region, an end is finally in sight to the displacement resulting from the wars in Croatia and Bosnia and Herzegovina. For those displaced from and within Kosovo, however, much remains to be resolved. Across the region, continued improvements in security, freedom of movement, enforcement of the rule of law, and inter-ethnic relations are still needed.

Experience in the western Balkans demonstrates that bringing displacement to an end requires sustained attention, advocacy, engagement from UNHCR, and from the broader international community. Above all, it shows the need for concerted political will on the part of the concerned governments, to close this chapter of their shared history. ◆

Return patterns in Afghanistan, South Sudan and Bosnia and Herzegovina provide evidence of the extent to which refugees and IDPs continue to move after return. Refugees may choose to return to their *country* of origin but not to their *community* of origin, or to leave the country again. Many return to urban areas rather than to rural places of origin. Large numbers of returnees in Afghanistan, for example, have made their way to cities such as Kabul, Nangarhar and Kunduz, although most did not originate from these towns. A similar pattern was observed in Liberia, where returning refugees saw Monrovia as 'the place to go for opportunities and individual advance'.[13]

To date, UNHCR's engagement with returnees in urban areas has been relatively limited, compared to its programmes in rural areas. This reflects in part the concern of governments to avoid additional pressure on urban infrastructures, and a tendency to view repatriation as a reversal of displacement, rather than as a transformative process.

However, the success and sustainability of return does not necessarily depend on integration into a community of previous residence. UNHCR accepts, for example, that refugees and IDPs who experienced urban or semi-urban lifestyles during their displacement may well move to towns and cities upon their return (*see chapter 6*). Such forms of mobility should only be regarded as a failure of the reintegration process if returnees feel they have no choice but to settle in these locations and would otherwise have preferred to return to their home areas.

LOCAL INTEGRATION

In 2005, UNHCR's Executive Committee agreed that states and UNHCR should 'work proactively' on local integration.[14] In the years that followed, however, many host countries continued to resist local integration while donor countries consistently encouraged efforts to find solutions in the refugees' regions of origin.

Host states are frequently reluctant to consider large-scale local settlement of refugee populations, especially if they consider that this would amplify communal tensions or competition for limited resources. Host communities may perceive refugees as having a negative impact on local development or as a presenting a threat to security. The unwillingness of many countries to permit local integration is reflected in policies of encampment which are in part intended to prevent refugees from putting down roots.[15] With the growing vitality of democratic governance and institutions in a number of host states in Africa, for example, attitudes toward the settlement of refugees increasingly find expression in national and local politics.

Yet, when refugees are given the opportunity to integrate in host communities, they often make important economic, social and cultural contributions. This has been observed in the case of Guatemalan refugees naturalized in Mexico, Angolan refugees in Zambia, and Sierra Leonean and Liberian refugees in West Africa, to cite just a few examples. In West Africa, freedom of movement in the context of the Economic Community of West African States (ECOWAS) offers particularly positive opportunities, as discussed later in this chapter.

UNHCR / S. SCHULMAN

Even where their presence is not officially authorized, refugees are not necessarily a drain on the local economy, and can actually boost it. In Kenya and in South Africa the highly entrepreneurial Somali community is reported to play an important economic role.[16] The presence of refugee camps can also contribute to local employment growth, a subject which is explored in a recent study on the area surrounding the huge Dadaab refugee complex in northeastern Kenya.[17]

▲ **Returned IDPs in Sri Lanka** have set up a small shop with the help of a UNHCR grant.

In some contexts, host government officials may attach political or economic value to the continued presence of refugees, and at least implicitly discourage them from taking up solutions, even where these are available. Humanitarian actors may then find themselves locked into patterns of assistance which perpetuate displacement. Recent reports on the Croatian refugee population in Serbia and on UNHCR's response to the protracted refugee situation in eastern Sudan draw attention to this risk.[18]

Despite policy restrictions aimed at preventing local settlement, integration invariably occurs to some degree when refugees remain in their country of asylum for years on end. A 2011 evaluation of UNHCR's response to long-staying Eritrean refugees in eastern Sudan, for example, highlighted extensive *de facto* integration. In that region, the day-to-day lives of refugee and host communities are remarkably intertwined, even as the Sudanese government remains reluctant to consider regularizing the residence status of the refugees.[19]

Moreover, many refugees have spent decades, or were born, in exile. Repatriation to a 'home' they do not know, and where they may not speak the language, clearly offers a less natural solution for them than remaining in communities where, over many years, they have established families and extensive social and economic ties. In this context, the government of Zambia's recent pledge to facilitate the local integration of up to 10,000 long-staying Angolan refugees, including some who have been born and brought up in Zambia as second and third generation refugees, is a welcome development.[20]

In recent years, UNHCR has paid renewed attention to local integration and its potential to solve refugee crises, particularly protracted ones, and has solicited more support from the donor community for this solution. Tanzania's decision to extend citizenship to 162,000 long-staying Burundian refugees is an example of how solidarity, both on the part of the host country and the donor community, can bring an end to a decades-old refugee problem.

BOX 3.2

Tanzania: ending a protracted refugee situation

The response to the 1972 influx

In 1972, armed conflict in Burundi between the Tutsi minority and the Hutu majority resulted in the death of over 100,000 persons. More than 150,000 Burundians, mostly ethnic Hutu, fled across the border into the United Republic of Tanzania. They were well-received by the Tanzanian Government led by President Julius Nyerere, which had adopted a progressive refugee policy in the spirit of African solidarity.

Rather than confining the refugees to camps, where they would be dependent on humanitarian aid, Tanzania allowed them to become self-sufficient in agricultural settlements. The refugees were allocated five hectares of land per family in three designated areas in central-western Tanzania (Katumba, Mishamo and Ulyankulu) that came to be known as the 'Old Settlements'. UNHCR and the international community provided assistance for basic infrastructure in the settlements, such as schools, clinics and boreholes for water.

Three decades later, natural population growth had brought the number of refugees in the Old Settlements to around 218,000. Most refugee families had achieved self-sufficiency, if not outright prosperity, by producing cash crops, mainly tobacco, and foods such as cassava, maize and beans. The younger generations, which make up about 80 per cent of the settlement population, were born and raised in Tanzania, attended state schools and became fluent in the official language, Swahili, further easing the path to integration. By 1985, the refugee community had become largely self-reliant and UNHCR was able to disengage from the settlements, turning to priorities elsewhere.

New approaches

Meanwhile, in the 1990s, Tanzania faced new influxes of refugees, with hundreds of thousands arriving once again from Burundi as well as from Rwanda and the Democratic Republic of the Congo (then Zaire). As the numbers grew, the policies and attitudes of the Government of Tanzania changed, moving away from the previous policy of promoting refugee self-sufficiency, which came to be seen as a disincentive for voluntary repatriation, and towards a strict encampment policy for new arrivals.

Despite having achieved a basic level of self-sufficiency, the status of those living in the Old Settlements remained that of refugees, appearing as such, year after year, in UNHCR's statistics. While refugee status provided them with protection from forced return, it did not give access to other rights, most notably employment outside the settlements. Unable officially to take up work in urban areas, it was not uncommon for educated young refugees seeking professional positions and able to speak the national language to present themselves as Tanzanians.

In June 2007, at the 11th meeting of the Tripartite Commission involving Tanzania, Burundi and UNHCR, convened in the context of promoting voluntary repatriation from the camps, it was agreed to commission a study of the Old Settlements. The purpose of the study was to assist the Tripartite Commission in developing a comprehensive strategy for the Burundians who had arrived in 1972, based on the durable solutions of voluntary repatriation and local integration, including naturalization. With the exception of around 8,500 of the 1972 refugees who had ended up in camps in northwest Tanzania, resettlement was not extended to the Burundians who arrived in 1972. Nor was the possibility of local integration open to those who arrived in the 1990s, and were living in camps rather than in the settlements.

Local integration and naturalization

Why did the Tanzanian Government agree to local integration for the inhabitants of the Old Settlements? There is probably more than one answer. First, it was consistent with the Government's stated objective at that time of establishing a 'refugee-free' Tanzania, taken in the positive sense of finding durable solutions for refugees in the country.

Second, there was also an appreciation of the fact that if all of the 218,000 refugees in the Old Settlements were to return to Burundi, in addition to those in the camps, this could have a destabilizing effect in Burundi at a time when Tanzania was encouraging a fragile peace process. By the end of 2007, Burundi had already received back some 293,000 returnees from Tanzania, and was facing many challenges with respect to reintegration.

Thirdly, it was well known that the 1972 Burundian refugee population contributed considerably to the Tanzanian economy, the majority being successful farmers, businessmen or professionals. (Tobacco production in Mishamo Settlement alone was 6,000 tonnes in 2009–2010, yielding tax revenue of 1.6 billion Tanzanian shillings.)

In late 2007, as recommended by the Tripartite Commission, in an initial step toward implementing the comprehensive solutions strategy, UNHCR launched a registration exercise and survey to capture the intentions of the refugees in the Old Settlements, and learn more about their socioeconomic and demographic profile. Out of 218,000 persons registered, close to 46,000 (21 per cent) opted for repatriation to Burundi, while 172,000 (79 per cent) chose naturalization and integration in Tanzania.

The findings and recommendations of the survey were endorsed in December 2007 by the 12th meeting of the Tripartite Commission. In February 2008, the Tanzania Comprehensive Solutions Strategy (TAN-COSS) was launched by UNHCR and the Tanzanian Government, along with a Supplementary Appeal for funding. Donors responded enthusiastically and the appeal was fully funded, with US$25 million for activities in Tanzania and US$8 million for reintegration activities in Burundi.

Taking the strategy forward

Before the programme could start, UNHCR needed to reopen offices in three remote locations near the Old Settlements and deploy staff. Voluntary repatriation to Burundi began in April 2008. It was a logisti-

UNHCR/G. SALERNO

◀ **A Burundian refugee** in the Katumba Settlement, Western Tanzania.

In order to take the comprehensive strategy forward, the Tripartite Commission established a Task Force to oversee the process and make sure that policy and operational matters were addressed. UNHCR and its partners also implemented community-based projects near the Old Settlements, including the construction of secondary schools, clinics, and water points, the upgrading of an airport and forestation projects. These projects were aimed at boosting local absorption capacity and reassuring the authorities that they would not be left alone in shouldering the costs of local integration.

By April 2010, the Minister of Home Affairs had naturalized more than 162,000 Burundian refugees, 98 per cent of those who had applied, with UNHCR paying a total of US$3.6 million in citizenship fees for them. The official list with the names of the newly naturalized was published in April 2010 and individual citizenship certificates were printed by the Immigration Department on high tech, forge-proof paper procured for Tanzania by UNHCR in Switzerland.

The last stage?

Still, the process was not over, as the Government of Tanzania had announced at the beginning of 2008 that the newly naturalized citizens would have to leave the Old Settlements, where they had been living for more than three decades, and relocate elsewhere in the country. The stated reasons for this related to security and ethnicity. It was also deemed that if the refugees remained *in situ*, the local community would continue to stigmatize them as refugees.

In September 2009, in a speech before the UN General Assembly, the President of Tanzania, H.E. Jakaya Kikwete, stated : 'my government has decided that, if accepted, they will be moved from the refugee camps and be resettled in various places in the country. We don't want them to remain with the refugee mentality. We also want Tanzanians to remove the attitude of continuing to consider them as refugees. This is going to be a very expensive exercise for which the support of the United Nations and others will be necessary.'

To address the issue of relocation, UNHCR in 2009 supported two meetings of Regional Commissioners to agree on how many newly naturalized former refugees each region of Tanzania would take. It also established a new working relationship with the Prime Minister's Office of Regional Administration and Local Government, as its main counterpart previously had been the Ministry of Home Affairs (MHA). Donors, notably the UK, provided funding for refugee assistance packages to facilitate the relocation of the newly naturalized.

cally complex operation, involving transportation of the refugees and all their belongings and livestock, using a combination of trucks and trains. There were also challenges in Burundi, especially in relation to land restitution. Eventually, however, 53,000 refugees repatriated from the Old Settlements, exceeding the initial planning figure of 46,000.

For those who had opted for naturalization, an expedited procedure to obtain citizenship was developed, within the framework of Tanzanian law. While faster than the regular naturalization process, it still required significant effort. Citizenship application forms were completed by 164,000 refugees, supported by Tanzanian witnesses. They had to renounce their Burundian nationality, declare an oath of allegiance to Tanzania in front of a Commission, and be fingerprinted. Their applications were reviewed by local officials, digitized and sent to Dar es Salaam for data entry by the Citizenship Processing Unit (CPU) within the Immigration Department. Finally, the applicants were individually screened by local Defence and Security Committees.

(Continued on page 74)

BOX 3·2 *(Continued from page 73)*

After some discussion, it was agreed that organizing UNHCR convoys for the relocation could draw attention to the new citizens and undermine their smooth integration in their new destinations. It was decided that the relocation would be self-driven, with the new citizens organizing their own moves. This was reflected in the 'National Strategy for Community Integration Programme' launched in June 2010 by the Tanzanian authorities and UNHCR, which spelled out the modalities for the relocation. It included a list of 16 regions (out of 21 in Tanzania) that would receive the newly naturalized, and a five-year budget (2010–2014) of US$144 million for individual assistance (cash grants, including transport assistance and start-up capital) and community-based projects in the regions of destination. This programme was also included in the UN Development Assistance Plan for Tanzania for 2011–2015.

In 2010 and 2011, UNHCR assisted the government with the preparatory work for the planned relocation, including information-sharing sessions with the local authorities and registration activities. However, in August 2011 the relocation was put on hold due to concerns raised by some members of Parliament and local officials about the extent of consultations at the local level and about how the relocation would proceed. The government has reiterated its commitment to the programme, including plans to complete the relocation by 2013, and has called on the international community to provide further support. As of the end of 2011, UNHCR was in discussions with the government to address these issues, so as to bring the local integration process to a successful conclusion.

Why is UNHCR still engaged with this caseload? After all, it could be argued that since the Burundians have been naturalized under Tanzanian law, they are no longer of concern to the organization. However, UNHCR recognizes that, given the scale of the naturalization and integration exercise for this group, a period of continued support is required. There is also a strong interest in ensuring that the local integration process is successful, to encourage other countries to take similar initiatives to resolve protracted refugee situations.

By the end of 2011, only 745 refugees who were living in Dar es Salaam at the time of the naturalization exercise had received their individual naturalization certificates. The majority of the 1972 Burundians were in a limbo situation. While they are Tanzanian citizens by law, *de facto* their ability to exercise their rights as citizens is limited until they receive citizenship certificates.

As is often the case, the last step of a durable solutions programme is the most challenging one. As an October 2010 evaluation noted, the comprehensive solutions strategy has been communicated as a success story, although the most difficult steps are still ahead. But, even if 'mission accomplished' might have been declared prematurely, it would be wrong to jump to the opposite conclusion. The Government has reiterated that it wants to see this process to completion. They, together with UNHCR and the international community, must stay the course in order to turn this story into an example of unprecedented solidarity. ◆

Although large-scale naturalizations, such as in Tanzania (*see box 3.2*), remain rare, many refugees are able to acquire the citizenship of their asylum country on an individual basis. Statistics reflecting the naturalization of refugees as distinct from other foreigners are hard to come by, since few states make this distinction in their record-keeping; nonetheless, it is clear that the granting of asylum followed by naturalization provides a durable solution for large numbers of refugees, particularly in countries of the industrialized world.

The contribution to durable solutions made by asylum granted on an individual basis is often neglected, and merits being factored into discussions on responsibility-sharing. According to statistics collected by UNHCR and published annually in its *Statistical Yearbook*, over the last ten years, 1.6 million persons have been recognized as refugees under the terms of the 1951 Convention by countries that implement individual asylum procedures; approximately half a million others received a complementary form of protection. The majority of these people will, in due course, acquire permanent residency or citizenship rights.

RESETTLEMENT

Resettlement is a vital protection tool for refugees whose life, liberty or other fundamental human rights are at risk in the country where they initially sought protection. It provides a durable solution for refugees for whom neither local integration nor voluntary repatriation is possible. As discussed in chapter 8, it is also a tangible expression of international solidarity with refugee-hosting countries.

In 2011, UNHCR estimated that 805,000 refugees under its mandate were in need of third-country resettlement. However, the sum total of places offered by states for refugee resettlement amount to only about 10 per cent of that figure on an annual basis. If resettlement is to make a more significant contribution to the provision of durable solutions, the number of places available will need to increase.

In 2010, 94 per cent of all resettled refugees went to just four countries: Australia, Canada, Sweden, and the United States of America. The US continues to resettle many more refugees than any other country; for the fiscal year 2012, it has set its resettlement ceiling at 76,000. Even though this figure includes a number of places earmarked for people still in their countries of origin (Cuba, Iraq or countries of the former Soviet Union) and who are thus not part of UNHCR's resettlement programme, the reality is that UNHCR's resettlement efforts remain disproportionately dependent on the engagement of one country: the United States.

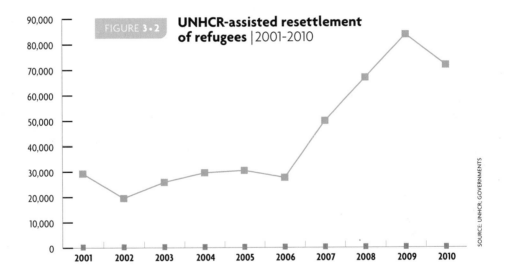

FIGURE 3•2 **UNHCR-assisted resettlement of refugees** | 2001-2010

SOURCE: UNHCR; GOVERNMENTS

UNHCR has consistently encouraged more countries to resettle refugees. As a result of this advocacy, the number of countries implementing resettlement programmes has grown from 15 in 2005 to 24 in 2012.[21] However, this has not yet had much impact on the overall number of resettlement places available, as the new resettlement countries are in general starting out with very small programmes, in an effort to build a solid basis for the integration of resettled refugees before expanding their programmes. Even with very modest numbers, there has been concern about the limited integration support available in countries with little previous experience of immigration and integration.

As resettlement is intended to be a durable solution, resettled refugees should be offered a viable prospect of integration and ultimately have the possibility to become citizens of their new country. This implies a responsibility on the part of the resettlement country to make sure that there is appropriate and sufficient integration support for resettled refugees, especially in the initial, often difficult, period immediately after arrival.

The focus on refugees' integration prospects sometimes leads receiving countries to

BOX 3•3

Resettlement from Nepal: a strategic approach

When refugees from Bhutan started arriving in Nepal in the early 1990s, the news scarcely made headlines outside the region. Such a silent refugee crisis often paves the way for what is euphemistically called a 'protracted' refugee situation, in which a combination of lack of political interest, declining funding for humanitarian aid and elusive durable solutions creates generations of refugees.

By the end of 1995, more than 90,000 people—around 18 per cent of Bhutan's population—had fled across the border into India and continued on to Nepal. Commonly known as *Lhotshampa* or 'people of the south', the refugees came from a variety of mostly Nepali-speaking minority groups in Bhutan. The vast majority of the refugees had been made stateless by Bhutan's 1985 Citizenship Act.

The refugees lived in seven camps in eastern Nepal. In 2007, when a complete registration was carried out, the refugee population had reached almost 108,000 persons, mostly because of natural population growth.

Even though the refugees shared the same language, religion and culture as the local population, their prospects of being allowed to settle in Nepal were slim. For many years Nepal also remained reluctant to let the refugees re-settle to third countries, fearing that this would undermine any prospect of voluntary return to Bhutan. There were numerous unsuccessful attempts to promote return, including through direct talks between the two countries.

In 2005, a 'Core Group' of countries decided to work together to resolve this situation. The eight countries—Australia, Canada, Denmark, the Netherlands, New Zealand, Norway, the United Kingdom, and the United States—announced their willingness to reset-tle refugees from Bhutan, in the hope that this would help to unblock the stalemate. The eight countries convened regularly in Geneva and Kathmandu. In Kathmandu, the ambassa-dors met with IOM, UNHCR and WFP Representa-tives in attendance, and became a powerful voice in support of the refugees.

In late 2007, Nepal agreed to allow resettlement, and the first departures took place in spring 2008. Within the refugee community itself, there were initially tensions between those who favoured resettlement and those who opposed it, and many remained undecided. The anti-resettlement group was concerned that resettlement would eliminate any chance of voluntary repatriation, although UNHCR reassured the refugees that it would continue to promote other solutions. By the end of 2011, more than 58,500 refugees had left Nepal for resettle-ment, and the remaining camp population had fallen to just under 55,000.

Why did the resettlement countries act in such a generous manner? What lessons can be learned from this experience? From a purely humanitarian perspective, the resettlement countries saw an opportunity to resolve a long-standing refugee situation. In addition, after years of discussion about the 'strategic use' of resettlement, it provided an opportu-nity to put theory to the test.

However, by the end of 2011, the extent of interest in resettlement among the remain-ing refugees and the very high acceptance rate meant that resettlement would be the principal durable solution for this refugee population. It is thus fair to ask whether resettlement has brought about wider solutions benefits, as was originally intended. Options for voluntary repatriation remain limited, while discussions are continuing with the government of Nepal on solutions for refugees who do not opt for resettlement.

Still, the large-scale resettlement has significantly reduced the camp population and provided tens of thousands of refugees with a durable solution. In 2010, Nepal en-dorsed camp consolidation and a Community Based Development Programme (CBDP) pro-posed by UNHCR, aimed at opening up social services and livelihood opportunities for the local population and the remaining refugees. Also in 2011, the government of Bhutan signalled its readiness to resume discussions on voluntary repatriation—an important step given that no refugee has been able to return in the past 20 years. ◆

select refugees for resettlement not only on the basis of their protection needs, but also on the basis of their presumed 'integration potential'. This approach is problematic for two reasons. First, from a point of view of principle, selecting refugees for resettlement on the basis of an assumption about their ability to settle successfully in a given country amounts to a serious deviation from the primary objective of resettlement as a tool of international protection. Secondly, it is difficult to assess an individual's 'integration potential' in ad-vance. For instance, while it is often assumed that a higher level of education enhances in-tegration prospects, this is not necessarily the case.

Civil society groups are actively engaged in refugee resettlement. They play a particularly important role in supporting the integration of resettled refugees at the grass roots level, and in encouraging governments to establish new refugee programmes or to expand existing programmes. For instance, a campaign entitled 'Save Me' launched in 2008 by civil society groups in Munich (Germany) resulted in dozens of city councils across the country proclaiming their willingness to receive resettled refugees in their communities. This campaign certainly influenced the German Federal Government's decision, announced in December 2011, to begin an annual resettlement programme as of 2012.

Recognizing that resettlement places are limited, UNHCR and partners have sought to use resettlement in a more 'strategic' manner–defined somewhat vaguely as an approach that 'maximizes the benefits, directly or indirectly, other than those received by the refugees being resettled'.[22] This is not altogether new. In the 1970s, a massive effort to resettle Vietnamese boat people was mobilized in order to persuade coastal states in Southeast Asia to allow the refugees to land. In the 1990s, UNHCR promoted resettlement of Bosnian refugees from Germany in part to ease pressures for minority returns to Bosnia and Herzegovina.

However, the strategic use of resettlement is now receiving much more attention for its potential as part of a comprehensive approach to resolving a protracted refugee problem, helping to improve the overall protection environment in the country of refuge or to improve prospects (and political and financial support) for other solutions, or both. The resettlement in 2007 and 2008 of about 8,500 of the '1972 Burundians' who had been living in UNHCR-assisted camps in Tanzania may have helped to open the path toward naturalization for the larger group in the 'Old Settlements'. More recently, the resettlement of refugees from Bhutan who had been staying in Nepal for more than two decades (*see box 3.3*) was intended to support a broader approach to solutions.

Resettlement also has particular relevance as a protection tool, enabling refugees to be quickly extracted from situations of danger. Several countries make specific provision in their programmes for emergency resettlement, and can respond rapidly to requests from UNHCR. In recent years, emergency resettlement has been supported by the establishment of three facilities to which refugees can be evacuated from their countries of first asylum. In 2008, UNHCR, the International Organization for Migration (IOM) and the government of Romania set up the first Emergency Transit Centre in the town of Timisoara. Refugees may stay up to six months while resettlement processing takes place. In 2009, similar arrangements were set up in the Philippines and in Slovakia.

Comprehensive strategies

UNHCR HAS SOUGHT TO UNBLOCK PROTRACTED REFUGEE SITUATIONS by pursuing comprehensive strategies which involve all three durable solutions. A durable solution, by definition, removes the objective need for refugee status by allowing the refugee to acquire or re-acquire the full protection of a state.

In the case of both local integration and sustainable repatriation, there is frequently a need to connect refugee solutions to broader peacebuilding and development efforts. This is now widely accepted, even if institutional arrangements at international and national levels have not always kept pace with this recognition. The UN Secretary-General has called for the UN system to play a 'more predictable and effective role' in this process.[23]

PEACE BUILDING

Peacebuilding is a multidimensional process focused on restoring the rule of law and governance systems as well as the economy, infrastructure, and public services of states emerging from conflict and that risk lapsing back into war.

In December 2005, the UN General Assembly and Security Council set up the Peacebuilding Commission, a new inter-governmental advisory body to help countries with post-conflict recovery and peacebuilding. UNHCR actively supports the work of the Commission, which is of direct relevance to the search for solutions to refugee problems. The Commission selected six countries as the focus of its initial work: Burundi, the Central African Republic, Guinea, Guinea-Bissau, Liberia, and Sierra Leone—all complex environments involving refugees, IDPs and/or returnees.

Governments with limited capacity to meet the socio-economic needs of their own citizens are more likely to resist the integration of refugees, and local populations may resent the perceived allocation of resources to refugees and returnees alike. In 2006, High Commissioner Guterres warned that 'large-scale population returns are difficult to sustain if development stalls and instability grows,' noting also that 'Without adequate resources (...) societies can unravel again, dormant conflicts can reignite, and civilians can be forcibly displaced once more'.[24]

The return of large numbers of refugees to countries that are devastated by years of war can place new pressures on scarce resources such as land and housing, increase competition for jobs, and lead to the establishment of shanty towns and squatter settlements. Old conflicts may reignite, or new social tensions and political violence may arise, leading to new waves of displacement. Preventing and resolving land disputes in the context of refugee returns, as has been the case, for instance, in Burundi and Liberia, takes on particular importance.

Security and stability are obviously preconditions for durable solutions. When refugees nonetheless return to unstable situations and fragile states, international development and humanitarian actors may have to devote more attention to finding ways to strengthen the 'resilience' of returning refugees and their communities to future emergencies. For all of these reasons, UNHCR has sought to ensure that issues related to refugees and returnees are an integral part of broader peacebuilding strategies.

LIVELIHOODS AND DEVELOPMENT

Since the 1980s, it has been clearly recognized that both local integration and voluntary repatriation require the full engagement of development actors. This is no less true today,

▲ **Somali refugee women** producing bricks for construction of shelters in Dadaab camp (Kenya).

in view of the fact that four-fifths of the world's refugees are located in the developing world, with nearly 20 per cent in Least Developed Countries (LDCs). Most refugee returns are to fragile post-conflict environments, such as Afghanistan, the Democratic Republic of the Congo (DRC), and South Sudan— states struggling to emerge from years of conflict that are poorly-equipped to support the reintegration of their citizens.

UNHCR is a humanitarian, not a development actor. Fulfilling its mandate to find 'permanent solutions' to refugee problems inevitably depends, at least in part, on the success of initiatives undertaken by partners such as UNDP and the World Bank.[25] Over the years, UNHCR has been the driving force behind numerous attempts to link refugee solutions to broader development programmes, with varying degrees of success.[26]

The Executive Committee's 2009 Conclusion on Protracted Refugee Situations once again 'urged humanitarian and development actors to pursue effective partnerships in the implementation of durable solutions (...)'.[27] The Committee also encouraged states, UNHCR and other partners to pursue proactive measures to reduce refugee dependency and enhance their protection and dignity.[28] The establishment in 2010 by the World Bank of a 'Global Programme on Forced Displacement' is an important step forward. The programme aims to improve the Bank's contribution to an 'enhanced development response to forced displacement that supports economically and socially sustainable solutions'.[29]

Within UNHCR operations in a wide range of countries, refugee livelihoods have taken on increased importance. Livelihood programming includes advocacy for access to work and a range of interventions that aim to preserve refugees' skills and productive assets, and to mobilize these assets in the search for durable solutions.

For instance, a comprehensive strategy is being launched to promote the socio-economic integration of Central African refugees in southern Chad, in collaboration with local institutions and a number of development actors. Based on the findings of a socio-economic survey, a range of interventions will be implemented to boost entrepreneurship, link agricultural production to markets, and strengthen socio-economic ties between refugees and host communities.

In 2010, UNHCR launched a new attempt to bridge the relief–development gap, unlock solutions for the displaced, and provide them with livelihood support. The Transitional Solutions Initiative (TSI), developed by UNHCR and UNDP along with the World Bank, is based on the recognition that displacement challenges cannot be addressed by humanitarian actors alone. [30]

BOX 3.4

Refugees in eastern Sudan:
a renewed search for solutions

With a view to finding solutions for Eritrean refugees in eastern Sudan, UNHCR has renewed its efforts to develop livelihood opportunities, reduce the refugees' vulnerability and reliance on outside aid, and encourage development actors to focus on the needs of refugees and host communities alike.

A sizeable population of Eritrean refugees has lived in eastern Sudan since the late 1960s, making it one of the world's most protracted refugee situations. Many of the refugees arrived during Eritrea's 30-year struggle for independence from Ethiopia; their number peaked at around 800,000 in 1990. By 2011, this refugee population had declined to around 70,000, most living in camps in Gedaref and Kassala States.

When the the war for independence ended in 1991, it was thought that the long-staying Eritrean refugees would opt to return to their country. Voluntary repatriation did begin in 1992, with 70,000 Eritreans going back from Sudan. But numbers soon decreased dramatically. Just 36,600 repatriated between 1993—the year of the referendum in which Eritreans overwhelmingly voted for independence—and 1999. Meanwhile, the number of Eritrean refugees arriving in Sudan started to rise again in 1998, as a result of the human rights situation in Eritrea and the outbreak of a new war. That conflict, which began as a border dispute between Eritrea and Ethiopia, ended two years later after causing tens of thousands of casualties and displacing

hundreds of thousands of people.

After the UN brokered an end to the border war in December 2000, some refugees returned to Eritrea, but they were quickly outpaced by a steady flow of new arrivals. The number of Eritreans seeking refuge in Sudan grew from around 1,000 in 2003 to over 90,000 during 2004–2010. Many of the new arrivals moved to urban areas of Sudan and onward to other countries and continents.

The long-staying Eritrean refugees have struggled to find durable solutions. They are not willing to repatriate in view of the human rights situation in Eritrea. Over the years, there have been few resettlement opportunities for them. Some defy the Sudanese government's encampment policy and move to urban centres, particularly Khartoum, where they stay without official authorization and work informally. Most, however, remain in the camps, dependent on humanitarian assistance, with few possibilities to engage in agricultural activities or to find other employment.

Keeping the situation in focus
UNHCR has redoubled its efforts to find durable solutions for the long-staying refugees, while at the same time striving to cope with the sizeable new influx. For those who arrived before 2005, the most viable strategy is to promote self-reliance and develop livelihood activities, with a view to facilitating eventual local integration.

Most of the long-staying Eritrean

refugees, in contrast to the newer arrivals, share ethnicity, language, culture, and religion with the local population. Many were born or brought up in Sudan and consider it their home. Some have already found a way of sustaining themselves at least to some degree, by means of agriculture or informal labour, although scarcity of fertile land and general poverty affect refugees and host communities alike. At the same time, as a complementary approach, UNHCR is developing a multi-year resettlement programme for those refugees with the least likelihood of being able to integrate in Sudan.

The renewed search for solutions started as early as September 2007, when UNHCR and the Sudanese Commissioner for Refugees (COR) elaborated a comprehensive Joint Solutions Strategy, which envisaged a shift from the provision of care and maintenance assistance to an approach based on self-reliance, as a precursor to local integration, as well as improvements in the asylum regime in the country.

Already at that time it was proposed gradually to integrate some of the refugee camps into national service provision systems, such as health and education, and to reorient aid to support refugee livelihoods. The strategy also called for using resettlement in a strategic manner, in the hope that it would help to open up opportunities for local integration. Above all, the approach sought to bring development aid to refugee-populated areas.

In 2008, the High Commissioner launched

The TSI is aimed at integrating the needs of the refugees, returnees and IDPs into broader reconstruction and development planning. It addresses these needs through community-level actions that also benefit local populations—people hosting refugees and IDPs as well as communities to which they return. A TSI pilot programme is underway in Colombia and eastern Sudan.

A key element of the TSI is the promotion of education and training, to enable refugees and returnees to become self-reliant and to contribute to their communities.

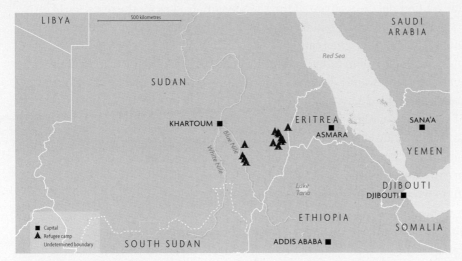

his Initiative on Protracted Refugee Situations, intended to put a spotlight on the worldwide problem of long-term displacement and to concentrate resources and efforts on securing solutions. Eritreans in eastern Sudan were selected as one of five protracted caseloads to address. This was followed by the elaboration in 2009 of a 'Multi-year Self-reliance Project for Long-staying Refugees in Eastern Sudan' which consolidated many of the earlier proposals.

The Transitional Solutions Initiative

UNHCR recognized that however effectively its activities were formulated and implemented, they would not lead to self-reliance on a large enough scale unless simultaneous steps were taken to stimulate economic and infrastructure 0growth in eastern Sudan. UNHCR thus embarked on the Transitional Solutions Initiative (TSI), a fresh effort to bridge the gap between relief and development and to build on the 2009 framework for refugee self-reliance.

Within the TSI, UNHCR is working mainly with UNDP and the World Bank to expand livelihood opportunities for refugees in camps in the east as well as for the surrounding communities. Agricultural development, livestock production, market-oriented vocational training and microfinance services are all part of this effort.

Drawing lessons from previous experience, UNHCR and UNDP are keen to improve coordination with state governments and with central line ministries, to build capacity among counterparts, and to mobilize sufficient resources for livelihood activities. Initial funding for the TSI in eastern Sudan has been provided by Norway and the IKEA Foundation. Donor countries have shown renewed interest in this region and some have established a Khartoum-based group, 'Friends of the East', to coordinate and strengthen aid.

While it is too early to assess the impact of the TSI in eastern Sudan, the challenges are clear. First, UNHCR will need to continue to advocate on behalf of refugee rights. Many refugees are living in camps which have been in existence for more than 40 years and are hard to distinguish from Sudanese villages. Some of the refugees consider themselves Sudanese for all practical purposes. UNHCR will continue to encourage the government to grant the refugees the right to work and to own land, to remove restrictions placed on their freedom of movement, and, as a longer-term objective, to give the refugees the possibility to become citizens. This advocacy will need to be accompanied by tangible economic, educational and environmental benefits for the host population.

Second, UNHCR will continue to promote sustainable refugee livelihoods, with a view to enabling the refugees to become self-reliant. If the camps are to be transformed into viable villages, it will be important to make sure that they are no longer dependent on humanitarian aid.

Third, UNHCR will have to make every effort to link its humanitarian activities to longer-term development and investment strategies; the goal must be to bring robust growth to eastern Sudan. To this end, UNHCR will need to engage with donors, development organizations, state-level governments and central authorities in Khartoum, including with ministries that have hitherto played a very limited role in refugee matters. The Sudanese government will also need to be assured that funding for the TSI and other refugee-related activities is additional funding, which does not detract from current humanitarian and development aid. ◆

While evaluation of UNHCR's activities in 1997 described education as 'the most critical element bridging the gap between relief assistance and durable solutions'[31] a new evaluation issued in 2011 found that a continued lack of high quality education for refugees still stands in the way of achieving durable solutions.[32]

In response to this situation, UNHCR has embarked on a new five-year education strategy. The new strategy places emphasis on increasing access to primary education, expanding access to secondary education and enhancing the quality of learning.

A FUNDAMENTAL CHANGE OF CIRCUMSTANCES

Both the 1951 Convention and the 1969 OAU Refugee Convention allow for the cessation of refugee status when positive, fundamental and durable changes have taken place in the country of origin, such that the original causes of refugee flight no longer exist. However, there may be individuals for whom refugee status will need to be maintained, in view of their particular circumstances, and a declaration of cessation is not a bar to new claims for refugee status. A declaration of cessation of refugee status can be seen in broad terms as the end point of a refugee situation.

Assessing a 'fundamental change of circumstances' is not always easy, and standards for invoking the 'ceased circumstances' clause contained in Article 1C of the 1951 Refugee Convention have traditionally been set at a high level.[33] Moreover, controversy can arise about the extent to which 'ceased circumstances' are declared under pressure from host countries eager to encourage repatriation or from countries of origin.[34]

Most recently, the 'ceased circumstances' clause has been invoked by UNHCR in the cases of Tajik refugees (in 2005), and Sierra Leonean refugees (in 2008). UNHCR has also elaborated new comprehensive strategies for resolving the refugee situations of Rwandans, Liberians and Angolans, including recommendations on the applicability of the cessation clauses.

In situations where cessation of refugee status is declared after protracted exile, and refugees have become integrated–*de facto* or *de jure*–in their countries of asylum, UNHCR's Executive Committee has urged that 'appropriate arrangements, which would not put into jeopardy their established situation, be [considered] (...) for those persons who cannot be expected to leave the country of asylum, due to a long stay in that country resulting in strong family, social and economic links there'.[35]

While the combination of durable solutions has been used before in an effort to address refugee situations, cessation of refugee status, assuming conditions are met, can also play a role in achieving durable solutions, acting as a catalyst to action. Invoking the cessation clause does not, in itself, provide a durable solution. However, it sends an important signal that the need for refugee protection, in general, has come to an end.

Refugee perspectives

A PERSISTENT CRITIQUE OF EFFORTS TO SOLVE REFUGEE PROBLEMS IS THAT the refugees themselves are insufficiently involved. Refugees often perceive resettlement processes as mysterious and bureaucratic. Local integration in the formal sense depends on the agreement of host state authorities, which refugees are usually powerless to influence. As far as voluntary repatriation is concerned, although UNHCR has made efforts to include refugee communities in peace negotiations on a number of occasions, when tripartite commissions are formed to negotiate conditions for return, they typically include

UNHCR, the country of origin and the country of asylum—but not representatives of the refugees themselves.

While the international community generally approaches solutions from either an individual perspective or a group level, refugees usually make their decisions at the family level. Women and older people are frequently left out of formal consultation processes, but at the family level, they play a key role in decision-making.

Within one family, there may be a deliberate and simultaneous pursuit of resettlement, voluntary repatriation and local integration, alongside other migration strategies—both regular and irregular.[36] A single family may include refugees, asylum-seekers, migrants and individuals who have not left home. Connected through complex social and economic networks that offer different coping strategies, they usually prioritize sustainable livelihoods as the most important aspect of their solutions to displacement.

Refugees understandably approach solutions in ways which they consider are most likely to maintain flexibility, maximize security and bring economic gains for their families. In some cases this can complicate formal durable solutions efforts. For instance, in the early years of the Afghan repatriation programme, before the introduction of advanced registration technology including biometrics in 2002, 'recycling' was a problem, as refugees criss-crossed the border to take advantage of repatriation assistance.

Refugees have at times sought access to resettlement by making unsubstantiated claims for family reunification, or by placing their offspring as 'foster children' with families eligible for resettlement. Refugees who are *de facto* locally integrated have informally acquired citizenship papers, as documented among Angolan refugees in Zambia and Eritreans in eastern Sudan.[37] In contrast, it has been suggested that some Croatian refugees of Serbian origin applied for citizenship in Serbia but did not complete the process—perhaps in the hope of retaining any benefits linked to their refugee status.[38]

The disjuncture between the approaches to solutions pursued by refugees and the international community can also drive refugees to wait for their preferred solution or to circumvent official criteria. In particular, refugees may hold out for resettlement; for example, in 2008, protesting Liberian refugees in Ghana demanded resettlement or a US$1000 voluntary repatriation package—rather than the US$100 on offer.[39] Refugees' insistence on resettlement has been noted in numerous settings, and can result in prolonged displacement.[40]

MIGRATION AND MOBILITY

When refugees are actively involved in the search for solutions, they invariably attach a high priority to one element in particular: mobility. One reason why refugees continue to attach such a high value to resettlement is that restrictive global migration policies limit their possibility to move through other channels.

In many refugee-producing regions—such as the Horn of Africa, West Africa, and Afghanistan—seasonal and circular migration patterns predate conflicts, continue through conflicts, and contribute significantly to meeting post-conflict needs and offering solutions.

In addition, migration and circular movement allow for a family's gradual reintegration in the country of origin, while maintaining access to more established markets and educational opportunities in the host country and providing a source of income for the family.

Numerous studies have highlighted the importance of remittances, some suggesting that remittances may be twice as efficient as aid in reaching intended recipients in particular instances.[41] Remittances are less likely to be affected by the corruption or high overheads sometimes associated with aid programmes. While remittances can exacerbate income inequalities within communities, it is clear that migration, particularly in post-conflict environments, offers a means of spreading a family's risk as well as insulating it from future shocks. It may also be problematic for returnees to sever all socio-economic ties developed with their former host communities.

▲ **Congolese returnee women in the DRC** receive agricultural training on land donated by the surrounding communities.

A growth has been documented in 'dormitory' or 'commuter' displacement, where refugees and IDPs live outside their community of origin, but make regular return visits. Whether they 'commute' to secure income, check on property, tend crops or care for family members, such mobile coping strategies can help refugees to stay in contact with their home area and may eventually contribute to sustainable repatriation. In late 2011, when Bosnia and Herzegovina, Croatia, Serbia and Montenegro committed to resolving protracted displacement in their region, the governments took account of the mobility and cross-border ties of people displaced as a result of the break-up of Yugoslavia, recognizing in particular their need to travel to places of origin to obtain personal documentation.[42]

The global policy trend over the past decade has been towards an increasingly restrictive approach to migration, prompting refugees and returnees to resort often to irregular migration in search of solutions. Irregular migration may result in exploitation and abuse by human smugglers and traffickers and heightens the risk of *refoulement*. If efforts to resolve displacement are aimed at ensuring that refugees and IDPs have access to meaningful rights, irregular migration offers no such assurance.

The existing durable solutions framework does not account for refugee mobility and international actors have tended to approach solutions to refugee problems with a sedentary bias.[43] While the everyday experiences of refugees and IDPs suggest that migration is often an important livelihood strategy, its potential benefits are constrained by a restrictive migration system and a humanitarian framework slow to recognize the positive aspects of mobility.

UNHCR has pointed out that mobility can play an important role in achieving durable solutions for refugees. In 2007 and 2008, papers prepared for the High Commissioner's Protection Dialogues suggested that refugees might find an interim or durable solution by attaining a secure status as migrants in their country of first asylum or elsewhere.

Since 2009, UNHCR has further explored the potential for migration channels to enhance refugee protection and access to solutions.[44] Migration is also closely connected to broader development goals; the role that migration can play in alleviating poverty is well-recognized, but this discussion has rarely extended to refugee or IDP mobility.[45]

Mobility is particularly relevant in those contexts where traditional solutions have proved most difficult to secure for refugees. Post-conflict states often lack capacity to meet their citizens' socio-economic needs; ensuring that returning refugees can retain access to markets and services in their (former) country of asylum can make repatriation more sustainable. Evidence from South Sudan, for example, shows that many refugees valued their access to education and employment opportunities elsewhere in the East African region, and looked for ways to retain these while moving towards establishing permanent residence in South Sudan. Mobility can strengthen the sustainability of returns by allowing refugees to control the timing and manner of their return, and enabling them to decide when it is safe enough to return permanently.[46]

An ambitious effort to address issues related to asylum and migration in a durable solutions context has been the Afghan Comprehensive Solutions framework, first launched by UNHCR in 2003. The framework recognizes the importance of addressing issues related to registered refugees while encouraging states to develop systems to manage the irregular migration of undocumented Afghans. The 2007 registration exercise in Pakistan which recorded the number of 'Afghans living in Pakistan' (rather than Afghan refugees), and the offer of work permits in Iran for registered Afghan refugees (Amayesh card holders) have been significant developments.

However, insecurity in Afghanistan has complicated the picture, along with domestic political and economic tensions in Iran and Pakistan which have led to increased 'asylum fatigue'. The host states reiterate that voluntary repatriation is their preferred solution, but there is increased acknowledgement of the importance of regulating and managing the movement of undocumented Afghans.

New regional and supranational approaches to citizenship and residency can also open up possibilities for durable solutions. For instance, under protocols of the Economic

Afghans: still on the move

UNHCR's largest voluntary repatriation programme of the past decade supported the return of over five million Afghans. Despite the political and security changes that led to these massive returns, Afghanistan remains the source of one of the most protracted and complex displacement challenges confronting the international community.

The most complex displacement situation

More than three decades after the Soviet invasion, there were still over 2.6 million Afghans registered as refugees in Iran and Pakistan at end 2011. A similar number of Afghans are believed to migrate irregularly within the region and beyond, primarily in search of work and economic opportunities. Worldwide, Afghans are still one of the largest groups of asylum seekers, and include an alarming proportion of unaccompanied minors. The number of IDPs within Afghanistan was estimated at over 400,000 in 2011.

This situation reveals much about post-conflict state-building, the complexity of contemporary population movements, the evolving security situation, and wider trends shaping the environment in which UNHCR and other humanitarian actors will work in the coming years. It suggests that the traditional formulae for resolving protracted refugee situations merit re-appraisal, and new arrangements for managing complex displacement patterns may be required.

Underpinning Afghanistan's long search for peace and stability are five trends affecting human security in the twenty-first century—demographic growth, climate change, urbanization, migration, and new forms of conflict and violence. These trends represent a formidable challenge for weak states struggling to establish their legitimacy, in the face of adverse political and security conditions. They also threaten to render obsolete an aid model that has long been central to voluntary repatriation as UNHCR's primary durable solution.

For much of the last 20 years, the paradigm of relief, rehabilitation, and development has underpinned the international community's approach to post-conflict state-building. Recently, an even more ambitious policy favoured by donor states that integrates diplomacy, defence, and development interventions in support of peacebuilding has emerged.

But experience in Afghanistan suggests that both of these approaches run into difficulties when the local political economy, culture, and traditions are not conducive to modern development practice, with its emphasis on technical and financial support to public institutions. Moreover, military actions have not contributed to overcoming deep-rooted political problems, and a formal and inclusive peace agreement remains elusive.

Repatriation and its challenges

Until recently, voluntary repatriation to Afghanistan continued at a relatively high level. Many refugees brought back much needed capital, assets and know-how acquired in exile. But these returns increased the country's population by an estimated 20 per cent; and the availability of housing, land, and services has rapidly been outpaced by demand. Competition for scarce natural resources has intensified, with frequent disputes between sedentary and pastoral farmers. The predominantly informal economy has provided insufficient employment opportunities for a largely unskilled labour force. Refugees returning from exile, IDPs moving due to the insurgency, and migration from rural areas have increased the population of Afghanistan's cities well beyond the reach of weak municipal service delivery. By 2006, it had already become clear that the country's absorptive capacity and public management were under serious strain.

At the end of the decade, reconstruction and development faced an array of political, governance, and security problems. Voluntary repatriation was no longer the positive indicator of Afghanistan's recovery it had been just a few years earlier. For many former refugees, durable social and economic reintegration and even access to basic services and livelihoods are increasingly difficult to achieve. In parallel, a mix of security,

Community of West African States (ECOWAS), refugees and former refugees from member countries could be enabled to stay in the countries where they have established business, social, and family networks.[47]

The ECOWAS Treaty is of course not a refugee instrument. At the same time, it promotes goals beyond economic integration which are relevant to UNHCR's aims, including solidarity and collective self-reliance, maintenance of regional peace, stability and security, and protection of human rights. The Treaty establishes the right of community citizens to enter and establish themselves in all 15 member states, and urges member states to implement this right with all appropriate measures.

economic and social factors has propelled a rise in (mostly irregular) out-migration. The volume and complexity of these movements have posed very real challenges for governments in the region, as well as for UNHCR, accustomed to looking at population movements through the lens of a legal and operational framework designed for refugees.

Mobility as part of the solution

Mobility, including seasonal cross border movement, has always been a feature of Afghan economic life, even during more stable periods. Over the last 30 years, refugee displacement has generated transnational links in the region and beyond. These have facilitated growth in trade and commercial networks, both formal and informal. Mobility has provided a risk-spreading and coping strategy for Afghan families and individuals through seasonal migration, remittances, and solidarity networks. By their very nature, these approaches depend on frequent cross-border movement and exchange, belying the standard model of asylum and/or permanent settlement in villages of origin upon return. But only modest advances have been made toward putting in place an official policy and legal framework, along with practical measures, to regulate such complex mobility. There has been some progress towards more predictable arrangements to manage the stay of long-term registered refugees. However, finding alternative immigration statuses for them has stumbled over defining their legal rights and administrative procedures. Similar

obstacles have hampered bilateral discussions about the management of irregular movements, even though Iran and Pakistan now assert that irregular migrants on their territory outnumber those registered as refugees. At the same time, political instability and the rise of the insurgency in Afghanistan have raised concerns about new protection needs within the refugee population.

The need for a comprehensive approach

Reflections on improving border management, and measures to identify refugees and disentangle them from broader migratory flows, have slowed in this region. Humanitarian concerns over potential displacement within and from Afghanistan and the need to preserve asylum space have again assumed growing importance. The familiar dilemma of maintaining voluntary repatriation to preserve space for refugee protection has re-emerged. But it has acquired sharper ambiguity in the face of deepening instability in Afghanistan and the role of mobility as a response to the economic situation.

Twice in the last two decades Afghanistan has slipped back into conflict after agreements that failed to address underlying political and structural tensions, a pattern seen in many other post-conflict situations. Afghans remain among the largest groups of asylum applicants worldwide, including persons coming directly from Afghanistan as well as from among the Afghan populations in Pakistan and Iran.

As UNHCR enters its fourth decade of delivering protection and assistance to Afghanistan's refugees and displaced, the need for political action to secure peace and stability remains paramount. In its continuing absence, transition from humanitarian assistance to development and reconstruction will remain an unfulfilled promise, and workable solutions for refugees and displacement will be hard to find.

In a renewed attempt to address this protracted refugee situation, UNHCR and the governments of Afghanistan, Iran and Pakistan embarked in 2011 on a quadripartite consultative process to develop a multi-year, multi-sector strategy. The Solutions Strategy for Afghan Refugees, to Support Voluntary Repatriation, Sustainable Reintegration and Assistance to Host Countries aims to anchor returnees in Afghanistan with sustainable livelihoods and to preserve protection space in the neighbouring states. A regional multi-donor trust fund is being established to draw on diverse expertise and development resources to implement community-based projects.

A sustainable future for people displaced from Afghanistan remains essential to the overall stability of the country. In the meantime, humanitarian and development actors may need to devote more attention to measures which reduce the vulnerability and strengthen the resilience of Afghan refugees, IDPs and returnees, to help them to withstand new stresses and emergencies. ◆

At end of 2011, there were some 250,000 refugees in West Africa, mainly originating from Côte d'Ivoire (160,000) and Liberia (60,000). Under ECOWAS protocols, as citizens of ECOWAS countries these refugees have the right to work and reside in other ECOWAS states, provided they satisfy certain requirements. By allowing refugees to take up the protection of their country of origin once again while continuing to live and work in another country in the region, such arrangements facilitate mobility and reflect the reality of refugees' social networks after prolonged exile.

Proposed moves towards an arrangement for free movement of labour for citizens in the East African Community could have similar implications for refugees in that region who are citizens of member states—such as Rwandans and Burundians. How these two regimes—refugee protection and free movement—might intersect in this region has yet to be fully explored. In the countries of the Association of Southeast Asian Nations (ASEAN), proposals for freedom of movement and establishment are also under discussion and, depending on how they develop, could have a positive impact on refugees from within the ASEAN region.

In the European Union, UNHCR and partners successfully advocated for amendment of the Directive on the status of third-country nationals who are long-term residents, so as to include refugees and subsidiary protection beneficiaries within its scope. This allowed them the possibility—within the terms of the Directive—to seek employment throughout the Union.[48]

UNHCR and Sweden have encouraged consideration of ways of enabling refugees to have access to regular migration channels, as an additional pathway to solutions.[49] It is usually difficult for refugees to avail themselves of migration schemes, whether for employment or educational purposes, as this generally requires the assurance that they have a country to which they are able to return, if and when their migration permit expires.

The way forward

THE FORMER UN HIGH COMMISSIONER FOR REFUGEES SADAKO OGATA frequently pointed out that there are no humanitarian solutions to political problems. Political will is needed to remove obstacles to durable solutions.

Notwithstanding this underlying challenge, durable solutions could be found for more than three million refugees since the last edition of *The State of the World's Refugees* appeared in 2006. In South Sudan, refugees and displaced people have returned to help build a new state; in Tanzania, Burundian refugees began the process of naturalization; in Nepal, refugees from Bhutan found solutions through a large-scale resettlement programme and started new lives in Europe, Asia and North America. In the Western Balkans, countries made tangible progress toward bringing protracted displacement to an end. And there are many more examples.

Yet any measured account of solutions must also focus on what has not been achieved: the failure to resolve some protracted refugee situations, the consequences of premature and fragile returns to areas still affected by conflict, the risk of refugees being labelled as irregular migrants and deported to danger, and the continued failure actively to engage refugees in discussions about solutions. It is also important to recognize that host communities in countries of first asylum often face severe economic and political strains that increase hostility towards refugees, while resettlement countries hesitate to expand their commitments in part for similar reasons.

Over the past five years, UNHCR has made resolving protracted displacement an institutional priority. As a result of these efforts, connections between durable solutions and other political, humanitarian and development processes are better understood. Making the framework for durable solutions more effective, however, will depend on strengthening global commitments in a number of key areas, as suggested below.

First, states must respect the institution of asylum and refrain from premature and involuntary returns. Asylum must offer refugees not just protection from life-threatening harm, but the possibility to lead a dignified life. Impatience with asylum demands, and the desire to take shortcuts in meeting legal obligations by pressing for returns, can prove costly not only in human and financial terms, but also in terms of regional peace and stability.

Second, in some long-term displacement situations, large numbers of refugees have 'inherited' their refugee status and have few—if any—personal connections to their 'country of origin'. In such contexts, recognizing the reality of local integration and helping refugees to regularize their status in the country where they have always lived would be a major contribution to durable solutions.

Third, despite many debates during the past three decades about bridging the 'relief-to-development gap' and embedding displacement in broader development and peacebuilding frameworks, progress has remained limited. It remains essential to place refugee solutions—local integration and voluntary repatriation—squarely on the development agenda.

Fourth, there is potential for resettlement to play a much bigger role in solutions. The number of countries participating in refugee resettlement could be significantly increased, as well as the number of places offered. The willingness and ability of civil society groups in many countries to support resettlement and, in particular, to help in the reception and integration of resettled refugees, should be widely embraced.

Fifth, refugee mobility should be incorporated into the solutions framework. While it is already recognized that migration plays an important role in development, it is important to recognize that flexibility and mobility can enable refugee families to tailor their own solutions—for instance facilitating voluntary repatriation for some family members while others continue to work or study elsewhere. Moreover, the involvement of expatriate communities can provide financial capital for reconstruction and actively contribute to peacebuilding. Regular migration channels may also offer refugees an alternative pathway to permanent residence and citizenship in a third country.

Finally, there is still a considerable gap between refugee understandings of solutions and institutional policies and programmes. Refugees need to be much more actively engaged in the search for solutions. It is important to take age and gender dimensions of refugee populations into account and to involve refugee women and older people in discussions.

In 1955, the first United Nations High Commissioner for Refugees, Gerrit Jan van Heuven Goedhart, identified many of the same challenges that impede solutions today. At the time, his response was to issue both a moral condemnation and a call to action. Refugee camps, he said, 'should burn holes in the consciences of those who are privileged to live in better conditions'.[50] His words remind us that solutions to refugee problems cannot be found without political will and an active commitment to international solidarity, cooperation, and responsibility-sharing. ■

▲ **This baby and her parents were among the many Biharis** in Bangladesh whose citizenship was confirmed by a 2008 decision of the High Court.

Resolving Statelessness

STATELESSNESS IS AN ANOMALY. Article 15 of the Universal
Declaration of Human Rights (UDHR) affirms that everyone has
the right to a nationality, and that no one should be arbitrarily deprived of nationality. Like the Declaration itself, the inclusion of the right
to a nationality in the UDHR was motivated by the impulse to respond to
the atrocities committed during the Second World War, among them
mass denationalizations and forced population movements.

Possession of nationality often serves as a key to enjoying many other
rights, such as education, health care, employment, and equality before the
law. As a result, people who are not considered to be nationals by any state—
stateless persons—are some of the most vulnerable in the world.

Stateless persons can be found on every continent and in virtually
every country. Whereas most people do not think about their citizenship
on a daily basis, for stateless persons, the lack of citizenship is an ever-
present concern.

Since its creation, UNHCR has worked to provide international protection and find durable solutions for stateless refugees who are covered by
its Statute and by the 1951 Refugee Convention. Soon after its establishment, UNHCR participated in the drafting of the two global instruments
on statelessness: the 1954 Convention relating to the Status of Stateless
Persons (1954 Convention) and the 1961 Convention on the Reduction of
Statelessness (1961 Convention)—which provide guidance on the rights of
stateless people and on how statelessness can be avoided.[1] In 1974, the UN
General Assembly designated UNHCR as the body to which stateless persons may turn under the terms of the 1961 Convention for assistance in
presenting their claims to state authorities.[2]

In the early 1990s, the break-up of the Soviet Union, the Socialist
Federal Republic of Yugoslavia, and Czechoslovakia, and the emergence
of new independent states, led to a dramatic increase in statelessness and
underscored the need for a more effective international response. As a result, in 1995, UNHCR's Executive Committee adopted a comprehensive Conclusion on the
Prevention and Reduction of Statelessness and the Protection of Stateless Persons.[3] That
Conclusion recognized explicitly that UNHCR's activities on behalf of stateless persons are

part of its statutory function of providing international protection. It requested UNHCR, *inter alia*, to promote accession to the 1954 and 1961 Conventions on statelessness, and to provide technical and advisory services to interested states on the preparation and implementation of nationality legislation.[4] The General Assembly endorsed this request.[5] Subsequent Executive Committee conclusions and General Assembly resolutions have further developed and refined UNHCR's mandate with respect to statelessness, and have identified four distinct areas in which the Office is authorized to act: the identification, prevention and reduction of statelessness and the protection of stateless persons.

The year 2011 marked the 50th anniversary of the 1961 Convention, and UNHCR took that opportunity to reinvigorate efforts to resolve situations of statelessness. The agency devoted particular attention to promoting accession to the statelessness conventions. As a result, the number of states parties to the 1954 and 1961 Conventions rose from 65 and 37 respectively at the end of 2010 to 71 and 42 at the end of 2011; a further 24 states pledged to accede to the 1954 Convention (or to work towards accession) and 33 did so with regard to the 1961 Convention.

The increase in accessions during recent years reflects growing awareness among states of the hardships faced by stateless people, and of the need to resolve their plight. Increasingly, governments recognize that their own interests are not served by having large numbers of stateless persons on their territories.

The international legal framework

THE STATELESSNESS CONVENTIONS

International law has traditionally recognized that states have broad discretion to define eligibility for nationality. However, laws and practices on citizenship must be consistent with the principles of international law. Although Article 15 of the UDHR guarantees that every individual has a right to a nationality, it does not prescribe how the responsibility for granting citizenship should fall upon any particular state.

Originally, norms to protect stateless persons were to be included in a protocol to the 1951 Convention. However, due to the complexities of statelessness and the urgency of refugee matters at the time, the 1951 Convention was adopted without inclusion of the planned protocol. Action on statelessness was delayed until 1954, when a Conference of Plenipotentiaries decided that it would be preferable to adopt a separate instrument to protect the rights of stateless persons—this became the 1954 Convention. A second separate treaty on avoidance of statelessness was adopted soon thereafter: the 1961 Convention.

The 1954 and 1961 Conventions together constitute the core of the international legal framework relating to statelessness. The 1954 Convention elaborates the protection regime for stateless persons, and its provisions are identical in many respects to those in the 1951 Refugee Convention. The 1954 Convention establishes an internationally recognized status for stateless persons, according them specific rights, such as access to courts, identity and travel documents, the right to employment, education, and freedom of movement.

Crucially, the 1954 Convention is the only international instrument which sets out the definition of a stateless person, as someone 'who is not considered as a national by any State under the operation of its law'.[6] Although the 1954 Convention has not been universally ratified, the International Law Commission has observed that its definition of a stateless person is now part of customary international law, meaning that it applies to all states, even those not party to the 1954 Convention.

The Article 1(1) definition set out above has sometimes been described as referring only to people who are stateless *de jure* (in a legal sense). An expert roundtable organized by UNHCR in May 2010 to provide further guidance on the concept and definition of a stateless person helped to clarify various aspects of the definition and its application.[7] Notably, the roundtable concluded that when determining whether someone falls under the definition, it is not only the letter of the law that must be examined but also state practice and more specifically, how an individual is viewed by state authorities. With this clarification, numerous ethnic minority groups and individuals, whose citizenship status was previously regarded as unclear, should be able to avail themselves of protection provided by the statelessness conventions.

The 1961 Convention creates a framework for avoiding future statelessness and places an obligation on states to prevent statelessness from arising as a result of their nationality laws and practices. Specifically, it obliges states parties to prevent children from becoming stateless at birth and to avoid statelessness as a result of loss or deprivation of citizenship later in life. Because statelessness often results from differing approaches to granting nationality, a common set of rules is essential. Despite low numbers of accessions to this treaty, its tenets have had a significant impact even in non-signatory states, many of which incorporate some of its bedrock safeguards—such as granting nationality to foundlings or avoiding statelessness when people change their nationality—in their domestic legislation.

UNHCR has worked to help states to implement and meet their obligations under these conventions. In December 2010, following the expert roundtable on the definition and concept of a stateless person, UNHCR organized a further meeting with experts to develop guidance on statelessness determination procedures.[8] A third meeting was held in May 2011 to examine safeguards under the 1961 Convention for preventing statelessness among children.[9] UNHCR will issue guidelines that take into account the conclusions of each of these meetings.

INTERNATIONAL HUMAN RIGHTS LAW AND REGIONAL INSTRUMENTS

In addition to the two conventions on statelessness, many international human rights instruments contain principles that limit states' discretion over nationality matters. Beyond the UDHR, there is the International Covenant on Civil and Political Rights, the International Convention on the Elimination of All Forms of Racial Discrimination, the Convention on the Elimination of All Forms of Discrimination Against Women, the

MAP **4•1**   **Parties to the 1954 and 1961 Statelessness Conventions** | 31.12.2011

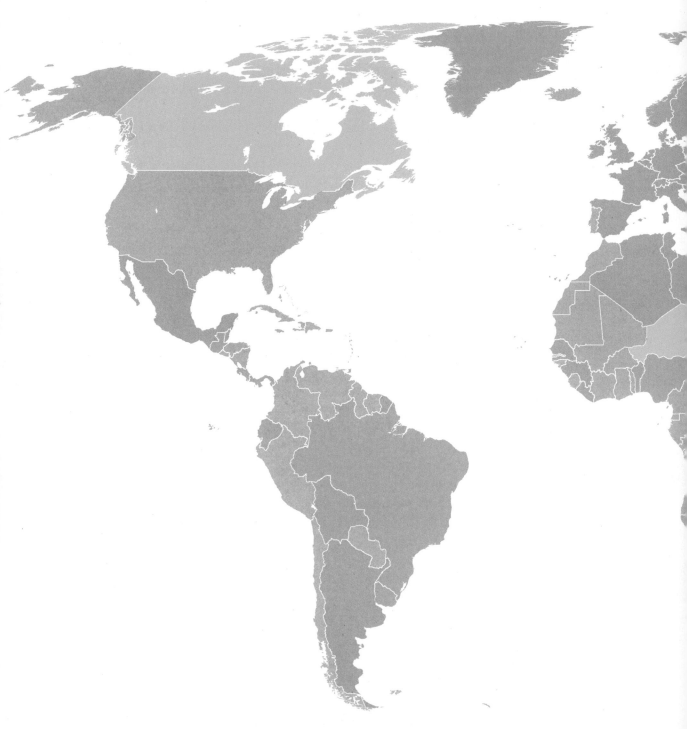

This map does not imply the expression of any opinion on the part of UNHCR or the United Nations concerning the legal status of any country or territory, or the delimitation of frontiers or boundaries, nor is it warranted to be error-free.

Parties to the **1954** and the **1961** Conventions (39 countries)

Parties to the **1954** Convention only (71 countries)

Parties to the **1961** Convention only (42 countries)

Not Parties to either the **1954** or the **1961** Conventions

Convention on the Rights of the Child, the International Convention on the Protection of the Rights of All Migrant Workers and Members of Their Families, and the Convention on the Rights of Persons with Disabilities. These treaties have progressively given content to the right to nationality, and in particular, to the right to be free from arbitrary deprivation of nationality.

The 1954 and 1961 Conventions are also complemented by standards contained in regional instruments. Numerous regional treaties recognize the right to nationality and establish additional obligations for states parties relating to the prevention of statelessness. In Africa, there is the African Charter on the Rights and Welfare of the Child; in the Americas, the American Declaration on the Rights and Duties of Man and the American Convention on Human Rights; in Europe, the European Convention on Nationality; in the Middle East and North Africa, the Arab Charter on Human Rights; and in the countries of the Organization of Islamic Cooperation, there is the Covenant on the Rights of the Child in Islam.

The most detailed standards relating to nationality have been adopted in Europe. The 1997 European Convention on Nationality regulates the acquisition and loss of nationality, and includes, amongst other provisions, a range of safeguards against statelessness, most of which mirror those contained in the 1961 Convention. Subsequently, the Council of Europe adopted the 2006 Convention on the Avoidance of Statelessness in Relation to State Succession, which contains the most detailed provisions of any international treaty on the prevention of statelessness in the context of state succession.

Despite what would appear to be a robust legal framework to guarantee the right to a nationality, statelessness persists almost everywhere. To address potential breaches of nationality-related rights, regional human rights bodies have recently become more active in highlighting and resolving the plight of those in protracted situations of statelessness. They have also addressed questions of enjoyment of human rights by people who are stateless. Human rights are guaranteed by international law to all individuals, but in practice they are often denied to stateless persons.

The first landmark nationality decision of the Inter-American Court of Human Rights was issued in September 2005 in the *Case of the Girls Yean and Bosico* v. *Dominican Republic*, which found that the Dominican Republic had applied nationality and birth registration laws in a discriminatory manner, leaving children of Haitian descent stateless, and violating a number of fundamental rights.[10]

The European Court of Human Rights (ECtHR) has also addressed nationality-related cases. In 2009, for example, it issued a judgment in *Andrejeva* v. *Latvia*, involving a stateless person (a 'permanently resident non-citizen' under Latvian law) who was denied pension entitlements equal to those of citizens. The court found that this amounted to discriminatory treatment in violation of the applicant's property rights in breach of the European Convention on Human Rights.[11]

In 2010, the ECtHR issued a judgment concerning a group of 'erased persons' in Slovenia—individuals residing in the country who did not acquire Slovenian citizenship immediately after independence in 1991, and were taken off the register of permanent residents. In *Kuric* v. *Slovenia* the Court concluded that the government's failure to regulate the legal status of these persons violated their right to private and family life, in light of the extensive network of relationships they had developed in Slovenia.[12] Upon request by the Slovenian government, this case was referred to the Grand Chamber of the ECtHR in 2011.

In *Nubian Minors* v. *Kenya* in 2011, the African Committee of Experts on the Rights and Welfare of the Child examined the situation of Kenyan Nubians who, despite having been brought to Kenya more than a hundred years ago to serve in the British colonial army, still had a tenuous citizenship status in the country, which prevented them from enjoying many of their rights.[13] This particularly affected Nubian children, who were not registered as Kenyans at birth and many of whom live in poverty with little access to education, health care, and public services. The Committee found that Kenya's failure to recognize these children as Kenyan citizens violated key provisions of the African Charter on the Rights and Welfare of the Child, and observed that statelessness is antithetical to the best interests of the child.

Causes of statelessness

STATELESSNESS HAS NUMEROUS CAUSES. States may simply cease to exist while individuals fail to secure citizenship in the successor states; political considerations may dictate changes in the way that citizenship laws are applied; an ethnic minority may be discriminated against and denied citizenship; or groups may live in frontier areas, with states on both sides of the border denying them citizenship. Statelessness can arise from differences in how laws regulate citizenship, for instance in cases where people live abroad but fail to register in a consulate, or where they renounce one nationality without having acquired another. In other cases, individuals may simply not be able to complete costly or complex administrative requirements for the acquisition or confirmation of nationality. Although the apparent causes of statelessness are often legal and technical, discrimination on the basis of gender or racial, ethnic, religious, linguistic, disability, and other grounds is frequently a key factor.

TRANSFER OF SOVEREIGNTY

The 1990s saw the turbulent break-up of the Soviet Union, Yugoslavia, and Czechoslovakia. These events, coupled with internal and external migration and other factors, produced millions of stateless persons. Although most individuals automatically became citizens of a newly independent state when its nationality legislation was adopted, large numbers of people throughout Central and Eastern Europe and Central Asia became stateless, with migrants and marginalized ethnic and social groups particularly affected.

The situation described above led to the adoption of two regional treaties to resolve statelessness issues in the 47 countries of the Council of Europe: the 1997 European

BOX 4•1

Citizenship and the creation of South Sudan

In January 2011, after decades of civil war, the people of South Sudan voted overwhelmingly for independence from the Republic of Sudan in the north. Six months later, on 9 July 2011, Africa's newest country was born: the Republic of South Sudan. The path to independence was not an easy one, and throughout the first year of independence, the possibility of renewed armed conflict between north and south was ever-present.

A related concern was that of statelessness. It was feared that, upon independence, tens of thousands or even hundreds of thousands of people living in both countries might suddenly find themselves without a nationality. There were concerns about gaps in the nationality laws of the two Republics, the availability of documentation to prove ancestry and place of birth, and the lack of awareness of the population about nationality issues. Unprecedented efforts were made at the local, national and international levels to prevent a nationality crisis from coinciding with the independence of South Sudan. While the worst-case scenario was effectively avoided, there is a need for continued advocacy and vigilance, as risks remain.

In identifying and addressing potential problems of statelessness, particular attention has focused on the large number of people of South Sudanese origin living in the north. The exact number is not known, but was estimated by the UN in 2011 to be around 700,000. Many had fled the conflict in South Sudan during the long civil war, and had lived for years as displaced persons in the north, especially in the capital Khartoum. Others had migrated to the north for economic reasons, in some cases as long as a century ago.

The risk of statelessness also extended to people from the north living in the south, as well as to those in trans-boundary communities. Regardless of where they were living, many people had effective links to both countries, for instance with one parent originating from the Republic of Sudan and the other from South Sudan. As independence approached, questions loomed large: would either of the two countries claim such individuals as their own? Would the affected population be able to acquire the necessary documents and exercise their nationality in practice?

With these challenges in mind, UNHCR has worked in concert with both governments to avoid widespread statelessness. It provided the nascent Government of South Sudan with technical advice on nationality legislation and cooperated with the former UN Mission in Sudan as well as with the new UN Mission established in South Sudan upon independence. It worked with UNICEF, UN Women, and embassies of interested countries, among other partners, to make sure that the provisions on nationality in the new country's Constitution and statutory law would comply with international standards. In doing so, it actively promoted the standards contained in the International Law Commission's Articles on the Nationality of Natural Persons in relation to the Succession of States.[i]

In June 2011, the Legislative Assembly of South Sudan adopted the country's first Nationality Act, providing a legal framework for the acquisition and loss of nationality in the newly independent country. In many respects, the Act demonstrated South Sudan's commitment to a human rights-focused approach to nationality. The new law allows for dual nationality and is gender-neutral, providing *inter alia* for the equal right of women and men to pass their nationality on to their children. Under the new law, persons of South Sudanese origin living in the Republic of Sudan automatically acquired South Sudanese nationality.

While the nationality law of South Sudan

Convention on Nationality and the 2006 Convention on the Avoidance of Statelessness in Relation to State Succession. While most cases of statelessness in the countries which emerged from the former Soviet Union, Yugoslavia, and Czechoslovakia have been resolved, more than 600,000 people remain stateless throughout the region.

Statelessness arising from state succession has also existed in Asia, the Middle East, and Africa.[14] For example, the 1971 conflict that led to the independence of Bangladesh from Pakistan left hundreds of thousands of Urdu-speaking Biharis in Bangladesh. Perceived as pro-Pakistan during the war, this group remained in Bangladesh for decades without nationality. Over the years, nearly 180,000 Biharis were repatriated to Pakistan, but that arrangement ended in 1993, leaving 250,000 to 300,000 in Bangladesh. A landmark High Court decision in 2008 confirmed that these Biharis were Bangladeshi citizens, and paved the way for their participation as voters in elections that year.

greatly reduced the risk of widespread state-lessness, it by no means eliminated it. In August 2011, soon after the independence of South Sudan, the Republic of Sudan amended its own law to provide that people recognized as citizens under the new nationality law of South Sudan would automatically lose their Sudanese nationality.

This change to the nationality law of the Republic of Sudan brought both practical and legal consequences. With the loss of Sudanese nationality, southern Sudanese who had been living in the north, often for decades, lost related rights and entitlements, including the right to own property and to public sector employment, as well as the ability to conduct basic official transactions. If they are not able to acquire documents demonstrating that they have South Sudanese nationality, they will be unable to legalize their status as residents in the Republic of Sudan.

In other words, with the loss of Sudanese nationality, risks of statelessness emerge. What will happen if the Republic of Sudan considers a person to be a citizen of South Sudan, but he or she is unable to show the necessary link under the nationality law of that country? Lack of civil documentation, such as birth certificates or identity papers, is commonplace in both Sudan and South Sudan, making it extremely difficult, if not impossible, to demonstrate that one's parents,

grandparents or great-grandparents were born in the south, a key criterion for acquisition of the nationality of the new state. If individuals lose Sudanese nationality and are unable to prove an entitlement to South Sudanese nationality, they will be stateless.

The international community has therefore recommended that care be taken to make sure that no one loses Sudanese nationality before it is clearly established that he or she has acquired the nationality of South Sudan. UNHCR continues to advocate with both governments to facilitate access to South Sudanese nationality documents for South Sudanese living in Sudan, among other issues. UNHCR is also working with Plan International to improve access to birth registration documents for South Sudanese communities in Sudan. Birth certificates can provide a vital proof of identity and can be used as evidence of entitlement to South Sudanese nationality.

In Khartoum, working with UNICEF, UNHCR has offered advice and support to the civil registration authorities to encourage fair and transparent procedures for the registration of births, confirming Sudanese nationality and issuing nationality documentation. UNHCR is also conducting awareness-raising sessions for community groups, legal aid organizations, and paralegals in areas where large numbers of South Sudanese reside. UNHCR is collaborating with UNDP to ensure that legal aid providers

advise South Sudanese populations in Sudan about their nationality status and related rights.

In Juba, the capital of the newly independent South Sudan, UNHCR is providing technical support to the Ministry of Justice, and has assisted the Ministry of Interior to elaborate implementing regulations for the new Nationality Act. Since independence, building the capacity of staff at the recently established South Sudanese General Directorate for Nationality, Passports and Immigration has assumed a particular urgency. UNHCR is also providing technical and financial support to enable the Directorate to organize field missions to areas where large numbers of returnees from the Republic of Sudan are living, in order to provide them with documentation. It is also important to make sure that civil society groups in South Sudan are well informed about the Nationality Act and related legislation.

UNHCR will remain engaged in supporting and monitoring the effective implementation of nationality laws in the Republics of Sudan and South Sudan, and will continue its efforts to reduce the risk of statelessness in both countries. ◆

i   International Law Commission, Articles on Nationality: Nationality of Natural Persons in relation to the Succession of States (1999), as annexed to UN General Assembly Resolution A/RES/55/153 of 30 January 2001.

The recent creation of South Sudan provides a contemporary illustration of the risk of statelessness in the context of state succession, and of the complexity of such situations.

CONFLICT OF LAWS

While state succession is a major event that can lead to the loss of citizenship, statelessness can also be caused by more mundane conflicts between the nationality laws of different countries. For example, states commonly apply one of two principles for granting citizenship at the time of birth: in legal terminology *jus soli* and *jus sanguinis*, the 'law of the soil' and the 'law of blood' respectively. Some states apply a hybrid of these two approaches. *Jus soli* provides that those born in the territory of a country have the right to citizenship of that country, generally with a few exceptions, such as the children of foreign diplomats.

Jus sanguinis confers citizenship based on the nationality of the parents. Certain restrictions are sometimes attached to the *jus sanguinis* transmission of nationality, such as limiting this to the nationality of the father or excluding children born out of wedlock.

Many children become stateless when they are born in a country which applies only the *jus sanguinis* principle, to parents who come from a country which places limitations on the *jus sanguinis* transmission of nationality in the case of children born abroad. The likelihood of children becoming stateless also increases when one parent is stateless. In such cases, safeguards in the 1961 Convention apply, to ensure that children acquire the citizenship of the state where they are born if they would otherwise be stateless.

ADMINISTRATIVE OBSTACLES

Statelessness arises because of conflicting citizenship laws, but it can also result from administrative and practical problems. In many contexts, individuals might be entitled to citizenship, but unable to undertake the necessary procedural steps. For example, states might require excessive fees to issue civil documentation or set unrealistic deadlines to complete procedures such as registration. In conflict or post-conflict situations, simple administrative procedures may be difficult to carry out. Failure to register children at birth is a pervasive problem in many developing countries where people live in remote areas with little access to civil registries or where illiteracy rates are high; this leaves many children without proof of where they were born and who their parents were. In many instances, individuals who cannot access state institutions and do not have identity documents are still considered to be nationals. But in circumstances where particular groups are acutely affected by discrimination or onerous bureaucratic procedures, statelessness can arise.

RACIAL AND ETHNIC DISCRIMINATION

Discrimination on racial or ethnic grounds is another cause of statelessness. Ethnic minorities may be arbitrarily excluded from citizenship; sometimes this discrimination is enshrined in law.

Stateless populations who have been excluded from citizenship since states were formed include minorities brought to the country during the colonial period to perform specific types of work, such as the formerly stateless Hill Tamils in Sri Lanka, whose situation was resolved through an innovative law reform and citizenship campaign in 2003. Similarly, Nubians in Kenya have faced many obstacles to confirming their citizenship, a situation that should change as a result of adoption of the new Constitution in August 2010 and of the new Citizenship and Immigration Act. In Côte d'Ivoire, the first post-independence nationality law in 1961 defined citizens of the new state by excluding persons who were born to foreigners. Hundreds of thousands of agricultural workers who had been brought to Côte d'Ivoire from neighbouring countries in colonial times were thereby denied Ivorian citizenship, a situation which contributed to a decade of armed violence in the country.

The importance of birth registration

A young Zimbabwean reads with delight the birth certificate she has finally obtained.

Birth registration is fundamental to the protection of children and to the prevention of statelessness. Every child has the right to be registered at birth and to acquire a nationality, as set out in the Convention on the Rights of the Child, the International Covenant on Civil and Political Rights, and in several regional human rights instruments. These rights apply to all children without discrimination.

Birth registration is generally distinct from the process by which a child acquires a nationality. Birth registration establishes legal proof of the place of birth and of the child's parents. It serves as documentary evidence underpinning the child's acquisition of the nationality of one or both parents (*jus sanguinis*), or of the state where the child was born (*jus soli*). In other words, birth registration in and of itself does not generally confer nationality on a child, but it is a key proof of the link between an individual and a state, and thereby serves to prevent statelessness. In some countries, a child is not considered to have acquired the nationality until the birth is registered.

Lack of birth registration puts children at risk of statelessness. This risk is particularly high among certain groups, including persons living in border areas, minorities, or nomadic and migrant populations, in particular when the populations concerned have actual or imputed ties to other states. In such contexts, establishing the origins of a child's parents and the place of a child's birth are essential elements in establishing nationality.

Failure to document a child's birth creates significant additional risks. Unregistered children often face difficulties in enrolling in school or obtaining healthcare. Without proof of legal identity, they are at heightened risk of child labour, early marriage, sexual exploitation, trafficking, recruitment into armed groups, and of being treated as adults when in conflict with the law.

The situation in Lebanon illustrates how a broad range of factors can hinder birth registration in practice. Many people are unaware of the importance of birth registration and the grave consequences of not registering their children's birth. They may be unable to afford the fees,

in particular those associated with late registration. But there are other factors as well. Births are registered by local authorities upon presentation of an attestation of birth. Some doctors refuse to issue attestations if the birth took place at home. Local authorities may decline to register children born out of wedlock, or to stateless parents, or children who are orphaned and abandoned. Recent efforts by the government of Lebanon and non-governmental partners to identify the reasons why births are not always systematically registered have led to the identification of ways to improve the situation.

Global data collected by UNHCR from 2008 and 2009 revealed low rates of birth registration among persons of concern to the organization, prompting UNHCR to commit to improving birth registration for those within its mandate. To that end, UNHCR has supported states to increase their capacity to register births. Refugees, returnees, stateless, and internally displaced persons have benefited from this assistance, often undertaken in cooperation with other agencies in the framework of nationwide registration campaigns. Support has taken a variety of forms, including technical advice, training for national authorities, logistical support and financial assistance.

In Georgia, for instance, UNHCR and its national implementing partner have worked to improve provision of birth registration, including in conflict-affected areas from which many people have been displaced. Working with the Civil Registry Agency under the Georgian Ministry of Justice, the project identified undocumented persons through outreach activities, provided legal advice, and registered births. In 2009, the government convened a workshop on registration, documentation, and citizenship, to remedy the obstacles encountered in registering births. Since then, the government agreed to waive the requirement of a child's health certificate as a precondition for late birth registration, expressed readiness to register birth data collected by doctors in villages, and improved cooperation among the agencies and actors involved in birth registration.

UNHCR has also carried out projects to support access to birth registration and other forms of civil documentation to prevent statelessness. In the Western Balkans, for example, with support from the European Union, UNHCR undertook a regional project to facilitate civil registration and improve the social inclusion of targeted minorities, particularly the Roma. The project sought to reduce the number of persons at risk of statelessness due to the absence of civil documentation. During the period 2008–2011, legal advice was provided to over 28,000 persons, of whom more than 13,500 received help to obtain civil registration papers, including birth registration.

Ensuring birth registration requires concerted action, with states playing a key role. UNHCR will continue working with partners to develop legal standards and good practices in order to improve birth registration and contribute to the prevention of statelessness. ◆

Indigenous groups have also, in some situations, been left stateless—such as in the case of some Hill Tribes in Thailand. Nomads whose way of life leads them to move across borders may be labelled 'foreigners' and not recognized as citizens in any of the countries to which they have links. In the Gulf States, for example, many of today's *bidoon* (stateless persons) are descended from nomadic tribes and lack legal status in the countries in which they live. This affects all areas of their lives: identity, family life, residence, education, livelihood opportunities, political participation, and freedom of movement.

Ethnic, racial, religious or linguistic minorities, in other cases, have been rendered stateless as a result of an arbitrary decision that deprives them of their nationality. In many of these situations, the loss of nationality has been ac-

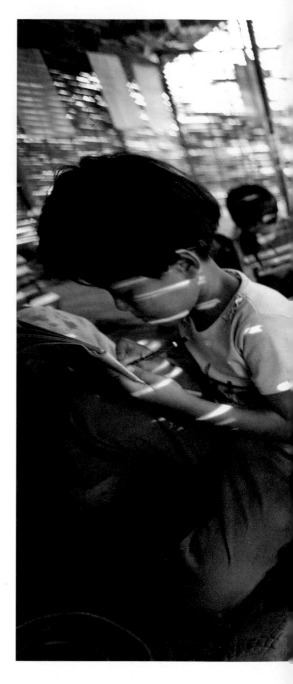

▶ **Stateless refugees from Bhutan** attend class in a refugee camp in Nepal.

companied by expulsion. Ethnic Nepalis living in Bhutan, for instance, were stripped of Bhutanese citizenship and expelled in the late 1980s and early 1990s. Most ended up as refugees in Nepal. In 1989, black Mauritanians were deprived of nationality and forced to leave the country for Senegal and Mali. Recently, many of the Mauritanian refugees have been able to return and reinstate their Mauritanian nationality, while by the end of 2011 more than 58,000 of the refugees from Bhutan had been resettled to countries in which they will over time be able to acquire citizenship (*see box 3.3*).

In Europe, after the Second World War, members of ethnic minorities were in some cases deprived of their nationality in a discriminatory—and thus arbitrary—fashion. From 1955, under Article 19 of the Greek Citizenship Law, persons of non-Greek origin were denationalized if they left Greece 'with no intent to return'. This had a particular impact on the Muslim minority. In 1998, when Article 19 was repealed, the citizenship of those denationalized was not automatically reinstated, and some remain stateless.

Minorities may face considerable obstacles in obtaining birth certificates or other documents necessary to acquire or confirm citizenship. Following the break-up of Czechoslovakia, the Soviet Union, and Yugoslavia, many Roma had difficulties in confirming that

UNHCR/J. RAE

they were citizens of one of the successor states. Although today most have citizenship in the countries in which they live, the risk of statelessness persists for some. A survey conducted by UNHCR in Serbia in 2010, for example, confirmed the problems faced by the Roma, Ashkali and Egyptian population and found that nearly 7 per cent were at risk of being stateless (*see box 4.4*).[15] This precarious situation can lead to a range of other violations of their human rights.

In the Caribbean, statelessness mostly affects children of Haitian migrants born outside of Haiti, who may face legal and practical obstacles to obtain birth registration or to be recognized as a national, either in the country where they were born or in Haiti. This predicament arises, for example, with respect to descendants of Haitian migrants in the Dominican Republic (*see box 4.3*).

GENDER DISCRIMINATION

Statelessness can also arise when citizenship laws do not treat women and men equally. Prior to the adoption of modern human rights instruments, many nationality laws dis-

---

BOX **4.3**

Persons of Haitian origin in the Dominican Republic

The long history of migration from Haiti to the Dominican Republic has resulted in a substantial population of persons of Haitian descent living in the country. Haiti and the Dominican Republic share the Caribbean island of Hispaniola, where Christopher Columbus landed in 1492. Haiti, which in 1804 became the first independent state in Latin America, occupies the western third of the island. The Dominican Republic, whose independence dates from 1821, occupies the eastern part.

Labour migration from Haiti to the Dominican Republic started in earnest early in the twentieth century, mainly in relation to the development of the sugar industry after the First World War. Although the sugar industry declined in the late 1980s, the Dominican Republic remained a consistent draw for people from Haiti, a country which has suffered waves of political unrest, virtually no economic growth, and more recently, a devastating earthquake.

Several generations of children with at least one parent of Haitian descent have been born on Dominican soil. Until August 2004, Dominican law provided that anyone born in the Dominican Republic, except for the children of diplomats and parents who were 'in transit', acquired Dominican citizenship through the *jus soli* principle. The 'in

transit' exception applied to children of parents who remained in the country for a period of 10 days or less.

This citizenship rule changed in August 2004 when the new General Law on Migration extended the 'in transit' exclusion to children born to parents classified as 'non-residents'. Since that time, children born in the Dominican Republic to 'non-resident' parents, defined to include temporary foreign workers, migrants with expired residency visas, undocumented migrant workers, and people who cannot prove their lawful residence, no longer acquire Dominican citizenship by virtue of birth in Dominican territory. A 2010 amendment enshrined this exclusion of children of 'non-resident' parents from Dominican citizenship in the Dominican Constitution.

People of Haitian descent in the Dominican Republic are not a uniform group. An individual's status before the law in the Dominican Republic can vary widely, depending on his or her parents' migratory status and civil documentation at the time of the child's birth. While there are different opinions about the degree of integration of these persons and their ties to the Dominican Republic, it cannot be disputed that many face considerable hardship on account of their inability to document their

citizenship. The fact that members of the same family frequently find themselves in different legal situations adds to the complexity.

As a result of the changes to the Dominican citizenship rules and systemic problems with civil registration, the exact number of persons of undetermined citizenship in the Dominican Republic is not known, and estimates vary widely. What is important is to ensure that none of these persons is made stateless through an act of deprivation of citizenship; that all, including children, have a nationality; and that all are able to receive documentation regarding their birth, without facing bureaucratic obstacles.

The situation of persons of Haitian descent is not unique to the Dominican Republic. While each country in the Caribbean region has its own laws and regulations regarding nationality, a similar situation exists in both the Bahamas and the UK Overseas Territory of the Turks and Caicos Islands, as well as in other countries in Latin America.

The roots of the problem of Haitian citizenship are complex. Haiti's Constitution establishes a *jus sanguinis* nationality framework. According to Article 11 of the Constitution, individuals possess Haitian

criminated on the basis of gender. This discrimination stemmed from the 'principle of unity of nationality of the family' according to which every member of the family should have the same nationality—that of the husband or father. Historically, it was believed that a family's allegiance should be to only one state because of the demands made on citizens in terms of military service. As a result, women often automatically lost their nationality upon marriage to a foreigner, and they automatically acquired, or enjoyed facilitated procedures to acquire, the nationality of their husbands. Further, nationality could only be conferred on children by the father, not by the mother.

Most progress in the elimination of gender discrimination in nationality laws has come from developments in international human rights law, often helped by vigorous advocacy

nationality at birth if they are born to a Haitian father or a Haitian mother who were themselves born Haitian and have not renounced their nationality. However, concluding that every child born of Haitian parents can acquire Haitian citizenship is an over-simplification that fails to take into account the legislative and administrative gaps in Haiti in relation to birth and civil registration. These have persisted ever since the country introduced its first civil registration legislation in 1805.

In practice, the issuance of appropriate civil documentation, including birth registration, and recognition of Haitian nationality are highly problematic. Due to shortages of human and financial resources, weak institutions, absence of clear regulatory frameworks, and socio-economic factors, the lack of civil documentation is very common among persons born in Haiti—whether living in the country or outside it. This affects Haitians' ability to exercise their human rights and presents a risk of statelessness. Weak and under-resourced consular services at Haitian Embassies and Consulates abroad can increase this risk for persons of Haitian descent born outside the country.

The problem of Haitian citizenship also has its roots in migration policies in the Caribbean region. Migration has alternately been regulated, de-regulated and instrumentalized by local authorities and powerful landowners or employers, frequently without consideration for the rights of the migrants and their family members.

UNHCR has argued that the determination of who is a Haitian citizen cannot be made only on the basis of race, surname, and language ability. It has to be made on the basis of applicable laws and regulations and fair evidentiary requirements, taking account of what is available in Haiti's civil registration records and what can be effectively sought from the authorities there. Assessing whether a person is a Haitian citizen requires establishing how he or she is viewed by the authorities of Haiti. UNHCR has advised governments to refrain from making this determination retroactively when the individual has already acquired another citizenship.

UNHCR is working to reduce the risk of statelessness among persons of Haitian descent by helping governments in the region to review relevant laws, administrative regulations and procedures. It also implements projects in the Dominican Republic, the Bahamas and in Haiti itself to assist undocumented individuals of Haitian descent to access their birth registration records or other civil documentation, to obtain recognition of their Haitian citizenship, and provides advice on options relating to citizenship. ◆

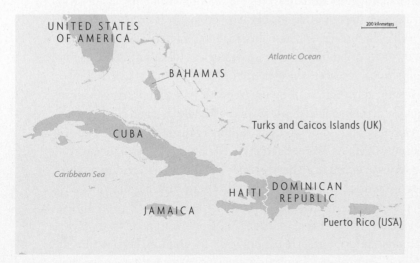

UNHCR/G. CONSTANTINE

from women's rights groups. In particular, Article 9 of the Convention on the Elimination of All Forms of Discrimination against Women (CEDAW) guarantees women's equality with men in respect of acquisition, change, or retention of their nationality (typically upon marriage to a foreigner) as well as in conferring nationality to their children. Despite these advances a recent survey by UNHCR found that over 40 countries still discriminate against women with respect to these elements.[16]

▲ **This Crimean woman was deported to Uzbekistan in 1944.** In 1997 she returned to Ukraine and eventually acquired citizenship there.

Fortunately, there is a growing trend for states to remedy gender inequality in their citizenship laws. In the Middle East and North Africa, a regional coalition of women's rights organizations has, for over a decade, waged the 'Women's Right to Nationality Campaign', advocating for law reform to achieve gender equality in nationality matters. Their efforts have been instrumental in achieving changes across the region. Laws have been reformed in Egypt (2004), Algeria (2005), Iraq (2006), Morocco (2007), and Tunisia (2010, for children born outside the country). Outside the Middle East and North Africa, countries as diverse as Indonesia (2006), Sierra Leone (2006, for children born within the country), Bangladesh (2009), Zimbabwe (2009) and Kenya (2010) have all amended their laws to grant women equal rights to pass their nationality on to their children.

Addressing statelessness

AS AWARENESS GROWS, MORE IS BEING DONE TO ADDRESS SITUATIONS OF statelessness around the globe. Responding to situations of statelessness involves the identification, prevention, and reduction of statelessness, and the protection of stateless persons.

IDENTIFYING AND COUNTING STATELESS PEOPLE

While the full scope of statelessness is only now becoming known, UNHCR has found the problem to be most pressing in Southeast and Central Asia, the Middle East, Central and Eastern Europe, and in certain countries in Africa. Because most countries in the Americas grant citizenship to all who are born on their territories, this region has the lowest incidence of people without a nationality.

Improving data on stateless populations is a major objective. Measuring statelessness is inherently complicated. However, baseline data on stateless populations is gradually improving. For example, the number of countries for which UNHCR has data on statelessness increased from 30 in 2004 to 65 in 2010. This was largely the result of the increased use of surveys and censuses of specific populations. A series of academic studies have also helped to identify and understand the scope of a number of situations of statelessness. [17]

From 2009 to 2011, identification activities were carried out by UNHCR in 42 countries. Those with the largest number of stateless people for which estimates are available are Estonia, Iraq, Latvia, Myanmar, Nepal, Syria and Thailand. In 2010, UNHCR had data reflecting 3.5 million stateless people around the world. However, a number of countries are known to have large but uncounted numbers of stateless persons. UNHCR believes that statelessness is widely under-reported and that there could be as many as 12 million stateless persons worldwide.

Accurate identification of who is stateless and formal recognition of a person's statelessness, particularly in countries which are party to the 1954 Convention, is crucial to ensuring that stateless persons can exercise their rights until they acquire a nationality. The identification of statelessness through formal determination procedures should result in official acknowledgement of an individual's stateless status through the issuance of appropriate documentation. This legal status confers rights and obligations on stateless persons, contributing to an improvement in their protection and livelihoods. Yet, very few countries have established procedures to determine statelessness. Those which have such procedures in place include France, Hungary, Italy, Latvia, Mexico and Spain.

UNHCR provides technical advice to states that wish to establish statelessness determination procedures, and this has yielded positive results in several countries. In Argentina, the regulations governing migration now provide for temporary residence to be granted to stateless persons. In Mexico, a statelessness determination procedure was introduced into the instructions issued to all immigration officers in 2010. In Slovakia, a statelessness determination procedure was established in the new Slovak Act on the Stay of Aliens. In Georgia and Moldova, formal statelessness determination procedures are also being

BOX **4.4**

The challenge of counting stateless people

Identifying people who are stateless and understanding the causes of their statelessness are prerequisites for resolving the problem in any given country. This is not as easy as it sounds. Most governments are unable to provide accurate information on stateless populations. Only a few have systems in place to determine statelessness and extend an official status to stateless persons. Although UNHCR and other UN agencies frequently carry out registrations of refugees and in some circumstances of internally displaced people, it is not common for them to register stateless persons.

Ways of identifying stateless populations

In recent years, an increasing number of projects have been developed with the explicit purpose of identifying stateless populations and surveying their protection needs. Such 'mapping' exercises can be costly and time-consuming and require careful planning. Statistics on stateless persons can be gathered using several different methods, including by analysing birth registration and civil registration data, through population census data, questionnaire-based surveys and approaches based on geographic information systems.

UN guidance on how to conduct population censuses outlines the importance of including questions related to citizenship, including statelessness.[i] However, the accuracy of the data depends on the reliability of the declarations made by the respondents. Whether someone is stateless or not usually needs to be determined on the basis of the laws and practice of a state, and self-identification may be misleading.

In a census, people may incorrectly identify themselves as stateless for a variety of reasons. For example, a person may not correctly understand the terms 'stateless person' and 'citizen', or may not know with certainty whether he or she is stateless. Proxy questions linked to the country of birth of the respondent or his or her parents, as well as a range of questions on prior residence, may be useful indicators of the individual's status and possible causes of statelessness. Such questions may also reveal the nature of links that stateless persons have to their country of residence and to other countries, providing insight into possible solutions through acquisition of nationality on the basis of birth, descent, residence or marriage.

A further challenge is that data gathered through proxy questions or self-identification often requires careful analysis and cross-checking. Determining whether individuals are citizens of a particular state often involves probing the state's view of the nationality status of particular populations. This may require contacting authorities where the stateless persons reside, or in other countries where they have a link through birth, descent, marriage or former residence. This can be a time consuming and labour intensive process.

Many individuals—including those who may be stateless—intentionally avoid registration or participation in censuses for a variety of reasons. Identification of persons as stateless might expose them to undesired government interference, making them reluctant to participate, for instance in situations where they live as undocumented migrants in a country and risk being detained or expelled if they are identified.

Data on statelessness can also be politically sensitive, in particular where statelessness results from discrimination and/or deprivation of nationality. In such contexts, government authorities may be reluctant to give researchers access to particular populations.

Recognizing the fundamental importance of proper identification of statelessness, UNHCR's Executive Committee has encouraged UNHCR to gain a better understanding of the nature and scope of this phenomenon, to collaborate with a wide range of partners in this effort, and to improve the way it gathers data on stateless persons.

adopted, as a result of UNHCR's collaboration with national authorities in those countries. Australia, Belgium, and Brazil and all pledged at UNHCR's 2011 Ministerial Meeting to create determination procedures in the near future.

Legal status as a stateless person is not a substitute for nationality, but determination procedures and status for stateless persons make a fundamental difference for the protection of individual rights. This is not necessarily limited to a grant of 'stateless status' under the 1954 Convention. Following dissolution of the Soviet Union, permanent residents of Estonia and Latvia who did not acquire the citizenship of any state were registered and given status as 'non-citizens' in Latvia and as 'persons of undetermined citizenship' in

'Mapping' statelessness: some recent experiences

A number of good practices in collecting data on stateless people have emerged from recent mapping exercises. One such example is a survey conducted in Serbia in 2010. Statelessness, or the risk of statelessness, was known to affect the Roma, Ashkali, and Egyptian (RAE) population in the country disproportionately. Due to marginalization and discrimination, as well as lack of information or familiarity with administrative procedures, the Roma do not always register their children's births, or have other personal documentation. In addition, many have links to more than one country, sometimes making it unclear which country they are nationals of. In such circumstances, many are unable to prove their nationality.

The objectives of the UNHCR-funded survey were to establish the number of persons who are at risk of statelessness because they lack documentation; to identify locations where such persons reside; to assess the awareness among this population of the need for personal identification documents and a nationality; and to identify reasons why individuals do not have personal documents. A key advantage for this survey was that the Government of Serbia already had estimates of the size and location of the affected population. The survey was therefore able to rely on statistical sampling methodology to identify random households to approach with its questionnaire. Extrapolating from the results,

the survey concluded that approximately 7 per cent of the RAE population in Serbia, or some 30,000 people, could be stateless or at risk of statelessness. This information has informed UNHCR planning and advocacy for civil documentation programmes to help to confirm nationality for this population.

The mapping of any situation involving statelessness presents challenges. For example, UNESCO has conducted two surveys to assess the prevalence and consequences of statelessness among Hill Tribe peoples of northern Thailand. Although government data on the baseline populations in this region were available and could be used to develop a sampling methodology, there were additional challenges such as language barriers, insecurity in the region, limited infrastructure, and distrust among the population to be surveyed. Nonetheless, the UNESCO research revealed that lack of citizenship is the major risk factor for highland girls and women in Thailand to be trafficked or otherwise exploited, mainly because it poses obstacles to obtaining education and lawful employment.

Other challenges may arise when efforts are made to gather information on stateless persons who are in an irregular situation. In 2010–2011, UNHCR and the NGO Asylum Aid carried out a project to identify the number and profile of stateless persons in the UK. The mapping exercise applied two distinct data collection methods. First, key informants such as immigration lawyers were interviewed

to gain a better understanding of challenges faced by stateless persons. Second, the snowball sampling method, a chain-referral system, was used to identify and interview a number of stateless persons, most of whom did not have a legal status in the country. Those interviewed included members of many known stateless populations around the world, such as the *bidoon* of Kuwait. While the mapping exercise did not yield an accurate estimate of the stateless population in the UK, it highlighted the need for a national procedure to determine the status of stateless persons. The survey also identified protection concerns among this population, and developed policy recommendations.

UNHCR is committed to improving its survey methodologies. Since 2010, UNHCR's Statelessness Unit and Field Information and Coordination Support Section have been conducting joint training for UNHCR staff and external partners on how to overcome challenges in mapping stateless populations and to set priorities for future projects. A survey by UNHCR of individuals lacking citizenship certificates in Nepal, surveys to identify stateless persons in Central Asian countries, Burundi, Cameroon, and Mozambique, as well as stateless persons in a migratory context in countries such as Belgium, the Netherlands, and the UK, were undertaken in 2011 or underway in 2012. ◆

i   'Principles and Recommendations for Population and Housing Censuses, Revision 2', United Nations, New York, 2008.

Estonia. In both cases, the status brought with it the enjoyment of most of the rights pertaining to citizens, including identity documents, secure residency, and the right to leave and to return to the country.

LAW REFORM

Most national action on statelessness in recent years has been in the area of law reform. Statelessness often occurs as a result of how the rules for conferral and withdrawal of nationality are formulated. Specific obligations to prevent and reduce statelessness are established under the 1961 Convention and international human rights treaties.

The 1961 Convention provides guidance on how states can prevent statelessness, and UNHCR uses its principles as a yardstick for reviewing and recommending reforms to the nationality laws of both state and non-state parties. Advocating for changes to legislation is a key way in which new cases of statelessness can be prevented and existing situations of statelessness resolved.

There has been a clear trend among both state and non-state parties to the 1961 Convention to bring their nationality legislation into line with Convention standards. In fact, the nationality laws of many states which are not parties include safeguards contained in the Convention.

In Kenya, for instance, a new Constitution was adopted in 2010 and brought about legal reform in a wide range of areas, including nationality and immigration. It was the first time that the nationality legislation had been revised since the original Kenyan Constitution was adopted in 1961. The new Constitution and Citizenship and Immigration Act incorporate several key safeguards against statelessness, including a provision to grant citizenship to foundlings, and gender equality in all nationality matters. The Citizenship Act also allows for acquisition of citizenship by stateless persons residing in Kenya since independence in 1963.

In 2010, both Lithuania and Georgia contributed to the prevention of statelessness by amending their citizenship laws. Although neither country is yet a party to the 1961 Convention, the new laws introduced a safeguard, in line with Article 7 of that Convention, preventing statelessness from occurring by only giving effect to an individual's renunciation of citizenship upon his or her acquisition of another nationality.

Law reform aimed at preventing statelessness can also reduce existing statelessness. New safeguards may be applied retroactively, granting citizenship to persons rendered stateless by previous gaps in the law. For instance, under a 1994 amendment to Brazil's Constitution, children born overseas to Brazilian parents could not obtain citizenship unless they returned to live in Brazil. Civil society groups in Brazil estimated that within a dozen years, 200,000 children had been made stateless. In 2007, when Brazil acceded to the 1961 Convention, the country's National Congress approved a constitutional amendment that replaced the residence requirement with consular registration as a precondition for the acquisition of citizenship. This reform applied retroactively, and helped many Brazilian children to acquire citizenship.

Indonesia has also taken fundamental steps to reform its nationality legislation. A significant number of the one million ethnic Chinese living in Indonesia were stateless or at risk of statelessness, as a result of restrictions in previous legislation. The 2006 citizenship law made it easier for affected members of the ethnic Chinese minority, who had lived in Indonesia for generations, to confirm their citizenship and acquire documentation to prove it. In addition, a provision which rendered Indonesians abroad stateless if they failed to register in a consulate over a period of five years was removed. In both cases, persons who had lost Indonesian citizenship or failed to acquire it at birth could apply to have it restored or to acquire it. Also, an equal right for men and women to transmit nationality to their children was introduced.

In Vietnam, thousands of Vietnamese women who had renounced their nationality in order to acquire that of their foreign husbands were left stateless when their marriages ended before they acquired the nationality of their husbands. Children of these women born outside Vietnam were unable to acquire nationality from their stateless mothers, and could not always acquire the nationality of their fathers. In 2009, the Vietnamese government reformed its nationality law to allow for re-acquisition of citizenship by women in such situations.

In Iraq, law reform has allowed people who had been stripped of their Iraqi citizenship to reacquire it. In 1980, the Faili Kurds, a mostly Shi'a minority living in Baghdad, Diyala Province, and the southern governorates of Wasit, Missan and Basrah, were stripped of their Iraqi citizenship by Decree 666 issued by Saddam Hussein. Their properties were seized by the government and many were deported to Iran, where they lived in camps as refugees. The 2005 Iraq Constitution and the 2006 Iraq Nationality Law repealed Decree 666, stating that all persons whose Iraqi nationality had been removed by the former government could have it reinstated. According to Iraq's Ministry of Displacement and Migration, about 20,000 formerly stateless families, or 100,000 individuals, reacquired Iraqi citizenship as a result.

In Syria, the President issued Decree No. 49 in April 2011, according to which stateless Kurds (*ajanib* or 'foreigners') registered in the civil records of the Governorate of Hassake were to be granted Syrian nationality. This decision to extend citizenship to part of the population of stateless Kurds is a step toward resolving a long-standing issue, dating back to the 1962 census, and which affects approximately 150,000 persons. According to official sources, by mid-September 2011, 59,000 applications for citizenship corresponding to some 103,000 persons had been received, and 51,000 Syrian identity documents had been issued. The measures taken in 2011 do not address the other segment of the stateless Kurdish population in Syria, the *maktoumeen* ('unregistered').

In some situations, rules for conferral of nationality have allowed stateless persons resident in the territory to be considered nationals, provided they were born there, resided there before a certain date, or descended from citizens. In many cases this is the preferred means of reducing statelessness, since it grants citizenship automatically, without cumbersome naturalization procedures.

Kyrgyzstan adopted comprehensive reforms in 2007 that enabled thousands of stateless people to acquire citizenship. Approximately 40,000 persons had lived in Kyrgyzstan without citizenship for more than a decade after independence, most of them ethnic minorities who had migrated from other parts of the former Soviet Union, and did not automatically acquire Kyrgyz citizenship or citizenship in any other successor state of the Soviet Union. Civil society groups advocated for a new citizenship law. The 2007 law recognized as citizens all former Soviet citizens who were stateless and had resided in Kyrgyzstan for five years or more. Since then, UNHCR has worked with the Kyrgyz government to enable thousands of persons to confirm their new nationality and obtain the relevant identity documents.

In Nepal, the promotion of law reforms which resolve and prevent statelessness has been ongoing. The 1990 Constitution limited transmission of citizenship by descent to men, repealing the prior grant of citizenship by birth on Nepalese territory. In 1995, it was estimated that the number of people with what are often called 'citizenship problems' in Nepal was between 3.4 million and 5 million. In 2006, Nepal adopted an interim Constitution reversing this policy. It resulted in a successful campaign to distribute citizenship certificates to nearly 2.6 million people who were eligible for citizenship on the basis of birth in Nepal before April 1990. UNHCR estimates that there were still approximately 800,000 persons without citizenship certificates in Nepal after the two-year window for registration expired in 2008. UNHCR is working with the Constituent Assembly and other actors to ensure that new cases of statelessness are not created by future constitutional changes.

Other states have specific procedures to facilitate acquisition of nationality following recognition as a stateless person. This generally occurs through naturalization. While most widely used in countries with small stateless populations, this approach can also be used on a large scale. Such procedures need to take account of the precarious situation of stateless people, for instance by reducing or waiving residency requirements and fees, and showing flexibility in the documentary evidence applicants are required to produce.

The Citizenship Law of the Russian Federation adopted in 2002 is an example of good practice. It specifically addressed the situation of hundreds of thousands of people in the country who remained stateless a decade after the dissolution of the Soviet Union. On the basis of simplified naturalization procedures, the law enabled former USSR citizens who were stateless to acquire citizenship if they resided permanently on Russian territory on 1 July 2002; they were also exempted from fees. By the time the procedure was discontinued in 2009, more than 600,000 stateless persons had received Russian citizenship.

WORKING IN PARTNERSHIP

There are now far more actors working on statelessness than just five years ago, including at UN level. In June 2011, the UN Secretary-General, Ban Ki-moon, issued a Guidance Note on statelessness, which resulted from extensive consultation within the UN system.[18] The Note sets out seven principles to guide UN action to address statelessness. It makes clear that addressing statelessness is a 'foundational and integral part' of UN efforts to strengthen the rule of law, and will be a blueprint for collaboration between UNHCR and other UN agencies in the years to come.

While UNHCR is the agency mandated to work with governments on issues of statelessness, cooperation and contributions from other UN agencies, regional organizations, and civil society will remain of vital importance. UNHCR coordinates with UN agencies such as UNICEF, the Office of the High Commissioner for Human Rights (OHCHR), UNESCO and the UN Population Fund (UNFPA). In Sri Lanka, for example, UNHCR and UNDP have implemented an 'Access to Justice' project where mobile registration clinics allow Hill Tamils not covered by the 2003 citizenship campaign to obtain identity documents, including refugees returning from India.

Regional organizations play a very important role in setting standards and raising awareness about regional and universal legal principles. The Council of Europe is the regional body with the longest and most consistent focus on standard-setting and monitoring of issues relating to nationality and statelessness. This engagement dates back to the development of regional standards on dual nationality in the 1960s, and to the adoption of two regional treaties on nationality and the avoidance of statelessness in situations of state succession in 1997 and 2006 respectively. The Council of Europe has also formulated two key recommendations addressing statelessness, the most recent in 2009 on the Nationality of Children.[19] For the past two decades, the organization has actively promoted the implementation of these standards when providing technical advice to states on nationality legislation.

The Council of Europe and UNHCR, as well as the Organization for Security and Cooperation in Europe (OSCE), have worked together since the 1990s on facilitating the return of Crimean Tatars and Meskhetian Turks to Ukraine and Georgia, from Central Asia—where they or their ancestors were deported to in the 1940s.

Other regional organizations have played a standard-setting role in the area of nationality and statelessness, albeit more sporadically than in Europe. As mentioned earlier in this chapter, the Inter-American Commission and Court of Human Rights, the African Commission on Human and Peoples' Rights and the African Committee of Experts on the Rights and Welfare of the Child have all issued important judgments, decisions, and opinions on nationality-related issues. Scope remains to develop further the engagement of regional bodies. In Southeast Asia, UNHCR is cooperating on several statelessness initiatives with the recently-established ASEAN Intergovernmental Commission on Human Rights.

Through a series of regional events held between 2009 and 2011, UNHCR and partners have sought to raise awareness of the situation of stateless people among states, international and regional organizations, and civil society actors, and to promote the exchange of good practices in addressing statelessness. Roundtables and expert meetings have been held in the Middle East and North Africa in cooperation with OHCHR, in Central Asia with the OSCE, in Southeast Asia with the National Human Rights Commission of Thailand, in southeastern Europe with the OSCE High Commissioner on National Minorities, and also in Southern Africa.

These have resulted in a number of concrete actions. The Regional Conference organized in Central Asia in December 2009 led to several initiatives to map statelessness in the region and to reform national legislation.[20] In 2011, UNHCR supported a government campaign to register all undocumented persons in Turkmenistan—many of whom are stateless. The 20,000 registered in this and a previous registration drive in 2007, if not confirmed as citizens of another state, will either be granted Turkmen citizenship or legal residence as stateless persons.

The Turkmenistan initiative is an example of the importance of inter-state cooperation to confirm the nationality status of individuals who may be stateless. In many such situations, persons can only be determined to be stateless through contact with the authorities of countries with which individuals have ties through birth, descent, prior residence, or marriage. In Turkmenistan, the vast majority of undocumented persons are from other republics of the former Soviet Union, and the necessary inter-state cooperation takes place through the diplomatic representations of the concerned states.

Similarly, one of the recommendations of the 2011 Zagreb Declaration, which emerged from a Regional Conference on Civil Status Registration and Documentation organized by UNHCR and the OSCE High Commissioner on National Minorities, with the cooperation of the European Commission, was the establishment of a regional mechanism for collaboration among governments in southeastern Europe.[21] In the region and beyond, many individuals face significant obstacles to obtaining civil status and identity documents, often because they have ties to more than one country. Inter-state cooperation is essential to ensure their confirmation as citizens of a state, and the issuance of documentation.

The global community is no longer silent on statelessness. Scholars, NGOs, the media, and affected individuals themselves are joining forces to gather information and develop more effective strategies to address statelessness. Advocacy groups have utilized the Universal Periodic Review process of the UN Human Rights Council, as well as UN treaty body mechanisms, to highlight problems of statelessness. This has, in particular, been done through reports to the Committee on the Rights of the Child, the Committee on the Elimination of Racial Discrimination, and the Committee on the Elimination of Discrimination against Women. At the same time, a growing network of international and national NGOs are working on the issue of statelessness, conducting awareness-raising and advocacy for government action.

UNHCR is collaborating with the universities of Maastricht and Tilburg in the Netherlands to establish a publicly available global analytical database of nationality legislation. The database will enable stakeholders, including governments, international organizations, academic researchers, legal practitioners, and civil society, to undertake accurate and timely analyses of nationality laws for a range of purposes, including that of advocacy for legislative reform.

The universal right to a nationality

THE EXPERIENCE OF THE PAST TWO DECADES SHOWS THAT MANY INSTANCES of statelessness can be prevented if existing standards are properly applied. International law prohibits discrimination by the state when conferring or withdrawing nationality; this stems from the universal principle of non-discrimination. Yet nationality laws frequently still contain discriminatory provisions or are applied in a discriminatory manner.

The treatment of stateless persons also requires effective action. A number of states refuse to allow stateless persons to return and reside on their territory, even when it is clear that their ancestors were born and raised in these countries. A related and as yet understudied problem is the detention of stateless persons, in particular those who are not permitted to return to their countries of habitual residence, and are subjected to repeated or indefinite periods of detention because they do not have legal status in the country in which they are detained. Such problems could be resolved through the application of the 1954 Convention and related human rights standards.

It is important that statelessness is not seen as an intractable political issue. It must be recognized as a problem with real, devastating, and lasting impacts on the lives of men, women and children without a state. Statelessness requires urgent and effective resolution.

At the Ministerial Meeting convened by UNHCR in December 2011 to mark the 50th anniversary of the 1961 Convention, many states made pledges to prevent and reduce statelessness, and to recognize the status of stateless people. More than 30 countries undertook to accede either to the 1954 or the 1961 Convention, or to both of these instruments.

These pledges demonstrate an increased willingness to address statelessness and a heightened global awareness of the plight of stateless people. Progress in the years to come will be measured by the implementation of these commitments. ∎

▲ **A camp in northwestern Yemen** for civilians displaced by conflict.

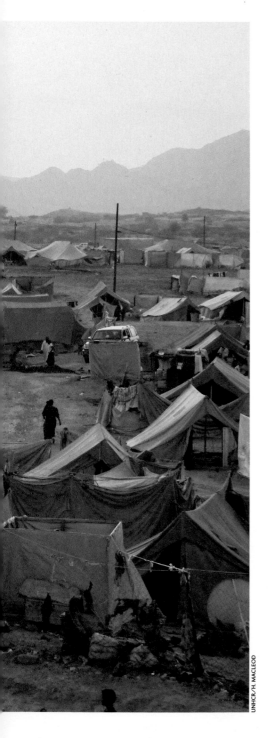

UNHCR/H. MACLEOD

CHAPTER 5

Protecting Internally Displaced Persons

I N RECENT YEARS, INTERNALLY DISPLACED persons (IDPs) have emerged as the largest group of persons receiving UNHCR's protection and assistance. At the start of 2011, UNHCR was operationally engaged with 14.7 million IDPs in 27 countries, in contexts ranging from the humanitarian emergency triggered by the combined effects of conflict and famine in Somalia, to the aftermath of inter-communal violence in Kyrgyzstan, to protracted displacement in Colombia.

According to the Internal Displacement Monitoring Centre (IDMC), a Geneva-based body that monitors internal displacement worldwide, the largest numbers of conflict-generated IDPs in 2011 were in Colombia and Sudan, Iraq, the Democratic Republic of the Congo (DRC), and Somalia.[1] Since 2009, the IDMC has also produced global estimates of the number of people displaced by sudden-onset natural disasters, a figure which vastly exceeds the number displaced by conflict.

In 2006, UNHCR assumed lead responsibility for the protection of conflict-generated IDPs within the UN humanitarian system's 'Cluster Approach', a mechanism designed to ensure a more predictable and better coordinated response to the needs of IDPs. It also assumed co-leadership for emergency shelter and camp coordination and management, with the International Federation of Red Cross and Red Crescent Societies (IFRC) and the International Organization for Migration (IOM) respectively. While UNHCR had been operationally engaged with IDPs on an *ad hoc* basis since 1972, this formalized

MAP **5·1** **Internal displacement** | 2011

BOSNIA A
HERZEGOV

HAITI

CÔTE
D'IVOIRE

CE
AFRI

COLOMBIA

R

D
T

Estimated populations of IDPs (end 2011)

4,000,000

2,000,000

400,000

*Serbia (AND KOSOVO: UNSCR 1244)

Sources: *Internal Displacement Monitoring Centre (IDMC), governments, UNHCR.*

*This map does not imply the expression of any opinion on the part of UNHCR or the United Nations concerning
the legal status of any country or territory, or the delimitation of frontiers or boundaries, nor is it warranted to be error-free.*

RUSSIAN FEDERATION

GEORGIA

SERBIA*

AZERBAIJAN

KYRGYZSTAN

IRAQ

AFGHANISTAN

PAKISTAN

MYANMAR

YEMEN

SUDAN

SRI LANKA

PHILIPPINES

SOUTH
SUDAN
UGANDA   SOMALIA

OF
GO
        KENYA
BURUNDI

ZIMBABWE

■ This map illustrates internal displacement in the 27 countries in which UNHCR implemented activities to protect and/or assist IDPs during 2011.

■ The map reflects conflict-related displacement with the exception of Haiti, where the circle represents persons displaced by the 2010 earthquake.

■ The circles depict estimated total IDP populations. UNHCR was not necessarily engaged with all of these persons in each country.

■ In several countries, the estimate includes recently returned IDPs, or those who are in the process of returning, as well as persons in IDP-like situations.

■ The number of IDPs in Zimbabwe is undetermined.

role raised questions about whether the organization would have the capacity and the resources needed to fulfil the task, and concerns that it might detract from the agency's core mandate concerning refugees.

Today, UNHCR's work with IDPs is well accepted across the organization and the wider international community. It is the parameters of UNHCR's engagement with IDPs—the scope and duration of its activities, its role with respect to protection in situations of natural disasters, and the extent of its involvement in the achievement of durable solutions—which are now the subject of healthy debate.

This chapter reviews the progress of the past six years in establishing a broad understanding of what the protection of IDPs means in practice, as well as the continuing need for national and international engagement to safeguard the rights and well-being of people who are displaced within the borders of their own countries. The emphasis of this chapter is on displacement caused by violence and conflict, although some of the issues discussed also pertain to displacement caused by natural disasters (*see chapter 7*).

From internal affair to international concern

WHILE REFUGEE PROTECTION IS A WELL-ESTABLISHED CONCEPT, the notion of protecting IDPs is less well understood. In practical terms, people displaced within their own countries by armed conflict and violence—or by natural disasters and development projects—have similar needs for shelter, food, and the protection of their rights, as refugees who have crossed international borders.

Refugee protection is international protection. Refugees find themselves in foreign lands, usually uninvited, and often unwanted. They have severed ties to their country of origin and cannot turn to its representatives abroad in case of difficulty.[2] Without national protection, they are in need of international protection. Elements of international protection are grounded in the institution of asylum, the 1951 Refugee Convention, its 1967 Protocol, and relevant regional instruments. UNHCR's standing to intervene in case of violations of refugees' rights arises from its Statute and the 1951 Convention.

By contrast, IDP protection is primarily national protection. Despite the similarity of their problems and needs, the situation of IDPs is fundamentally different from that of refugees. Because they remain within their own country, the principal responsibility for protecting and assisting them rests with their government—even if it lacks capacity to do so, or was responsible for their displacement.

For a long time, the imperative of state sovereignty was enough to silence the international community in the face of internal displacement. During the Cold War, internal displacement was considered an 'internal affair', and state sovereignty was used as a shield against international scrutiny and engagement. IDP protection emerged on the international agenda only in 1989 with the end of the political stalemate between East and West.[3]

With the shifting paradigms of the post-Cold War period, the internal dimension of sovereignty—the duty of states to protect their population, in accordance with their obligations under international human rights and humanitarian law—came to the fore. The term 'sovereignty as responsibility' was coined by Francis Deng, the first Representative of the UN Secretary-General for Internally Displaced Persons.[4]

Today, the UN General Assembly and other bodies recognize that the international community, notwithstanding the primacy of national responsibility, has a legitimate interest in IDPs and the protection of their rights.

This shift did not happen overnight. Important steps included the creation, by what was then the UN Human Rights Commission, of the mandate of the Representative of the Secretary-General on Internally Displaced Persons in 1992. UNHCR launched its first massive IDP operation in Bosnia and Herzegovina a year later, and large IDP operations in other parts of the world quickly followed. The 'Guiding Principles on Internal Displacement' were presented to the Human Rights Commission in 1998.[5] The UN's Humanitarian Reform was adopted by the Inter-Agency Standing Committee (IASC) in 2005, and designated UNHCR as global lead or co-lead agency for protection, emergency shelter and camp management. Many countries adopted laws or policies on internal displacement. Finally, binding regional instruments on internal displacement were adopted by the International Conference on the Great Lakes Region in 2006[6] and the African Union (AU) in 2009.[7]

These steps signalled a growing recognition that refugee protection is complemented by IDP protection—and that IDP protection is neither a substitute for asylum nor undermines that institution. At the same time, because protection serves both groups in factually similar but legally different contexts, UNHCR's long experience with refugee protection—including participatory, community-based and age, gender and diversity-sensitive approaches—has been recognized as making the agency particularly well-suited to lead protection responses also on behalf of IDPs.

Dimensions of solidarity

TO BE DISPLACED IS A DEVASTATING EXPERIENCE. From one day to the next, IDPs, like refugees, lose their homes, livelihoods and community ties. They flee in search of safety, and should not be forced to return as long as risks to their life, security, liberty and health exist.[8] They need shelter, food, access to medical care, education and other basic services, help to replace lost documents, as well as protection from discrimination because of being displaced. Their property must be protected and eventually returned to them, or they should be compensated for its loss, once the crisis is over. Over time, the needs of the displaced can change and humanitarian assistance often dwindles. IDPs may find themselves in a worse situation six months or a year after the initial emergency. Sometimes

IDPs who have found safety have to flee again. Most of all, like refugees, they need to be able to find a durable and sustainable solution ending their predicament.

PROMOTING A COMPREHENSIVE RESPONSE

Each case of internal displacement is unique: the cause of displacement may be armed conflict, violence, human rights abuses, or other man-made causes such as development projects or actions to preserve the environment, as well as natural disasters. Displacement may affect only a few families or millions of people. It may last days, weeks or months or become protracted, leaving people marginalized for decades. IDPs may stay in camps, or be dispersed in rural areas, often housed with host families, or live among the urban poor. Displacement can have a particularly devastating impact on women and children who constitute the large majority of displaced populations.

With such a diversity of scenarios and patterns of displacement, the response to internal displacement must be comprehensive. It cannot be limited to one or several elements of humanitarian assistance, but should address all aspects of displacement. The response should last as long as needs and problems caused by the displacement itself remain unresolved; it should ensure care for all displaced people irrespective of the cause of their displacement and whether they find shelter in or outside of camps, in rural or in urban areas.

THREE DIMENSIONS OF SOLIDARITY

A comprehensive response to IDPs requires solidarity on three levels: between the host community and the displaced themselves; solidarity of governments with their displaced citizens; and solidarity of the international community with IDPs in need of assistance and protection.

The solidarity shown by *communities* is particularly critical for IDPs, whether communities hosting them or those to which they eventually return. Internally displaced who are not supported by families, friends or communities can face increased risks to their safety and well-being. Where IDPs have lost ties to their own communities and the protection that comes with communal affiliation, host communities can restore some degree of that protection and should be helped, where possible, to do so. In the north of Yemen, where most IDPs settle outside camps, many sheikhs of receiving communities expressed their understanding that the displaced are not unwelcome intruders, but victims of armed conflict unable to return home for the moment. In the DRC, support provided by UNHCR in the form of construction materials and non-food items has helped to sustain the generosity of host families,

UNHCR/J. BJÖRGVINSSON

▲ **Haitians displaced by the 2010 earthquake** are taken in by a host family outside the affected area.

improving their own living conditions and enabling them to take in a displaced family.

Communities can benefit from hosting arrangements as well. In the Indonesian region of Aceh, following the 2004 tsunami, livelihood support to IDPs in host families not only sustained them, but had a 'multiplier effect' on the community, supporting overall recovery. Elsewhere, community-based services, rather than services and structures in camps, have benefited host communities, facilitated the integration of IDPs, and minimized or helped to repair inter-communal tensions.

BOX **5 • 1**

Iraq: the Diyala Initiative

In 2009, the government of Iraq, with support from UNHCR and other UN agencies, launched the 'Diyala Initiative' in an effort to support the return, reconciliation, and reintegration of displaced persons in Diyala Governorate in central Iraq. Between 2009 and the closure of the initiative in 2011, some 185,000 people returned to Diyala.

Priority was attached to Diyala because the area suffered some of the country's worst sectarian violence between 2005 and 2008. Thousands were killed and around a quarter of a million people, or 20 per cent of the province's population, were displaced as a result of sectarian fighting and attacks by insurgents. Most of those displaced remained in Iraq, although some fled to Syria or other countries in the region.

The Diyala Governorate is also of geopolitical importance. It borders Baghdad to the west and Iran to the east. To the north is the Kurdish Regional Governorate of As-Sulaymaniya, and to the north-west is the Governorate of Salah ad-Din. Diyala's pre-war composition was diverse: predominantly

Sunni Arab, with Shi'a Arab, Kurdish and Turkmen minorities.

In 2008, as security in most parts of Diyala improved, large numbers of people began to return. The fate of the mostly Shi'a villages of Al-Buri and Ahmad Khalaf gives a good idea of the scale of the challenges they faced. In July 2007, insurgents attacked these villages.

They cut the water supply and killed 20 males, all belonging to the Skuk tribe, which lost a total of 475 men during the period 2004 to 2008. Residents fled to Baghdad, Babylon and elsewhere. Up to 90 houses in the two villages were destroyed. An adjacent village called Abu Dhaba was completely razed, with every house blown up. When the villagers

Following inter-communal violence in Kenya in 2007–2008, efforts concentrated on re-establishing solidarity among communities and on community-based reconciliation processes. Post-conflict reconciliation has been challenging in many other contexts, such as in in Iraq, where sectarian violence has created deep wounds.

Today, the primary responsibility of *national authorities* to assist and protect internally displaced people is widely accepted, if not always uniformly understood or respected in all its dimensions. This responsibility is rooted in the sovereignty of each state to govern its own population and its duty to take care of it. The duty of care thus informs the responsible exercise of sovereignty. Yet some governments continue to limit access for international humanitarian actors, even where such actors could help to save lives.

The responsibility to assist and protect the displaced is a demanding one. Particularly following a disaster, or in the midst of conflict, there may be times when even the most willing government is unable to do so adequately.[9] Limited financial and human resources, the scope and impact of disaster, or competing priorities can affect the extent to

began to return they found they had lost every-thing: their homes, livestock, farming equip-ment, wells, irrigation canals, and pumps along with the social fabric of their community.

Profound divisions had emerged as a result of the violence which had often pitted village against village and neighbour against neighbour, affecting people who had gone to school together, married each other, worked together, celebrated and mourned together for years. The Diyala Initiative was intended to pool national and international resources to promote reintegration and reconciliation, rebuilding not only the infrastructure but an environment of social cohesion, respect for human rights and the rule of law.

Through Cabinet Order 54, the govern-ment set up a Higher Committee to oversee the initiative, bringing together officials from various central government departments and provincial authorities. The government com-mitted over US$30 million, mainly to compen-sate people for their losses. Support for service delivery and rebuilding of infrastruc-ture was provided by UN agencies (especially UNHCR, UNICEF, the World Food Programme and the World Health Organization) and the International Organization for Migration (IOM) through a coordinated programme, which attracted strong donor backing.

The Diyala Initiative addressed multiple problems. By promoting returns it mitigated humanitarian problems elsewhere, reducing the number of displaced squatting in Baghdad and in other towns. It reduced unemployment by helping farmers to get back to their previous livelihoods. In an environment that was extremely tense, it promoted social justice and reconciliation; and by not allowing abandoned towns and villages to persist as a security vacuum which could be taken over by militants, it promoted stability.

UNHCR and the government drew up lists of hundreds of affected villages and agreed on key objectives. These included protecting the right to adequate housing through construc-tion of 'starter homes' for the most vulnerable; supporting basic services (health, education, water, sanitation); creating liveli-hood opportunities, especially through rehabilitation of the agricultural sector; and facilitating access to justice. The National Reconciliation Committee and other govern-ment officials helped communities to reach agreement on how to tackle the divide that had emerged during the conflict.

Some mayors and local council members went to great lengths to cooperate with UNHCR and other humanitarian actors. Not all local government officials were familiar with

the villages and squatter settlements in their areas, and the Initiative helped to introduce them to their constituents. Iraqi NGOs that implemented projects provided employment for local people and acquired valuable experi-ence in development work and community relations. But the government's limited capacity to support and sustain the project remained a serious challenge.

Visits to villages in the province nonethe-less illustrate the impact of the initiative. For instance, in 2006, the mainly Sunni village of Bayaa was infiltrated by insurgents who kidnapped men, killed the school principal, and destroyed 50 out of 60 houses. Most of the families fled north to Sulaymaniya. Bayaa had been a farming village where residents grew fruit and vegetables and tended livestock. They lost everything, including all their tractors, generators and water pumps. About 24 families returned after UNHCR provided them with starter houses. Others waited for more houses to be built in order to return. 'We started agriculture again,' one man said, 'we started from below zero.'

The Diyala Initiative brought significant gains in terms of reconciliation and recon-struction in the province. The challenge will be to maintain these gains in the face of ongoing sectarian tensions in Iraq. ◆

which national authorities are able to assume their responsibility towards the displaced.

In other contexts, the national authorities may be unwilling to act. Where govern-ment forces or their proxies are the perpetrators of displacement, the authorities may deny the existence of IDPs or turn a blind eye to their plight. And in situations character-ized by the fragility or collapse of government institutions, or lack of governmental terri-torial control, there is no effective recognized authority to assume the responsibility to as-sist and protect IDPs.

In such contexts, the engagement of the international community to protect and assist the internally displaced is legitimate. International solidarity is called for when na-tional authorities are willing but not able fully to assume their responsibilities. Where na-tional authorities are *unwilling* to do so, or where there is a complete lack of governmental institutions to assume this responsibility, the international community may have an obli-gation to step in. In the latter case, humanitarian actors including ICRC and UNHCR may have to deal with non-state armed groups exercising effective control over certain areas and populations, and remind them of their obligations *vis-à-vis* civilian populations under international humanitarian and international criminal law. Depending on the context, humanitarian action has to be shaped accordingly; it may be as support to the national authorities, as complement to insufficient national efforts, or as a substitute for absent or dysfunctional state institutions.

The role of the international community

PROTECTION BY WHOM?

In recent years, the 'international community' has worked to strengthen its response to internal displacement, and to make it predictable and reliable. The international community encompasses a wide range of actors: international organizations providing protection and assistance, governmental and non-governmental aid agencies, development actors working to enable sustainable solutions to displacement, and donors—all may be involved to varying degrees. In some situations, the Security Council and its peacekeeping or peacebuilding missions may be involved, meaning that military actors work alongside civilian and humanitarian players (*see chapter 1*). In a number of countries, the UN's new Peacebuilding Commission is engaged. Strong cooperation and effective coordination among all of these actors is essential but not always easy. In Haiti, following the earthquake in 2010, shelter coordination meetings at one point included over 200 mostly expatriate participants, while issues of language and access to meeting facilities limited local NGO participation.

In times of emergency, humanitarian actors are expected to distribute food, truck water, erect tents and provide medical care. Such action is life-saving and helps to fulfil basic social and economic rights, but it is insufficient to protect civil and political rights. In the 1990s, during the armed conflicts in the Balkans, the phenomenon of the 'well-fed dead', people who had enough to eat but whose lives and safety were at risk, became particularly apparent.[10] Since then, protection has evolved to include advocacy for civil and political rights, for example by combating rape used as a weapon of war in places such as eastern DRC or addressing the abduction of children by the Lord's Resistance Army for the purpose of using them as child soldiers or sexual slaves.

Nevertheless, where life and limb need to be protected, humanitarians quickly reach the limits of their competencies and the presence of police and even military forces may become essential. In recent times, UN peacekeepers have been mandated to protect civilian populations, with some mandates referencing the protection of IDPs, for instance in Chad, DRC, and Côte d'Ivoire. Security Council Resolutions have repeatedly called for the protection of IDP camps, informal sites and settlements—not only from infiltration by armed elements, but also from forced recruitment, attack and other violations of human rights. In Côte d'Ivoire, UN troops have been mandated to work closely with humanitarian actors to assess threats and tensions in areas of IDP return, ultimately seeking to address these in a UN system-wide protection strategy.

Internal displacement does not disappear with the close of the emergency phase, nor do the protection needs of the displaced. The former Representative of the UN Secretary-General on the Human Rights of Internally Displaced Persons, Walter Kälin, observed that displaced people he met years or even decades after the emergency appeared worse off than they had during the conflict, when the humanitarian actors had a strong presence.[11]

The phasing out of humanitarian assistance, without the parallel stepping-up of recovery and development activities, risks creating a gap in the protection of the displaced, and increases the chance of protracted displacement. The early involvement of recovery and development actors is essential to support the rebuilding of public institutions necessary for the rule of law and of public services. Peace and reconciliation activities must reflect the situation of IDPs, who should be given a voice when peace agreements are negotiated.[12]

HUMANITARIAN REFORM

'[I]nternally displaced persons and their needs often fall into the cracks between different humanitarian bodies,' former UN Secretary-General Kofi Annan concluded in his 2005 report entitled *In Larger Freedom*.[13] The report triggered a reform process which, at its core, was an institutional reform, intended to address two major failings. First, humanitarian responses were not sufficiently predictable; some crises received much attention and support, while others remained almost invisible, even though the needs were the same or even greater. Second, inadequate coordination among humanitarian actors led to overlaps in some areas and gaps in others, meaning that available funds were not always used efficiently. The aim was to make the humanitarian response system more predictable, accountable and transparent through better coordination.

The three pillars of the reform were: (i) a strong system of UN Humanitarian Coordinators (HCs) at the country level in situations of complex humanitarian emergencies; (ii) a Central Emergency Response Fund (CERF) providing for a reserve to fund emergency interventions rapidly and to address 'underfunded' situations; and (iii) what has come to be known as the 'Cluster Approach'.

The Cluster Approach is a coordination arrangement set up by the UN to address humanitarian emergencies, including those with substantial numbers of IDPs. It covers eleven thematic areas of humanitarian work including water, sanitation and hygiene; nutrition; emergency shelter; camp coordination and management; and protection. With lead agencies for each cluster designated at the global and national levels, this approach is intended to improve the overall humanitarian response through enhanced predictability, timeliness and effectiveness. This new approach calls for strengthened partnerships, leadership, clearly delineated responsibilities for needs assessment and strategy development, and greater accountability for delivery of services.[14]

At the country level, clusters are led by one UN agency, sometimes with NGO co-chairs. Subject to caveats of access, security and funding, the lead agency acts as a 'provider of last resort' to avoid gaps in the response, when no other organization is able to act. The Cluster Approach is to be used in major new emergencies as well as in ongoing situations where a UN Humanitarian Coordinator has been appointed. By the end of 2011, the Cluster Approach had been implemented in 43 situations, though not all were still active.

Unlike in refugee situations where, according to its Statute, UNHCR is responsible for providing international protection, the Protection Cluster serves to identify and assess protection needs of IDPs, and to initiate and coordinate responses. UNHCR leads the Protection Cluster in situations of armed conflict; where requested, it may also do so in cases of natural disaster.[15] At the global and country levels, agencies with specific expertise have agreed to serve within the Protection Cluster as focal points for thematic areas: child protection (DRC), gender-based violence (UNICEF and the UN Fund for Population Activities), mine action (UN Mine Action Service), and housing, land and property (UN-Habitat).

The cluster system has achieved a great deal since 2005. IDP protection—a concept virtually unknown 20 years ago—has become accepted as an important task at the international, regional and national levels. The Global Protection Cluster has been active in developing or contributing to important standards and operational guidance, including the 2008 UNHCR *Handbook for the Protection of Women and Girls* and the 2010 *Handbook for the Protection of Internally Displaced Persons*. It has developed general guidance for national Protection Clusters and provides them with advisory and technical support, including for example through deployment of experts in disabilities and ageing or gender advisers. A training programme on protection in natural disasters has recently been developed to support cooperation and joint planning with local organizations and national governments.

On the other hand, challenges remain. UNHCR's experience and that of other humanitarian actors in protecting IDPs is still limited when compared to experience of more than 60 years in refugee protection. Unlike for refugee protection where it holds the primary mandate and responsibility, UNHCR is just one actor, albeit an important one, when it comes to IDP protection; and this is not necessarily recognized by all governments in all situations. The International Committee of the Red Cross (ICRC), with its solid protection mandate and long-standing experience in situations of armed conflict, may often be better positioned to address protection needs of the displaced as part of the affected civilian population.

Despite a multi-year consultative process led by the ICRC on the meaning of 'protection' involving some 50 humanitarian and human rights organizations,[16] stakeholders do not necessarily agree about what protection entails in practice, and how priorities should be determined.[17] To date there has been a tendency to determine priorities in light of the mandates and the work plans of participating partners rather than on the basis of assessed needs. In some countries, protection activities have been limited to child protection and protection from gender-based violence—important but nonetheless only part of a comprehensive protection approach. Protection also entails understanding how the context shapes needs and responses. This is not limited to armed conflict situations, as protection needs also arise in natural disasters. Protection needs are frequently context-specific; for example, mine clearance, activities to promote reconciliation, provision of documentation, or access to housing, land or property.

In 2011, six years into the humanitarian reform process, UNHCR, as the leader of the Global Protection Cluster, initiated an extensive review of the role and impact of this Cluster. In 2012, with a new mission statement and strategy, one of the key challenges of the Global Protection Cluster will be to ensure a comprehensive protection approach, as described above. UNHCR has also prioritized advocacy and resource mobilization, recognizing that field Protection Clusters have struggled to show tangible results either because they lack funding or because they cannot operationalize protection in ways that have real impacts, thus creating a vicious circle between lack of funding and inadequate outcomes.

The responsibility to lead the Protection Cluster at both global and country levels has placed many new demands on UNHCR. As a result, in 2011, the agency created new posts dedicated to cluster leadership in several key countries, and developed training programmes in areas such as coordination, leadership and protection in natural disasters. Many UNHCR staff have strong leadership skills and expertise in the area of IDP protection, but as expectations of the organization's performance in this area grow, more needs to be done to build institutional capacity.

The legal dimension of protection

TOWARD BINDING INSTRUMENTS

Internally displaced persons are rights-holders. They are entitled to enjoy all international human rights and humanitarian law guarantees, in addition to legal entitlements they possess in their country as citizens and habitual residents. Over the past decade, significant progress has been made in strengthening the international legal framework.

The 1998 UN Guiding Principles on Internal Displacement, intended to serve as an international standard for the treatment of IDPs, are widely accepted. At the UN's Millennium Summit in 2005, heads of state and government recognized them as an 'important international framework for the protection of internally displaced persons'.[18] The Guiding Principles have been re-affirmed by regional bodies such as the Organization of American States and the Council of Europe.[19] The International Conference on the Great Lakes Region and the African Union (AU) went a step further and developed binding instruments. The 2006 Great Lakes Protocol on the Protection and Assistance to IDPs established a legal framework in the Great Lakes Region of Africa to ensure implementation of the Guiding Principles, and requires their transposition into national legislation.

The AU Convention for the Protection and Assistance of IDPs in Africa ('Kampala Convention') of 2009 is a more comprehensive instrument. It establishes responsibilities and obligations of states parties and other actors to prevent internal displacement, protect and assist IDPs and to promote durable solutions as well as regional solidarity and cooper-

BOX 5·2

The Kampala Convention:
a legal framework for solidarity

In 2009, African states adopted a pioneering new international instrument on internal displacement. Known as the Kampala Convention, the *African Union Convention for the Protection and Assistance of Internally Displaced Persons in Africa* continues the continent's tradition of setting normative standards on forced displacement.

The Convention was approved at the African Union (AU) Summit on forced displacement held in Kampala, Uganda, in October 2009. Forty years earlier in Addis Ababa, the (then) Organization of African Unity had adopted the *Convention Governing the Specific Aspects of Refugee Problems in Africa*.

The Kampala Convention addresses the full cycle of internal displacement: from prevention to solutions. UNHCR was closely associated with its preparation, helping states and the AU Secretariat to ensure consistency with international standards, especially the 1998 UN Guiding Principles on Internal Displacement. The Convention transforms the issues covered by the Guiding Principles into 'hard law' and enlarges the normative framework by incorporating some new provisions.

The Convention sets out the primary responsibility of states to prevent displacement; to protect the human rights of IDPs; and to seek lasting solutions to the problem of displacement. While addressing the protection and assistance needs of IDPs, in particular those who may have specific vulnerabilities, such as women, children, and pastoral communities, the Convention also requires states to take into account the needs of host communities. Signatories must enact implementing legislation and designate an appropriate institutional focal point at the national level.

The Convention covers all aspects of state responsibility toward IDPs. It prohibits arbitrary displacement, requires states to provide protection and assistance to IDPs, promotes lasting solutions, and recognizes the right of IDPs to receive compensation for violations of their rights. It applies to displacement generated by a range of causes, including armed conflict, human rights violations, natural disaster and climate change, and takes a progressive approach in recognizing the responsibility of states to 'prevent political, social, cultural and economic exclusion and marginalisation, that are likely to cause displacement(...)'. States are required to put in place early warning systems, emergency preparedness and management measures and disaster reduction strategies.

The Convention also covers the obligation of states to ensure the accountability of non-state actors such as armed groups, multinational companies, private security companies and others for acts of arbitrary displacement or complicity in such acts.

Beyond the responsibility of states, the Convention provides a platform for regional cooperation. One of its objectives is to 'establish a legal framework for solidarity (...) and mutual support between the States Parties in order to combat displacement and address its consequences.' The Convention reiterates the right set out in the Constitutive Act of the African Union for the Union to intervene in a member state, pursuant to a decision of the AU Assembly, where genocide, war crimes and crimes against humanity occur.

The Convention explicitly seeks to preserve and expand space for humanitarian action. States Parties must ensure respect for humanitarian principles, including to 'protect and not attack or otherwise harm' humanitarian personnel. They are to allow unimpeded access of relief supplies and facilitate the role of local and international humanitarian actors. Where states are not able to provide sufficient protection and assistance to IDPs, they are to cooperate in seeking the assistance of humanitarian agencies and other relevant actors. The Preamble specifically refers to UNHCR's protection expertise as a source of support.

The obligations set out in the Convention must be translated into domestic laws. In some countries, this will mean extensive legislative reform. Significantly, the Convention requires States Parties to create and maintain an updated register of all IDPs within their jurisdiction, and to issue IDPs with documentation for the exercise of their rights.

At the end of 2011, 32 countries had signed the Kampala Convention while eight had deposited their instrument of ratification at the African Union. The Convention enters into force 30 days after the deposit of the 15th instrument of ratification. ◆

ation. States parties are required to incorporate the Convention into their domestic law and adopt national policies or strategies on internal displacement.

The past decade was thus marked by strong international and regional recognition of the Guiding Principles and the development of legally binding instruments at the regional level. Individual states such as Germany and Iraq have even attributed to the Guiding Principles the character of customary law. While these developments are only a beginning, they are important steps in the path of moving from soft to hard law.

EVOLVING NATIONAL INSTRUMENTS

A major protection gap frequently faced by IDPs is the absence of opportunities to have their rights ensured, implemented, or–when needed–legally enforced at the domestic level. A key measure to address this gap is the translation of the UN Guiding Principles and regional instruments on internal displacement into national laws, policies and strategies. Further necessary steps are the identification of national institutional focal points, and adequate funding for implementation of laws and policies addressing internal displacement.

Today, more than 20 countries, including Azerbaijan, Colombia, Georgia, Iraq, Peru, Serbia, Sudan, and Uganda, to cite just a few, have adopted laws or strategies that address internal displacement.[20] Others, for instance the Central African Republic, Kenya and Yemen, were in the process of doing so at the end of 2011. Still others have provisions in their disaster management legislation which relate to displacement. The growing number of countries with national legislation on internal displacement is a positive and continuing trend, particularly in Africa where states parties to the Great Lakes Protocol and the Kampala Convention are obliged to enact such laws. While adopting a law is a sovereign act, and an indication that a government takes its responsibility seriously, international organizations and NGOs can play a helpful role in the development of national laws and policies, as UNHCR has historically done in support of refugee-related legislation and the establishment of national asylum institutions.

While some national laws and policies remain largely symbolic because they are too general or are not properly implemented, others have had a real impact on the situation of the displaced. For instance, Colombia's law on internal displacement dates back to 1997 and has been amended since then in light of the UN Guiding Principles and changes in the displacement situation.[21] Despite some gaps in implementation, this law has significantly influenced the institutional response to internal displacement and strengthened IDP protection, including by increasing the visibility and priority attached to the problem. The law acknowledges the particular needs of the displaced and provides a stable framework to protect them. While the law demands a response from the entire Colombian state, it enabled the creation of specific institutional arrangements to assist and protect Colombian IDPs.[22]

In Kenya, a proposed national policy on the prevention of displacement and protection and assistance for IDPs was pending adoption by the Government at the end of 2011. It was the result of an inclusive consultative process and a high level of commitment of several Ministries, the Kenya National Commission on Human Rights, representatives of IDP communities, national and international civil society, and the UN. The Kenyan national policy will be the first instrument established in the post-Kampala Convention era, and is likely to be a model for other countries.

UNHCR has played an essential supportive role in Colombia and in Kenya, as well as in Georgia (*see box 5.7*) and many other countries affected by internal displacement. Where governments request assistance in drafting laws, strategies and policies pertaining to IDPs, the Protection Cluster and UNHCR as cluster lead should indeed provide support. This puts high demands on the Protection Cluster at the global and the country levels, both of which may need additional capacity and expertise to support governments in such endeavours. In the coming years, this will be particularly true in Africa where the implementation of the Kampala Convention will trigger widespread legislative action.

JUDICIAL OVERSIGHT

Laws without judicial oversight and rights that cannot be enforced remain largely ineffectual. Domestic courts and judicial or quasi-judicial human rights bodies at the regional and UN level remain underused in IDP protection. However, there are encouraging signs of increased engagement.

At the domestic level, the role of Colombia's Constitutional Court stands out. In 2004, it handed down a landmark decision declaring that the massive, longstanding and repeated disregard of IDPs' fundamental rights was an 'unconstitutional state of affairs'.[23] It issued a series of orders aimed at improving the situation of IDPs and pledged to monitor and verify compliance with these orders.[24] The Court acknowledged the Guiding Principles as part of applicable Colombian Law and as the main source of authority to determine both the scope of displaced persons' rights and the state's obligation to protect them.[25] Regional human rights courts and bodies have started to play a more active role in protecting the human rights of IDPs. For instance, with reference to Colombia, the Inter-American Court of Human Rights has characterized displacement as a human rights violation, affirmed the right not to be displaced, and the obligation of the State to contribute to the creation of conditions for prompt and voluntary return in conditions of safety and dignity. It has highlighted the vulnerability of Afro-Colombian and indigenous populations to displacement.[26] On many occasions, the Court has issued provisional measures to protect communities at risk of being displaced, asking states 'to adopt, without delay, the measures necessary to protect the life and personal integrity of all the members of the[se] communities'.[27]

The European Court of Human Rights has dealt with cases concerning restitution of or compensation for property left behind by IDPs.[28] In one case, it held that even though displacement may have been justified by reasons of military necessity, a human rights violation occurred owing to the refusal to give the displaced access to their village and the ensuing 'serious and harmful effects that have hindered the applicants' right to enjoyment of their possessions for almost ten years, during which time they have been living in other areas of the country in conditions of extreme poverty, with inadequate heating, sanitation and infrastructure'.[29]

The African Commission on Human and Peoples' Rights, in a 2010 ruling dealing with the forcible removal of an indigenous community from their ancestral lands where a game park was created, held that 'the failure to provide adequate compensation and benefits, or provide suitable land for grazing' amounted to a violation of the right to development under the African Charter on Human and Peoples' Rights.[30]

UN treaty bodies regularly address internal displacement in the course of examining state reports, but IDPs themselves have rarely used the individual communication

IDPs and Colombia's Constitutional Court

Colombia has one of the most highly developed legal and institutional frameworks for the protection of IDPs. The country's Constitutional Court has actively promoted this framework through a variety of actions, most notably through a ground-breaking judgment handed down in 2004.

Under the procedure known as 'acción de tutela', individuals in Colombia are able to petition the Constitutional Court for the protection of their rights. By the end of 2003, the claims of more than a thousand IDP families had made their way to the country's highest court.

In view of the magnitude of internal displacement in Colombia—estimated by the government in 2011 at 3.8 million—the potential for individual claims was virtually unlimited, and the Constitutional Court considered that reviewing individual cases was not the most efficient way to address human rights violations. It has therefore focused on promoting state laws and policies that guarantee IDPs the full enjoyment of their rights. The Court's January 2004 Decision known as T–025/04 exemplifies this 'structural' approach.

Decision T–025/04 followed a review of 108 cases which had been grouped together for the Court's examination. Each case in turn represented numerous IDP families from around the country. These families sought the Court's action against a wide range of state and municipal authorities, alleging that the authorities had failed in their duty to protect the displaced population, and had not responded effectively to the IDPs' appeals for material as-

sistance, access to livelihoods, health care, and education, among other services.

In its judgment, the Court held that the IDPs had suffered 'multiple and continuous' violations of their human rights, owing to the failure of the competent authorities to address their needs. It found their living conditions to be 'inhumane' and their treatment to be 'unconstitutional'. The Court was particularly attentive to the situation of indigenous and Afro-Colombian communities as well as other vulnerable people such as the elderly, female heads of households, and children. The Court did not attribute the rights violations to any single authority but found that they were the result of structural shortcomings, and ordered the design of policies to remedy the situation and the correction of institutional failures.

As a result of Decision T–025/04, IDP issues are now a core part of the public policy agenda in Colombia. The resources allocated by the central government to respond to the needs of IDPs grew from US$177 million in 2004 to US$950 million in 2011. A system of indicators was established to measure the extent to which IDPs are able to enjoy their rights. Policies were adjusted in numerous sectors, such as health, education, housing, land, and registration. Most recently, in 2011, the government adopted the historic Victims and Land Restitution Law.

When the Court issued its judgment T–025/04 it simultaneously established two new mechanisms to ensure compliance with its orders. The first consists of public hearings, held regularly since June 2005, to assess compliance with T–025/04. These hearings enable

the displaced population, national and international NGOs, as well as government officials, the Ombudsman, and UNHCR, among others, to give their views. The second instrument consists of periodic Rulings by the Court giving its assessment of progress in fulfilling the requirements of Decision T–025/04.

One of the structural shortcomings identified by Decision T–025/04 was the absence of specific policies relating to the most vulnerable IDPs. In a Ruling in 2006 (218/06), the Court noted that progress in this respect had been inadequate; from 2008 onward the Court began to issue orders to ensure sufficiently differentiated responses. For example, in its follow-up Ruling 004 of 2009, the Court established special protection for indigenous peoples and warned that at least 35 indigenous groups were in danger of physical and cultural extinction as a result of the impact of conflict and displacement.

Despite the Court's action and the government's efforts, UNHCR's monitoring activities show that the conflict continued to take a heavy toll on indigenous groups. In the first six months of 2011 alone, at least 900 people from groups at risk of extinction were displaced, and 20 killed. The Court has issued specific rulings for the protection of the Awa, Jiw and Hitnu indigenous communities.

A great deal has been achieved for Colombia's IDPs, but much remains to be done. The Constitutional Court will no doubt be called upon to continue its unique oversight of the government's response to the country's massive internal displacement. ◆

mechanisms to have their case assessed through a decision which, although not legally binding, would have considerable authority.

In contrast, international criminal courts have started to hold individuals accountable for egregious cases of arbitrary displacement. The International Criminal Tribunal for the Former Yugoslavia (ICTY) has sentenced persons for war crimes and crimes against humanity that displaced members of ethnic minorities.[31] The prosecutor at the International Criminal Court (ICC) has brought indictments against high ranking individuals suspected of having committed the crimes of deportation and transfer of civilians[32] in north-ern Uganda, Sudan and the DRC.[33] More recently, the ICC confirmed charges against Kenyan politicians and a journalist for their role in the violence which followed the disputed December 2007 presidential election. The charges include forcible transfer of population.[34]

The operational dimension of protection

LEGAL NORMS AND POSSIBLE JUDICIAL ENFORCEMENT ARE ESSENTIAL, but not sufficient, to protect IDPs. Legal protection must be complemented by activities on the ground during and after humanitarian emergencies. Protection has been defined in an operational sense[35] as humanitarian activities that aim 'at obtaining full respect for the rights of the individual in accordance with the letter and spirit of relevant bodies of law' including human rights law and international humanitarian law.[36]

A fundamental question remains as to the relationship between protection and assistance. Are traditional humanitarian activities–such as distributing food and setting up camps–also 'protection' because they contribute to fulfilling the rights to food and adequate shelter? While humanitarian assistance in many situations has a protective value, a narrower and sharper notion of protection in the context of internal displacement is needed. Protection is about securing human rights and, where possible, enabling rights-holders to secure them for themselves. If, for example, a community displaced by government forces is in dire need of medical services, a humanitarian approach would ensure that it is visited by health workers whereas a protection approach would focus on negotiating access for the people themselves to medical services available in a nearby town under government control.

For practical purposes, humanitarian organizations often distinguish four categories of protection activities relating to IDPs.[37]

First, activities addressing past, present or future harm in contravention of human rights guarantees. This includes actions aimed at providing security, preventing and stopping violence and exploitation, and helping victims of violence. Examples include monitoring the human rights situation of IDPs and taking up cases of violations with competent authorities; advocating with armed forces and non-state armed groups not to target civilians and their property and allowing humanitarian organizations to reach displaced people or communities at risk. It also includes steps to enhance security in IDP camps and settlements, for instance by setting up separate sanitation areas for women and men, ensuring lighting of public areas, or organizing night patrols to prevent sexual and gender-based violence. It would also cover intervention with relevant authorities in cases of forced evictions of IDPs from their housing, including to ensure that any unavoidable evictions are carried out in accordance with international standards, and that IDPs are provided with alternative housing.

BOX **5•4**

Protection monitoring in IDP situations

More than a century ago, the human rights pioneer Roger Casement based his ground-breaking reports on Congo and Peru on painstakingly collected first-hand information about the abuse of local populations. Much has changed since Casement's day, but the need for timely information on human rights violations remains a staple of humanitarian work.

For UNHCR to carry out its role as the lead agency for protection, it needs to have first-hand information about the situation of IDPs. 'IDP protection monitoring' refers to the observation and assessment of the situation of communities and individuals who have been displaced— usually by conflict but also by natural disasters. Protection monitoring collects information on the causes, locations, and dynamics of displacement, and on the types of problems that IDPs encounter. It enables the gathering of information about specific incidents as well as the observation of trends over time. It requires direct contact with affected populations.

IDP protection monitoring is now a key feature of UNHCR's work in many operations around the world, but it is never an end in itself. Monitoring seeks to inform interventions to stop or mitigate abuse, whether through advocacy with state or non-state actors, or the establishment of operational programmes.

Governments and civil society have progressively taken on more responsibility for monitoring the welfare of IDPs. National human rights bodies and local NGOs are very often engaged, and UNHCR tries to reinforce their capacities rather than setting up parallel systems. For example, UNHCR has partnered with the Afghan Independent Human Rights Commission to monitor refugees returning from Iran and Pakistan, as well as internally displaced populations and communities which were never displaced but might be suffering similar patterns of deprivation or rights violations.

In situations where IDPs live outside of camps or in remote or dangerous locations, imaginative approaches to monitoring are needed. In Somalia, UNHCR and its partners devised a system for Population Movement Tracking (PMT), which relies on an extensive network of community contacts to follow the frequency and causes of movement of vulnerable populations in areas where information cannot be obtained through direct observation.

The PMT is complemented by a Protection Monitoring Network through which partners report on the situation of civilians affected by violence. Partners can draw on a small Emergency Grant Fund to provide assistance in urgent cases they encounter in the field. Many of these are victims of sexual and gender-based violence who need medical or psychosocial support. During 2010, for instance, monitoring partners referred 181 survivors to specialized services using the Emergency Grant Fund.

In the Democratic Republic of the Congo (DRC), protection monitoring has also empowered local partners to reach out to displaced communities, despite numerous security and logistical challenges. Monitoring is the foundation for advocacy to raise the visibility of protection concerns with donors, the Security Council and others, including the military.

In the DRC, the Protection Cluster established a joint planning exercise with the UN Stabilization Mission (MONUSCO) whereby monitoring data is used by peacekeepers to identify areas that they 'must', 'should' and 'could' protect. This has contributed to enhancing the peacekeepers'

effectiveness and accountability. UNHCR and its partners also intervene directly with national military forces. For example, information collected by the Protection Cluster led a Congolese National Army colonel to demand that commanders of a military operation in North Kivu follow up on reports of human rights violations against civilians.

In Côte d'Ivoire, widespread violence after the 2010 presidential election resulted in the displacement of nearly one million persons. UNHCR quickly reinforced its monitoring capacity using mobile teams. In mid-2011, in the aftermath of the violence, monitors identified protection problems that were impeding IDP returns. In some cases, land and productive forests had been occupied by newcomers, causing friction when IDPs tried to return to their villages. UNHCR reported these incidents to local authorities, who then mediated between the two groups to defuse tensions that in some cases had complex ethnic undertones. This activity became a crucial part of UNHCR's efforts to promote community reconciliation.

In western Côte d'Ivoire, irregular checkpoints were sometimes used to subject returning IDPs to extortion. The presence of militias in local communities was also a major obstacle to the sustainable return of IDPs. Monitoring allowed UNHCR to map the roads and communities where these problems were most prevalent. After raising this concern with local authorities and the UN Operation in Côte d'Ivoire (ONUCI), the checkpoints that had been identified as most problematic were removed, and UN peacekeepers increased their patrols in villages where abuse by armed elements had been reported by UNHCR monitors. UNHCR has also used monitoring data to design and implement protection and human rights training for the country's armed forces.

In some cases, protection information can be obtained from ongoing assistance projects. For example, in Colombia, UNHCR has provided legal aid to IDPs for over a decade through local partners in the Red de Derecho y Desplazamiento (the Law and Displacement Network). These partners are present in 13 locations in Colombia including those with the highest concentration of IDPs. Analysis of the kind of complaints that IDPs bring to the legal aid centres showed that in numerous cases, authorities were interpreting the definition of IDPs restrictively, when deciding whether to include individuals in the national IDP registry. In Colombia, being left out of this registry has a negative impact on eligibility for humanitarian assistance, housing and income generating projects, and access to basic services. UNHCR shared its analysis with the Colombian Constitutional Court. The Court used this data in a series of rulings concerning how the IDP definition should be applied.

Protection monitoring is vital for informing humanitarian interventions. At the same time, since monitoring is often carried out in areas prone to violence, it can involve serious risks. IDPs and monitors alike may face retribution from alleged perpetrators or rejection within their communities. Thus, protection monitoring systems must incorporate measures to minimize risks to monitors and affected populations according to the principle of 'do no harm'. When this principle is respected, protection monitoring can be an essential mechanism to give voice to populations displaced by violence or natural disasters. ◆

BOX 5•5

The strength of local capacities in Mindanao

'The wars forced us out of our homes three times in seven years. After the third time, we decided to take matters into our own hands', said Adela Nayal, a 70-year-old woman from the municipality of Pikit on the Philippine island of Mindanao, pointing to the dilapidated house she was forced to vacate in 2000.

Mindanao is the southernmost island of the Philippines archipelago. It is bigger than Sri Lanka, has a population of 21 million, and has been a battleground since the sixteenth century, when Spanish settlers fought the local Moro residents—an ethno-linguistic community of 13 tribes practising Islam. Since the late 1970s, well-organized armed groups renewed their call for a free Moro State (Bangsamoro). The resulting conflict is one of the world's longest running civil wars, even if it is relatively unknown. It has led to the loss of thousands of lives and the displacement of hundreds of thousands of people.

The municipality of Pikit in central Mindanao is one of the most impoverished in the Philippines. It was a critical battleground between the government and rebel forces of the Moro Islamic Liberation Front (MILF) during the conflicts of 1997, 2000, 2003 and 2008. Over 40,000 people were displaced in the Pikit municipality in 2000 alone, and fractures between the Muslim and Christian communities grew.

UNHCR began its engagement in Mindanao in 2010 in the context of a renewed effort by all parties to reach a peaceful settlement, and in recognition of the increasing vulnerability that displaced communities were facing.

Working closely with local NGOs and communities, UNHCR was struck by the resolve of local people to find ways to mitigate the effects of war. UNHCR began supporting communities in their efforts to prevent new displacement and to find solutions for those who were already displaced.

One successful community-based initiative has taken place in Pikit. Following the 2000 conflict, Adela together with a small multi-faith team began a series of dialogues on establishing a 'culture of peace' in their war-affected community. They met with the military, rebels, religious leaders, community organizations, farmers' associations, and even with local children and youth to discuss how to protect their community from and during conflict. On 4 February 2002, the local communities declared that the village of Nalapaan would be respected as a 'zone of peace'— an area where none of the parties would fight. On 29 November 2004, this zone was expanded to cover six additional villages.

With the exception of a few minor violations, the zone of peace has been respected by all parties to the conflict. The ground rules are simple and rarely need to be enforced. While armed personnel are not prevented from entering the zone, they are required to respect the community and are not permitted to conduct military operations or to use their weapons. 'Culture of peace' trainings are conducted frequently by the residents for school children, visitors as well as military and rebel forces residing near the zone. UNHCR has assisted Adela and her team to establish peer-to-peer contacts with other conflict-affected communities in Mindanao that want to create zones of peace of their own.

It is becoming evident that low-cost solutions developed by local communities are often more easily accepted, and can offer better protection, than larger-scale 'textbook' approaches frequently adopted by international agencies. Visitors from 80 countries including Bangladesh, Colombia, Sri Lanka, Timor-Leste and Uganda have visited Adela's community to learn more about how the zone of peace was established and how it is maintained.

Women play a critical role in these initiatives. 'Men in our community are viewed with suspicion by the rebels and the army, so we women often lead negotiations and maintain good relations with all parties all the time,' explained one Muslim woman. In another instance, the women of an indigenous Moro community declared a 'sex strike'—withholding sex until their spouses peacefully resolved a local conflict. In still other cases, UNHCR has assisted communities to petition the authorities to re-establish water, education, and healthcare facilities in their villages so they can return.

The key lesson learned from these experiences is that local communities have tremendous capacity, and creative abilities, to create a protective environment. UNHCR will continue to support and nurture this capacity. ◆

A second category of protection activities addresses *lack of physical access* to goods and essential services such as food, water and sanitation, shelter, health and education. Actions aim at removing legal or practical barriers to these goods and services as well as securing access for humanitarian actors to areas where IDPs are in need. For instance, this category would encompass the organization of food distribution and communal kitchens in a way that ensures that women, children, persons with disabilities, and older persons are able to get their share. It would include advocacy with authorities to allow IDP children to go to school even if they do not have a birth certificate or other documents, or intervention with health and social service providers to help rape survivors even if they have no money to pay for services.

A third category of activities addresses the *lack of possibilities for IDPs to exercise their rights*. This includes measures to strengthen IDPs' capacities in this respect, improving the provision of information to IDPs and their consultation and participation in decisions affecting them. It addresses the lack of effective remedies against violations of IDP rights, including access to courts and reparation for violations. This can be as simple as providing bus fare allowing victims to travel to appear in court. Humanitarian organizations may provide free legal aid to IDPs; advocate with the justice system to investigate and prosecute human rights violations committed against IDPs; or support competent authorities in issuing birth certificates, identity cards and other personal documentation.

Finally, there is a category of protection activities which addresses *discrimination* against certain IDPs, and includes steps aimed at ensuring that people are not singled out for harm, unable to assert their rights, or otherwise disadvantaged because of their race, ethnicity, sex, language, religion, political or other opinion, national or social origin, property, disability, birth, age or similar status, including the fact of having been displaced.

As the examples show, protection activities may aim at responding to ongoing violations of the rights of IDPs, providing remedies for violations that have already occurred or preventing future violations by building an environment conducive to full respect of the rights of the internally displaced.

Durable solutions: restoring the rights of IDPs

ENDING DISPLACEMENT

From a protection perspective, finding lasting solutions that bring an end to internal displacement is essential and an important form of reparation for the rights violations suffered by IDPs. Helping people to rebuild their shattered lives, however, is a difficult and complex process. Simply returning to one's former home, or taking the decision to remain and settle where one was displaced, does not mean that the problems caused by displacement are automatically solved. Return, for instance, does not necessarily mean that IDPs are able to reclaim their property, live in safety, re-establish livelihoods allowing for self-sufficiency, or avoid discrimination.

For these reasons, the humanitarian community has considered that displacement does not end with return, but only when former IDPs no longer have displacement-specific needs—that is, needs they would not have if they had not been displaced.[38] Thus,

BOX 5•6

Ending displacement in northern Uganda

More than 1.8 million people were displaced in northern Uganda during the brutal 20-year conflict between the government and the Lord's Resistance Army (*LRA, see box 1.3*). At the peak of the displacement, 251 sites were gazetted as IDP camps in northern Uganda.

The 2006 Cessation of Hostilities Agreement between Uganda and the LRA brought improvements in security and humanitarian access to affected populations. Although sporadic LRA incursions from the DRC continued in 2008 and 2009, the Agreement marked the start of IDP returns from the congested camps to transit sites closer to home and ultimately, for the majority, back to their villages of origin.

The challenge of mass returns

UNHCR scaled back its programme of assistance to IDPs in Uganda in December 2011, as the vast majority had returned home, even though a final peace deal had not been signed between Uganda and the LRA.

By end 2011, only some 30,000 IDPs still lived in four remaining camps or at transit sites close to their land. In some cases, further returns are dependent on the resolution of issues related to inter-clan land conflicts, the presence of minefields, fear of raids by Kari-mojong warriors, or the occupation of land in return areas by the army.

After such a long conflict, and such long-term displacement, the process of return presented major challenges. Infrastructure, community resources, and coping capacities in northern Uganda had been severely depleted. Returnees needed essential services such as safe water, health centres, and schools. Disputes arose over land entitlements, the most valuable resource in an agrarian economy, and the rule of law needed strengthening.

Displacement and return also disrupted many features of traditional life in northern Uganda. Prior to their displacement, families had lived scattered across great distances, relied almost entirely on farming, and cared attentively for their elders and vulnerable family members. But especially in the initial stage of returns, as IDPs were struggling to re-establish their livelihoods, vulnerable family members were often left behind in the camps, where it was easier for them to receive assistance. This explains why many of those remaining in camps are categorized as 'extremely vulnerable' people, including elderly and disabled individuals, or others with special needs.

Promoting durable solutions

Uganda's National Policy for Internally Displaced Persons, adopted in 2004, commits the government to promote the right of IDPs to return voluntarily to their homes or places of habitual residence, or to settle in another part of the country. Starting in 2006, UNHCR and other UN agencies worked to fill critical gaps in services to facilitate IDP returns, building or rebuilding primary schools, health centres, police outposts, access roads and other facilities.

Aware that physical returns do not automatically resolve all problems created by displacement, the UN agencies, local authorities and civil society organizations undertook a durable solutions assessment in 2010. A household survey was used to evaluate achievement of eight conditions outlined in the IASC Framework for Durable Solutions for Internally Displaced Persons, and to determine whether IDPs continued to have needs specifically linked to their displacement, or if they faced challenges that could result in renewed displacement.

Overall, the assessment found that the majority of former IDPs no longer had protection and assistance needs that were directly related to their displacement, with the no-

finding durable solutions is a gradual process which can take three forms: (i) return with sustainable reintegration in the place of origin, (ii) sustainable local integration in the area to which IDPs were displaced, or (iii) sustainable settlement and integration in another part of the country.

In 2009, the Inter-Agency Standing Committee adopted a 'Framework on Durable Solutions for Internally Displaced Persons' which stresses that this process can only be effective if IDPs are able to make an informed and voluntary choice about which solution to pursue, and can participate in the planning and management of durable solutions. The Framework sets out four conditions necessary for IDPs to achieve a durable solution: (i) long-term safety, security and freedom of movement; (ii) an adequate standard of living, including adequate food, water, housing, health care and basic education; (iii) access to

table exception of land-related disputes. It also found that most had chosen to return home, with 97 per cent of respondents confirming that they had been able to opt for the solution they wanted, although government support was only available for returns.

Still, the assessment identified significant unmet needs among the returnees as well as critical development challenges.

First, it pointed out that safety and secu-

In preparation for returning home, IDPs in Oyam (northern Uganda) dismantle their former dwellings.

rity were fragile in areas of return. The returnees perceived that their safety had improved overall, and that the general security situation did not adversely affect their routine activities. But numerous unresolved conflicts were reported between clans and between individuals. Increased sexual and gender-based violence was also reported, often linked to alcohol abuse. Moreover, a majority of respondents feared that security

could deteriorate if the LRA returned. The lack of a clear system of transitional justice for human rights violations committed during the conflict posed a further challenge.

Second, the assessment found that land disputes were the most common cause of tension, and formal legal mechanisms were often inadequate to deal with land issues arising in the context of such rapid and massive returns.

Third, basic services which had been (continued on page 140)

employment and livelihoods; and (iv) access to effective mechanisms that restore their housing, land and property or provide them with compensation.[39]

This is a broad framework within which to work toward solutions. In some contexts it has become clear that for IDPs to benefit, without discrimination, from durable solutions they must also be able to replace personal and other documentation; reunite with family members from whom they were separated during displacement; participate in public affairs at all levels on an equal basis with the resident population; and access effective remedies for displacement-related violations.

The Guiding Principles stress that IDPs have the right to a free and informed choice between the options of return, local integration, or settlement in another part of the country. Such choice is not possible without information, consultation and participation of the

BOX 5•6 *(continued from page 139)*

destroyed during the conflict remained limited in areas of return. Many communities continued to face difficulties in having access to clean water, health care and education. Some returnees even travelled back to camps and former camps to benefit from basic services.

Fourth, most people considered themselves unable, or barely able, to make a living. Almost half of the sample considered that their livelihood situation was worse than before displacement. The overwhelming majority of those polled relied on farming as their main source of income, but most only produced enough for subsistence, pointing to lack of capacity to buy livestock and farm in-

puts. In general, northern Uganda remained poorer than other parts of the country, with insufficient food production and heavy reliance on seasonal rains.

With this backdrop, UNHCR redoubled its efforts to promote durable solutions, through local capacity building and sensitization, mobile legal assistance clinics, and protection monitoring in the remaining IDP camps. It also provided basic integration assistance in return areas and support to help persons with specific needs remaining in camps and transit centres to find durable solutions.

Supporting government efforts

UNHCR had established its presence in

northern Uganda in June 2006 to help the government to cope with the displacement crisis. The previous year, Uganda had been identified as one of six pilot countries for implementation of the Cluster Approach in the context of the UN's humanitarian reform. UNHCR was tasked with leading two clusters at district level: the Protection Cluster and the Camp Coordination and Camp Management Cluster.

In October 2007, the government set out the Peace, Recovery and Development Plan for northern Uganda. Its objectives were to consolidate state authority; rebuild and empower communities; revitalize the economy; and build peace and reconciliation.

UNHCR/P. TAGGART/OCTOBER 2008

displaced. Often, however, IDPs are forced to go back to their former homes, sometimes prematurely, because support is exhausted or terminated prematurely at the site of displacement, or because governments are eager to present a return to normality. In other cases, refugee status or temporary or subsidiary protection for persons who sought refuge abroad is revoked and they 'are forced to return home without conditions or programmes in place for their reintegration, thus leading to situations where returned persons end up in protracted internal displacement.'[40]

▲ **An internally displaced woman in Tbilisi, Georgia,** who fled the conflict in Abkhazia during the nineties.

This provided a framework within which all partners could work constructively. However, the government and international partners did not start to implement recovery programmes until 2009, and their full impact was yet to be felt in 2011. A review conducted that year by the authorities found that law and order as well as trust in government had been strengthened, and that service delivery and infrastructure were improving, but conflict drivers such as land disputes, youth unemployment, and reintegration of ex-combatants still needed attention.

In 2010, all humanitarian coordination functions were handed over to the government, after the last year of implementation in Uganda of the UN's 'cluster' system and phasing out of the UN Consolidated Appeal Process for the country. The efforts of district local governments, working with humanitarian agencies and war-affected communities, were considered decisive for improving conditions in the region. Uganda's Human Rights Commission took the lead responsibility for IDP protection at the central and regional levels. UNHCR and its partners from the former Protection Cluster have worked to strengthen the capacity of the Human Rights Commission.

Continued actions to help returned IDPs have been integrated into the government's long-term development and recovery programmes. The UN is working with development partners to ensure a common understanding of the peacebuilding gaps and of priorities for intervention. The 2010–2014 United Nations Development Assistance Framework for Uganda (UNDAF) supports the government's priorities. International financial institutions and bilateral donors are funding recovery and development in northern Uganda.

At both national and international levels, UNHCR continues to encourage support to maintain the sustainability of returns in Uganda, helping to end one of Africa's longest-standing displacement crises. ◆

THE POLITICS OF PROTRACTED DISPLACEMENT

In at least 40 countries people have lived in internal displacement for more than five, ten or even 15 years. All too often, they remain socially and economically marginalized, with a standard of living of the non-displaced poor.[41] This happens where conflicts are frozen or processes to find durable solutions have stalled. In such situations many IDPs live in inhumane conditions, have no realistic chance of earning a living, and their children are excluded from proper education. In short, their human rights, in particular their economic, social and cultural rights, are not respected. This is particularly true in countries where keeping IDPs in limbo is part of a deliberate policy motivated by the conviction that if they are allowed to integrate in their place of displacement, they will never return home, or the belief that showing their suffering to the world will push the international community to put pressure on the other side of an ongoing or frozen conflict.

In reality, however, allowing IDPs to live normal lives does not limit or undermine their right to return. Rather, people who are able to regain control of their lives and become self-sufficient are in a much stronger position eventually to achieve a durable solution, including return, than are people who remain dependent on outside aid or become a burden to local communities. Policies aimed at keeping people in limbo for years or even decades cannot be justified. Protection in situations of protracted displacement means advocating to improve the living conditions of all IDPs and to integrate them into the mainstream of society, even while they wait for the opportunity to return home.

Protracted displacement can also be a consequence of the failure of governments and the international community to invest in rebuilding areas destroyed by conflict or natural disasters. As has been noted in the case of returning refugees, a transition from humanitarian assistance to development interventions is often missing; food aid, health and other services to IDPs are phased out while the necessary reconstruction of infrastructure,

BOX 5.7

International advocacy
and national policy in Georgia

At the end of 2011, around six per cent of Georgia's population of roughly 4.7 million were internally displaced, or some 274,000 people. This large-scale displacement crisis arose from still unresolved conflicts over Abkhazia and South Ossetia which took place in two phases—first in the early 1990s and again in August 2008.

From the early 1990s on, the government tried to address the most urgent needs of the displaced population, and arranged for about half of them to be provisionally accommodated in collective centres. This housing was intended to be short-term, as most of the displaced hoped to be able to return soon to their homes.

As time went on, however, and without a political agreement which would allow for return, despair mounted among the displaced. Most of the collective centres housing IDPs were located in remote parts of the country with few opportunities for employment. Conditions in many of the centres were deplorable, and there was a lack of investment in maintenance and repair. From a socio-economic point of view, the IDPs had become marginalized citizens who had few prospects for integration in the places where they were living. Although the international community initially provided considerable financial support, interest in Georgia's IDP problem progressively waned.

UNHCR strongly encouraged the government to develop a longer-term strategy to improve the living conditions of the displaced. It urged the authorities to enable the IDPs to become self-sufficient in their new places of residence, while maintaining the goal of dignified and safe return to their

homes. The Representative of the UN Secretary-General on the Human Rights of IDPs (RSG) supported this approach. In 2006, a State Commission was established and, after a year of intensive work, a State Strategy on IDPs was adopted. UNHCR, the RSG and members of the international community cooperated with Georgia on the development of this strategy, which provided an opportunity for frank analysis of the plight of the IDPs.

Although the State Strategy was intended to enable IDPs to find solutions pending return, some in the Georgian government remained hesitant to translate it into action. It quickly became redundant, when a new round of conflict broke out in August 2008 and triggered a second wave of displacement. Paradoxically, this crisis also opened a window of opportunity, as international donors showed renewed willingness to help Georgia to address the needs of its internally displaced.

A joint UN/World Bank assessment was completed immediately in September 2008, looking at the situation of the newly displaced as well as those from the earlier conflicts. This helped to mobilize fresh donor support. The government prepared an updated, comprehensive Action Plan for the Implementation of the State Strategy on IDPs, in cooperation with key donors, Georgian civil society, the RSG, UNHCR, and IDPs themselves. This plan was adopted in December 2008.

The focus of the Action Plan was on housing, mostly the rehabilitation and privatization of collective centres, but it also opened up the possibility for international agencies and NGOs to engage in other sectors, under the leadership of UNHCR, to support the integration of IDPs in their places of residence.

UNHCR seized this opportunity and launched a set of pilot projects under the label 'Shelter Plus', combining housing solutions with income-generating activities. The government recognized that while the provision of durable housing is essential, other dimensions of integration, such as access to education, social and medical services and above all to livelihood opportunities, must be addressed as well.

Experience in Georgia shows the importance of partnerships. It was decisive to bring together all interested parties—the RSG, international NGOs, Georgian civil society, donors, Georgia's Ombudsman, UNHCR, and representatives of the IDPs themselves—to communicate consolidated messages and to offer concrete help. Looking ahead to the extension of the government's Action Plan into 2012–2014, there is an opportunity not only to review the approach to housing solutions, but also to decentralize services for IDPs, improve lines of communication between the government and IDPs, and develop integration efforts further.

At the same time, the plight of Georgia's displaced has been kept in focus in the context of wider peacebuilding efforts. 'International Discussions' on Georgia started in October 2008, in accordance with the August 2008 ceasefire agreement. These discussions, convened in Geneva, are co-chaired by the UN, the European Union, and the Organization for Security and Co-operation in Europe. A Working Group on displaced persons and refugees was set up in the context of these discussions, with UNHCR as co-chair. This has provided a forum at which UNHCR has consistently worked to promote respect for the rights of Georgia's displaced people. ◆

institutions and investment in livelihood opportunities is insufficient or absent. One author has noted that IDPs 'who may have received generous humanitarian assistance at the height of a humanitarian crisis are often forgotten as soon as the guns fall silent or the flood waters recede' and 'enter a vicious cycle of dependency on aid and protracted displacement' because of the absence of interventions aimed at re-establishing livelihoods and basic services, and 'a failure of the donor community to adequately fund early recovery strategies and activities'.[42]

In Georgia, the government's policy since the early 1990s was seen as contributing to the social and economic dependency of IDPs, making local integration difficult.[43] However, in 2007, the government endorsed a new strategy aimed at enabling IDPs to integrate into mainstream society while upholding the option of return (*see box 5.7*).

In summary, there is a need for robust efforts to restore the economic, social, and cultural rights of IDPs, and to end their marginalization. While progress has been made in recent years in a number of countries, this will have to remain high on the agenda of UNHCR and other humanitarian organizations.

Future prospects

Situations of internal displacement are very volatile, and the overall number of internally displaced people remains alarmingly high. At any given moment, return movements and new displacements are occurring, sometimes even within the same country. Despite the many challenges, there are clear opportunities for enhancing action on behalf of IDPs and many positive developments have taken place.

The growing recognition of the importance of protecting IDPs is encouraging, as evidenced by the adoption of national laws and policies, as well as regional instruments. In particular, the commitment of African states to the Kampala Convention provides a unique opportunity to strengthen domestic protection capacities. The recent trend toward improved living conditions for IDPs in protracted displacement in countries such as Azerbaijan, Bosnia and Herzegovina , Georgia and or Serbia is encouraging as well.

Continued efforts are needed to reinforce the response of national institutions and international actors, including UNHCR, to internal displacement. The relief-to-development gap needs to be narrowed, and the politics of protracted displacement overcome. Making perpetrators of arbitrary displacement accountable and providing restorative justice for their victims deserves more attention. Since most IDPs do not live in camps or collective shelters, governments and the humanitarian community need to be better prepared to identify, assist, and protect IDPs living outside camps, including in urban areas, and to support their needy hosts. Finally, the prospect of climate change and the potential for large-scale internal displacement triggered by its effects (*see chapter 7*), raises questions about the operational and financial capacities of the humanitarian system. Continued solidarity at the community, national and international levels remains vital to address all of these challenges. ■

CHAPTER 6

Urbanization and Displacement

A S THE WORLD HAS URBANIZED, SO TOO HAVE PATTERNS OF DISPLACEMENT. Increasingly, refugees, returnees, and the internally displaced are not living in camps, where UNHCR has long experience designing and implementing programmes to meet their needs, but in urban areas. They typically stay in impoverished and crowded neighbourhoods where governments already struggle to provide basic services, and where there is often resentment at the presence of migrants and refugees.

In September 2009, UNHCR adopted a new policy on Refugee Protection and Solutions in Urban Areas to take account of these realities.[1] In December 2009, the High Commissioner devoted his annual Dialogue on Protection Challenges to the topic of refugees and other people of concern to UNHCR living in urban areas.[2] A key aim was to foster cooperation with new partners who have not been among UNHCR's traditional interlocutors, and first and foremost with municipalities. At the Dialogue, the High Commissioner made a commitment to evaluate UNHCR's programmes for refugees in a number of cities, and progressively to implement the new policy worldwide.[3]

It is difficult to know the precise number of refugees who live in urban areas. Many have stayed in cities for years without coming to the attention of UNHCR or other agencies. Information collected to date suggests that the long-held assumption that refugees and displaced people in cities are predominantly single young men is not correct. These populations also include many women, children and older people, some in highly vulnerable circumstances. However, it is often easier for men to have access to government or UNHCR offices, and they tend to be more vocal about their needs and thus more visible. Women, the elderly, unaccompanied children and persons with disabilities are easily overlooked.[4]

◀ **IDPs walking** to a UNHCR-supported learning centre in Soacha, Colombia.

Like their often equally impoverished neighbours, refugees and displaced people frequently struggle to survive in cities.[5] Providing aid to them and to their host communities may resemble development activities more than the traditional task of protecting, feeding, and sheltering refugees living in camps. Moreover, it can be challenging to manage the expectations of urban dwellers knowledgeable about their rights, but not necessarily

Changing policy and practice in Delhi

India hosts sizeable refugee populations in both rural and urban areas, although the country is not a party to the 1951 Refugee Convention or its 1967 Protocol. In recent years, the population of concern to UNHCR in India's capital city has grown more diverse, and UNHCR has sought to apply its new Policy on Refugee Protection and Solutions in Urban Areas.

In late 2011, refugees and asylum seekers in Delhi numbered around 22,000, including some 11,000 Afghans, 10,000 Myanmarese, and around 1,000 Somalis and others. Afghans seeking protection have been allowed to enter India over several decades, and, once recognized as refugees by UNHCR, they have been permitted to remain. Many come from urban backgrounds and are relatively well settled, especially the Sikhs and Hindus among them. The Myanmarese, who are mainly ethnic Chin from a rural background, face a wider range of problems—from poverty to discrimination to gender-based violence. Somali refugees encounter additional marginalization and face the greatest difficulties.

While India has no national legislative framework pertaining to refugees, asylum seekers and refugees are in principle protected under Article 21 of India's Constitution, which upholds the right to life and applies equally to citizens and non-nationals. Refugees and asylum seekers are allowed access to public services, and many are able to find work in the informal sector.

However, without specific legal measures, the overall situation of asylum seekers and refugees in urban areas remains precarious, and they may be affected by acts of racism and xenophobia. Delhi's Afghan and Myanmarese refugees are able to apply for residence permits, issued at the government's discretion, for periods of a year or two; but Somalis and other refugee groups are not entitled to apply for them. More broadly, the situation of refugees in Delhi contrasts with that of much larger numbers of Tibetan and Sri Lankan refugees who receive direct protection and assistance from the government in rural areas.

UNHCR's involvement with refugees in Delhi dates back to 1981, when the agency re-established its presence in India after a five-year absence, and responded to an influx of refugees following the Soviet invasion of Afghanistan in 1979. At that time, UNHCR mainly provided Afghan refugees in the city with a monthly subsistence allowance. Ten years later, the UNHCR programme in Delhi assisted some 26,000 Afghans and 80 per cent of the programme's budget was spent on subsistence allowances.

The situation changed in 1993, after UNHCR conducted a survey of the Afghan refugees in Delhi to identify those who were—or could become—self-sufficient, and to identify the most vulnerable Afghans for whom continued support was essential. Most long-stayers who were assessed to be self-reliant had their subsidies terminated,

---

about the constraints which limit the protection and material assistance UNHCR can provide. 'It is not the kind of work the global refugee system is comfortable with', one observer has noted.[6]

The presence of refugees, IDPs and returnees in cities is part and parcel of the global process of urbanization. In some cases it is accelerating urbanization, while also transforming the composition of populations of cities.[7] People who move to urban areas for protection-related reasons frequently choose not to return to rural areas, even if security there has improved. The presence of IDPs in urban areas of Darfur highlights this phenomenon. In northwest Pakistan, many IDPs are abandoning rural life. The same is true of returning refugees in various countries. Evidence from repatriation programmes for Afghan and Sudanese refugees shows that returnees gravitate towards urban areas, either because they have become accustomed to urban life while in exile or because they have no land to which to return.[8] The same phenomenon has been observed in West Africa and elsewhere.

Displacement can exacerbate the phenomenon of 'urban primacy'—the concentration of a significant proportion of the national population in one city. There are many examples of cities whose rapid growth has been driven, at least in part, by influxes of refugees, returnees and internally displaced people. Demographic data is incomplete, but such

a decision that was not received without tensions.

In 1995, India joined UNHCR's Executive Committee, and in recent years UNHCR has strengthened its cooperation with India, as an important global partner. UNHCR and India have held high-level bilateral consultations since 2008, and the High Commissioner made official visits in 2006 and 2009.

In the absence of national laws on refugee status in India, UNHCR continues to take on the responsibility for determining whether asylum seekers in Delhi qualify for protection as refugees under UNHCR's mandate. The agency has invested in strengthening the efficiency and quality of its registration, identification, and determination systems. The government respects UNHCR's decisions, and recognizes the documents it issues to refugees and asylum seekers.

In line with its new urban refugee policy, UNHCR also promotes access for refugees to mainstream public services provided by the government. Despite their entitlement, refugees and asylum seekers in Delhi often find it difficult to use services such as health care and education, without special guidance and language support. UNHCR and its partners encourage primary and secondary schools to accept refugees and asylum seekers, and provide 'bridge lessons' and tuition support. Similarly, UNHCR has worked with partners to provide counselling and translation services, in order to enable refugees and asylum seekers to use public health facilities. UNHCR has also established refugee centres in various local communities in Delhi, so that refugees have support services—such as childcare, training, and counselling—in areas where they live.

At the same time, UNHCR advocates on behalf of the refugees with government authorities and civil society organizations. The agency's efforts to raise awareness among the city's police, for example, encouraged refugees to turn to law enforcement authorities to intervene with unscrupulous landlords or when faced with other problems.

Given the protracted nature of the conflicts in the refugees' countries of origin, prospects for voluntary repatriation remain limited, and resettlement is only available for very small numbers. UNHCR has therefore invested in promoting refugee self-reliance, working with partner organizations to support employment programmes, including vocational training and job placement, as well as innovative 'production centres' where refugees make clothes and other items for sale.

Self-reliance remains difficult for the refugees who have to vie for jobs in the informal sector along with hundreds of thousands of Indian migrants who move from the countryside to the capital city every year. Refugees tend to earn very low wages that do not cover their basic needs, including the city's high rent and transport costs. Similarly, retail items produced by refugees have to compete on Delhi's high-quality low-price market, and refugee entrepreneurs have no official access to credit. Qualified professionals, mainly Somalis and Afghans, have even fewer prospects, since they are not allowed to work in the formal sector.

In Delhi, as elsewhere, implementation of UNHCR's new policy on protection and assistance for refugees living in urban areas remains a work-in-progress. Offering a formal legal status and work permits for urban refugees would constitute a valuable step forward. ◆

cities include Abidjan, Bogotá, Johannesburg, Juba, Kabul, Karachi, Khartoum, Luanda, Monrovia, Nairobi, and Sana'a. Whole regions may become urbanized as a result of protracted displacement. For example, IDP camps—once located on the outskirts of Darfur towns—have been absorbed into agglomerations.[9]

The specificities of providing protection and assistance to refugees sheltering in cities are such that UNHCR must develop new ways of working and new partnerships. In particular, UNHCR needs to advocate effectively for refugees' access to mainstream services. Yet often the agency lacks interlocutors among municipal authorities, police, regulators of market and labour practices, health and education administrations, and other service providers. A particular challenge arises because many cities with large refugee populations are in states that have not acceded to the 1951 Refugee Convention, or which do not implement refugee status determination processes. Where such systems do exist, they may be strained by high numbers, which can create administrative backlogs.

This chapter looks at the challenges of recalibrating UNHCR's policy and programme delivery to respond to urban displacement. While the focus of the chapter is on refugees, much of its content is also applicable to internally displaced people (IDPs) living in urban areas, as well as to former refugees who have returned to cities and towns in their countries of origin.

Evolution of UNHCR's urban refugee policy

UNHCR FIRST FORMULATED A POLICY ON URBAN REFUGEES IN 1997. That policy acknowledged the right to freedom of movement under international law, but implied that flows of refugees to cities were undesirable, and regarded the movement of refugees out of camps as 'irregular'. Reflecting the priority given at that time to camp settings, it warned about the high cost of helping refugees in urban areas. Refugee advocacy groups, and even UNHCR staff, were critical of the 1997 policy. UNHCR evaluations noted that its implementation was inconsistent, and that it often had damaging effects on populations of concern.[10]

Confronted with growing numbers of urban refugees and facing mounting pressure to respond to their needs, UNHCR in 2009 forged a new set of operating principles. The title itself–UNHCR Policy on Refugee Protection and Solutions in Urban Areas–signalled a fresh approach. The policy is rights-based and refugee-respecting, and recognizes the need for UNHCR staff to revisit old assumptions and to acquire new skills. It commits the agency to advocate for the expansion of 'protection space' for refugees living in cities. The notion of 'protection space' does not have a legal definition; it is used by UNHCR to denote the extent to which an environment exists which is conducive for the internationally recognized rights of refugees to be respected and their needs met.

The policy emphasizes that UNHCR's mandated responsibilities towards refugees are universal and do not depend on a refugee's place of residence. In particular, it stresses the importance of recognizing that refugees have different needs and capacities, depending on their age, gender, and other characteristics–reflecting the approach known within UNHCR as Age, Gender and Diversity Mainstreaming (*see box 0.1*).

The following table was prepared in 2007 by the UNHCR Office in Nairobi, Kenya. It encapsulates in clear terms some of the thinking about refugees and internally

PREVIOUS ASSUMPTIONS	NEW ASSUMPTIONS
Urban refugees tend to be single young men.	Urban refugees are a very diverse population, including women and men, girls and boys, and people with a variety of specific needs.
Urban refugees are passive; they are waiting for UNHCR to solve their problems.	Urban refugees have developed a variety of coping mechanisms to protect themselves and establish livelihoods in urban settings.
Urban refugees want resettlement and use manipulative behaviour to get it.	While resettlement is attractive, many refugees have built their lives and communities in the country of asylum.
Urban refugees may be aggressive, meaning UNHCR staff must take additional security precautions when visiting refugee communities.	Urban refugees welcome interaction with UNHCR staff in their own communities, and it is generally safe to visit them using the usual precautions for an urban environment.
UNHCR already knows everything it needs to know about urban refugees.	UNHCR can use multiple sources of information, including mapping, indicators, and community work, to learn about refugee communities in greater depth, giving particular attention to persons who may not approach the office regularly.
Urban refugees come to UNHCR if they have problems.	Many of the most vulnerable refugees are unable to approach the office at all, while others approach UNHCR infrequently.

displaced people in urban areas which led to adoption of the new policy. [11]

Refugee camps are often in remote locations, reflecting in some cases the desire of governments to concentrate refugees in one or several areas, and to keep them isolated from local society. In camp environments, determining the numbers and needs of refugees is relatively straightforward, and particularly vulnerable people can be identified and given supplementary assistance. Operational partnerships with NGOs and state agencies have been fine-tuned over the years for work in refugee camps. Apart from some dramatic exceptions, the humanitarian community for the most part can muster the resources and meet the basic needs of refugees when they are clustered in camps.

In cities, however, humanitarian actors must develop new methodologies to identify people in need and provide services to them. Refugees are often hidden among populations who live in marginalized urban settlements—an estimated one billion people worldwide. In some contexts, UNHCR's action is constrained by state policies that oblige refugees to remain in camps, and at times criminalize their presence outside them. Distinguishing persons of concern to UNHCR from migrants in urban areas can be difficult, and both categories of people may wish to keep a low profile.

Despite these challenges, UNHCR has begun to recalibrate its operations towards urban areas. Like other humanitarian agencies, it is beginning to develop ways to identify and support vulnerable refugees and IDPs in urban areas, and to advocate for governments to recognize their presence and protect their rights. UNHCR's new policy highlights the importance of identifying refugees in urban areas who would otherwise remain 'invisible', and addressing the reasons for their non-identification: fear of detention or deportation; fear of mistreatment by host communities; perceptions that registration offers no advantages; legal frameworks that blur the distinction between refugees and migrants; and inconsistent interpretation and application of the 1951 Refugee Convention.

UNHCR's experience in responding to the exodus of Iraqi refugees after 2003 played an important role in propelling the agency to formulate and then to implement its new policy for urban refugees. A defining feature of UNHCR's programme in Jordan, Lebanon, and Syria has been its urban dimension. At the height of the displacement, host governments estimated that up to 1.6 million Iraqis had sought refuge in these three countries—nearly all of them in the capital cities of Amman, Beirut and Damascus. Many were urban professionals, some of whom came with substantial personal assets that were rapidly depleted. Others were much less well off, and some were rural people who had not previously lived in an urban environment. UNHCR worked closely with the host government authorities to secure access to state services for the refugees.

Needs assessment, delivery of assistance, and monitoring, can be more costly and time-consuming in urban areas than in refugee camps. Profiling exercises can be politically sensitive and often produce incomplete data, or information that quickly becomes outdated, given the high mobility of urban dwellers. Anecdotal evidence from Jordan and Syria indicated that as their resources were depleted, refugees moved frequently in search of more affordable housing.

The demand for resources to respond to the needs of urban refugees is certain to rise, as UNHCR's new policy calls on staff to be more proactive in identifying refugees living in urban areas and in meeting their needs. While UNHCR now has an updated policy that addresses urban refugees, there is an even greater number of IDPs in urban areas who also require attention.

Protection and assistance in cities

REFUGEES IN URBAN AREAS FACE A WIDE RANGE OF PROTECTION RISKS, OFTEN broader than and distinct from those faced by refugees living in camps. These include: prohibitions on movement and residence; lack of documentation; threat of arrest and detention; harassment; exploitation; hunger; inadequate shelter; limited access to formal health and education systems; vulnerability to sexual and gender-based violence (SGBV) and to HIV/AIDS; and human smuggling and trafficking in persons.

For humanitarian actors trying to address these risks, communicating with refugees living in cities is critically important, but much more difficult than when refugees are confined in camps. Camps often have structures, even if rudimentary, which enable refugee representation and participation. Urban refugees are often preoccupied by the struggle for daily survival and tend to be very mobile. Categories of people of concern can be blurred, for instance, when former refugees return home to situations of internal displacement. Reaching out to refugee women, particularly in cultures where they rarely leave home unaccompanied by a male family member, is especially challenging.

It may also be difficult for refugees to make contact with UNHCR, NGO or government offices. Lack of literacy and education, and absence or weakness of structures to represent refugees, may prevent them from completing administrative paperwork, requesting interviews, or addressing correspondence to UNHCR, the host government, or other actors. Travelling to UNHCR or government offices or to NGOs can be time-consuming and costly for refugees.

At the same time, many urban refugees are well-educated and regularly use the internet. They are aware of their rights, and if access to services is not improved, tensions can mount. Managing large crowds in or around a UNHCR or NGO office, or a government department, can require particular sensitivity, and local police often do not have experience in handling such situations. Struggles over the distribution of scarce resettlement slots can easily dominate the relationship between urban refugees and UNHCR.

Mobilizing financial resources for programmes to benefit refugees in urban areas is a new challenge for UNHCR and its partners. It is often compounded by host government laws and policies which limit refugees' access to work permits and hence their ability to meet at least some of their own needs.

A further problem can be attitudinal: the willingness to 'turn a blind eye' and ignore the existence of urban refugees, even though they are well known or 'hidden in plain view' as a Human Rights Watch report described urban displaced populations in Kampala,

Uganda, and in Nairobi, Kenya.[12] Policy makers may lack administrative frameworks to distinguish refugees and IDPs from other migrants in cities. Some politicians may find it expedient to support local groups who protest the presence of migrants and refugees in their neighbourhoods. Prejudicial terminology is sometimes used by politicians who believe that ascribing social ills to refugees and threatening robust action against them will win votes.

BOX **6·2**

Asylum in Ecuador: spotlight on Quito

Ecuador faces economic problems, one of the highest population densities in Latin America, and the spill-over effects of violence in Colombia. Nonetheless, the country has kept its border open to people seeking international protection. As one of the first countries to incorporate the broader refugee definition recommended by the 1984 Cartagena Declaration into its domestic legislation, Ecuador considers people who have fled their country because their lives, safety, or freedom were threatened by generalized violence, to merit protection as refugees.

In 2011, Ecuador hosted the largest refugee population in Latin America, with some 55,000 recognized refugees and around 20,000 pending asylum applications. Nearly all these refugees and asylum seekers are Colombians. Many more are believed to be living in the country but have not approached the authorities. Ecuador's border areas have been seriously affected by the influx from Colombia, but two-thirds of the refugees move on and live dispersed in urban areas, first and foremost in the capital city, Quito.

To cope with the influx, the government launched an Enhanced Registration Programme, improving access to refugee status determination and documentation through an expedited, mobile one-day process. Since it was launched in 2009, this process has enabled the registration of more than 27,000 refugees and served as the entry point into a system of human rights protection for a highly vulnerable and marginalized population.

Despite steps taken by the central government, refugees face many challenges to enjoying their rights and integrating into local communities. Refugees in Quito and other parts of Ecuador frequently face discrimination, mainly related to stereotypes which many Ecuadorians hold about Colombians. Afro-Colombian refugees residing in Quito often suffer double discrimination. Refugees may have protection risks that go unattended if they are unable, or do not know how, to access local services. This is particularly true for the women and children who make up 70 per cent of the refugee population.

In recent years, in view of the complexity of dealing with large numbers of asylum seekers, refugees and migrants, as well as Ecuadorians returning from abroad, Quito has responded by leading a process of coordination involving local institutions, civil society and church organizations, and UNHCR. This resulted in the adoption of a Municipal Decree to protect the rights of populations in the context of what it terms 'human mobility', allowing for the inclusion of refugees and migrants into social programmes implemented in the poorer neighbourhoods of Quito.

This local legislation represents an important advance for refugee protection, and has set a precedent for other cities in Ecuador. In general, Quito's more than 20,000 refugees live in the city's most marginal areas where basic services such as health, education, and decent housing are limited, despite government efforts to improve them. They face serious difficulties in achieving a minimum level of self-reliance. Stable employment is hard to find, as many refugees lack the right documentation or skills. Many opt for self-employment or take insecure temporary jobs in the informal sector.

Since the Municipal Decree was published, Quito has supported numerous actions to promote the quality of asylum. The Municipality has organized regular seminars on Human Mobility, as a venue for discussion on ways to include refugees in existing social programmes. A Human Mobility Observatory has been set up, to systematize knowledge and information about mobility in the city. UNHCR has supported two 'Human Mobility Houses' in Quito where refugees can receive orientation, legal aid and psychosocial support. The Municipality has supported public awareness campaigns, such as the 'Living together in solidarity' campaign, to explain to the population what it means to be a refugee.

In 2010, the Municipality of Quito, in co-ordination with UNHCR, organized the 'Meeting of Cities of Solidarity: Human Mobility and Asylum', in the framework of the World Forum on Migration which took place in Quito. The Municipality proposed this meeting of Latin American cities to share best practices, experiences and challenges in the application of public policies with respect to the protection of people on the move. Among the subjects discussed were local governments' role in the protection of urban refugees, as well as assistance and integration; mixed migration movements; and prevention and protection of victims of human trafficking and smuggling. The meeting concluded with the adoption of a declaration calling on Latin American cities to recognize the rights of refugees and migrants and address their need to take part in local development projects. ◆

DOCUMENTATION AND FREEDOM OF MOVEMENT

Unlike refugees living in camps, refugees in urban areas are virtually certain to have contact with state actors such as police, local government officials, workplace and marketplace inspectors, or providers of health care, education, electricity and water. For those who are undocumented, fear of contact with agents of the state is often pervasive. Without identity papers or residence permits, it is generally impossible to sign a lease, cash a cheque, receive remittances, obtain credit, travel legally, seek formal employment, or perhaps even to access the internet or have a SIM card.

Undocumented urban refugees are vulnerable to arrest and detention, and to the solicitation of bribes as well as various forms of intimidation to avoid arrest. Births of refugee children may not be registered, and a considerable number of refugee children therefore grow up without proof of identity.

Provision of documents attesting to identity and status can help to prevent and resolve many protection problems. It is the primary responsibility of states to provide refugees with documentation, but in situations where the authorities are unable or unwilling to do so, UNHCR issues its own identification and status documents. In some cases these are recognized by the state, and in others they are not. Documents issued by UNHCR are not necessarily regarded as evidence of entitlement that would allow refugees to move freely or to work.

Article 26 of the 1951 Convention stipulates that Contracting States shall accord to refugees lawfully in their territory the right to choose their place of residence and to move freely within their territory, subject to regulations generally applicable to foreigners. However, states often put policies in place that tightly restrict movement and residence for refugees. For example, a UNHCR evaluation found that restrictions imposed by authorities in Tajikistan made it hard to see how the new urban policy could be implemented there.[13] In Sudan, asylum seekers entering eastern Sudan from Eritrea or Ethiopia are required to lodge their asylum applications in this region, and may not do so in Khartoum.

SHELTER

Displacement to cities frequently results in people squatting on land owned by others. Many refugees and IDPs are forced to settle on peripheral land which is unsuitable for residential development, such as on waste sites; along rivers, canals, roads, or railways; or on steep slopes. In such locations, residents are often exposed to high levels of risk from natural disasters, as well as the problems of living without security of tenure. Unable legitimately to access electricity or water networks, refugees and IDPs, like other equally vulnerable residents, may attempt to connect to these networks illegally.

Housing and property issues present obstacles to solutions for displaced populations wherever they are, but they pose particularly complicated challenges in urban environments. Refugees, IDPs, and returnees must compete in the low-cost housing market but often do not have enough money for a deposit or the necessary local references. Regulations requiring proof of residence or citizenship may restrict access to formal tenancy arrangements. As a result, people of concern to UNHCR are frequently exploited by landlords.

As cities grow, the once-marginal land settled on by the urban poor, including IDPs, refugees, and returnees, may acquire increasing value. The end of conflict that makes refugee returns possible can also lead to inflation of urban land prices, a scramble for available plots, and result in secondary or tertiary displacement. Returning refugees may become IDPs due to property disputes. Urban renewal campaigns and other official eviction programmes can have a dire, and sometimes massive, impact on refugees and IDPs. For example, it has been estimated that 665,000 IDPs were forcibly relocated in Khartoum between 1989 and 2005, and around 700,000 people lost their homes or livelihoods in Harare during Operation Murambatsvina–Operation Restore Order–from 2005.[14]

HEALTH AND NUTRITION

UNHCR's goal in urban settings is for refugees to have access to health services at least on terms equivalent to nationals. Monitoring the health and nutritional status of refugees dispersed across urban areas is much more challenging than if they lived in camps; but, it is clear that refugees in many cities face difficulty obtaining health care. Since refugees often do not have access to government medical facilities, social security systems, or health insurance schemes, they are left dependent on basic services provided by UNHCR and other humanitarian agencies. Access to government health institutions is sometimes only possible if the refugee is accompanied by UNHCR or NGO staff and able to pay for it— whether officially or informally. Provision of medical assistance in government facilities may be limited to short term emergency situations while chronic diseases go untreated, especially among older refugees.

Mental health care is particularly scarce, though the extent of post-traumatic stress disorder among refugees is known to be high. Studies have noted worrisome levels of domestic violence among urban refugees linked to unresolved trauma and loss of traditional family roles, alcoholism, and fractured social relations.[15]

Following adoption of its 2009 urban refugee policy, UNHCR developed a strategy to improve access to health services for urban refugees and other persons of concern. This strategy relies on advocacy, capacity building, monitoring and evaluation of service delivery. Thus, UNHCR advocates on behalf of refugees to ensure that authorities make services available to refugees; supports and strengthens existing national services; and assesses the health status of refugees to ensure their needs are being met. Access to quality primary health care and emergency health services remains the priority for UNHCR and its partners, but more resources are needed to increase the capacity of existing systems.[16]

In camps, there is usually intense scrutiny of the nutritional status of refugees, and at least basic health care is provided by humanitarian agencies. International agencies commit to internationally agreed minimum nutritional standards. Cuts in food entitlements to encamped refugees are often highly visible, and may result in protests from the NGO community and in the media.

In cities, however, hungry refugees can easily go unnoticed. In urban areas, IDPs and refugees rarely receive food support, and those who do may be particularly vulnerable people supported by charitable groups. Knowledge of what urban refugees and IDPs eat and their nutritional status is still very limited. Researchers in Kampala, for example, reported in 2011 that 57 per cent of urban refugee families ate just one meal per day.[17]

Donor and media interest may determine the level of food aid provided. Iraqi refugees in Cairo and in Sana'a, who have attracted less attention than those in Amman and Damascus, have complained that they do not receive food support. Persistent nutritional crises in urban areas do not provoke emergency responses; IDPs in Khartoum have been reported to be worse off than those in the Darfur camps who have attracted considerable international interest. On average, the level of severe malnutrition among IDP children in Khartoum was reported by one study to be 11 times that for Khartoum State as a whole.[18]

LIVELIHOODS

UNHCR and many others use the term 'livelihood' to mean 'the capabilities, assets and activities required for a means of living'.[19] Many humanitarian actors attach priority to promoting livelihoods and fostering self-reliance. Self-reliance refers to the capacity of an individual, household or community to meet basic needs—including food, water, shelter, personal safety, health, and education—in a sustainable manner. UNHCR seeks to develop and strengthen livelihoods for persons of concern in order to reduce their vulnerability and long-term reliance on external or humanitarian assistance.

It is widely acknowledged that the right to work is integral to protection and durable solutions. The right to work is set out in Article 23(1) of the Universal Declaration of Human Rights, as well as in Article 6 of the International Covenant on Economic, Social and Cultural Rights. The 1951 Convention (Articles 17, 18 and 19) guarantees refugees 'favourable treatment' with respect to employment, meaning that they must be treated at least as well as other lawfully-staying foreign nationals regarding their right to participate in wage-earning and self-employment activities.

For urban refugees and returnees, protection and livelihoods are intertwined. In order to pay for food and shelter they must work. A 2009 UNHCR study found that refugees were working illegally in cities in around 100 countries, making them vulnerable to exploitation and abuse.[20] The lack of access to livelihood activities impacts negatively on the sustainable reintegration of returnees and contributes to further displacement.

Most urban refugees get by through entrepreneurial vigour and working in the informal economy, often competing with local people for hazardous and poorly paid manual labour jobs. The qualifications they earned at home are rarely recognized, so that even a highly educated refugee will have no choice but to work in a low-skilled position, perhaps as a street vendor without formal authorization, a taxpayer identification number, or a municipal permit. Urban refugees have little opportunity to receive credit. The great majority struggle to pay for rent, food, transportation, school fees and uniforms for their children, as well as the bribes that are often demanded by officials with whom they interact.

The ability of persons of concern to put their skills and capacities to use depends on the opportunities available to them in their host environment, which in urban areas usually means access to employment opportunities—formal or informal. Urban environments may seem to offer more opportunities to make a living, but the right to work and the achievement of self-reliance remain unattainable for many persons of concern, either owing to restrictive national legislation or to the lack of appropriate skills.

Refugees are not a homogenous group. Their capacities, vulnerability and resilience vary. Therefore, comprehensive livelihood assessments are critical to enable UNHCR and its partners to develop joint planning with key stakeholders.

Advocacy is an important part of livelihoods interventions in urban areas, aimed at addressing policy and legal issues at the national and municipal levels and at increasing refugee access to existing facilities and services, often through partnerships with financial institutions, technical and vocational training providers, social services such as day-care centres, and career counselling or job placement facilities.

EDUCATION

Over the years, considerable attention has been paid to the development of education programmes for refugee children living in camps. For many of those living in cities, however, especially in the developing world, access to education has remained largely a hit-or-miss affair, with many refugee children of primary school age not attending school at all.

UNHCR's priority is to mainstream refugee children into the national education system, with special attention to the basic right to primary education. In many countries, refugee children are able to enrol in local schools. Problems frequently arise, however, when the schools are not able to provide them with learning programmes which enable them to catch up with their local peers and to participate effectively in the classroom.

In some countries, there is no regulatory framework governing the admission of refugee children to state schools. Refugee and displaced children may face discrimination from school administrators or from teachers who do not want them in their classrooms, or harassment and bullying by other students. In some cases, refugee parents may therefore prefer private schools over government schools if they are able to pay the fees.[21]

In Kuala Lumpur, Malaysia, where urban refugees and asylum seekers number around 95,000, refugee children are not allowed to enrol in government schools. To fill this gap, UNHCR has encouraged and assisted the refugee community to provide education for their children. Refugee groups have set up some 90 community schools with support from UNHCR and its 'Adopt a School' programme, which matches willing Malaysian individuals and support groups to a refugee community school. Although UNHCR continues to advocate for refugee children to have access to public schools, which is the preferred option, the community schooling arrangement goes some way to ensuring that children do not fall too far behind in their studies. At the end of 2011, around 5,800 refugee children were enrolled in these refugee-run schools. Schooling also provides a means to bring together refugees and their Malaysian hosts around the shared value of education.

Since adopting its new urban refugee policy in 2009, UNHCR has stepped up its advocacy for refugee children to have access to local educational institutions, and has tried where possible to boost the capacity of schools to admit refugee children and youth. Limited data makes it hard to quantify rates of enrolment, retention, or completion, but UNHCR has set itself targets to raise enrolment and ensure gender parity in environments where data can be obtained.

UNHCR's budget to support urban education activities remains quite modest, even though it has increased considerably in recent years. By way of example, in 2009 only US$40,000 of UNHCR's total education expenditure of US$3.7 million in Kenya was allocated to urban education. In 2011, the urban education budget rose to US$220,000. This is still inadequate but nonetheless represents a five-fold increase. The level of UNHCR support for urban education varies from country to country as a result of funding constraints, the attitudes of national education ministries, and the activities of other UN agencies and NGOs. Funding to support secondary or tertiary education for refugees remains limited and only available in well-resourced operations.

GENDER

Women displaced to cities frequently report that they face sexual and gender-based violence, harassment, and intimidation. In many cities, it appears easier for refugee and displaced women to find employment than for men. This may be explained in part by the nature of the work available, typically as household servants. But it may also be the case that women are often perceived to be at less risk of random arrest and detention. However, domestic employment can expose refugee women to significant risks of exploitation, including sexual abuse.

In some urban settings, refugee women have few choices but to engage in 'survival sex' to support their families.[22] Further, the risk of being trafficked appears to be higher for urban refugee and IDP women than for other women. Some UNHCR urban programmes include the establishment of safe houses for women who are survivors of violence, but it is clear these facilities do not reach all those in need.

In many contexts, the lack of employment opportunities for men and adolescents compounds problems of gender-related violence. In patriarchal societies, the effect of women becoming the sole or principal breadwinner can be destabilizing for men and diminish their self-esteem. There is at least anecdotal evidence from Somali and Iraqi urban refugee communities linking this to an increase in domestic violence. The full extent of this phenomenon and the impact of prolonged periods of idleness and helplessness on men and their sense of masculinity and self-worth remain to be investigated more fully.

Urban refugee men and women consulted by researchers in six cities during 2008–2010 called for more to be done to provide medical care, counselling, and legal support to survivors of sexual and gender-based violence.[23] This was reiterated by participants in the Dialogues with Refugee Women sponsored by UNHCR in seven countries as part of its commemoration of the sixtieth anniversary of the 1951 Refugee Convention in 2011.[24]

UNHCR/A TANNER

The impacts of displaced populations

KNOWLEDGE ABOUT THE IMPACT OF REFUGEES, IDPs, AND RETURNEES IN CITIES remains limited. More effort is needed to understand the relationship between the presence of refugees and displaced people and the prices of food, water and energy, or the impact on labour markets and residential rents. Most analysis to date has focused on the refugees and IDPs themselves, rather than on the impacts of their presence in host communities or the nature of host country concerns.

▲ **IDPs waiting for work**
on a street in Kabul, Afghanistan.

The financial implications of urban refugee and displaced populations are not well understood. There are clearly severe strains on central and local government budgets, but there may also be a tendency to exaggerate these effects to bolster appeals for international assistance. In the absence of empirical information, it is often hard to separate perceptions from reality.

It is clear that displacement processes are transforming the population of many cities. Refugees, IDPs and returnees do not necessarily share the language, culture and ethnic origin of their hosts. Kabul's current population, for the first time in its history, is now highly heterogeneous, unlike much of Afghanistan. Such demographic changes have the potential to exacerbate tensions between communities. In Kampala, for instance, IDPs displaced from northern Uganda have reported discrimination in education and employment, and being called 'Kony'—the leader of the brutal Lord's Resistance Army.[25]

Tension between established city-dwellers and newcomers is a global phenomenon,

BOX 6.3

Refugee outreach workers in Damascus

UNHCR developed new methods for reaching out to Iraqi refugees in Syria's capital city, Damascus, mobilizing refugee women to identify and assist vulnerable fellow refugees living among the city's more than two million inhabitants. The 'Outreach Volunteer Initiative' which started in 2007 is a model which could be replicated in urban settings elsewhere.

The exodus from Iraq

The outflow of refugees from Iraq following the US-led military intervention in 2003 intensified sharply in 2006, reflecting an upsurge in sectarian violence in Iraq. The refugees fled mainly to neighbouring countries, with the largest numbers settling in and around the Damascus and the country's second-largest city, Aleppo. Only some of the refugees came forward to be registered by UNHCR. That number peaked in 2008, by which time UNHCR had registered more than 200,000 Iraqi refugees, or around 55,000 families—mostly in Damascus. Many, but not all, were well-educated and came from urban areas in Iraq, where they had previously held good jobs and enjoyed a relatively high standard of living.

A very large proportion of the refugees had experienced or witnessed egregious acts of violence in Iraq, and suffered emotional and physical consequences. In 2009, more than 30 per cent of the Iraqi refugees registered with UNHCR were assessed as being particularly vulnerable—up to 50 per cent when

medical conditions were included. Many reported having survived torture and/or sexual or gender-based violence in Iraq.

In Syria, the refugees were safe but faced other problems: social isolation, a lack of supportive community structures, shifts in gender roles within families, deterioration in socio-economic status, and deepening poverty. The psycho-social well-being of many refugees was affected, notably men who often expressed feeling 'not useful' any more.

Almost 10 per cent of the families UNHCR registered in Syria reported mental health and psychosocial difficulties, such as symptoms of anxiety, depression, and other mood disorders, as well as physical exhaustion or pain. In some extreme cases, their suffering led them to harm themselves or others. Suicide attempts, child abuse, and other forms of domestic violence were reported.

Adapting to a new situation

Unlike many other situations of mass influx, the refugees were not accommodated in camps. UNHCR had little prior experience in dealing with large populations of refugees in urban areas and no blueprint to follow. The agency struggled to find the best way to make contact with the refugees, determine their needs, understand their intentions, and identify the most needy. Its difficulties in reaching the widely dispersed urban refugee population, combined with an under-resourced psychosocial sector, few NGO part-

ners, and a limited community-based support system, meant that UNHCR's office came under pressure from large crowds of refugees who approached it every day.

Following the International Conference on addressing the humanitarian needs of Iraqi refugees and IDPs convened by the High Commissioner in April 2007 to draw attention to the crisis, international interest grew and UNHCR was able to mobilize substantial resources, rapidly scale up its activities, deploy more staff to the field, and develop innovative programmes to address the specifically urban characteristics of the situation.

One of these innovations was the establishment of a network of outreach volunteers and support groups composed of qualified refugees. Others involved setting up refugee community centres for social and recreational activities, and mass information campaigns addressed to refugees—using mobile phone text messages. UNHCR also opened an ambitious one-stop-shop facility on the outskirts of town, where the diverse needs of refugees could be attended to, from registration to counselling to food distribution.

Reaching out to the most vulnerable

But the most vulnerable refugees did not necessarily come forward for help. UNHCR realized that it would need support from

and not limited to situations where refugees and displaced people are present. Many attacks on urban refugees and IDPs, however, go unreported. The scale of assaults on Zimbabwean migrants and refugees in South Africa in 2008 was unusually well-documented and shortcomings in the response were identified, but this is not always the case in cities where xenophobic violence occurs.[26]

Host governments often assert that refugees are a costly burden on their national resources, push inflation up and put excessive pressure on public services, wages and infrastructure. In some cities there is a widespread belief that newcomers, including refugees,

within the refugee community to make contact with them. The Outreach Volunteers Programme, created in September 2007, was aimed at identifying vulnerable refugees in urban settings.

The initiative started when UNHCR invited some Iraqi refugee women to a focus group discussion, and proceeded to recruit volunteers to seek out vulnerable and hard-to-reach refugees. By 2009, UNHCR had engaged 76 volunteer caseworkers, covering 38 neighbourhoods in and around Damascus. The volunteers dealt directly with up to 7,000 cases per month, mainly through counselling, home visits, and by providing community support and services. Only a relatively small number of refugees had to be referred to UNHCR for follow-up action.

The volunteers were selected according to their willingness, ability, and acceptability to the refugee community. Preference was given to the recruitment of refugee women, who had easier access to at-risk households, in particular those headed by women.

All in all, 135 volunteers were given orientation on UNHCR's mandate and code of conduct, training in communication and on effective ways to offer support and engage their community. They signed an agreement committing themselves to confidentiality and non-discriminatory approaches to refugees. Although they did not receive a salary, they did receive a small sum to cover transport and telephone expenses.

The functions of the volunteer workers included identifying and visiting particularly vulnerable refugees; providing counselling and practical assistance; facilitating refugee access to services; identifying and mobilizing community resources; improving UNHCR's understanding of the refugee population; and supporting UNHCR's public information work. In addition, the programme helped to restore hope and dignity among the refugee community at large, and among the volunteers themselves, who were not otherwise authorized to take up employment in Syria.

Strengthening national capacities

The volunteers played a particularly important role in addressing psychosocial difficulties among the refugees. Normally, UNHCR would address such problems by referring individuals in need of care to local mental health practitioners. But this was not possible in all cases in Damascus, as the Syrian mental health sector was under-resourced, with just 89 psychiatrists in the country for a population of around 22 million in 2010. The minimum ratio recommended by WHO is 25 times that number.

In 2008, in a further innovation, UNHCR established a Psychosocial and Mental Health Programme, which relied on resources within the refugee community to help other refugees, and also included a national capacity-building component.

By 2011, 17 of the 135 refugee outreach volunteers had been trained by the Psychosocial and Mental Health Programme in psychosocial support and first aid, and were helping to identify vulnerable refugees, provide counselling to refugees through home visits, and liaise with existing local mental health and psychosocial services. A larger group of refugee volunteers managed an Outreach Counselling Centre, set up by UNHCR in a refugee-hosting neighbourhood of Damascus, where 16 different psychosocial and recreational activities were available to refugees.

The national capacity-building element of the programme helped to strengthen local mental health and psychosocial support services, through training and curriculum development. Senior mental health professionals received training in working with refugees, and they in turn were able to support non-specialized front-line staff.

With the extra capacity provided by refugee volunteers and the enhanced national capacity, UNHCR's Psychosocial and Mental Health Programme had benefited over 6,000 refugee families by the end of 2011.

Lessons learned

UNHCR does not view refugee outreach workers as a panacea. In Syria, their work was not easy to monitor, and there was significant turnover as refugees departed for resettlement. The preference for engaging refugee women, while justified under the circumstances, also raised questions in the context of the application of UNHCR's Age, Gender, and Diversity Mainstreaming policy.

Nonetheless, the initiative proved to be a valuable means of reaching out to the refugee population. An internal evaluation found that it not only helped to bring a sustainable form of assistance to the most vulnerable refugees but also empowered the volunteers themselves, strengthened refugee representation and advocacy, improved relations within the refugee community, and between the refugee community and UNHCR. ◆

---

take away jobs from locals. Yet refugees can also have a positive impact, as demonstrated by research into the livelihoods of refugees from the Democratic Republic of the Congo living in Nairobi. Such is the popularity of their music and fashion that Congolese musicians, tailors, barbers, and hairstylists are much in demand; Congolese musicians contribute to the local economy by attracting customers and generating profits for local club and hotel owners. Refugees pay housing rent, use public transport, and purchase goods and services.[27] In Johannesburg, there is also evidence that refugees and asylum seekers are increasing employment opportunities for locals.[28]

Good practices

RECENTLY, MORE EFFORT HAS BEEN MADE TO DOCUMENT SUCCESSFUL APPROACHES to meeting the protection and assistance needs of refugees living in urban areas. Information is still limited, and there is always a risk of exaggerating the impact of successes until it is possible to consider long-term effects and sustainability of interventions. Nonetheless, some evidence of good practice has emerged. Resources and awareness-raising will be needed to ensure that interventions of the kind described below are scaled up and replicated more broadly.

ENGAGING WITH MUNICIPAL AUTHORITIES

In 2009, the High Commissioner's Dialogue was preceded by a meeting of mayors from cities that host large populations of refugees and IDPs. Since then, UNHCR offices have started working with many more municipal authorities, in particular in Latin America where cities have signed up to become 'Cities of Solidarity' under the 2004 Mexico Plan of Action (*see box 8.1*). The Cities of Solidarity initiative focuses on promoting local integration of refugees settled in urban areas, through access to education, healthcare, and sustainable income-generating activities.

In Colombia, UNHCR, the Representative of the Secretary-General on the Human Rights of IDPs, Colombian academics, and civil society organizations have worked in partnership to foster dialogue with municipal leaders on how to implement Colombia's progressive IDP legislation.[29]

In Costa Rica, the municipality of Desamparados—in the city of San José—created the 'House of Rights' in collaboration with UNHCR, the national bar association, an NGO partner called 'Asociación de Consultores y Asesores Internationales' (ACAI), and the University of Costa Rica, which established a legal clinic there. Since then, other partners have joined the House of Rights, a place where refugees can obtain legal aid and advice to help them find employment or access public services, among other activities.

ADVOCACY

In Kenya, the international community and local civil society have worked together to promote positive change for urban refugees, particularly in Nairobi. A strong coalition has emerged, including refugee representatives, churches, human rights activists, and politicians. They have urged Kenya to work with UNHCR and other UN actors to adopt a rights-based urban refugee policy. Recognizing the vibrancy of many refugee businesses, UNHCR and the Refugee Consortium of Kenya have called on the government to register and document refugees' businesses so that they will also pay taxes and not be coerced into paying bribes.

DOCUMENTATION

Documentation is particularly important for urban refugees and asylum seekers, who are likely regularly to come into contact with authorities. UNHCR encourages national authorities to issue documentation to urban refugees. For instance, in Ghana it has been

Surviving in the city: refugees in Nairobi

Despite an official policy of accommodating refugees in camps in remote parts of the country, every day hundreds of refugees and asylum seekers arrive in Nairobi in search of security and opportunity. Many are former city-dwellers who feel uncomfortable in the rural camps, having lived and worked all their lives in urban areas.

Kenya has tolerated an increasingly large refugee population in Nairobi and other urban centres. At the end of 2011, there were 50,000 refugees and asylum seekers registered with UNHCR in Nairobi and an unknown—but probably at least as large—number of unregistered refugees.

Most refugees in Nairobi survive through casual labour in the informal sector, although the income they earn is rarely sufficient to sustain their families. Many live in over-crowded dwellings, often without access to basic sanitation or other services. In many ways, their lives are not very different from those of Kenya's urban poor. But, as refugees, they face particular challenges to survive in the city.

Refugees often arrive in Nairobi alone or with just a few family members. They are likely to be cut off from the traditional support structures provided by clan or tribe and frequently do not have personal documentation. Refugees are easily exploited by landlords and employers.

During 2006–2011, UNHCR registered more refugees in Nairobi than in its entire 43-year history of working in Kenya. As a result of its urban refugee initiative, UNHCR has developed a better understanding of and relationship with the refugee population in Nairobi. It has established productive new partnerships with local government, the security services and judiciary, service providers, civil society and the NGO community.

Much of the progress in expanding protection space for refugees in Nairobi has resulted from advocacy by UNHCR and its partners for refugees to be able to benefit from national service structures, such as health care, education and law enforcement mechanisms. By supplementing and supporting these services, UNHCR has enhanced goodwill and awareness among local administrations and communities, and substantial numbers of refugees are now able to use public services such as City Council Health Clinics and primary schools on equal terms with Kenyans. Regular meetings with local police and the establishment of a network of community paralegals have helped to reduce police harassment of refugees, extortion, arbitrary arrests and detention. Most refugees, provided they are registered, are now able to stay in Nairobi without fearing deportation or relocation to the rural camps.

A key element of UNHCR's work in Nairobi has been to encourage refugee self-reliance. UNHCR and partners promote skills development, credit schemes, small grants and access to banking services, and help refugees to obtain the necessary documentation to be able to start small businesses.

A further development has been the shift from working out of a central location in Nairobi to an outreach approach which emphasizes the capacities of refugee communities, local authorities and partners. In many cases, networks of refugee volunteers are able to advise fellow refugees and help them to obtain information and services. UNHCR is increasingly using text messaging and posting information on its website to keep refugees informed of matters which concern them, saving refugees precious time and money in a city where transport costs are soaring and every working day counts.

The Government of Kenya is a key partner in this effort. It now formally takes the lead on registration and provides registered refugees with government-issued identity documents. Kenyan social services have a strong interest in child protection, including refugee children, and local Children's Officers are actively engaged in identifying care arrangements for unaccompanied and separated children and in resolving legal issues related to custody or child abuse.

There remain, of course, many challenges, some related to current political and security developments in the Horn of Africa. Somali refugees in particular are viewed with distrust. The ongoing drought and economic crisis compound hostility toward refugees in urban areas. For these reasons it is important to keep communication channels open between refugees, local populations and the authorities.

While UNHCR has expanded its activities in Nairobi, the capacity and funds available to the Office are not commensurate with the demands. It is a constant challenge for the organization to decide how much of its scarce resources to allocate to an urban programme which, at end 2011, served around 50,000 refugees, in a country where more than ten times as many refugees were living in remote, overcrowded camps. ◆

agreed that the Ghana Refugee Board will take over the full responsibility for issuing documentation to refugees and asylum seekers by mid-2012.

In Ecuador, where many Colombians live without papers and are unable legally to access employment, UNHCR has worked with the authorities and civil society to operate mobile registration clinics for people unable to access asylum systems otherwise, whether because they lack the resources or because they fear detention. In the course of a one-day process, applicants are interviewed and receive a government document attesting to their refugee status or a document indicating they have applied for asylum (*see box 6.2*).

INVOLVING BENEFICIARIES

UNHCR actively encourages the participation of refugees living in urban areas in matters which concern them. In Sana'a, Yemen, UNHCR has invested in mechanisms to enable them to interact with the Yemeni authorities about issues which are important to the refugee communities. UNHCR has fostered the emergence of representative and democratically elected committees that act as interlocutors with the government and provide a means for community mobilization. Like Yemeni civilians, refugees were affected by the widespread political violence in the country throughout 2011. When security constraints forced UNHCR staff to withdraw temporarily from certain areas, the committees continued to function, identifying the most vulnerable refugees and temporarily relocating them to safer environments.

Similarly, UNHCR in Colombia fostered an IDP community organization in the city of Cartagena, enabling IDPs to negotiate with municipal and utility authorities to obtain access to water and energy supplies.[30]

In Kuala Lumpur, UNHCR encouraged refugees living in the city to organize associations to represent their communities, thereby facilitating liaison and cooperation with UNHCR on matters of protection, education, health, community development, and livelihood. Refugees participate in deciding how to allocate the modest amounts available in UNHCR's Social Protection Fund, which provides support for refugee-run projects in the areas of education, health, livelihoods, and youth activities.

USING NEW TECHNOLOGIES

In Syria and Jordan, UNHCR has successfully used new technologies to register and communicate with refugees dispersed in urban areas, and to provide assistance to them. Electronic vouchers have enabled refugees to redeem coupons for food in state-run outlets, UNHCR-supplied cash cards have allowed refugees to withdraw cash grants directly from banks, and UNHCR has kept refugees informed about matters concerning them through text messages.

UNHCR is drawing on its experience with the Iraqi refugee operation to find ways to operate more cost-effectively in urban settings more generally. One lesson is that distributing cash assistance using debit cards can be more cost-effective than manual aid distribution, and do more to preserve the dignity of beneficiaries. Vouchers redeemable in shops can make more sense than handing out food or non-food items that many refugees will immediately sell—at a loss—in order to raise cash to purchase items that they consider more essential for their families. But not all displaced populations in urban settings have access to cash machines, vouchers or even mobile phones.

BOX 6•5

Understanding displacement: urban mapping

UNHCR has prepared detailed maps of dozens of refugee camps and IDP sites in recent years, charting the location of refugees. Mapping the whereabouts of refugee and displaced populations in urban areas is much more difficult, but can be even more essential in order to design effective protection and assistance programmes.

Mapping the distribution of refugees and services available to them in urban areas is challenging precisely because refugees are not confined within camps and are not necessarily registered with UNHCR or partners. Moreover, service providers are usually not managed or coordinated by UNHCR.

In big cities, refugees often live across much wider areas than in camps. There may be no official street address system, or the local way of describing where people live might not be easily translated into UNHCR's registration systems. Host country regulations might impose constraints on UNHCR's collection of data about refugees. UNHCR is not always able to obtain global positioning system (GPS) data or base maps for administrative divisions.

In recent years, UNHCR has developed tools to overcome some of these challenges. For example, the agency has established simple grids for dividing a city into zones for mapping purposes, and asks refugees to point out their place of residence on this map at the time of registration, thus facilitating UNHCR's access to these individuals or families later on, even if they do not have a formal address.

UNHCR has found it particularly useful to map the locations where refugees reside, along with relevant local infrastructure and facilities, such as schools, clinics, police stations, and community organizations. In addition, it has proven helpful to map places where violent incidents or threats to safety have occurred in order to understand and address protection risks faced by persons of concern.

UNHCR has collected and organized data about refugees' residence and registration in nine large cities: Addis Ababa, Aden, Bangkok, Cairo, Douala, Kuala Lumpur, Nairobi, Sana'a and Yaoundé. Technical connectivity has been established between registration and mapping tools, allowing field operations automatically to update maps with registration data. Registered users can view these maps in UNHCR's GeoPortal.

The evolving numbers and profiles of the registered populations—including their gender and age, country of origin, ethnicity and religion, occupation, education level, and any special needs—can be monitored over time, and easily shared with partners, without specialized technical support.

UNHCR staff and partners can see the distribution of refugees and services available within a community, helping them to identify gaps and plan further services to meet needs. Since the information is presented in visual form, the relationship between the location of people of concern in a city and the capacity of existing services can be easily understood; it can also be easily shared with others who might need this information for the purposes of planning and decision making.

Mapping has yielded some important findings, notably that there is often a sharp disconnect between where refugees live and where available services are located. In Cairo, for example, most refugees live in one or two parts of the city, and these are far from the UNHCR office and many of the service providers. In Kuala Lumpur, UNHCR has used mapping information to make suggestions to city authorities on the optimal location for new community services.

Mapping has also revealed that refugees and other displaced populations tend to gather in particular districts, and may even be concentrated in particular buildings within those districts. This information has helped UNHCR to find particularly vulnerable refugees who have not approached UNHCR on their own. Urban outreach programmes can be better targeted when UNHCR focuses its efforts on locations where refugees are known to reside.

This type of focused urban outreach has been used in Nairobi since 2007, when initial mapping revealed places where refugees were living, including individual buildings with high concentrations of refugees. When UNHCR staff visited the buildings and met refugees in their homes, the limits of earlier outreach efforts became evident. Few of the refugee women interviewed were aware of how to access affordable health care in Nairobi, or of the potential benefits of registration with UNHCR. Through such visits, UNHCR discovered a 'safe house' in which 18 refugee women were living, only one of whom was registered with UNHCR; the women indicated that they felt safe there, that they supported each other, and that the landlord empathized with them and had reduced their rent by half. Such insights enable UNHCR to design more effective shelter strategies in urban areas.

UNHCR's data management and mapping approach in cities is user-friendly. It can be maintained and its layers updated locally with little support from technical experts. UNHCR field offices and their partners can easily share up-to-date data in an aggregated and anonymous form. No costly or sophisticated software is required to exchange or view the information. The mapping tool can facilitate concerted actions, based on a common understanding of where refugees live, what their needs are, and where services are available. ◆

UNHCR/T. BAHAR

MICROFINANCE

In Costa Rica, UNHCR has been working with a microfinance institution and an NGO partner to facilitate access to microfinance services for refugees; the services are also available for migrants and Costa Rican citizens. The latest assessment of the programme shows that on average 2.2 jobs were created per loan disbursed. It is estimated that more than 10% of persons of concern to UNHCR in Costa Rica participate in this project. In Jordan, UNHCR concluded an agreement with the Jordanian MicroFund for Women (MFW), to make it easier for Iraqi refugee women to have access to loans and business support. The MFW also provides information and training to help the women manage their businesses.

▲ **A refugee woman** from Myanmar looks out over rooftops in Delhi.

HEALTH CARE

Ensuring that persons of concern in urban areas can have access to mainstream health services is a stated UNHCR objective. In Costa Rica, where refugees and asylum seekers mainly live in urban areas, they are able to turn to the Costa Rican national health system for emergency care; access is also offered to all children under 18 years, and all women in need of reproductive health services. The country's national health insurance scheme is mandatory for all citizens and residents—including refugees—with costs shared by employers, employees, and the state. Refugees with capacity to pay do so. The state is expected to cover costs for persons who are not able to pay, and destitute refugees may register for their costs to be covered by the state.

EDUCATION SUPPORT

UNHCR encourages the admission of refugee children to local schools in urban areas. With this in mind, in Damascus and Amman, schools were rehabilitated and classrooms added to help schools to cater for large numbers of Iraqi refugee children. In Delhi, UNHCR partners provide day-care for children in areas where refugees are concentrated. This not only ensures a safe environment for young children while their parents work or study, but also provides pre-school education which eases the children's later entry into the Indian educational system. Children are taught in English and Hindi to enable them to use government education and health services.

New players, new partnerships, new paradigms

To respond to the protection and assistance needs of refugees living in urban areas, humanitarian agencies, development agencies, and host governments will need to work together more closely and more consistently. UNHCR has encouraged other UN actors—including UN-HABITAT, OCHA, UNESCO and UNICEF—to engage with urban refugee and displaced populations, and has sought to develop linkages between actors working on displacement and those working more broadly on urban planning and administration, poverty reduction, and emergency preparedness.

The perception that refugee protection and assistance in cities requires a humanitarian response—more than a development response—stems from the assumption that refugee movements reflect short-term humanitarian emergencies. But evidence from many cities shows that refugees and other displaced people remain long after the emergency phase of a crisis is over.

UNHCR has stressed that the relationship between displacement and urbanization needs more analysis, and that efforts must continue to build a better evidence base from which to develop operational guidance to support livelihoods and mitigate tensions between host and refugee communities. While some urban refugee populations have been the subject of extensive research, little is known about others. The NGO Refugees International has noted: 'First and foremost, refugees need to be found. This means sending teams into urban areas and reaching out, like social workers, to identify vulnerable refugees and register them'.[31]

The implementation of UNHCR's new urban refugee policy is in the early stages, and it will require new partnerships and substantial awareness-raising, including among public servants. Many municipal officials and law-enforcement personnel who interact with urban refugees are unfamiliar with international refugee and human rights law. In some circumstances, UNHCR is able to provide basic training but the need for sensitization in this field is significant.

UNHCR's policy shift has helped to stimulate new thinking on urban displacement within host governments, donor governments, and other humanitarian actors. The International Labour Organization has acknowledged the impact of displaced populations on urban labour markets and employment standards. Recent studies commissioned or undertaken by UNHCR, UN-HABITAT, the Humanitarian Policy Group, the Women's Refugee Commission, universities and other actors have increased policy makers' understanding of the challenges and how to respond to them, although the focus has been on a relatively small number of cities. There is hope that the momentum generated by UNHCR will be met with significant new investment from donors.

At the global level, UNHCR is working with a range of UN and non-governmental partners as part of a Reference Group for Meeting Humanitarian Challenges in Urban Areas (RG MHCUA), which was set up under the auspices of the Inter-Agency Standing Committee (IASC), the central UN-convened hub of stakeholders that shapes global humanitarian policy making. The IASC is promoting a strategy agreed in 2010 which stresses the need to develop multi-stakeholder partnerships for enhanced effectiveness of humanitarian responses in urban areas, and better coordination with development actors.[32]

UNHCR has recently published guidance to staff on health, education, and livelihoods support services in urban areas. Other major humanitarian players, such as the International Federation of Red Cross and Crescent Societies, UN-HABITAT, the Norwegian Refugee Council, and Médecins Sans Frontières, to cite only a few, are also developing and cataloguing good practices. It is important that the preparation of tool-kits by various agencies is well-coordinated, to avoid contradiction or duplication. UNHCR sees a natural role for itself in facilitating the exchange of information and policy debate concerning urban refugees.

As in many contexts, the availability of funding will be critical. In some countries, decentralization processes are giving municipalities more responsibility for responding to the needs of refugees and internally displaced people, but without necessarily also providing additional central government funding. At the international level, it is generally easier to secure donor funding for emergency responses than for urban interventions. Despite massive expansion of UNHCR's engagement in Kenya resulting from intensification of the Somalia emergency, for example, the agency had a budget in 2011 of less than US$14 million for Nairobi, a city where the number of newly arriving refugees is estimated to exceed one thousand per month.[33] Nairobi has been adopted as a pilot city by the UN's Reference Group, but as of late 2011, funding still had to be found for the initiative.

UNHCR's new policy cautions that its objectives cannot be attained by the agency alone. If its ambitious goals are to be achieved, the policy document states, 'an appropriate resource base will be required, coupled with effective cooperation and support from a wide range of other actors, especially those host governments and city authorities in the developing world that so generously host the growing number of urban refugees'.[34]

At a policy level, UNHCR has made a major shift. The picture revealed by the new focus on urban areas is challenging, and at times grim. But recognition of the phenomenon, its scale and the need for partnerships and solidarity is a crucial step.

When it comes to cities, the UN family as a whole will need to rethink some of its long-held assumptions. For instance, it has tended to see displacement caused by conflict and displacement caused by natural disasters as distinct phenomena. But when the victims flee to urban areas, distinguishing between them is difficult. The next chapter looks in detail at the challenges posed by displacement caused by natural disasters and linked to the effects of climate change. ■

CHAPTER 7

Climate Change, Natural Disasters, and Displacement

LIMATE CHANGE IS EMERGING AS THE DEFINING ISSUE OF OUR TIMES.[1] While there is debate within the scientific community about its pace and impact, a strong consensus exists that human activity, especially greenhouse gas emissions, is causing long-term changes to the earth's climate. Global warming is expected to result in an increase in the frequency and severity of sudden-onset disasters such as hurricanes, cyclones, and flooding. It is anticipated that changes in the earth's atmosphere, caused by rising emissions, will cause the sea level to rise; increase the acidity of oceans; lead to salination of fresh water supplies, coastal, and riverine erosion; as well as accelerate drought, desertification, and long-term land degradation.

Global warming affects both developed and developing countries, but poorer countries are less able to cope with its consequences. As the UN Human Rights Council has observed, the impacts of climate change are apt to exacerbate existing inequalities and to be felt most acutely by the poor and vulnerable.[2]

Climate change will add to the scale and complexity of human displacement.[3] More people are already displaced each year by natural disasters than by conflict, and it is projected that the effects of climate change will, over time, trigger large-scale movements of people both within and across borders. UNHCR believes that the international community needs to ensure a stronger and better-coordinated response to the displacement that results from sudden-onset disasters and from the effects of climate change.

◀ **A boy in the ruins of his home** after it was hit by Cyclone Nargis in Myanmar.

For that reason, UNHCR included climate change and displacement among the subjects considered by a series of expert roundtables on the occasion of the organization's 60th anniversary in 2011.[4] The conclusions of these discussions contributed to the Nansen Conference on Climate Change and Displacement convened in June 2011 by the government of Norway.[5]

UNHCR's core mandate does not encompass displacement caused by natural disasters and climate change, but UNHCR has a clear interest in the movement of people related to these factors. Environmental degradation can fuel social tensions and conflict, which in turn can give rise to flows of refugees and IDPs. Even where the cause of displacement—whether internal or across borders—is purely environmental, the affected populations may have protection needs and vulnerabilities similar to those of people whose flight is provoked by violence or human rights abuses. As the UN Emergency Relief Coordinator and the UN Secretary-General's former Representative on the Human Rights of Internally Displaced Persons have pointed out, 'human rights don't disappear the moment an earthquake, a hurricane or a tsunami strikes'.[6]

People forced to leave their homes because of disasters such as floods, droughts, or earthquakes are often called 'environmental refugees' or 'climate refugees'. UNHCR does not favour this terminology, as the word 'refugee' is defined in international law as a person who satisfies the criteria under the 1951 Convention, the 1969 OAU Convention, or UNHCR's Statute. Nor would UNHCR favour an initiative to redefine the term 'refugee', as this could undermine the international protection regime. 'External displacement' is a more accurate way to refer to the phenomenon of cross-border movements driven by a wide range of natural hazards.

Whatever terminology is ultimately used, displacement generated by climate change and natural disasters is likely to test the capacity of the international humanitarian system for many years to come.

BOX **7•1**

Key developments in the international response to climate change

The Stockholm Conference on the Human Environment (1972): The Stockholm Conference was the first major UN conference to highlight environmental challenges. It adopted 26 Principles 'to inspire and guide' international action to preserve and enhance the environment and recommended the creation of the United Nations Environment Programme (UNEP), which was set up by the UN General Assembly the same year.

The Montreal Protocol on Substances that Deplete the Ozone Layer (1987): The Montreal Protocol on Substances that Deplete the Ozone Layer, an international treaty, was proposed to limit the use of substances responsible for ozone depletion. By 2011, 196 countries had signed the Protocol.

The Intergovernmental Panel on Climate Change (1988): The Intergovernmental Panel on Climate Change (IPCC) was established by UNEP and the World Meteorological Organization, and endorsed by the UN General Assembly, to provide scientific knowledge on climate change for the international community. By 2011, 194 countries were members of

the IPCC, and experts from all over the world contributed to its work.

The United Nations Framework Convention on Climate Change (1992): The United Nations Framework Convention on Climate Change (UNFCCC) was adopted by the UN Conference on Environment and Development—or 'Earth Summit'—held in Rio de Janeiro, Brazil. The UNFCCC is an international treaty aimed at reducing global warming and addressing its consequences. It recognizes that industrialized countries are the source of most greenhouse gas emissions and puts the onus on them to reduce these emissions. The Convention entered into force in March 1994, and by 2011 nearly all countries had signed it.

The Kyoto Protocol to the UNFCCC (1997): The Kyoto Protocol to the UNFCCC aims to address global warming by setting binding targets for the reduction of greenhouse gas emissions. Based on the principle of 'common but differentiated responsibilities', it places a heavier responsibility on developed nations than on developing countries. It entered into force in 2005.

The International Strategy for Disaster Reduction (1999): The International Strategy for Disaster Reduction (UNISDR) was established to serve as the focal point in the UN system for the coordination of disaster reduction activities.

The United Nations Climate Change Conference in Cancún (2010): The Conference of the Parties to the UNFCCC held its sixteenth meeting in Cancún, Mexico. It reaffirmed mitigation targets, agreed on new financing mechanisms, and for the first time, affirmed that migration, displacement and planned relocations could be considered as strategies for 'adaptation' to climate change.

The United Nations Climate Change Conference in Durban (2011): The UNFCCC met in Durban, South Africa, and agreed to begin work on a new climate arrangement to be adopted by 2015, which would have legal force and require emission cuts from both developed and developing countries. It also agreed on modalities for a 'Green Climate Fund' to finance climate change mitigation and adaptation projects. ◆

Why is UNHCR concerned about climate change?

CLIMATE CHANGE BY ITSELF DOES NOT CAUSE PEOPLE TO LEAVE THEIR HOMES. Rather, the effects of climate change exacerbate existing vulnerabilities to create situations where people judge that it is time to move—either because they cannot survive where they are or because they would be better off elsewhere.

People usually make decisions to move based on a combination of factors. While the international system clearly distinguishes between voluntary movement of people (termed 'migration') and forced movement ('displacement'), in the case of climate change, it may be more accurate to think in terms of a continuum. People may see signs of impending disaster and decide to leave their communities before the area becomes uninhabitable: pre-emptive movement can be a rational adaptation response. Or there may be cases where the initial decision to leave is voluntary, but climate change makes livelihood, and hence return, impossible. Still, observers expect that most of those moving because of the effects of climate change will remain within the borders of their own countries.

The earth has gone through periods of global warming and cooling in past millennia (e.g. the ice ages), but experts believe that environmentally-induced migration and displacement could take on unprecedented dimensions—both in terms of scale and scope. 'It could have significant effects on the global economy, international development, and national budgets as well as on political and state security'.[7] Researchers, governments, UN agencies, and NGOs have all made predictions about the potential scale of such movements; these predictions vary widely, ranging from 25 million to one billion by the year 2050. For example, the total number of persons who could be permanently or temporarily displaced due to flooding by the end of the twenty-first century has been estimated by the United Nations Development Programme (UNDP) at 330 million, if global temperatures were to rise by three to four degrees.[8]

Climate change is an accelerator of other global trends that create or affect refugees and internally displaced persons (IDPs), including urbanization, economic inequality and conflict. Climate change may fuel conflicts that generate both refugees and IDPs. Few would deny, for example, the role of environmental degradation and competition for scarce resources in the conflict in Darfur, which has led to large-scale movements of refugees and IDPs. Drought and famine in the Horn of Africa in 2011 provided further evidence of the deadly interplay of deteriorating environmental conditions, political instability, and conflict (*see box 7.2*). Moreover, refugee protection needs may arise where a government's actions in dealing with climate-related events could be considered as a form of persecution. For example, denial of assistance to a specific ethnic or religious group among those suffering the effects of climate change may amount to persecution under the 1951 Convention.

People forced to leave their communities because of extreme weather events or other natural hazards have very clear needs for material assistance. It is less well-recognized that they often have protection needs akin to those of people displaced by conflict. Protection concerns may arise, for instance, because of the heightened vulnerability of women,

BOX 7•2

Drought and displacement in the Horn of Africa

In the Horn of Africa, the environment, conflict, and population displacement are interrelated in complex ways. Within Somalia, pervasive governance failures and violence belie the notion of purely 'environmentally-induced' displacement (*see box 0.2*). But along with intensifying conflict in 2011, a severe drought became a famine in parts of south-central Somalia, and this correlated with a major increase in displacement. The role of environmental factors in shaping displacement in this situation, and across the wider region, is increasingly apparent and troubling in its implications.

Increasing environmental stresses

Across the Horn of Africa, complex environmental changes are having major effects on the agricultural and pastoral livelihoods that support some 80 per cent of the population. Over centuries, livelihood systems have adapted to cope with harsh ecological conditions and recurrent drought. Rural people have sophisticated methods to optimize the use of water and land, and have developed a range of strategies to deal with more severe circumstances. Households under stress will often skip meals, drive livestock to water sources, and sell off productive assets; tap into family and community support networks; and move on a temporary basis to new areas where customary law may enable them to access resources and assistance.

But the environmental stresses are increasing. Processes of desertification and degradation impose cumulative, long-term pressures on rural livelihoods. Acute, sudden-onset threats to livelihoods exist in the form of intermittent floods in some areas. But the major threat is from slow-onset drought, occurring in intensifying cycles. Drought used to come once every ten years or so, and the occurrences were even given names; but drought is now a very frequent aspect of life. The 2011 drought was particularly severe, and escalated into famine in some areas of Somalia due to inadequate policy responses coupled with conflict.

Coping mechanisms

Standard coping strategies are increasingly inadequate to address the environmental stresses that households encounter. Years of war and drought have eroded the asset base of many rural households, with fewer able to weather crises or help others in need. International humanitarian assistance has come to play a critical role in rural livelihoods.

Many whose livelihoods have been destroyed are forced to migrate to seek humanitarian assistance in IDP settlements. At the same time, a slower-paced process of urbanization is underway, as rural people experience progressive impoverishment and high levels of hardship, and move to urban areas where they join the ranks of the urban poor. While environmental shifts are typically associated with internal migration, in the case of Somalia, there is a substantial international dimension. During 2011 alone, nearly 300,000 people sought refuge in neighbouring countries, the majority congregating in camps in border areas of Kenya

and Ethiopia which are also under severe environmental stress.

Conflict and displacement may exacerbate environmental change, with resulting unregulated charcoal production further reducing tree cover, and land-grabbing leading to overgrazing on the remaining rangeland. In addition, human responses to changing environmental conditions may trigger conflicts, as competition for scarce resources intensifies, and some groups assert themselves by force in a context where the rule of law is weak. In Somalia, while conflict over resources has long been a feature of pastoral life, the ready availability of automatic weapons has made the consequences of such clashes much more severe.

Conflict complicates rural people's standard strategies for dealing with environmental stress. It can disturb the migratory patterns and strategies of pastoralists, making it dangerous for them to move to places where they can find water. In Somalia, conflict has made it harder for rural people to reach places where assistance is provided, because it involves crossing frontlines, insecure territory, or checkpoints established by armed groups or the authorities. Conversely, climate change can affect conflict coping strategies; in earlier years many people from urban areas sought refuge from fighting with relatives in rural areas, but the erosion of rural asset bases leaves rural households struggling to host them.

Many families have been hit simultaneously by drought and conflict, so their experiences of each are closely intertwined: for them, displacement is often the result of both environmental and conflict factors. Drought and hunger may be the immediate trigger for movement, although the groundwork was already laid by experience of conflict and abuse over the years. In other cases, an upsurge in violence may trigger movement, but against a background of long-term strains on livelihoods. The causes of movement have important implications for the desirability and feasibility of return.

Institutional responses

Conflict provides the context in which institutional responses to environmental challenges evolve, shaping how policy-makers act in relation to supporting rural livelihoods and protecting displaced people.

Many people's livelihoods depend on the pastoral and agricultural economy—even in the context of environmental challenges—and with appropriate support, these could thrive. There are opportunities to intervene at various points in the cycle of environmental stress. While effective early warning systems have been put in place, delayed policy responses have failed to prevent or mitigate the impact of drought on livelihoods, leading to displacement. In Somalia, domestic actors prioritized political struggle and international actors were slow to register the gravity of early warnings. To avoid future disasters, early warnings will need to be acted upon.

Moving more smoothly from emergency humanitarian response to effective and timely rehabilitation will also be crucial. Future food security is jeopardized when farmers are not able to plant crops due to

UNHCR/B. BANNON/AUGUST 2011

displacement or lack of resources. Rehabilitation efforts have tended to be short-term in nature: food aid, some cash relief, emergency water provision and medical care, or seed distribution. These important short-term measures need to be connected with longer-term frameworks for increasing the resilience of rural communities.

Local communities play a critical role in mediating environmental processes at the micro-level, and their cooperation and insight are vital to the success of interventions aimed at mitigating the impact of environmental changes and improving resilience. But much stronger and higher-level political action is needed to respond effectively to the impact of environmental change.

In Somalia, the lack of a coherent national government and the limited capacity of the regional authorities in Somaliland and Puntland are major obstacles. Actions that degrade the environment are allowed to continue, drought is permitted to escalate into famine, and there is little in the way of economic planning to support the agriculture and pastoralist sectors. Furthermore, Somalia is not a party to the UN Framework Convention on Climate Change, the country has no national adaptation programme of action or climate change policy in place, and it is fully absorbed with current political and military challenges.

Meanwhile, the international community bears a clear responsibility for many of the climate-related changes that are having such a severe effect in the region. The carbon footprint of the average Somali is minuscule by comparison with nationals of developed countries. The onus is on developed countries and those in rapid transition to transform their consumption and production practices, and contribute to mitigating their consequences in poorer parts of the

▲ **Two Somali refugee girls** run through a dust storm in the Ifo settlement near Dadaab, Kenya.

world. International aid responses to drought in the Horn of Africa have tended to come too late, and in the form of humanitarian assistance. Longer-term environmentally-sensitive livelihoods programming, although hampered by political insecurity in many areas, could achieve a substantial impact in some parts of the Somali territories. This should include the environmentally stressed refugee-hosting areas in Kenya's North Eastern Province and Ethiopia's Somali Regional State.

While those displaced internally because of conflict or environmental factors are IDPs under the UN Guiding Principles and the Kampala Convention, the legal position of people who move across borders in the wake of environmental stress and crisis is more ambiguous.

The practice of African governments has generally been to allow those fleeing natural disasters to cross borders on a temporary basis, although this is not considered part of their legal obligations under the OAU Convention. The distinction between people displaced as a result of conflict and those who flee drought is not always clear. In many cases, people move across borders for a combination of reasons, including human rights abuses, fear of persecution, conflict, and the consequences of drought. But the distinction is politically significant as it is often presumed that people displaced by drought will return more easily than those displaced by war or persecution. Such thinking may underestimate the devastating effect of the drought and displacement on families and their livelihoods, and the challenge of effective rehabilitation—especially in the context of a volatile and protracted conflict such as in Somalia. This further highlights the critical role of broader political processes in addressing displacement. ◆

children, the elderly, and the disabled; because victims have lost important personal documentation in the disaster; or because they become separated from their families.

UNHCR has expertise which can help to respond to displacement caused by both sudden-onset and slow-onset disasters. This experience relates to legal protection but also to the provision of shelter, livelihoods for displaced people, the use of participatory and people-oriented planning methods, and the promotion of regional cooperation among states in the search for solutions.

UNHCR's experience may also be relevant in the context of planned relocation of populations. Such relocations are already undertaken in some situations where land becomes uninhabitable as a result of climate change, and they may increase in the future. For example, food shortages in the Carteret Islands, off the coast of Papua New Guinea, have led the government to try to resettle the population on the mainland. These food shortages have stemmed from declining fishing and agricultural production, the loss of coastal lands and unusually high 'king' tides which are attributed to the effects of climate change.[9] In other countries, ranging from Mozambique to Argentina, communities have been relocated to prevent their exposure to natural disasters, especially flooding.[10]

Finally, UNHCR is also concerned about climate change because, like other humanitarian organizations, it has a responsibility to minimize the environmental impacts of its own actions. UNHCR is therefore seeking to adapt its operations accordingly (*see box 7.3*).

Understanding displacement caused by climate change

DIFFERENT CATEGORIES OF POPULATION MOVEMENT COULD OCCUR OR INTENSIFY as a result of climate change. The five categories set out below can be helpful for understanding the types of movements, and the associated protection needs.[11]

People may be displaced by *hydro-meteorological disasters*, such as flooding; hurricanes, typhoons, and cyclones; or mudslides. Such movements are usually temporary in nature. While most can be expected to occur within the borders of a country, there may also be cross-border movement.

Displacement may be caused by *environmental degradation and slow-onset disasters*. These causes of displacement could include reduction of water availability, desertification, long-term effects of recurrent flooding, sinking coastal zones, and increased salination of ground water and soil. This is expected to result in people moving to other regions of their country or to other countries if no options are available for internal relocation, and most likely on a permanent basis.

In the case of *inundation of small island states* by rising sea levels, the entire population of an island might be forced to move permanently elsewhere (*see box 7.4*).

Where some areas become uninhabitable either because of sudden- or slow-onset

BOX 7·3

'Climate-proofing' UNHCR's operations

In its submission to the 'Rio+20' UN Conference on Sustainable Development, to be held in Brazil in June 2012, UNHCR pledged to make sound environmental management an integral part of its humanitarian operations. If not properly managed, refugee and IDP camps and settlements can do significant damage to the environment, and competition for natural resources can be the source of conflict within displaced populations and with host communities. This is particularly the case with respect to trees that are cut to provide firewood or to build shelters.

Evidence from many locations shows that sexual and gender-based violence is directly linked to the need for women and children to scavenge for firewood. Moreover, they often spend more than half of every day collecting firewood; this time could more usefully be invested in education and income-generating activities. Introducing energy-saving approaches and alternative energy sources for cooking and lighting can reduce protection risks and preserve natural resources.

Fuel-efficient stoves, both locally-manufactured and imported, have been distributed to refugees in countries such as Bangladesh, Chad, Djibouti, Ethiopia, Kenya, and Togo. A pioneering ethanol-burning stove distributed in camps in eastern Ethiopia, for example, lowered indoor air pollution, protected refugee women, and reduced tension with local residents over firewood—and could also run on ethanol produced as a by-product of the local sugar industry. In Bangladesh, environmentally friendly briquettes made of rice husks cover domestic energy needs in refugee camps. In Chad and Nepal, refugees use solar cookers.

UNHCR is a partner in the Global Alliance for Clean Cookstoves, a public–private initiative led by the UN Foundation which aims to introduce clean and efficient stoves to 100 million homes by 2020, including in refugee and IDP settings. In 2011, UNHCR launched its own campaign entitled Light Years Ahead, to raise funds for solar lighting and fuel-efficient stoves for refugees in seven African countries. In its first year, this initiative received more than 1.6 million dollars contributed by private donors, allowing UNHCR to install over 200 solar street lights in refugee camps, distribute nearly 15,000 solar lanterns to refugees, and provide more than 8,300 refugee women with fuel-efficient stoves.

Forest rehabilitation is a crucial part of UNHCR's operations. Forestry provides essential resources for refugees and host communities, including fuel and shelter materials as well as a source of income. In eastern Sudan, a programme launched in 1985 planted trees over more than 28,000 hectares of once-barren land. In Chad, one of the hottest and driest places on earth, UNHCR distributes seedlings of lemon, mango, and papaya trees to refugees and IDPs; some 400 hectares have been reforested. Since 2007, UNHCR has participated in the Billion Tree Campaign initiated by the UN Environment Programme. With UNHCR's support, over 23 million trees have been planted by refugees since 2007 in countries across Africa. It is clear that if given the opportunity, refugees and IDPs can contribute to sustainable development and to a green economy.

Better environmental management in refugee-impacted areas does not come from UNHCR alone. In 2005, UNHCR and CARE International developed the Framework for Assessing, Monitoring and Evaluating the Environment in Refugee-related Operations (FRAME). This guidance tool encourages all stakeholders—UNHCR, host governments, NGOs, and refugee men and women of all ages—to participate in improving the environment in their communities.

Promoting sound environmental management in refugee camps requires the active engagement of host communities, to reduce the risk of conflict between refugees and local families over natural resources. Awareness-raising and environmental education is therefore often conducted together with host communities. In western and northern Ethiopia, for example, a youth-driven co-existence programme promotes care and concern for the environment through sensitization and dialogue between refugees and their host communities.

The challenge for UNHCR is not only to reduce the environmental impact of its operations but to adapt them to the reality of climate change, including in key areas such as water, sanitation, and agriculture. UNHCR has begun to build climate change adaptation and disaster risk reduction measures into its operations through its 'area-wide adaptation' approach. This is based on recognition that the way in which refugee and IDP sites are established and administered has an effect on the environment and on refugees' vulnerability to natural disasters.

The 'climate-proofing' of UNHCR operations requires cooperation not only with host country authorities and partner agencies. Collaboration is also needed with academics, engineers and other experts who can help to design solutions to some of the most pressing problems faced by refugees and IDPs, to support them in building sustainable livelihoods, and to adapt to the challenge of climate change. ◆

disasters, *evacuation and relocation* of people to safe areas may be needed. Such movements may be temporary or permanent, depending on conditions in the area of origin.

Finally, displacement of varying duration may occur when armed conflict and violence are triggered by a *shortage of essential resources* (water, food) due to climate change.

UNHCR PHOTO

▲ **A reforestation project**
in a refugee-hosting area
of eastern Sudan.

The relevance of this category has been highlighted by the former
Representative of the Secretary-General on the Human Rights of Internally Displaced Persons.[12]

Each of the categories listed above poses its own challenges in
terms of protection and long-term solutions. People displaced within the borders of their
own countries—whether by sudden-onset natural disasters or conflict—are defined as
IDPs; and thus the applicable normative framework, as confirmed by the Inter-Agency
Standing Committee (IASC), is provided by the UN Guiding Principles on Internal Displacement, which affirm the responsibility of governments to protect and assist IDPs
within their territories.[13]

However, in countries likely to be affected by climate change, migration and displacement may be sensitive issues; government policies to address internal migration and displacement may not be adequate; and the fragility of states may mean that the political
commitment to effective human rights protection is weak.[14] The Guiding Principles state
that when governments are unable to provide such protection and assistance, they have a
responsibility to seek international assistance. In this respect, UNHCR plays an important
role in providing support to government efforts to protect and assist IDPs in conflict situations, and has acquired considerable experience also in the context of natural disasters (*see
chapter 5*).

Some of those displaced across an international border by armed conflict and violence triggered by the effects of climate change may fall within UNHCR's mandate and the traditional refugee law framework, or qualify for existing complementary forms of protection.[15] But others who are forced to move outside their countries because their home areas become uninhabitable—whether because of the effects of sudden-onset disasters, environmental degradation caused by slow-onset disasters, or because their national territories can no longer sustain them—fall into a legal gap; there is no applicable protection framework. There is evidence that environmental vulnerability produced by climatic variation is already resulting in increased displacement across borders. One recent study, for example, reported that environmental reasons are important drivers of out-migration from Ghana, and that climatic changes in East Africa are influencing the cross-border migration patterns of pastoralists.[16]

While many of those displaced by sudden-onset disasters are likely to move temporarily and remain within the borders of their countries, long-term environmental degradation could lead to permanent displacement or relocation of some groups, both internally and across borders. In fact, the slow-onset disasters are likely to produce the largest movement of people, and to pose the greatest challenge to the international system.

BOX **7•4**

The particular case of small island states

The situation of small island states has received considerable attention as a potentially dramatic example of climate change-induced displacement. Scientific studies, including those of the Intergovernmental Panel on Climate Change (IPPC), indicate that sea levels are rising and will continue to do so.

Already in 2001, the IPPC highlighted that small island states are among the areas most vulnerable to the effects of climate change, although they are responsible for less than one per cent of the world's greenhouse gas emissions. The IPPC drew attention to the fact that land loss from sea-level rise on atolls and low limestone islands could disrupt virtually all economic and social sectors. In such a case, the panel warned, potential options for the population may be limited to migration.

The prospect of sea-level rise threatens small low-lying islands in unique ways. Average elevation on Tuvalu and the Maldives Islands, for example, is only about one metre, and therefore leaves these countries at risk of

both sudden-onset disasters—such as tsunamis triggered by earthquakes—and of rising sea levels resulting from global warming.

While the possibility that these islands will 'sink' or be inundated by rising sea levels has generated much attention, such events will not occur overnight. Instead, it is likely that global warming will create a multitude of problems—damage and destruction of coral reefs, increasing salinity of water, decreased food production, harm to the tourist industry—that will lead people to leave their islands long before they are submerged by rising sea-levels. In fact, the tipping point for migration and displacement is considered more likely to result from declining availability of fresh water than from flooding. An ominous sign of this was the declaration of a national emergency in Tuvalu in September 2011 due to continuing drought, critically low community water supplies, and damaged desalination units.

The particular vulnerability of small

islands underlines the need for mitigation measures to reduce the likelihood of sea-level rise, for community preparedness and contingency planning initiatives, and for governments to increase their capacity to plan, monitor and respond effectively to climate change-induced displacement. Small island vulnerability also underscores the importance of looking at adaptation measures which could enable populations to remain where they are—though such measures may be prohibitively expensive. It also points to a need to consider scenarios in which large-scale relocation may be necessary, although the history of population relocations in the Pacific region, for example, is not a positive one.

The fundamental question is whether these situations will be met by *ad hoc* reactions, or by a coherent international response designed to respect the rights of the affected populations, including the right to their national identity. ◆

Natural disasters and displacement

A DISASTER HAS BEEN DEFINED BY THE IASC AS 'A SERIOUS DISRUPTION of the functioning of a community or a society causing widespread human, material, economic or environmental losses which exceed the ability of the affected community or society to cope using its own resources'.[17] The terms sudden-onset and slow-onset disaster are widely used to contrast, for example, an earthquake, which occurs in a matter of minutes, and a drought, which may develop over years; but there is no accepted dividing line between sudden-onset and slow-onset disasters.

The number of sudden-onset disasters has increased dramatically in recent decades. According to many experts, this is the result of global warming and a particular effect on rainfall patterns resulting in an increase in hydrometeorological disasters. For example, both the severity of tropical storms–typhoons, hurricanes, cyclones–and the frequency of severe storms are increasing as a result of the warming of the earth's atmosphere and oceans.[18] While 133 natural disasters were recorded in 1980, the number has increased to over 350 per year in recent years.[19]

Although 'natural disaster' is a widely used term, it is in fact shorthand for the more technically accurate term 'disaster triggered by natural hazards'. Natural hazards do not in themselves constitute disasters; rather human actions exacerbate the effects of natural phenomena to create disasters. For example, deforestation caused by human actions may lead to a heavy rainfall that results in a landslide; the destruction of a mangrove forest may remove a natural barrier that in turn increases the impact of a cyclone. Patterns of human settlement affect whether or not a natural hazard constitutes a disaster. For example, torrential rain falling in a sparsely inhabited rainforest is probably not a disaster, while the same level of rain in a large urban centre could cause catastrophic flooding.

Marginal areas in urban settings are likely to be most seriously affected in disasters as the rate of urbanization increases worldwide, and ever more people live in these marginal settings (*see chapter 6*). Urban environments pose particular challenges for those seeking to respond to natural disasters. Congestion can impede access to affected communities; marginal areas in the world's big cities are often territories controlled by criminals, gangs, traffickers, and insurgent groups, which creates security risks for humanitarian actors; and it is often difficult to identify the most needy in urban settings. In Haiti, for example, urban programmes aimed at assisting those made homeless by the January 2010 earthquake may have ended up creating new IDPs, as people left their homes in the hope of receiving assistance.

The impact of natural disasters is a function of both the severity of the natural hazard and the capacity of a population to deal with it. The notion of vulnerability, 'the characteristics and circumstances of a community (...) that make it susceptible to the damaging effects of a hazard',[20] is thus key to understanding the impact of natural disasters on communities. While most attention is focused on mega-disasters–such as the 2011 earthquake in Japan or the 2010 floods in Pakistan–less attention is given to smaller-scale disasters that may have a great impact on their communities. For example, the 2007 tsunami in the

Solomon Islands displaced 4.6 per cent of the population; if that percentage is extrapolated to Germany, for example, the corresponding number of people displaced would have been around four million. Moreover, the cumulative effect of multiple disasters occurring in the same communities is poorly understood.[21]

▲ **The town of Beichuan** in Sichuan province (China) after the May 2008 earthquake.

Recently, efforts have been made to collect data on the number of people displaced by natural disasters, but only for sudden-onset disasters.[22] There are no systematic data on cross-border displacement caused by disasters, nor on how long disaster-induced displacement lasts. It is usually assumed that displacement due to natural disasters is temporary, although there is considerable anecdotal evidence that at least some displacement following disasters lasts into the longer term. For example, a year after the Haiti earthquake, some 800,000 people were still living in over 1,000 settlements, mostly in tents, throughout the country's capital.[23]

Even though standard practice in large-scale disasters is to provide temporary shelters, such as tents, many of those displaced by natural disasters find shelter with family or friends, or among host communities rather than in camps. While it is difficult to count those displaced by sudden-onset disasters such as cyclones or hurricanes, it is even more difficult to estimate the numbers displaced by slow-onset disasters where people may migrate, especially to cities, as a result of both environmental and economic factors.

BOX 7•5

Cyclone Nargis

Cyclone Nargis made landfall in the Irrawaddy Delta region of Myanmar, the country's lowest expanse of land, during the night of 2 May 2008. The cyclone caused widespread devastation and death, destroyed livelihoods, and severely disrupted economic activities and social structures, including in the former capital Yangon.

With strong winds accompanied by heavy rain, the damage in the Delta region was compounded by a 12-foot tidal wave. Official estimates were that 140,000 people died, and joint assessments found that 2.4 million severely affected people were in need of assistance, including 800,000 who were displaced by the cyclone. Available information indicated that more women died than men.

International agencies and NGOs present in the country quickly launched an emergency response, using staff and resources available in the country at the time of the disaster. On 5 May, the government announced that it would welcome international assistance, and made a specific request to UNHCR for help. The magnitude of the devastation, the authorities' appeal for support, the limited presence of humanitarian agencies in the country, and initial restrictions on visas for additional aid workers established a clear humanitarian imperative for UNHCR to respond.

In the first weeks of the emergency, agencies present in Myanmar did their best to bring immediate relief to the affected populations. UNHCR concentrated on providing plastic tarpaulins for emergency shelter, mosquito nets, blankets and cooking pots. By the end of 2008, UNHCR had delivered relief items to 100,000 households.

Initially, it appeared that the authorities considered that assistance should consist of financial support for government efforts, as in the early phase of the emergency it did not facilitate the issuing of visas for incoming aid workers, or relax limitations on travel of foreigners to the affected areas. Even though national staff did not face the same restrictions, these limitations resulted in an initial shortage of personnel with experience in dealing with such emergencies.

In late May, during the visit of UN Secretary-General Ban Ki-moon, an agreement was reached with Myanmar's senior leadership on international access to affected areas and on the modalities of the relief operation. It would be managed through a special coordination mechanism, termed the Tripartite Core Group (TCG), consisting of representatives from the Association of Southeast Asian Nations (ASEAN), the UN, and the government. This arrangement proved effective in building trust and enabling constructive solutions to be found.

Following the Secretary-General's visit, UNHCR gained access to the affected areas and immediately established small offices in Bogale and Laputta, two of the hardest-hit townships. This allowed UNHCR to identify vulnerable survivors and address their needs directly, or refer them to other agencies for appropriate care. Protection matters such as involuntary relocation, closure of temporary settlements, and forced returns were raised with the government through the TCG mechanism and, in a number of cases, could be solved.

Partnerships were established with NGOs working in the country and with emerging community-based organizations, with the objective of reaching as many affected people as possible. UNHCR also was able to initiate training on emergency response for various government officials assigned to work under the newly established National Response Committee.

Protection needs arising from natural disasters have many similarities with those resulting from other forms of forced displacement: security from sexual- and gender-based violence and exploitation; equality before the law; the right to essential services; the right to food, water, and health care; the right to work; and housing, land and property rights. In Myanmar, a dialogue with the government on such issues would have been inconceivable a few months earlier, but the new working environment made these topics somewhat less controversial and UNHCR could bring its experience to bear in dealing with protection of the cyclone victims. Protection interventions made by UNHCR and others on behalf of IDPs met with some success. Lost documentation or lack of documentation was a major problem in the Delta, and UNHCR provided support wherever it could.

As in many other situations, complex property issues arose in the aftermath of the disaster. Property in many villages has never been registered and owners do not usually hold deeds. UNHCR was able to benefit from the services of an official from the Land Department, to help to tackle some of these problems. Through the Land Adviser, UNHCR could support and train NGOs, village leaders, and others on land issues.

A 'Protection of Children and Women Cluster', co-chaired by UNICEF and Save the Children, and an informal 'Vulnerability Network' set up by the Humanitarian Coordinator, were brought together into an overarching Protection Cluster in December 2008. The Protection Cluster was chaired by UNHCR, with the Department of Social Welfare as the government counterpart. As the emergency operation wound down, the Protection Cluster was transformed into a nationwide protection working group, which served as a platform for engagement with the authorities.

In short, the terrible tragedy of Cyclone Nargis provided an opportunity for dialogue with a wide range of local and national authorities on many issues, and helped to open up 'protection space' in Myanmar's Delta and beyond. ◆

UNHCR'S ENGAGEMENT IN NATURAL DISASTERS

When UNHCR has an established presence and programme in a country struck by a disaster, the agency has frequently offered its support to the authorities as a sign of solidarity and as part of broader UN efforts. In such situations, UNHCR cannot ignore the host communities among whom refugees and other persons of concern live; it is a basic humanitarian imperative to respond to people in distress. In addition, UNHCR has expertise which can be useful in addressing the protection needs of local populations displaced by natural disasters.

UNHCR's presence in countries affected by the 2004 Indian Ocean tsunami enabled the agency to respond rapidly. Similarly, UNHCR was able to mount a response after the 2005 Pakistan earthquake because it had experienced staff and supplies of desperately-needed tents and other items available. In the summer of 2010, and again in 2011, UNHCR participated in inter-agency effort for flood relief in Pakistan. Following government requests for aid, UNHCR also responded to disasters which were much less publicized, such as flooding in Uganda and Ghana in 2007, and in Benin and Montenegro in 2010.

A UNHCR-commissioned review of 58 natural disasters in 2005–2010 reported that UNHCR had an operational involvement in 13 and provided support in another five.[24] However, the study found there was no consistency in the timing of UNHCR's involvement, that UNHCR was not a part of the United Nations Disaster Assessment and Coordination (UNDAC), and that unpredictable funding limited UNHCR's engagement.

The UN's humanitarian reform process designated UNHCR to take the lead at both the global and field levels on protection issues in complex emergencies arising from conflicts. No corresponding lead at field level was named for protection in natural disasters; rather, a consultative process was established by which the UN's three protection agencies—UNHCR, UNICEF, and the Office of the High Commissioner for Human Rights—would consult to determine which was best-placed to take the lead in a specific emergency. In practice, this has meant delays and a lack of predictability in response.

For that reason, and in view of UNHCR's field presence and operational expertise, the High Commissioner expressed willingness to take on a more predictable role in responding to the protection needs of people displaced by natural disasters. That suggestion generated considerable discussion within the international community; some feel that UNHCR's expertise is particularly relevant to disasters; others are concerned that increasing UNHCR's engagement with natural disasters could detract from its refugee protection mandate. At a June 2011 meeting of members of its Executive Committee, UNHCR put forward a set of considerations to guide its involvement in situations of natural disaster, but no consensus could be reached. At the October 2011 plenary session of the Executive Committee, the High Commissioner noted a lack of agreement on the way forward and affirmed that UNHCR would therefore continue to respond on a case-by-case basis.[25]

PROTECTION CONCERNS AND VULNERABILITIES IN NATURAL DISASTERS

The 2004 Indian Ocean tsunami contributed to raising international awareness about the importance of protection in situations of natural disaster. Until then, the assumption was that protection is central to complex emergencies stemming from conflicts, but the main challenge in natural disasters is to deliver relief supplies quickly.

The many evaluations of the tsunami response discovered a range of protection issues, which have also been evident in subsequent natural disasters. For instance, when a disaster occurs, families may be separated, and trafficking of children can increase. Sexual and gender-based violence is endemic in most temporary shelters. Pre-existing patterns of discrimination are often reinforced, and responders may lack adequate means to identify, protect, and assist those with special needs; there may be discrimination in access to assistance because of ethnicity, religion, and caste. In the aftermath of a disaster, the loss of documentation—such as birth certificates or identity cards—frequently makes it difficult for people to have access to public services and exercise their rights.

Protection of housing, land and property rights can be particularly problematic, especially in cases of forced relocations, evictions and premature returns, but also in the context of recovery. People who lack a recognized title to their property or who do not own their homes, such as renters and squatters, have a hard time recovering their property or finding housing following a disaster. Gender inequities often arise—for example, when women are not permitted to inherit property from deceased spouses.

As noted earlier, the UN Guiding Principles on Internal Displacement apply to people displaced by natural disasters as well as by conflict. The national authorities are responsible for protecting and assisting those living within their borders, and they have a responsibility to ask for assistance when their capacity is stretched. However, governments may be reluctant to consider people driven from their homes by natural disasters as IDPs, either because they consider the displacement to be of a very temporary nature, or because of the term's association with conflict and human rights abuses.[26]

These complexities led the Representative of the UN Secretary-General for the Human Rights of IDPs to develop the Operational Guidelines for the Protection of Persons affected by Natural Disasters, intended as practical guidance to humanitarian agencies on how to help governments to fulfil their responsibilities for the protection and assistance of people affected by natural disasters in their country.[27] UNHCR participated actively in the drafting and field-testing of these Guidelines, which were adopted by the IASC in late 2010.

The Guidelines explain clearly how natural disasters affect human rights. They do not distinguish between people who are displaced and those who remain behind, but make clear that people who are forced to leave their homes are particularly vulnerable. They also stress that natural disasters exacerbate existing vulnerabilities, and that this needs to be considered in emergency response.

In other words, disasters do not affect all people in the same way. For example, in the case of an earthquake, inhabitants of poorly constructed housing are more likely to be injured or killed than those of solidly-constructed buildings. The people most likely to live

UNHCR/S. PHELPS

▲ **In 2010, Pakistan suffered the worst flooding in a century.** In August 2011, heavy monsoon rains again flooded the country, displacing millions of people.

in sub-standard housing are the poor and marginalized. There are also gender and age inequities. In the case of the 2005 Pakistan earthquake, for example, women were more likely to suffer injuries caused by collapsed housing than were their husbands, who were often working outside the home. In floods and tsunamis, women are more likely to drown as a result of lesser physical strength (to hang on to branches), cultural traditions (less likely to learn how to swim) or family responsibilities (more likely to be holding on to children). Similarly, those with physical disabilities, the elderly and children may suffer disproportionately.[28]

The Operational Guidelines offer a helpful typology—indeed, a hierarchy—of protection actions to be taken in situations of natural disasters. The first priority is to protect life, personal security, and the physical integrity of affected populations. The second priority relates to ensuring the right to the basic necessities of life, such as food, shelter, and health

BOX 7•6

Helping flood victims in Pakistan

In the summer of 2010, Pakistan was hit by the worst flooding in 100 years. The floods affected more than 20 million people in four provinces: Khyber Pakhtunkhwa, Balochistan, Sindh and Punjab. Along with local residents, many Afghan refugees were affected, as were Pakistani IDPs who had fled internal strife in the north-western part of the country in 2009. Around 1.8 million homes were destroyed and an estimated 2,000 people lost their lives as a result of the floods.

Faced with the scale of the catastrophe, UNHCR could not stand on the sidelines. UNHCR has operated in Pakistan for more than three decades, mainly to provide protection and assistance to refugees from Afghanistan. At the end of 2011, Pakistan hosted 1.7 million registered Afghan refugees.

After the government appealed for international help, UNHCR launched its largest programme ever in the context of a natural disaster, valued at US$186 million, as part of the broader UN response. High Commissioner

António Guterres visited Pakistan in September 2010 to express his solidarity, commenting: 'Nobody was prepared for such a level of destruction and for such difficult conditions for the people affected. Everybody is doing their best, but the best everyone is doing cannot match the dramatic needs that we are facing.'

UNHCR's assistance reached over two million of the most vulnerable flood-affected people in organized camps, public buildings, or informal camp-like settlements. Many others lived with host families or camped along deserted roadways. As always, the first responders came from the local level, including district government officials, the military, philanthropists, and countless members of the local population.

Pakistan's military took a strong lead in coordinating the emergency response, while the government's National Disaster Management Authority and Provincial Disaster Management Authority took charge of relief and recovery activities in the flood-affected areas.

The UN eventually activated all 11 aid 'clusters' to coordinate the international engagement.

UNHCR **was tasked to lead** the Protection Cluster during the emergency phase at the national and provincial levels. Given the extremely large number of protection actors—120 agencies—UNHCR initiated a Strategic Advisory Group composed of government, national and local NGOs, and key agency representatives, which acted as a steering committee for the Protection Cluster. UNHCR also led the Camp Coordination and Management Cluster and the Emergency Shelter Cluster in two provinces, Khyber Pakhtunkhwa and Balochistan.

Aid workers were understandably concerned about preventing a second wave of deaths due to standing water, the lack of safe drinking water and sanitation facilities, as well as cramped living conditions that could facilitate the spread of disease. Ensuring that people had shelter from continuing rains was a primary concern.

---

care, and to primary education. A third category encompasses the protection of rights related to land and property, as well as livelihoods and secondary education. A fourth category includes basic civil and political rights, such as freedom of assembly and the right to political participation.

Cross-border displacement: a normative gap

RESEARCHERS AND HUMANITARIAN ACTORS HAVE LONG BEEN CONCERNED ABOUT the effect of climate change on human mobility. However, those responsible for negotiating climate change agreements, primarily from national environment and finance ministries, have been slower to address the potential impact of climate change on the movement of people. It was only at its sixteenth meeting in 2010 that the Conference of Parties of the United Nations Conference on Climate Change acknowledged the importance of addressing the movement of people caused by climate change, and recognized that such

A key protection issue for UNHCR was the fact that many citizens had lost their personal documentation in the floods, including birth certificates, marriage certificates, and land titles, as well as government-issued identity cards. Many government records were also damaged or destroyed. Apart from making it hard for people to prove land ownership and settle property disputes, thereby delaying returns, people who did not have their Computerized National Identity Card (CNIC) could not have access to the government's Citizen Damage and Compensation Programme, supported by the World Bank, which included a cash assistance component known as *Watan*—meaning 'country' in Urdu.

To receive cash assistance, recipients needed to have a CNIC. For many who had lost their cards, it was too expensive or administratively difficult to replace them on their own. Women, particularly single women and female heads of household, were the most likely to lack the necessary documentation, as women and children were traditionally listed on men's cards.

UNHCR decided to put its experience with refugee registration and documentation to use, to provide support to the government for registration of flood victims, in particular to enable them to access the *Watan* programme. UNHCR advocated for the inclusion of the most vulnerable persons affected by the floods in this scheme, and for the issuance of identity cards to those who did not have them, or who had lost them during the emergency. UNHCR and NGO teams regularly visited the registration centres to provide legal counselling and advice.

UNHCR mobilized the Protection Cluster to provide technical advice and conduct field monitoring during the implementation of the *Watan* scheme, and conducted several rapid protection assessments. A comprehensive report by UNHCR and the Protection Cluster detailed how the scheme was implemented and made several recommendations for how such schemes could be improved in future scenarios, in Pakistan or elsewhere.

UNHCR is convinced that cash assistance can be an efficient way to provide rapid support to people affected by large-scale emergencies. In the Pakistan floods, conventional aid distribution mechanisms were rendered inadequate both by the scale of the disaster and by the fact that so many areas were inaccessible. The size of the emergency simply exceeded procurement, production, delivery, and logistic capabilities. Yet the victims could not wait weeks or months for help.

Infrastructure in the country was generally functioning and food and other supplies were available on the markets. In this context, cash assistance represented value for money and was usually preferred by the beneficiaries to in-kind assistance. Although in-kind assistance certainly contributed to supporting coping mechanisms and reduced household expenditures and vulnerability, the life-saving element of such aid was probably limited.

Still, many agencies continue to feel more comfortable with in-kind assistance and some hesitate to change their approach. Also, while the registration exercise during the Pakistan emergency was a logistical triumph, it is true that flawed registration criteria can lead to inclusion and exclusion errors.

Equipped with the lessons learned from this experience, UNHCR is encouraging further improvements, to ensure that the most vulnerable among affected populations are able to benefit from cash assistance without discrimination, including people who live in isolated communities cut off from infrastructure. ◆

---

displacement will take different forms and require actions at different levels.

The Conference invited all parties to undertake measures '(...) to enhance understanding, coordination and cooperation with regard to climate change-induced displacement, migration and planned relocation, where appropriate, at national, regional and international levels'.[29] This was an important step and may encourage governments and other actors to consider mobility as a strategy for adapting to the effects of climate change.

The International Law Commission, in its ongoing work on a text that might serve as the basis for the development of binding international law on the protection of persons in the event of disasters, has considered an article on the duty of states to seek international assistance when they are unable to cope single-handedly.[30] Another important development is the effort by the International Federation of Red Cross and Red Crescent Societies to develop and promote international disaster response law, to facilitate actions of emergency responders and to affirm the responsibility of governments to oversee the disaster response.[31]

While international law clearly establishes the responsibility of each state for the protection of its citizens, including those who are internally displaced, a potential gap exists with respect to the protection of persons who are displaced across borders owing to natural disasters and the effect of climate change. For this reason, immediately after the earthquake in Haiti in January 2010, UNHCR and the UN High Commissioner for Human Rights appealed to governments not to return people to Haiti against their will.[32] This appeal was widely respected.

Courts around the world have made clear—and UNHCR concurs—that the 1951 Convention does not cover persons fleeing natural disasters. The High Court of Australia has stated: 'No matter how devastating may be epidemic, natural disaster or famine, a person fleeing them is not a refugee within the terms of the Convention'.[33] However, numerous states have recognized the need to offer such persons another form of protection.

There are many examples of states granting permission to remain, or at the very least granting a stay of deportation, to persons whose country of origin has been hit by a natural disaster or another such extreme event.

In the United States of America, for instance, Temporary Protected Status (TPS) may be extended to foreigners who are in the US when an 'environmental disaster' occurs in their country. This was the case for nationals of Honduras and Nicaragua, following Hurricane Mitch in 1998, and for nationals of El Salvador after a series of earthquakes in 2001.[34] At the request of their governments, this temporary stay has been regularly extended as a way of supporting these countries even after the immediate effects of the disasters. After the 2010 Haiti earthquake, the US government granted TPS to Haitians in the country at the time of the quake, but also issued a strong warning that Haitians seeking to enter after the earthquake would not automatically be accepted. During the period designated for TPS, beneficiaries are protected from being removed, and may obtain authorization to work and to travel. A grant of TPS does not affect an application for asylum.

Other countries have also included provisions in their immigration law to provide temporary protection in the wake of an environmental or natural disaster. For instance, Argentine law provides a remedy for persons who, although not in need of protection as refugees, are temporarily unable to return to their countries due to the consequences of natural disasters or environmental disasters caused by man. Similarly, Swedish law contains a provision extending protection to people who are unable to return to their country of origin because of an environmental disaster, although to date it has not been used. Finnish law also provides that a person may be granted protection for the same reason.[35] Canada, the Czech Republic and Romania have analogous provisions in their legislation.

A broader international framework providing guidance for the protection of those displaced across national borders because of environmental causes could help states to understand and meet their responsibilities in this area. At present there seems to be scant political support for a new binding international instrument, but there is nonetheless a need for guidance which, even if not legally binding, could promote coherence in approach and provide practical suggestions to governments.

One possibility, raised at the Nansen Conference in Oslo in June 2011, is to use the Guiding Principles on Internal Displacement as a model for developing a set of principles relating to people who are displaced across borders by the effects of climate change and other environmental hazards. The principles could, for example, define particular groups of concern, affirm the basic human rights of displaced persons, and specify responsibilities for protecting them. The development of such principles would be a concrete way of encouraging international solidarity.

UNHCR has indicated that it would be prepared, in line with its statutory responsibility for the progressive development of international law in areas of its concern, to work with states and other actors to develop a guiding framework or instrument to apply to situations of external displacement other than those covered by the 1951 Convention, in particular regarding displacement resulting from climate change and natural disasters.[36]

BOX **7.7**

The Nansen Principles: a way forward?

The Nansen Conference on Climate Change and Displacement in the 21st Century was convened in June 2011 by the government of Norway, coinciding with the 150th birthday of Fridtjof Nansen, the Norwegian scientist, explorer, and humanist who was appointed High Commissioner for Refugees by the League of Nations in 1921.

The Conference in Oslo brought together experts and representatives of governments, civil society, and UN agencies to consider the humanitarian consequences of climate change. Chaired by the United Nations Assistant Secretary-General for Disaster Risk Reduction, Margareta Wahlström, the Conference proposed the following ten Principles to guide future action, known as the 'Nansen Principles':

I. Responses to climate and environmentally-related displacement need to be informed by adequate knowledge and guided by the fundamental principles of humanity, human dignity, human rights and international cooperation.

II. States have a primary duty to protect their populations and give particular attention to the special needs of the people most vulnerable to and most affected by climate change and other environmental hazards, including the displaced, hosting communities, and those at risk of displacement. The development of legislation, policies and institutions as well as

the investment of adequate resources are key in this regard.

III. The leadership and engagement of local governments and communities, civil society, and the private sector are needed to address effectively the challenges posed by climate change, including those linked to human mobility.

IV. When national capacity is limited, regional frameworks and international cooperation should support action at the national level and contribute to building national capacity, underpinning development plans, preventing displacement, assisting and protecting people and communities affected by such displacement, and finding durable solutions.

V. Prevention and resilience need to be further strengthened at all levels, particularly through adequate resources. International, regional and local actors have a shared responsibility to implement the principles enshrined in the Hyogo Framework for Action 2005–2015: Building the Resilience of Nations and Communities to Disasters.

VI. Building local and national capacity to prepare for and respond to disasters is fundamental. At the same time, the international disaster response system needs to be reinforced. The development of multi-hazard early warning systems linking local and global levels is critical.

VII. The existing norms of international law should be fully utilized, and normative gaps addressed.

VIII. The Guiding Principles on Internal Displacement provide a sound legal framework to address protection concerns arising from climate—and other environmentally-related internal displacement. States are encouraged to ensure the adequate implementation and operationalization of these principles through national legislation, policies and institutions.

IX. A more coherent and consistent approach at the international level is needed to meet the protection needs of people displaced externally owing to sudden-onset disasters. States, working in conjunction with UNHCR and other relevant stakeholders, could develop a guiding framework or instrument in this regard.

X. National and international policies and responses, including planned relocation, need to be implemented on the basis of non-discrimination, consent, empowerment, participation and partnerships with those directly affected, with due sensitivity to age, gender and diversity aspects. The voices of the displaced or those threatened with displacement, loss of home or livelihood must be heard and taken into account, without neglecting those who may choose to remain. ◆

A test for international solidarity

THE LINE IS DIFFICULT TO DRAW BETWEEN DISPLACEMENT CAUSED BY CLIMATE change and displacement resulting from natural disasters. In many regions of the world, cycles of monsoon rain trigger floods on a regular basis. It is hard to ascertain whether heavier-than-usual floods have resulted from long-term changes in climate or from normal variations in natural phenomena. In the 2010 Pakistan floods, there was a widespread feeling that the floods were unusually severe because of climate change, but it is hard to draw the causal connection.[37] The relationship between climate change and drought is also difficult to ascertain.

What is evident is that there are protection gaps—especially for people displaced across international borders, whether by sudden-onset natural disasters or by longer-term effects of climate changes. There is a need to address these gaps now, in preparation for possible future increases in such movements. National laws and policies will need to be adapted and strengthened to respond to displacement caused by climate change. Regional and sub-regional norms will need to be developed so that governments can hold one another accountable for the way in which they respond to displacement caused by climate change.

Climate change is likely to test global solidarity in ways that are radically different from anything experienced before. Countries and regions affected by climate change will need support, including from those actors most responsible for contributing to global warming. Much more effort will need to be made to mitigate the effects of climate change and to reduce the risk of disasters, and the work of the International Strategy for Disaster Risk Reduction should be supported. Further work will be needed to develop guidance for states affected by people moving because of the effects of climate change.

At the international level, no single institution has responsibility for matters related to climate change; it is a global challenge that involves many areas of international governance. Since the founding of the UN in 1945, the international community has struggled to find appropriate ways to address diverse global threats, ranging from the nuclear arms race to the depletion of the ozone layer by chlorofluorocarbons. In 1987, governments were able to unite in adopting the Montreal Protocol on Substances that Deplete the Ozone Layer to protect the earth's atmosphere, thereby reaching what a former UN Secretary-General called 'perhaps the single most successful international agreement to date'.[38] This achievement reflected a shared understanding of a common threat that transcended traditional conceptions of national sovereignty.

Speaking at the UN Security Council in November 2011, High Commissioner António Guterres said 'the process of climate change and its role in reinforcing other global imbalances constitutes an important threat to international peace and security.' And so far, he said, 'the international community has lacked the political will and cooperative spirit required to reduce the pace of that process'.[39]

Addressing the effects of climate change will require the world once again to think beyond the confines of national sovereignty, not least out of a sense of intergenerational equity. New forms of multilateral cooperation will be needed to respond effectively to displacement, and to the other human consequences of climate change. Developing a humanitarian response to such challenges is important, but the international community will also need to address the implications of climate change for global peace, security, justice, and human rights. Climate change sets a particularly stern test for solidarity. ■

CHAPTER 8

State Responsibility and International Solidarity

O N 11 July 2011, a Spanish Navy frigate operating in the Mediterranean rescued more than 100 people of various nationalities. They had fled the conflict in Libya in an unseaworthy boat and had been in distress at sea for several days. According to press reports, the frigate, the *Almirante Juan de Borbón*, operating under the authority of the North Atlantic Treaty Organization (NATO), was ordered to bring the passengers to Malta.

Malta did not allow the frigate to dock, maintaining that disembarkation should take place in Italy or Tunisia; only a few passengers with serious medical conditions were brought ashore in Malta. NATO then sought disembarkation in several other European countries, including Italy and Spain, without success. On 16 July, NATO ordered the frigate to head for the Tunisian coast, where it transferred the passengers to a Tunisian naval vessel. The passengers were disembarked in Tunisia.

Many of the facts of this case remain unclear. Where exactly did the rescue occur, and in which country's Search and Rescue Areas? Which countries were approached by NATO or by the Spanish authorities with a request for disembarkation? Why was disembarkation denied? Of what nationalities were the passengers? How many were refugees or asylum seekers? Was consideration given to the fact that Tunisia—a much poorer country than Italy or Malta—had already taken in many more people fleeing Libya than had all the NATO member countries combined?

◀ **Somalis boarding a boat to flee to Yemen** in November 2007. Only eleven of more than one hundred passengers survive the journey.

This incident affected a relatively small number of people, but it illustrates the persistent tension between state sovereignty and efforts to ensure international protection. It also illustrates why greater international solidarity is needed.

The international refugee protection system is founded on national responsibility, that is, on the compliance of states with their legal obligations towards refugees and others at risk. At the same time, the system depends on international solidarity, described by the UN General Assembly as a 'fundamental value by virtue of which global challenges must be managed in a way that distributes costs and burdens fairly (...)'.[1]

Solidarity is needed because responsibility for refugees is not evenly distributed; it rests with whatever state a person seeking protection is able to reach. The countries most affected by refugee flows appeal regularly for more international support, yet no clear parameters exist for how states should help one another with hosting refugees. There are often different assessments of the need for solidarity, depending on the visibility—and the politics—of each crisis.

The UN High Commissioner for Refugees has identified the solution to growing tensions in the global refugee regime as, 'quite simply, more international solidarity'.[2] This chapter looks at how solidarity can help states to shoulder their responsibilities for refugees. It reviews the international community's recognition, over time, of the need for solidarity, the impact on countries and communities of hosting large numbers of refugees, and the principal forms of responsibility-sharing. The chapter concludes with a discussion of prospects for strengthening international solidarity in order to improve protection and to find lasting solutions for millions of the world's most vulnerable people.

Recognition of the need for solidarity

IT WAS NOT UNTIL EARLY IN THE TWENTIETH CENTURY THAT AN INSTITUTIONAL framework for addressing refugee problems came into being, with High Commissioners for Refugees appointed by the League of Nations. In the 1920s, these High Commissioners had some success in fostering international cooperation and most notably, the adoption of an identity document for refugees—the Nansen Passport.

In the 1930s, the League of Nations grievously failed to find solutions for people trying to flee Nazi Germany. The absence of solidarity was most evident at the 1938 Evian Conference, convened to discuss the problem of Jewish refugees. Although 32 nations participated, only the Dominican Republic made a pledge to take in refugees, and many countries were openly opposed to their admission. This failure cost countless lives.

Massive population movements during and in the wake of the Second World War resulted in the establishment of UNHCR in 1951.[3] UNHCR was tasked with working closely with governments to address the problem of refugees, in line with one of the central purposes of the UN as set out in its Charter: to achieve international cooperation in solving problems of a humanitarian character.[4] In UNHCR's Statute, the General Assembly listed eight specific ways in which governments could support UNHCR's work, including by becoming parties to international conventions for the protection of refugees and by admitting refugees to their territories.[5]

The Second World War was also the context for framing the 1951 Refugee Convention. Its Preamble makes clear that national responsibility and international solidarity are mutually reinforcing concepts. It notes that 'the grant of asylum may place unduly heavy burdens on certain countries', and that a satisfactory solution cannot be achieved without international cooperation.[6] This language set the framework through which national responsibility should be supported, not supplanted, by international cooperation.

A similar approach was articulated in the 1969 Convention Governing the Specific Aspects of Refugees Problems in Africa, which provides that: 'Where a Member State finds difficulty in continuing to grant asylum to refugees, such Member State may appeal directly to other Member States and through the OAU, and such other Member States shall in the spirit of African solidarity and international co-operation take appropriate measures to lighten the burden of the Member State granting asylum'.[7]

In Latin America, the adoption of 'soft law' instruments such as the 1984 Cartagena Declaration on Refugees, and more recently the 2004 Mexico Plan of Action (*see box 8.1*), have also paved the way for responses to forced displacement which build on the concept of 'regional solidarity'.[8]

BOX **8·1**

Dimensions of solidarity in Latin America

Latin America has a long tradition of regional cooperation and solidarity with refugees. In 1984, as proxy wars in Central America were forcing millions to flee their countries, a Colloquium on refugee protection was convened in Cartagena, Colombia. The Colloquium resulted in the Cartagena Declaration on Refugees (*see chapter 2*). In the same tradition, on the 20th anniversary of the Cartagena Declaration in 2004, 20 countries endorsed the Mexico Declaration and Plan of Action to Strengthen the International Protection of Refugees in Latin America.

Today, Latin America hosts the smallest number of refugees of any region, although one country—Colombia—has one of the largest populations of IDPs. The Mexico Plan of Action was an effort to frame a regional response, rooted in the principles of state responsibility and regional solidarity, to the ongoing humanitarian crisis created by the situation in Colombia.

The Mexico Plan of Action encouraged the further development of national legislation pertaining to refugees and of refugee status determination mechanisms. At the regional level, it endorsed three innovative approaches to durable solutions, entitled 'Cities of Solidarity', 'Borders of Solidarity', and 'Solidarity Resettlement'.

The Cities of Solidarity programme signalled the political will of countries in the region to promote self reliance and local integration for refugees living in urban areas, by enabling them to exercise their social, economic, and cultural rights. It recognized that two-thirds of all refugees and asylum seekers in Latin America live in cities, along with around half of Colombia's IDPs, and that training, recognition of refugees' qualifications, employment, microfinance, and the engagement of civil society are all needed to support integration.

Since the adoption of the Mexico Plan of Action, much has been done to improve the situation of urban refugees. All countries in the region grant refugees the right to work, and nine countries extend this right to asylum seekers as well. Numerous municipal and provincial authorities have taken steps to facilitate access of asylum seekers, refugees, and IDPs to local education and health services. Civil society groups help persons of concern to UNHCR to exercise their rights.

The Borders of Solidarity programme involves both Colombia and its neighbours. It seeks to respond to the humanitarian needs of people living in the border areas of Colombia who are at risk of displacement, as well as of Colombians in need of international protection who are living in the border areas of neighbouring countries—in particular Ecuador, Panama, and Venezuela. Local populations in these isolated and often very poor regions also benefit from the implementation of income-generating activities, infrastructure improvements, and other actions, for instance to improve health care and education facilities, or to provide clean water and sanitation.

The Solidarity Resettlement programme was created to expand refugee resettlement prospects for Colombian refugees within the region. Since 2005, around 1,100 Colombian refugees have been resettled in one of the region's five resettlement countries: Argentina, Brazil, Chile, Paraguay, or Uruguay. At the request of UNHCR, Chile and Brazil have also resettled Palestinian refugees from Iraq (*see box 8.3*).

Several 'twinning' meetings sponsored by Norway have enabled resettlement countries from different parts of the world to exchange experiences with their Latin American counterparts.

The Mexico Plan of Action has provided a flexible framework for solidarity and partnership. The scale of displacement in and from Colombia continues to be a very serious concern. But the degree to which governments in the region have established public policies to facilitate refugees' access to their rights, and the active role of local authorities and civil society in promoting durable solutions, are encouraging signs and set a positive example for other regions. ◆

As the nature of violence and forced displacement evolved, increasing numbers of people became internally displaced. The responsibility of national authorities for their own citizens was clear, but in many cases they could not discharge it unaided, and in some cases they were unwilling to discharge it at all.

For those forcibly displaced within their own country there is no international regime comparable to that for refugees. The 1998 Guiding Principles on Internal Displacement thus apply the notion of international cooperation in support of national responsibility (*see chapter 5*). Principle 25 states clearly that the primary responsibility for internally displaced persons (IDPs) lies with national authorities, but also suggests that there is a duty to accept international support under certain circumstances. 'International humanitarian organizations and other appropriate actors have the right to offer their services in support of the internally displaced', it says, adding that '[c]onsent thereto shall not be arbitrarily withheld, particularly when authorities concerned are unable or unwilling to provide the required humanitarian assistance'.[9]

With the end of the Cold War, the dynamics of refugee policy, and of international solidarity, changed. The interests of refugees and countries in the developed world no longer converged as clearly as they had in the past.[10] Western countries responded to the dramatic increase in irregular migration in the early and mid-1990s by introducing and enforcing measures to restrict access by asylum seekers and others to their territories, or to return them to countries through which they had travelled. Some refugee-hosting countries in the global South saw these measures as reflecting a double standard, given what was expected of them, and in recent years discussions about refugees have tended to become more polarized.

In 2000, UNHCR launched a series of Global Consultations on International Protection in order to explore ways to revitalize the international protection regime. A far-reaching 'Agenda for Protection' emerged from these Consultations, was endorsed by UNHCR's Executive Committee, and welcomed by the General Assembly in 2002. The Agenda for Protection set out six broad goals, of which the third was 'Sharing burdens and responsibilities more equitably and building capacities to receive and protect refugees'.[11] It called, in particular, for refugee issues to be anchored within national, regional and multilateral development agendas. The Agenda for Protection was followed by the 'Convention Plus' initiative.

The Convention Plus initiative was intended to develop international policy in areas identified in the Agenda for Protection as requiring attention because they were not fully covered by the Refugee Convention. The goal was to promote responsibility-sharing and comprehensive solutions to refugee problems. The initiative focused on three areas: resettlement; irregular secondary movements; and the use of development assistance to help achieve durable solutions. While there was a wide measure of agreement in principle, the initiative did not result in any firm agreement on burden-sharing.[12] Nor have subsequent initiatives.

UNHCR's Executive Committee has nonetheless consistently endorsed the value of international responsibility-sharing and in 2004 adopted its most detailed and solution-oriented treatment of the subject. Conclusion No. 100 (LV) of 2004 on 'International Co-operation and Burden and Responsibility Sharing in Mass Influx Situations' draws particular attention to contexts where responsibility-sharing can contribute to resolving refugee problems. It highlights first the need for financial assistance and other forms of support for voluntary repatriation, in view of the primacy of that durable solution. It also calls for assistance to support local integration where it is feasible, including development assistance; for more effective and strategic use of resettlement as a tool of burden- and responsibility-sharing; and for the mobilization of support for the rehabilitation of refugee-impacted areas in host countries.

More recently, in December 2010, participants in the High Commissioner's Dialogue on Protection Challenges endorsed a broad notion of burden- and responsibility-sharing across the full cycle of forced displacement, including prevention, protection and solutions. They noted that while financial aspects of burden-sharing are essential, humanitarian and political components are also important.[13] An Expert Meeting convened by UNHCR in 2011 agreed that strengthened international cooperation is a pressing issue for countries of origin and refugee-hosting countries alike, but pointed out that its meaning and scope required further definition and a better understanding was needed of the available tools.[14]

If the need for international solidarity is recognized, there are major obstacles to translating this into situation-specific action.[15] Without a clear framework for burden-sharing, states may be tempted to resort to burden-shifting—seeking to pass their responsibilities for refugees on to other states or to UNHCR and other international organizations. The involvement of UNHCR and others in emergency relief operations is a necessary manifestation of international solidarity. But involvement is problematic if over-burdened states expect UNHCR to bear the primary responsibility for open-ended 'care and maintenance' programmes, while denying refugees opportunities for self-sufficiency. It is also problematic if states expect UNHCR to undertake refugee status determination rather than develop that capacity themselves.[16]

Assessing the impact of hosting refugees

ONE OF THE MOST IMPORTANT ISSUES TO ARISE IN RELATION TO INTERNATIONAL solidarity concerns the costs incurred by refugee-hosting states and the impact of large-scale refugee influxes on their society, economy and environment.

There is no agreed methodology to assess the impact of refugees on different countries, or to compare the contribution made by individual countries to the refugee protection system. Even the distinction commonly made between refugee-hosting and donor countries is not clear cut: most donor states also host refugees and refugee-hosting states make significant financial and other contributions.[17] It is also difficult to measure how far costs incurred by countries hosting large refugee populations are offset by humanitarian or development aid. For a variety of reasons, some countries attract greater and more sustained international support than others.

BOX 8•2

Mass influx in Liberia

Volumes are written about refugee-hosting in Africa. Many authors describe the 'golden age' of refugee-hosting at the time of independence struggles and in the immediate post-colonial period. They point out that the refugee definition contained in the 1969 OAU Convention reflected refugee situations on the continent resulting from decolonization, and suggest that newly independent states' willingness to host refugees at that time can best be understood in that context.

Over the past two decades, large-scale refugee movements have continued in Africa, as a result of civil conflict and governance crises, but host states have adopted ever more restrictive policies. Governments have explained this policy shift by pointing to the scale and lasting nature of the refugee situations; limited support from international donors; and the security problems associated with major refugee flows.

Against this backdrop, Liberia's open door to refugees who fled the violence in Côte d'Ivoire which followed the presidential elections there in November 2010 stands out as a strong demonstration of solidarity. Liberia's response was all the more remarkable as the country was still consolidating its own fragile peace and development, after years of civil war and economic devastation.

It was on 29 November 2010 that staff at UNHCR's field office in Saclepea, Liberia received a call from immigration officials based at the border with Côte d'Ivoire, alerting UNHCR to what was to become a major refugee influx. Some 400 women and children had crossed that day from Côte d'Ivoire into Nimba County, a chronically poor region of eastern Liberia. In the next two months, 40,000 refugees entered Liberia.

Arrivals mounted steadily as the conflict worsened in Côte d'Ivoire. By 1 April, Nimba County alone hosted over 62,000 refugees—nearly as many as the local population. Addressing villagers in the border region in March 2011, High Commissioner António Guterres told them: 'In a world full of egotism, where rich countries are closing their doors, you have opened yours and shared what you have, and what you do not have.'

All told, within six months, 173,000 refugees crossed into Liberia. Most were initially sheltered in scores of villages located along the border, where the local people had kinship ties with the refugees. The villagers shared food with the refugees, but local absorption capacity was stretched, and some communities were reported to be using their seed rice to feed the newcomers.

Liberia's response was without doubt influenced by its own experience. During the country's 14-year civil war, more than 300,000 Liberians found refuge in Côte d'Ivoire, and were hosted by many of the same communities that fled into Liberia in 2010 and 2011. Nearly all of Liberia's estimated 3.8 million people were affected in one way or another by the long conflict.

When the refugee emergency began in 2010, UNHCR and other international actors were quick to point out that the conflict in Côte d'Ivoire posed a potential risk to Liberia's ongoing peacebuilding process. The High Commissioner called for international support to avoid any destabilizing effect. The UN Mission in Liberia, established by the UN Security Council after the Accra Peace Agreement ended Liberia's civil war in 2003, stepped up its military and police presence along the 700km border, with a view to preventing arms smuggling, and increased its cross-border cooperation with the UN Mission in Côte d'Ivoire (ONUCI).

Numerous international agencies were working in Liberia when the influx started, but their focus was mainly on development activities, not emergency response. Many humanitarian agencies, including UNHCR, had reduced their presence in Liberia as development work scaled up. The refugee emergency posed operational challenges for UNHCR, including questions about how to align the agency's mandated leadership role for refugees with a UN presence structured around an integrated peacekeeping mission and the 'Delivering as One' model.

With the vast majority of refugees located in host communities rather than camps, there was a heightened need for effective collaboration between international agencies and local authorities, as well as an opportunity to attract aid and infrastructure improvements to remote areas that had benefited from little development support since the end of the civil war. The coordination of sectoral responsibilities initially was problematic, but ultimately the response to the refugee crisis managed to draw constructively on the technical capacities of different agencies.

The mobilization of international attention and financial resources for the refugee emergency was another challenge, at a time when much of the world's attention was focused on the crisis in Libya and on the aftermath of Japan's devastating earthquake. However, donors rallied to support the emergency response, contributing a total of US$39 million in 2011 to UNHCR's operation on behalf of refugees from Côte d'Ivoire in Liberia. ◆

A telling indication of the impact of refugees is, however, given by correlating their numbers with their host country's per capita Gross Domestic Product (GDP) or with its national population. States with a relatively low per capita GDP accommodate a disproportionate number of the world's refugees. At the start of 2011, developing countries hosted 80 per cent of the 10.5 million refugees under UNHCR's mandate. The 20 countries with the highest number of refugees in relation to GDP were all in the developing world, and more than half were least-developed countries (LDCs). Of the ten countries with the largest number of refugees compared to the national population, nine were categorized as emerging and developing economies by the International Monetary Fund.

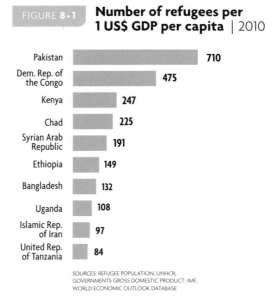

FIGURE **8·1** **Number of refugees per 1 US$ GDP per capita** | 2010

Pakistan	710
Dem. Rep. of the Congo	475
Kenya	247
Chad	225
Syrian Arab Republic	191
Ethiopia	149
Bangladesh	132
Uganda	108
Islamic Rep. of Iran	97
United Rep. of Tanzania	84

SOURCES: REFUGEE POPULATION: UNHCR; GOVERNMENTS GROSS DOMESTIC PRODUCT: IMF, WORLD ECONOMIC OUTLOOK DATABASE

However, it is not always a straightforward matter to compare refugee populations at national level, as data on the naturalization of refugees is not readily available. UNHCR's figures for refugees in 24 industrialized countries are thus estimates, based on the assumption that recognized refugees become citizens of their new countries after ten years.

Comparisons of refugee numbers at national levels can also obscure the fact that the most significant impacts of the presence of refugees are usually felt at the local level, in the refugee-hosting communities themselves. There, the refugees may even out-number nationals. Their presence can have many different and sometimes contrasting effects. For example, nationals may face increased competition for employment, while employers may benefit from a new source of willing and often low-cost labour. The impact may vary markedly within the same country.

At the national level, the costs of refugee-hosting fall

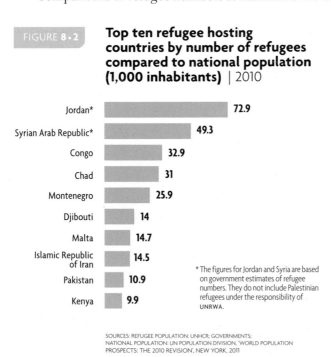

FIGURE **8·2** **Top ten refugee hosting countries by number of refugees compared to national population (1,000 inhabitants)** | 2010

Jordan*	72.9
Syrian Arab Republic*	49.3
Congo	32.9
Chad	31
Montenegro	25.9
Djibouti	14
Malta	14.7
Islamic Republic of Iran	14.5
Pakistan	10.9
Kenya	9.9

* The figures for Jordan and Syria are based on government estimates of refugee numbers. They do not include Palestinian refugees under the responsibility of UNRWA.

SOURCES: REFUGEE POPULATION: UNHCR; GOVERNMENTS; NATIONAL POPULATION: UN POPULATION DIVISION, 'WORLD POPULATION PROSPECTS: THE 2010 REVISION', NEW YORK, 2011 into three broad categories. First, there are those which accrue to the state administration, as countries must pay salaries and meet other expenses of their departments and officials responsible for refugee-related tasks. Second, there are costs to the economy, environment and infrastructure. These are not limited to situations where refugees are hosted in camps, even if the impacts are most obvious in that setting. Where large numbers of refugees live dispersed among the local population, governments also incur considerable costs, such as for the provision of education, health care and other essential services. Some costs are not immediately evident, for instance where refugees benefit from commodities subsidized by the government, such as bread or fuel. Third, there may be far-reaching political costs for the host state in terms of its security, social fabric, and relationships with other states.

The impacts of refugee situations that remain unresolved for years are less visible than those of emergencies, but they are no less serious for the host states and for the affected individuals (*see chapter 3*).[18] Large-scale refugee flows can also have wider destabilizing effects, as witnessed in the 1990s in the Great Lakes region of Africa. This is particularly the case when the ratio of refugees to the local population is high, or the ethnic or religious background of the refugees is different from that of the local population, as for example with the exodus from Kosovo to the former Yugoslav Republic of Macedonia in 1999.

Investigation into refugee-hosting has tended to focus on negative elements, but it can also have positive impacts. A World Bank report notes that 'displacement may contribute to economic growth benefitting both the displaced and the host region, and may also in the event of return, successful local integration, or resettlement in third countries, bring valuable human and economic capital to the recovery process'.[19]

Finally, consideration of the impact of refugee-hosting rarely extends to developed countries, although as demonstrated in chapter 2, some industrialized countries receive considerable numbers of asylum seekers, and grant asylum or offer resettlement on a large scale. Most research has been into the cost of maintaining asylum systems or of the process of integration, but there are also significant social, economic and demographic impacts which merit further study.

Responsibility-sharing in practice

HOSTING LARGE NUMBERS OF REFUGEES IS IN ITSELF THE MOST FUNDAMENTAL manifestation of 'responsibility-sharing in practice'. The important role played by low-and middle-income countries in sustaining the international protection regime is not always recognized. Many of the countries which host the majority of the world's refugees are struggling with the effects of climate change, volatile commodity prices and the global recession. If they are to pursue generous policies toward refugees, they must be adequately supported.

Responsibility-sharing mechanisms could aim either to address the *impacts* of the unequal distribution of refugees, or to achieve a *more equitable distribution* of the refugee 'burden' itself, or to do both.[20] In practice, international cooperation has focused on addressing the impact of refugee-hosting, and on supporting local integration and sustainable voluntary repatriation, through various forms of financial and technical support for the most affected countries.

Responsibility-sharing through the physical relocation of refugees and asylum seekers has mainly occurred through resettlement, but rarely on a large enough scale to reduce the burden on host countries significantly. Discussion of other ways to achieve a more equitable physical distribution of refugees has remained largely theoretical, confined primarily to the European Union.

FINANCIAL AND TECHNICAL SUPPORT

Financial support for the costs of protecting and assisting refugees and returnees has long been a part of international cooperation, through humanitarian and development assistance as well as through peacebuilding and peacekeeping actions.

The mechanisms for fiscal burden-sharing in the humanitarian sphere have evolved from largely *ad hoc* arrangements to well-established systems, both bilateral and multilateral, but they remain dependent on voluntary contributions.

Over the past decade, several innovations have been introduced in the funding of humanitarian operations. The 'Good Humanitarian Donorship' initiative launched in 2003 is now an informal donor forum and network of 37 countries which recognize that, 'by working together, donors can more effectively encourage and stimulate principled donor behavior and, by extension, improved humanitarian action'.[21]

In early 2006, the UN set up its Central Emergency Response Fund (CERF), which has helped to ensure more timely and reliable assistance to populations affected by natural disasters and complex emergencies. The CERF contains both a grant and a loan facility. It does not replace other sources of aid, but enables operations to be jump-started. Through this mechanism, states and other donors contribute to a fund managed by the UN, rather than to a specific agency or activity. Besides the CERF, the UN manages smaller, country-specific Common Humanitarian Funds and Emergency Response Funds. The development of pooled funding helps to make the emergency response system less dependent on the vagaries of individual contributions.

In 2009, UNHCR introduced its Global Needs Assessment (GNA), a planning process which forms the basis for the organization's annual budget. To the greatest extent possible, the GNA assesses the comprehensive needs of refugees and other people of concern to UNHCR around the globe. The agency appeals for funding on the basis of this assessment, rather than adjusting its budget to the amount of funds it thinks it could mobilize. This approach has allowed the international donor community to gain a better understanding of the impact of its support, as well as the consequences of funding gaps.

In 2010, UNHCR received US$1.86 billion in voluntary contributions, an increase of almost US$150 million compared to 2009. The 2011 provisional tally was US$2.088 billion. These are very significant amounts but they still covered under 60 per cent of the identified global needs.

Broad-based financial support for multilateral humanitarian action is an important demonstration of international solidarity. Yet in 2011, three-quarters of all contributions received by UNHCR came from just ten donors, and more than half were provided by just four: the United States, Japan, the European Commission, and the United Kingdom. For UNHCR and other humanitarian actors, identifying new sources of revenue remains a priority, especially in times of fiscal constraint, and because of the need to broaden support.

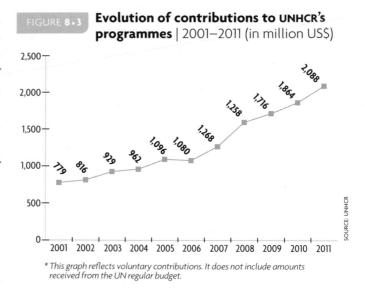

FIGURE 8.3 **Evolution of contributions to UNHCR's programmes** | 2001–2011 (in million US$)

This graph reflects voluntary contributions. It does not include amounts received from the UN regular budget.

SOURCE: UNHCR

Humanitarian aid is necessary but not sufficient to address refugee problems. It is generally agreed that it should be possible to reduce the burden on host states and achieve durable solutions by providing development aid which benefits refugees, returnees, and local populations.[22] The relative lack of success of this approach to date may be explained at least in part by the fact that refugees are often located in areas which are not a priority for host governments. But it is also often the case that the aid provided to host countries is insufficient or the recipient countries fear that refugee aid will be at the expense of existing bilateral or multilateral assistance intended to benefit their citizens.

Along with financial support, many countries provide technical assistance to help host states to improve their ability to receive and protect refugees, and to resolve refugee problems. Building capacity is a long-term process that involves numerous local, national, regional, and international actors, and should be integrated into broader development goals. It is important at all stages of the refugee cycle.[23]

Capacity-building can encompass a wide range of activities, for example, from the development of emergency response capabilities to the establishment of national asylum systems, to support for refugee resettlement, integration and community development. Capacity-building cannot be imposed or imported from outside; if it is not locally 'owned', it may be perceived as an exercise in 'burden-shifting'. Without local action and commitment, even the most determined and coherent engagement by the international community is unlikely to succeed.

RESETTLEMENT

Resettlement provides protection and durable solutions for refugees. It is also an important means by which states can share responsibility with refugee-hosting countries.

Resettlement has been a feature of the refugee landscape since after the Second World War, and UNHCR has helped many millions of refugees to resettle since 1951.

The General Assembly had resettlement in mind when, in the Resolution establishing UNHCR, it called on governments to cooperate with the High Commissioner by admitting refugees to their territories.[24] The reference to promoting the 'assimilation' of refugees within new national communities was also a reference to resettlement.[25]

No legal obligation exists for states to participate in resettlement, and their engagement in resettlement has waxed and waned over the years. In the immediate aftermath of the Second World War, the resettlement of refugees and displaced persons not only served a humanitarian purpose, but also helped to fill labour market gaps in Western European countries and beyond. During the Cold War, refugee resettlement was often seen as serving political as well as humanitarian aims. After the terrorist attacks in the United States in 2001, resettlement declined sharply, as participating countries focused on minimizing any possible security risks.

UNHCR/B. DIAB

Even though the number of resettlement places available globally has risen again, it remains far below the number of refugees for whom resettlement would be the most appropriate durable solution. UNHCR believes that resettlement can and should play a greater role as an instrument of responsibility-sharing. Over the past decade, UNHCR has successfully encouraged more countries to participate in refugee resettlement (*see chapter 3*). By 2012, 24 countries had established annual resettlement programmes: two in North America, three in Asia, five in Latin America, and 14 in Europe.

▲ **Palestinian refugee children** in the Al-Tanf camp at the border between Iraq and Syria.

BOX 8·3

Finding solutions for Palestinian refugees who fled Iraq

Between 2007 and 2011, thousands of Palestinian refugees fled Iraq, and were stranded at the country's borders with Syria and Jordan. Finding solutions for the refugees put international responsibility-sharing to the test. It also required the engagement of both UN refugee agencies: UNHCR and the UN Relief and Works Agency for Palestine Refugees in the Near East (UNRWA). Within Jordan and Syria, Palestinian refugees fall within UNRWA's area of operations. Those outside UNRWA's areas, including in Iraq, are within UNHCR's competence.

Palestinian refugees arrived in Iraq in several waves. The first came in 1948, fleeing from the northern part of today's Israel. A second group arrived in 1967, fleeing the third Arab–Israeli war. A further influx came from Kuwait and other Gulf countries in the aftermath of the 1991 Gulf War. By the time of the US-led military intervention in March 2003, an estimated 34,000 Palestinian refugees were living in Iraq.

The Palestinians were not formally recognized as refugees by the government of Saddam Hussein, but they were protected on the basis of resolutions of the League of Arab States. Although they were not given access to Iraqi citizenship, the Palestinians enjoyed a relatively high standard of treatment and a significant measure of integration. They were given residence permits, the right to work and to education, access to social services and to government-owned housing as well as subsidized rent. For these same reasons, some Iraqis resented their presence.

As sectarian violence in Iraq intensified after 2003, the Palestinian refugees became targets. Already in May 2003, UNHCR expressed concern about their safety, and started delivering humanitarian aid to those who had been forced to leave their homes and were camping in open areas or in abandoned buildings in Baghdad. Between March and August 2003, when UN staff were evacuated from Baghdad after the bombing of the UN compound, UNHCR had registered 23,000 Palestinians in Iraq, mostly in the capital.

Palestinian refugees in Iraq faced steadily increasing threats to their security. Many were dismissed from their jobs and evicted from subsidized housing. Attacks on Palestinian neighbourhoods, kidnappings, murders, and threats proliferated. Many fled, mostly to neighbouring Jordan and Syria, though some travelled as far as India. This movement became a steady flow, and by the end of 2010, the population of Palestinian refugees in Iraq had fallen to around 10,500.

Stranded without solutions
Some of the first Palestinian refugees to flee to Syria in 2003 were housed in Al-Hol camp in Al-Hassakah governorate. As arrivals continued, the authorities stopped admitting the Palestinians, leaving refugees stranded in desperate conditions in two camps at the Iraq–Syria border: one just inside Iraq at Al-Waleed, around three kilometres from the border, and another at Al-Tanf, in the no-man's-land between Iraqi and Syrian border posts.

More than 1,000 Palestinian refugees were also stranded at the border between Jordan and Iraq, where they had started to arrive in 2003. Jordan admitted several hundred refugees who were married to Jordanian citizens, but only allowed the remainder into the country in 2005, placing them in a refugee camp at Al-Ruweished—70 kilometres inside Jordan. The refugees, mainly urban professionals, became increasingly frustrated at their situation. A UNHCR Representative sympathized, saying 'After all, it's our job to find

However, there remains a serious imbalance in the global resettlement effort, with around two-thirds of all resettled refugees taken in by the US and only 10 per cent by countries in Europe. Expanding refugee resettlement in Europe remains a key UNHCR objective.

In 2010, refugees of 100 different nationalities were resettled; the largest groups were from Iraq, Myanmar, Bhutan, and Somalia. They were resettled out of 88 countries of first asylum and were taken in by 22 countries of resettlement. This diversity has helped to dispel any impression remaining from the Cold War period that countries engage in resettlement only when it serves their political interests. The collaboration of numerous governments, NGOs and UN agencies in the resettlement of Palestinian refugees who fled Iraq after 2003 (*see box 8.3*) is an example—albeit on a small scale—of the use of resettlement to resolve a particularly dire humanitarian problem.

UNHCR cannot always count on a positive response to its emergency resettlement

solutions for refugees. But to do this, we are dependent on a state, or states.'

The plight of the refugees became desperate, especially those at Al-Waleed and Al-Tanf. These isolated camps, located on the edge of the Damascus-to-Baghdad highway, had poor shelter and sanitation facilities. Conditions were scorchingly hot in summer and freezing in winter. On several occasions floods devastated the border camps, while fires in Al-Tanf and Al-Ruweished took several lives and injured dozens.

An international response

The situation had not improved by December 2006, and UNHCR issued an aide-mémoire appealing to states to demonstrate solidarity. In April 2007, when the High Commissioner convened an International Conference on the Humanitarian Crisis in Iraq, he again drew attention to the plight of the Palestinian refugees in Iraq, and those stranded at the borders.

In May 2008, Sudan offered to relocate some of the refugees from Al-Waleed to Khartoum on a temporary basis. Sudan, the PLO, and UNHCR concluded a Statement of Principles on the proposal. A Sudanese delegation met refugees in Al-Waleed to explain the offer. Four refugee representatives visited Khartoum in January 2009 and conveyed their impressions on return to Al-Waleed. Although appreciative of the

offer, refugees in the camp were reluctant to accept it; they did not wish to be refugees in yet another country. NGOs also opposed the proposal, arguing that relocating the Palestinian refugees to Sudan would simply shift them from one marginalized situation to another—particularly in the absence of clarity as to the rights they would enjoy. However, exploration of the Sudan option may have helped to spur resettlement countries to come forward to assist the refugees.

By the second half of 2008, only 381 of the refugees had been resettled. The largest numbers went to Brazil and Chile, but other countries, such as Iceland and New Zealand, took in vulnerable individuals. In October, UNHCR again appealed for greater international cooperation to find new homes for the stranded refugees. Soon thereafter, a 10-country EU fact-finding mission, mandated by EU Ministers of Justice and Home Affairs, visited Jordan, Syria, and the Al-Tanf camp. Delegates were deeply moved by what they saw, particularly at Al-Tanf, and many urged their governments to help. Following the mission, the EU Ministers pledged to resettle 10,000 refugees from Iraq, including Iraqis and Palestinians. NGOs, journalists and documentary film-makers from several countries visited the border camps, and their reports added to the pressure for action. Cell-phone videos made by the refugees themselves contributed to international awareness of their plight.

In 2009, prospects for solutions appeared to be improving. In July 2009, the US confirmed it would admit up to 1,350 refugees from among those living at Al-Waleed and in Baghdad. Some refugees were moved to emergency transit centres in Romania and Slovakia, and this helped to decongest the camps. Syrian authorities also agreed to stop transferring to Al-Tanf Palestinian refugees from Iraq found in an irregular situation inside Syria.

The Al-Tanf camp was finally closed on 1 February 2010 by which time most of the 1,300 refugees who had lived in the camp had been resettled. Those who remained on the day it closed were relocated to Al-Hol in northern Syria. Most of the population at Al-Waleed could be resettled as well, though the camp stayed open.

At the end of 2011, there were still small numbers of Palestinian refugees from Iraq at Al-Hol camp and Al-Waleed, and UNHCR continued its efforts to find solutions for them, hoping to be able to close both remaining camps in 2012.

In all, the Palestinian refugees from Iraq found new homes in 18 countries in the Americas, Europe and Asia. Even if progress in responding to the needs of the stranded Palestinians was initially slow, the international response ultimately demonstrated that when a broad effort is made to share responsibility, solutions can be found. ◆

appeals. In 2011, the Office launched a 'Global Resettlement Solidarity Initiative' to find new homes for refugees—mainly Somalis and Eritreans—who had fled the conflict in Libya and were provisionally sheltered in Egypt and Tunisia. UNHCR called for 8,000 places to be made immediately available (a number later reduced to just 5,000), but with the notable exceptions of Norway and the US, most countries were reluctant to make new commitments. The low number of places offered by the 27 EU Member States led the EU's Commissioner for Justice and Home Affairs to comment that Europe 'did not pass the test' of solidarity.[26]

The Annual Tripartite Consultations on Resettlement, coordinated by UNHCR and chaired each year by a different resettlement country, help to ensure that resettlement is used in the most effective way. States, NGOs and UNHCR participate in these Consultations, which started in 1995 and have become an ever-more important vehicle for cooperation in the area of resettlement, and highlight the value of partnership between state and civil society actors.

OTHER COOPERATIVE ARRANGEMENTS

Formal arrangements to allocate responsibility for hosting refugees or asylum seekers are rare. Only two such arrangements have been concluded to date, and both involve countries of the developed world. One was concluded in 2002 between Canada and the United States of America.[27] The second is EU's 'Dublin II Regulation', in which 31 European states now participate (*see box 8.4*).[28]

These arrangements are similar in that they are based on the principle of inter-state trust, aim to make sure than the claims of asylum seekers are examined in a substantive procedure in (only) one country, and set out the criteria for establishing which state is

BOX **8•4**

The European Union's 'Dublin II' Regulation

Article 80 of the Treaty on the Functioning of the European Union—the Lisbon Treaty—provides that the policies and practices of the Union in the area of asylum are governed by the principles of solidarity and fair sharing of responsibility. But recent developments with respect to the 'Dublin II' Regulation are straining the concept of solidarity within the European Union (EU).

The Regulation allocates responsibility for examining asylum applications among 31 participating countries.[i] It was adopted in 2003 and replaced the 1990 Dublin Convention, which initially concerned just 12 countries.

The objectives of the 'Dublin II' Regulation are to ensure that asylum seekers have access to procedures for assessing their claims, to prevent them from lodging claims in several countries, and to determine as quickly as possible the state responsible for examining an application. The perceived need for the system arose as border controls in parts of Europe progressively disappeared, and governments feared that asylum seekers would file multiple claims, or move around the continent looking for better conditions and chances of receiving protection—known as 'asylum-shopping'.

The general rule established by the Regulation is that the responsible country is the one where the applicant first enters the territory of the participating states, in the case of irregular entry. If the applicant enters legally, responsibility rests with the state which issued the entry authorization. Specific criteria apply for unaccompanied children or separated families, to ensure respect for the best interests of the child and family unity.

While the Regulation assigns responsibility for examining asylum claims, it does not contain any mechanism to ensure that responsibility is fairly distributed. In fact, because most asylum seekers arrive overland and cross the external EU border without authorization, if the Regulation could be implemented as intended, responsibility for hosting asylum seekers and considering their claims would fall mostly on countries located at the EU's external borders.

The Regulation was supposed to avoid the controversy that had plagued the Dublin Convention. That Convention was adopted before the decision to establish a Common European Asylum System, and was criticized for having 'knowingly and willfully disregarded divergences among Member States' protection systems'.[ii] However, the 'Dublin II' Regulation has come in for similar criticism.

Like its predecessor, the Regulation is based on the principle of mutual trust. It relies on the presumption that all participating states will fulfil their responsibilities toward asylum applicants in a similar manner. Over the years, this presumption has been challenged, first in national courts and then at regional level. Both of Europe's regional courts have now confirmed that under the system established by the Regulation, a sending state may not simply assume that a receiving state will respect its international obligations.

In January 2011, the European Court of Human Rights (ECtHR) ruled in *M.S.S.* v. *Belgium and Greece* that a transferring state must *verify* that a receiving state complies with its international obligations.[iii] One state may not send an asylum seeker to another state, the Court said, if that would expose the individual to a risk of torture, inhuman or degrading treatment. Such treatment is clearly prohibited by Article 3 of the European Convention on Human Rights (ECHR). But the Court's finding that violations of Article 3 were possible *within* the EU shook the foundations of the Dublin system. Moreover, the Court made it clear that the asylum seeker does not have to present evidence of the would-be receiving state's failure to comply with its obligations; the presumption of compliance can be rebutted by external sources. In that

responsible for determining asylum claims. Observers have expressed concern at the risk that responsibility-sharing agreements will be based on the lowest common denominator for treatment of applicants and their claims.[29] Still, such agreements can help to avoid unilateral burden-shifting and reduce the risk of chain *refoulement*.

Another potential framework for responsibility-sharing was established by the EU in 2001, in a Directive on temporary protection in the event of a mass influx. The Directive intended to ensure a 'balance of efforts' among Member States in the case of a large-scale influx, but it has not been activated to date.[30] It was adopted after the *ad hoc* experiences with temporary protection for persons from the former Yugoslavia, and sought to

Dublin II Regulation: Participating States

information including NGO reports, materials prepared by the European Commission, and information provided by UNHCR.

In addition to these landmark rulings, further decisions were issued both by national courts and the ECtHR in late 2011 and early 2012, suspending Dublin transfers to EU Member States other than Greece, on the grounds that appropriate standards of treatment could not be guaranteed for asylum seekers.

These developments are very significant for the operation of the Dublin II Regulation, and for the Common European Asylum System as a whole. They have led EU officials and Member States to acknowledge that more effort must be invested in making sure that the obligations set out in EU asylum law are respected in practice throughout the Union. ◆

context, the Court gave particular weight to the views of UNHCR.

In December 2011, the Court of Justice of the European Union (CJEU) further clarified that the principle of mutual trust cannot be relied upon in an automatic way. In *N.S.* v. *Secretary of State for the Home Department* (UK) and *M.E. and others* v. *Refugee Applications Commissioner* (Ireland), the CJEU also addressed the lawfulness of transfers of asylum seekers to Greece under the 'Dublin II' Regulation, this time in the framework of EU law, including the Charter of Fundamental Rights and its Article 4, which also prohibits torture and

inhuman or degrading treatment or punishment.

The CJEU ruled that an EU Member State may not transfer an asylum seeker to another Member State in a situation where it 'cannot be unaware' of systemic deficiencies in the asylum procedure and reception conditions there.[iv] In other words, if there are reasonable grounds for believing that the asylum seeker would face a risk of treatment in violation of Article 4 of the Charter, the State may not go ahead with the transfer, and must examine the claim itself. The Court looked at how the risk of inhuman or degrading treatment can be assessed, and drew attention to sources of

i   The formal title is 'Council Regulation (EC) No. 343/2003 establishing the criteria and mechanisms for determining the Member State responsible for examining an asylum application lodged in one of the Member States by a third-country national'. Participating states are the 27 EU Member States plus Iceland, Liechtenstein, Norway and Switzerland.

ii G. Noll, 'Formalism v. Empiricism: Some Reflections on the Dublin Convention on the Occasion of Recent European Case Law', *Nordic Journal of International Law*, 70, 2001, 161.

iii *M.S.S.* v. *Belgium and Greece*, Application no. 30696/09, Council of Europe: European Court of Human Rights, 21 January 2011.

iv *N. S.* v. *Secretary of State for the Home Department and M. E. and others* v. *Refugee Applications Commissioner, Minister for Justice, Equality and Law Reform*, C-411/10 and C-493/10, European Union: European Court of Justice, 21 December 2011.

establish a more predictable arrangement. Governments did not take up suggestions voiced in 2006–2007, including by UNHCR, that the Directive could be activated in response to the arrival of Iraqi asylum seekers.

Solidarity in the area of asylum is now a principle of primary EU law.[31] In late 2011, the European Commission adopted a Communication on 'Enhanced intra-EU solidarity in the field of asylum'[32] which calls for more practical cooperation and financial solidarity among the EU's members, as well as for the continuation of arrangements for the intra-EU relocation of beneficiaries of international protection as a means of addressing 'particular pressures' on any given Member State.[33]

There have been periodic discussions in Europe about new forms of access to asylum procedures, often termed 'embassy procedures' or 'protected entry procedures'.[34] In this model, asylum seekers and refugees would be able to apply directly from their first country of asylum to enter another potential asylum country. In theory, this could provide some relief to host countries with large refugee populations, but it has rarely been applied.

Strengthening international solidarity

SOLIDARITY IN THE INTERNATIONAL REFUGEE REGIME IS NOT AN END IN ITSELF, but a means to improve the availability and quality of protection. Three important principles underpin UNHCR's efforts to promote international cooperation and solidarity. First is the recognition that international cooperation is a complement to states' responsibilities and not a substitute for them, and that states should not devolve their core responsibilities onto international organizations. Second, the underlying objective of cooperative arrangements must be to enhance refugee protection and prospects for durable solutions. Third, cooperative arrangements must always be guided by the basic principles of humanity and dignity, and be aligned with international refugee and human rights law.

In 2011, UNHCR launched a renewed effort to strengthen international solidarity. An Expert Meeting on responsibility-sharing reviewed the lessons learned from past cooperative arrangements and pointed out that clear ownership and leadership by states is a condition for the success of such arrangements.[35] This may be easier to achieve on a regional rather than on the global level.

The discussions also made clear that effective international cooperation on refugees requires recognition that though forced displacement creates humanitarian needs, it is above all a political problem. Addressing it demands efforts on numerous fronts, including by national authorities responsible for foreign and internal affairs, security, defence, and the environment, as well as those dealing with international development and humanitarian affairs. In addition, it needs the engagement of many non-state actors. Cooperation within the UN system itself is also vital, to ensure that measures to address the needs of refugees, returnees, and IDPs are included within the UN's common strategic vision for any given country.[36]

BOX **8·5**

The Asia–Pacific Regional Cooperation Framework

Asia generates and hosts the largest number of refugees and the second largest number of migrants worldwide. Population movements have been both a motor of economic growth and development, and a challenge to state sovereignty and security. These movements are the by-product of a complex, overlapping mix of factors that include population growth, urbanization, climate change, water scarcity, food and energy insecurity, conflict, human rights violations, and natural disasters. Preserving or enhancing protection space for refugees in such a complex environment requires navigating between migration dynamics, state interests, and protection imperatives.

There is a long tradition in Asia of providing protection on an *ad hoc* basis to refugees. Afghan refugees are still the largest single group of concern to UNHCR worldwide. There are also protracted refugee situations in Bangladesh, India, Nepal, and Thailand. In recent years, the largest UNHCR refugee status determination operation in the world has been in Malaysia. Two of the largest resettlement operations have been conducted in Asia, involving refugees from Bhutan resettled out of Nepal, and refugees from Myanmar resettled out of Thailand.

Policy prescriptions that might work in other regions do not easily apply in Asia. Many countries do not have a legal framework governing refugee protection, and accession to the 1951 Convention and/or its 1967 Protocol remains rare. The few countries that are signatories lack the institutional capacity or political impetus effectively to implement these commitments. Attitudes are still influenced by the 1989 Comprehensive Plan of Action for Indochinese Refugees—with its focus on orderly migration programmes, temporary protection in first countries of asylum, return of non-refugees to their countries of origin, and resettlement of recognized refugees outside the region. Some countries in the region are reluctant formally to acknowledge that they have become countries of destination or settlement for refugees.

UNHCR **remains *de facto* the main protection actor in the region**, often operating in an unpredictable environment due to the absence of legal frameworks. Repatriation and resettlement are the only durable solutions accepted by most Asian states. However, given the situation in the main countries of origin and the limited places available for resettlement, many refugees will not be able to benefit from either of these solutions.

Faced with narrow legal protection and uncertain prospects for solutions, a highly mobile, often young population of asylum seekers and refugees moves irregularly in search of better standards of protection and durable solutions, often heading for middle-income countries such as Thailand and Malaysia, or through Indonesia to Australia. This movement, together with the substantial rise in irregular migration over the last decade, has underpinned regional dynamics that have led to the development of a Regional Cooperation Framework for the Asia–Pacific region.

In 2002, following an increase in unauthorized boat arrivals in Australia, the Bali Process—an informal regional grouping of interested countries—was established to develop practical measures to help states in the region to tackle smuggling and trafficking in persons and related transnational crime. Since then, it has become clear that law enforcement and border control

measures alone will not reverse the trend of increasing numbers of people undertaking hazardous sea journeys. Nor are they sufficient to address the challenges to good-neighbourly relations, or respond to the public outrage, when people in distress at sea are not rescued in time—or not rescued at all. Human smuggling and trafficking networks flourish, capitalizing on human despair and the diversity of national responses to refugees and irregular migration. Recognizing that disparities in the treatment of refugees contribute to irregular movements, states participating in the Bali Process have since 2009 paid increasing attention to refugee protection, resettlement, repatriation, and reintegration.

The rise in irregular migration is not only a challenge to refugee protection. In the Asia–Pacific region, it has also presented an opportunity for practical cooperation among states sharing similar problems to address their shared concerns. In March 2011, at the fourth Bali Process Ministerial Conference, participating states decided to develop an inclusive but non-binding 'Regional Cooperation Framework'. The Conference agreed that border control and law enforcement initiatives were important measures to combat people smuggling and trafficking, but that they needed to be complemented by practical cooperation to respond to humanitarian needs.

The Regional Cooperation Framework seeks to reconcile state interests in safeguarding national security and the integrity of their borders, with protection imperatives, in order to minimize the need for hazardous irregular movements. It thus moves away from the *status quo* in some countries, which for years placed responsibility for refugee protection within UNHCR's realm only, and encourages its greater ownership by states.

Following the Ministerial Conference, UNHCR proposed the establishment of a Regional Support Office (RSO) to serve as the institutional focal point for strengthening practical cooperation on refugee protection and international migration. This was accepted by the Bali Process *Ad Hoc* Group in October 2011. The Regional Support Office will be set up under the oversight of the Co-Chairs of the Bali Process and in consultation with the IOM and UNHCR. It will focus on information-sharing on refugee protection and international migration, capacity building and exchange of best practices. Pooling of technical resources, pilot projects and joint activities are also envisaged, with an emphasis on specific caseloads or topics such as irregular movements by sea. It is expected that the RSO will start working in 2012.

The presence of major, overlapping drivers of displacement, the size of the populations at risk, as well as the strength of transnational criminal networks in the Asia–Pacific region have led states to move towards closer cooperation to deal with population movements. In this process, and with concerted UNHCR efforts, refugee protection has increasingly gained recognition as a constituent part of any effective state response. The recently-adopted Regional Cooperation Framework and proposed Regional Support Office provide a basis for promoting greater state ownership of refugee protection, and encouraging equitable responsibility-sharing across the region. Political leadership will be needed to continue looking beyond national boundaries, domestic agendas, and narrow law-enforcement concerns when deciding on concrete activities for the Regional Support Office. ◆

BOX 8•6

Refugees and asylum seekers in distress at sea

People fleeing threats to their lives and freedom use whatever means are available, including undertaking dangerous sea journeys. Terrible tragedies have regularly been reported from the Gulf of Aden, as Somalis try to flee to Yemen, judging the turmoil in that country to be a lesser risk than the chaos in their own; and from Asia. According to the Parliamentary Assembly of the Council of Europe, in 2011 alone, some 2,000 boat people perished in the Mediterranean while trying to reach Europe from North Africa.

Refugees and asylum seekers risk their lives in this manner when legal channels for entry are not open to them. In many cases they turn to smugglers who charge them a high price in exchange for a promise of safe passage, but then place them on overcrowded, unseaworthy vessels, without qualified skippers or navigators. Boats run out of fuel, engines break down and passengers are stranded without food or water. Precarious vessels break apart in stormy seas or when they hit rocky coasts. Dozens of lives were lost close to Australia's Christmas Island in December 2010, and up to 200 people drowned off Java, Indonesia just a year later.

Every shipmaster is obliged to render assistance to persons in distress at sea. This longstanding maritime tradition is also a duty enshrined in international law; it must be carried out without regard to nationality, status, or the circumstances in which the persons in distress are found. It is based, *inter alia*, on two core treaties: the 1982 United Nations Convention on the Law of the Sea (UNCLOS) and the 1974 International Convention for the Safety of Life at Sea (SOLAS). The shipmaster's obligation to render assistance is complemented by the obligation of state parties to set up search and rescue services and to coordinate rescue operations in their area of responsibility.

When the passengers and crew of a commercial vessel are rescued, their disembarkation in a nearby port and return to their countries is a straightforward matter. But the situation is often different when a vessel in distress is carrying—or believed to be carrying—refugees, asylum seekers, or other people without documentation who cannot or do not want to return home. In such cases, passing vessels have frequently shown reluctance to rescue people, anticipating difficulties in disembarking them, and wary of the costs that could be incurred in the process. In some cases, after a rescue has been undertaken, the flag state has had to negotiate for days or weeks to arrange for disembarkation.

The picture is complicated by the fact that very often, refugees and asylum seekers travel alongside others who are not seeking protection, but use the same channels in an effort to start a new life elsewhere. However, the phenomenon of 'mixed migration' does not alter the obligation to aid persons in distress at sea.

Rescue situations often trigger the responsibilities of different states: the state in whose Search and Rescue Area the vessel in distress is found; the flag state of the rescuing vessel; and other coastal states in the region. This makes it easy for responsibility to be referred from one state to another without any one taking action.

Member states of the International Maritime Organization (IMO) tried to address this situation by amending the relevant legal framework but could agree only that states were obliged to 'coordinate and cooperate' with regard to rescue at sea. Even this agreement is hard to translate into practice, as states remain reluctant to permit disembarkation, particularly if they are already coping with large numbers of people arriving directly on their shores.

States hesitate to allow the disembarkation of asylum seekers, refugees, and irregular migrants, since this is followed by the need to house and care for the passengers, assess claims for asylum, and provide assistance to persons requiring medical care or who have other special needs. Beyond the stage of initial reception and status determination, states worry that they will have to assume longer-term responsibility for asylum or for the return of persons who are found not to be in need of protection.

Greater international cooperation is clearly needed to address these problems. At a meeting of international experts convened by UNHCR in Djibouti in late 2011, the agency put forward a 'Model Framework for Cooperation in Rescue at Sea Operations involving Asylum Seekers and Refugees', based on UNHCR's 10-Point Plan of Action on Refugee Protection and International Migration (*see chapter 2*).

The Model Framework suggests that a number of states could enter into a cooperative arrangement through which each would commit to specific but differentiated responsibilities. States could agree on a list of possible ports for disembarkation in their region, and on ways to support countries of disembarkation, for example by providing assistance for reception arrangements, agreeing to receive persons recognized as refugees, and/or facilitating the return of those not in need of protection.

The Model Framework would also ensure that rescued people are treated with dignity and are not disembarked in or transferred to places where they might face persecution, torture, or other serious harm. It could also include measures to seek to account for people reported missing and, where necessary, to ensure the proper treatment of human remains.

The Model Framework could facilitate cooperation among states and encourage better implementation of their obligations. While UNHCR and other agencies can advocate for such arrangements, their implementation will require the political will of one or more governments prepared to lead the process. At the Djibouti meeting, some states expressed an interest in working towards a collaborative arrangement for specific regions. It is hoped that this interest can be translated into practice, for the alternative—no collaborative action—will continue to have high political, financial, and above all human costs. ◆

UNHCR has consistently stressed the need for development cooperation policies to take full account of the efforts which host countries make in receiving refugees, and the impact of forced displacement on their societies. The significant investment in infrastructure and services required for refugees in developing countries must also benefit the local population. Assurances that aid for refugees will be additional to other forms of assistance can contribute to an improved climate for local integration.

It is also evident that other forms of responsibility-sharing are needed to preserve the refugee protection regime. In recent years UNHCR has intensively promoted collaboration to address mixed migratory flows, in order to safeguard access to asylum (*see chapter 2 and box 8.6*). This poses significant challenges, notably in the context of rescue at sea and interception. UNHCR has consistently reminded states that they remain bound by their international obligations no matter where they act, including on the high seas. UNHCR has set out its position on the extra-territorial application of the *non-refoulement* obligation in a 2007 Advisory Opinion[37] and more recently in an intervention before the European Court of Human Rights.[38] In early 2012, that Court confirmed that a state cannot evade its responsibilities under international law by acting extra-territorially.[39]

Rescue at sea was once automatic, an unquestioned duty of seafarers. This is no longer always the case, while even after rescue, jurisdiction and state responsibility to provide a place of disembarkation are frequently disputed. The dramatic loss of life in the Mediterranean, the Gulf of Aden, and elsewhere underlines the urgent need for states to work together to develop a fair division of responsibility for saving those whose flight has placed them in peril on the sea.

NEW MOMENTUM FOR INTERNATIONAL SOLIDARITY?

At the end of 2011 a Ministerial Meeting was organized by UNHCR with the aim of strengthening both national responsibility and international solidarity with respect to refugees and stateless people. All UN member states were invited to the meeting, and 155 participated.

Drawing on the practice of the Human Rights Council and the International Conference of the Red Cross and Red Crescent Societies, and in an effort to promote national responsibility, states were invited to make specific and measurable pledges of changes in policy and legislation and to improve the treatment of refugees and stateless people. One hundred and three states made concrete pledges on a wide range of refugee protection and statelessness issues, an important reiteration of governments' commitment to the cause of international protection.

A significant number of pledges related directly to improving national protection responses. States demonstrated their commitment not only to the global framework for refugee protection but also to making it work effectively.

Many pledges related to durable solutions for refugees. Some 20 countries, particularly in Africa, committed to facilitating local integration for long-staying refugees. Another 18 states pledged to improve access to resettlement, including by making additional places available.

The most significant breakthrough related to statelessness, in the past a neglected aspect of UNHCR's mandate. The two international treaties relating to statelessness—the 1954 Convention relating to the Status of Stateless Persons and the 1961 Convention on the Reduction of Statelessness—have long been under-subscribed. During 2011, the number of states parties to these instruments rose to 71 and 42 respectively, with more than 30 other countries pledging to accede or to make progress toward accession. There is a new dynamic to resolving the anomaly of statelessness.

Beyond the question of accession to the treaties, more than 40 states made other commitments related to statelessness at the Ministerial Meeting. Notable pledges were made to reform nationality laws in order to bring an end to gender inequality in nationality legislation, in particular to enable women to transmit their nationality to their children.

The consideration of 'new factors' that give rise to displacement provoked lively discussions at the Meeting. Norway, together with Germany, Mexico and Switzerland, made a joint pledge to cooperate with interested states and relevant actors, including UNHCR, to obtain a better understanding of cross-border movements provoked by new factors such as climate change and environmental degradation.

In the Ministerial Communiqué issued by the Meeting, UN member states pledged to help countries that host large numbers of refugees to meet their needs, while working to promote refugee self-sufficiency. The states recognized new challenges in providing protection and achieving solutions, and urged the international community to deepen its understanding of displacement and strengthen means to address it in a changing global context. The Communiqué also highlighted the need to devote renewed attention to the causes of displacement and statelessness.

The pledges made by states were statements of policy rather than legally binding commitments. In the years ahead, UNHCR will face the challenge of holding states to their declarations, and ensuring that they are translated into concrete action.

In conclusion

A BOOK ABOUT FORCED DISPLACEMENT CAN HAVE NO OBVIOUS ENDING. FORCED displacement continues, and its nature changes. The international community's response must evolve accordingly, to ensure that protection and assistance are available for all persons who are driven from their homes.

The primary responsibility rests with states: those receiving refugees as well as the countries of origin of refugees and IDPs. They must understand and exercise national sovereignty in a way that protects the rights of refugees and stateless people on their territories, as well as of their own citizens, including those displaced internally and those who were formerly refugees in other countries. At the same time, the wider international

BOX **8•7**

Ministerial Communiqué:
Intergovernmental Event of December 2011

1. **We, the Ministers and representatives of Member States of the United Nations**, gathered in Geneva, Switzerland, on 7 and 8 December 2011, for a ministerial-level meeting facilitated by UNHCR to mark the 60th anniversary of the *1951 Convention relating to the Status of Refugees* and the 50th anniversary of the *1961 Convention on the Reduction of Statelessness*.

2. **We reaffirm** that the *1951 Convention relating to the Status of Refugees* and its *1967 Protocol* are the foundation of the international refugee protection regime and have enduring value and relevance in the twenty-first century. We recognize the importance of respecting and upholding the principles and values that underlie these instruments, including the core principle of *non-refoulement*, and where applicable, will consider acceding to these instruments and/or removing reservations.

3. **We recognize** that the *1961 Convention on the Reduction of Statelessness* and the *1954 Convention relating to the Status of Stateless Persons* are the principal international statelessness instruments, which provide important standards for the prevention and resolution of statelessness and safeguards for the protection of stateless people. We will consider becoming a party to them, where appropriate, and/or strengthening our policies that prevent and reduce statelessness.

4. **We express our concern that millions of people** live without a nationality, which limits enjoyment of their human rights, and we will work towards addressing statelessness and protecting stateless persons, including, as applicable, through national legislation and strengthening mechanisms for birth registration.

5. **We are committed to strengthening and enhancing** international protection and assistance to refugees through international cooperation in a spirit of solidarity, responsibility and burden sharing among all States and to improving ways to support countries hosting refugees, including in protracted refugee situations.

6. **We commend the countries** that host large numbers of refugees for their generosity and acknowledge the security, socio-economic and environmental impact of the presence of large-scale refugee populations on these countries. We will work alongside these countries to meet the assistance and protection needs of refugees. We will endeavour to promote refugees' self-sufficiency, with the aim of investing in their future durable solutions.

7. **We remain deeply concerned** that too many refugee situations have become protracted, and will strive to work with UNHCR and development actors, as appropriate, to resolve refugees' plight and realize durable solutions in more effective and comprehensive ways, consistent with international law and relevant UN General Assembly resolutions. We will cooperate with countries of origin to foster conditions for voluntary repatriation, which remains the preferred solution, and pursue resettlement, in tandem with other solutions, and local integration where feasible. In this context, we recognize the need to address the root causes of refugee situations in accordance with international law.

8. **We express our appreciation** for the leadership shown by UNHCR and commend the Office for its ongoing efforts. We further commend the staff and implementing partners of UNHCR for the competent, courageous and dedicated manner in which they discharge their responsibilities.

9. **We, while recalling the global nature of the refugee problem**, note the efforts undertaken by UNHCR in partnership and cooperation with international, regional and national stakeholders.

10. **We note that today's challenges** in providing protection and achieving solutions continue to be serious, interconnected and complex. In this regard, we recognize the importance of enhancing international solidarity, strengthening action in accordance with the principles enshrined in applicable instruments and finding durable solutions. We will reinforce cooperation with each other and work with UNHCR and other relevant stakeholders, as appropriate, to deepen our understanding of evolving patterns of displacement and to agree upon ways to respond to the challenges we face in a changing global context.

11. **We extend our gratitude** to the Government and people of Switzerland for generously hosting the UNHCR ministerial meeting to commemorate the 60th anniversary of the *UN Convention relating to the Status of Refugees* and the 50th anniversary of the *Convention on the Reduction of Statelessness.* ◆

community must demonstrate solidarity by helping states to shoulder these responsibilities in a consistent and effective manner.

While the need for solidarity is recognized in theory, it has yet to materialize in sufficient measure in practice. The states that could help

UNHCR/G. GORDON/MARCH 2011

◀ **A Liberian motorcycle taxi driver** gives a lift to an older refugee from Côte d'Ivoire.

provide it have not always seen it as a priority for the necessary commitment of resources. Those states that need international solidarity most have limited leverage to attract it. The shortfall in solidarity has itself high costs: the tensions in the international refugee regime will continue to grow and no country will be immune from the impact. International solidarity alone cannot overcome all the problems, but without it they cannot be addressed.

This book has identified a number of critical challenges in combating forced displacement. The first and greatest arises from the proliferation of complex internal conflicts and situations of political violence in which civilians are not adequately distinguished from combatants or are targeted directly. Reducing the vulnerability of civilians—whether refugees, IDPs, or returnees—must remain a central priority for states, UNHCR, and all concerned.

Second, asylum seekers face a difficult and often hostile and unpredictable reception. The 1951 Convention and/or its 1967 Protocol have been ratified by 148 states, but more than one-third of all refugees under UNHCR's mandate are hosted in non-signatory states. These states generally offer protection from *refoulement*, but do not always provide asylum in the sense of a legal status accompanied by a clear set of rights. States, including many signatories of the 1951 Convention, respond in different ways to people fleeing violence and conflict, thereby leaving many without the protection they need. Protection must be provided to all who need it.

Third, for the majority of refugees, protracted exile has become the norm because none of the traditional durable solutions has been made available. Voluntary repatriation is at its lowest level in 20 years. Local integration is resisted by many host countries, despite evidence that refugees can—with the right conditions—contribute to development. Resettlement is only offered to a small portion of the world's refugees. Countries of origin, host countries, and donor nations must work more effectively together to find durable solutions.

Fourth, many individuals still lack the protection of citizenship. There are stateless people on every continent, and in virtually every country. Having a nationality is the key to enjoying other rights, and stateless people are therefore among the world's most disadvantaged. Without citizenship they have no future. Compared to some other challenges, their problems should be relatively easy to resolve.

Fifth, tens of millions of people worldwide remain forcibly displaced within their own countries. The number displaced by conflict—estimated in 2011 at some 27.5 million—is more than twice the number of refugees under UNHCR's mandate. Protecting and assisting the internally displaced is often even more challenging than coming to the aid of refugees, but no less important.

Sixth, growing numbers of refugees, returnees, and IDPs are struggling to survive in urban areas, where it is often difficult for aid agencies to identify and help them. They face a wide range of threats to their security and well-being, and are particularly vulnerable to exploitation. These threats and their vulnerability must be reduced.

Seventh, it is clear that climate change will add to the complexity of human displacement. More people are already displaced as a result of sudden-onset natural disasters than by conflict, and it is projected that the effects of climate change will, over time, trigger massive movements of people. There are gaps in the international system, especially with respect to the protection of people who move across borders as a result of climate change and natural disasters. These gaps must be filled.

Finally, the nature and scale of refugee flows, internal displacement and statelessness put national and international systems under considerable pressure. No government can deal with these problems in isolation. While the world has changed in ways that could not have been imagined when the UN was established, the purposes and principles written into the UN Charter in 1945 remain just as relevant today: 'to maintain international peace and security (...) to achieve international co-operation in solving international problems of an economic, social, cultural, or humanitarian character, and in promoting and encouraging respect for human rights and for fundamental freedoms for all, without distinction as to race, sex, language, or religion'.

This book would not be complete without paying tribute to the manifold forms of solidarity shown by ordinary citizens toward refugees, IDPs, and stateless people in many countries and at many levels, a subject which deserves a book in its own right. The solidarity displayed by concerned individuals ranges from small gestures of human kindness to organized support activities conducted by civil society groups in their enormous diversity the world over. Whether it is Liberian villagers welcoming refugees from Côte d'Ivoire, citizens of Iceland helping resettled Palestinian refugees from Iraq to feel at home, or people in Malaysia supporting informal schools for refugee children, acts of person-to-person solidarity ultimately make the most meaningful contribution to improving the state of the world's refugees. The compassion and solidarity shown by so many individuals for the displaced must be matched by states. ■

INTRODUCTION

1 Statute of the Office of the United Nations High Commissioner for Refugees, UN General Assembly Resolution 428 (V) of 14 December 1950.

2 Quoted in 'The Nansen Conference: Climate Change and Displacement in the 21st Century' (Chair's Summary)', Oslo, 5–7 June 2011.

3 United Nations, Department of Economic and Social Affairs, Population Division, 'World Population Prospects: The 2010 Revision', New York, 2011.

4 Internal Displacement Monitoring Centre (IDMC), 'Displacement due to Natural Hazard-induced Disasters: Global Estimates for 2009 and 2010', June 2011.

5 Food and Agriculture Organization (FAO), '2050: Climate Change Will Worsen the Plight of the Poor, Future of Agriculture and Food Security Closely Linked to Climate Change,' 30 September 2009; see also FAO, 'Agriculture to 2050: the Challenges Ahead', Diouf Opens High-Level Forum on Food's Future', 12 October 2009.

6 Inter-Agency Standing Committee (IASC), 'Protection of Internally Displaced Persons: Inter-Agency Standing Committee Policy Paper', December 1999, 4. The definition was originally adopted by a 1999 Workshop of the International Committee of the Red Cross (ICRC) on protection which itself was the culmination of a three year consultative process.

7 UNHCR, 'Age, Gender and Diversity Mainstreaming Forward Plan 2011–2016', September 2011.

8 J. Sanness, 'The Nobel Peace Prize 1981: Presentation Speech', 10 December 1981.

CHAPTER 1

1 Internal Displacement Monitoring Centre (IDMC), Global Statistics for 2011. The IDMC was established in 1998 by the Norwegian Refugee Council, and monitors internal displacement worldwide.

2 *The State of the World's Refugees: Fifty Years of Humanitarian Action* (Oxford: Oxford University Press, 2000) covers this evolution in depth.

3 On a far smaller scale, in 1990 UNHCR began supporting 'open relief centres' in areas of conflict in Sri Lanka.

4 As an early example, the global media coverage of the plight of Iraqis on the border with Turkey in the spring of 1991 largely determined the nature of the political and humanitarian responses. Similar and often live coverage of the conflicts during the break-up of the former Yugoslavia that began the same year had a major impact on support for the humanitarian response, which was widely seen as a substitute for political action. More recently, there was intense media coverage of the 'Arab Spring' and the crisis in Libya, including the humanitarian aspects.

5 The challenge of operating in insecure environments has been the subject of a number of recent studies. An authoritative example, covering humanitarian action in general, is 'To Stay and Deliver: Good practice for humanitarians in complex security environments', an independent study commissioned by the UN Office for the Coordination of Humanitarian Affairs (OCHA), undertaken by J. Egeland (former UN Emergency Relief Coordinator), A. Harmer, and A. Stoddard, published in February 2011. For a comprehensive examination from UNHCR's perspective, see V. Tennant, B. Doyle, and R. Mazou, 'Safeguarding Humanitarian Space: a Review of Key Challenges for UNHCR', UNHCR Policy and Development Evaluation Service, PDES/2010/01, February 2010.

6 The *World Development Report 2011* defines organized violence as 'the use or threat of physical force by groups' including 'state actions against other states or against civilians, civil wars, electoral violence between opposing sides, communal conflicts based on regional, ethnic, religious, or other group identities or competing

economic interests, gang-based violence and organized crime, and international, non-state, armed movements with ideological aims'. The World Bank, *World Development Report 2011: Conflict, Security, and Development: Overview*, Washington DC, 2011, xv.

7   UNHCR Executive Committee, 'Note on International Protection', 31 May 2011, UN Doc. EC/62/SC/CRP.12, paras 35 and 36.

8   The World Bank, *World Development Report 2011*, 2, 5 and 18.

9   V. Türk, Director of International Protection, UNHCR, Address: 'Protection Gaps in Europe? Persons Fleeing the Indiscriminate Effects of Generalized Violence', Brussels, 18 January 2011.

10 J. Egeland et al., 'To Stay and Deliver', 4.

11 S. Pantuliano et al., 'Counter-terrorism and humanitarian action: tensions, impact and ways forward', Humanitarian Policy Group (HPG) Policy Brief No. 43, Overseas Development Institute, October 2011, 12.

12 The term 'humanitarian space' was coined in the 1990s by Rony Brauman, former president of the influential NGO Médecins Sans Frontières (MSF). He described it as a space in which MSF was free to evaluate needs, monitor the distribution and use of relief supplies, and have a dialogue with the people.

13 For an argument that it is not shrinking, see: D. Hubert and C. Brassard-Boudreau, 'Shrinking Humanitarian Space? Trends and Prospects on Security and Access', *The Journal of Humanitarian Assistance*, 24 November 2010.

14 The executive summary of 'To Stay and Deliver' states that 'While simultaneously calling for respect for humanitarian principles, in the recent past many humanitarian organizations have also willingly compromised a principled approach in their own conduct through close alignment with political and military activities and actors'. This judgement is echoed by S. Jessen-Petersen in 'Humanitarianism in Crisis', United States Institute of Peace, Special Report No. 273, 4, June 2011: 'Many humanitarian agencies and their donors too easily and uncritically accept the conditions for involvement set by the military in those increasingly frequent operations where security forces are part of the integrated response to a crisis'.

15 Note from the Secretary-General, 'Guidance on Integrated Missions', 9 February 2006, cited in C. de Coning, 'Civil-Military Relations and UN Peacekeeping Operations', *World Politics Review*, 19 May 2010.

16 See E. Barth Eide et al., 'Report on Integrated Missions: Practical Perspectives and Recommendations – Independent Study for the Expanded ECHA Core Group', May 2005.

17 J. Lim, Assistant High Commissioner (Operations), UNHCR, Keynote address: 'Contemporary Challenges for Humanitarian Engagement in Insecure and Complex Environments', Webster University 16th International Humanitarian Conference: Humanitarian Space, 27 January 2011.

18 It is not only the UN flag that no longer provides the protection it once did; of grave significance in the context of humanitarian action in conflict is the fact that the symbol of the ICRC no longer always provides protection.

19 A. Stoddard, A. Harmer and K. Haver, Humanitarian Outcomes, 'Aid Worker Security Report 2011: Spotlight on Security for National Aid Workers: Issues and Perspectives', London, August 2011.

20 A. Stoddard, A. Harmer and V. Di Domenico, 'Providing aid in insecure environments: 2009 Update', HPG Policy Brief No. 34, Overseas Development Institute, April 2009.

21 In 1996, UNHCR staff reported that Serb mercenaries they encountered in what was then Zaire explained their hostility towards the UNHCR personnel as a consequence of UNHCR's actions in the Balkans during the break-up of the former Yugoslavia, which they perceived as anti-Serb.

22 *World Development Report 2011*.

23 2005 World Summit Outcome, UN Doc. A/RES/60/1, 24 October 2005, in particular para. 138. For a relevant examination of the concept, see S. Harris Rimmer, 'Refugees, Internally Displaced Persons and the "Responsibility to Protect"', UNHCR New Issues in Refugee Research, Research Paper No. 185, March 2010.

24 J. Egeland et al., 'To Stay and Deliver', 24.

25 Few studies on the challenges to humanitarian space examine the possibility of a principled

suspension. One that does is S. Jessen-Petersen, 'Humanitarianism in Crisis', 7–8.

26 J. Egeland et al., 'To Stay and Deliver'.

27 Associated Press, 9 November 2011, 'Interview: UN Refugee Head Says Agency Emphasizing Humanitarian Aid after Kandahar Attack'.

28 United Nations, 'Human Rights Due Diligence Policy on UN support to non-UN security forces (HRDDP)', 2011.

CHAPTER 2

1 N. Grubeck, *Civilian Harm in Somalia: Creating an Appropriate Response*, Washington DC: Campaign for Innocent Victims in Conflict (CIVIC), 2011.

2 M. J. Gibney, *The Ethics and Politics of Asylum: Liberal Democracy and the Response to Refugees*, Cambridge: Cambridge University Press, 2004, 2.

3 E. Feller, 'The Refugee Convention at 60: Still Fit for its Purpose?' Presentation at Workshop on Refugees and the Refugee Convention 60 years on: Protection and Identity, Prato, 2 May 2011.

4 1951 Convention relating to the Status of Refugees, 189 *UNTS* 150 (also referred to as the 1951 Convention or the Refugee Convention); 1967 Protocol relating to the Status of Refugees, 606 *UNTS* 267 (referred to as the 1967 Protocol).

5 Ministerial Communiqué, 8 December 2011, HCR/MINCOMMS/2011/6.

6 'UNHCR Hails Mexico's Accession to International Refugee Instruments', UNHCR Press Release, 20 April 2000.

7 UN High Commissioner for Refugees, 'Submission by the Office of the United Nations High Commissioner for Refugees in the case of *Hirsi and Others* v. *Italy*', March 2010, endnote 48.

8 *Plaintiff M70/2011* v. *Minister for Immigration and Citizenship; and Plaintiff M106 of 2011* v. *Minister for Immigration and Citizenship*, [2011] HCA 32, Australia: High Court, 31 August 2011, para. 244.

9 Organization of African Unity, Convention Governing the Specific Aspects of Refugee Problems in Africa ('OAU Convention'),

10 September 1969, 1001 *UNTS* 45. Article 1 repeats the 1951 Convention definition and in its paragraph 2 states: 'The term "refugee" shall also apply to every person who, owing to external aggression, occupation, foreign domination or events seriously disturbing public order in either part or the whole of his country of origin or of nationality, is compelled to leave his place of habitual residence in order to seek refuge in another place outside his country of origin or nationality.'

10 Ibid., Article II(1) and (5), and Article V.

11 Cartagena Declaration on Refugees, Colloquium on the International Protection of Refugees in Central America, Mexico and Panama, 22 November 1984, OAS/Ser.L/V/II.66, doc. 10, rev. 1, pp. 190–193. Part III paragraph 3 of the Declaration states: 'Hence, the definition or concept of a refugee to be recommended for use in the region is one which, in addition to containing the elements of the 1951 Convention and the 1967 Protocol, includes among refugees persons who have fled their country because their lives, safety or freedom have been threatened by generalized violence, foreign aggression, internal conflicts, massive violation of human rights or other circumstances which have seriously disturbed public order.'

12 European Union: Council of the European Union, 'Presidency Conclusions', Tampere European Council, 15-16 October 1999.

13 Arab Convention on Regulating Status of Refugees in the Arab Countries, Adopted by the League of Arab States, 1994, reproduced in *Refugee Survey Quarterly*, 27/2, 2008.

14 Organization of the Islamic Conference, 'Resolution No. 15/10-P (IS) On the Problem of Refugees in the Muslim World', adopted by the Tenth Session of the Islamic Summit Conference, Putrajaya, Malaysia, 16–17 October 2003. An earlier Resolution No. 32/7-P (IS) with the same title was adopted on 15 December 1994.

15 Asian–African Legal Consultative Organization (AALCO), '[Revised] 1996 Bangkok Principles on the Status and Treatment of Refugees' 24 June 2001.

16 An Expert Meeting convened by UNHCR and the International Criminal Tribunal for Rwanda (ICTR) in Arusha, Tanzania in April 2011 noted the strong interaction between international

humanitarian law, international criminal law and the refugee regime. While stressing that each regime has its specific purpose, participants noted important synergies and suggested a number of areas where international human rights law, international humanitarian law and international criminal law can assist in the interpretation and application of refugee law. See: UNHCR and the ICTR, 'Expert Meeting on Complementarities between International Refugee Law, International Criminal Law and International Human Rights Law: Summary Conclusions', Arusha, Tanzania, 11 – 13 April 2011.

17 In 2011, UNHCR and the Council of Europe convened a Roundtable involving experts from regional human rights courts and bodies from Europe, Latin America and Africa. See: 'Joint UNHCR/Council of Europe Colloquium on the Role of Regional Human Rights Courts in Interpreting and Enforcing Legal Standards for the Protection of Forcibly Displaced Persons, Conference Report, 15–16 June 2011, Strasbourg, France', published in December 2011.

18 United Nations High Commissioner for Refugees, *Handbook on Procedures and Criteria for Determining Refugee Status under the 1951 Convention and the 1967 Protocol relating to the Status of Refugees*, January 1992, rev. 1, para. 189.

19 B. Rutinwa, '*Prima Facie* Status and Refugee Protection', New Issues in Refugee Research No. 69, UNHCR Evaluation and Policy Analysis Unit, October 2002.

20 E. Feller, 'Doing Protection Better', Address to the 62nd session of the Executive Committee of UNHCR's Programme, Geneva, October, 2011.

21 European Union, Council Directive 2004/83/EC of 29 April 2004 on Minimum Standards for the Qualification and Status of Third Country Nationals or Stateless Persons as Refugees or as Persons Who Otherwise Need International Protection and the Content of the Protection Granted, Article 2(e) and 15 (c).

22 *Elgafaji* v. *Staatssecretaris van Justitie*, C-465/07, European Union: European Court of Justice, 17 February 2009.

23 UNHCR, 'Safe at Last? Law and Practice in Selected EU Member States with Respect to Asylum-Seekers Fleeing Indiscriminate Violence', Brussels, July 2011.

24 UNHCR, Guidelines on International Protection No. 2: 'Membership of a Particular Social Group' Within the Context of Article 1A(2) of the 1951 Convention and/or its 1967 Protocol Relating to the Status of Refugees, 7 May 2002, HCR/GIP/02/02.

25 European Union, Council Directive 2004/83/EC of 29 April 2004, Article 10 (1)(d).

26 For example, RRT Case No. 98/24000, Australia: Refugee Review Tribunal, 13 January 2000.

27 For example, Commission des Recours des Réfugiés (France), 25 March 2005, 513547, *Mlle G.*; Cour Nationale du Droit d'Asile (France), 1 July 2008, 571904, *K.* See also: Verwaltungsgericht, Frankfurt (Oder), 11 November 2010, VG4K 772/10.A; Verwaltungsgericht, Ansbach, 21 August 2008, AN 18 K 08.30201.

28 See e.g. *Matter of S-E-G-, et al.*, 24 I&N Dec. 579 (BIA 2008), United States Board of Immigration Appeals, 30 July 2008.

29 See e.g. UNHCR, *Granados Gaitan* v. *Holder*: Brief of the United Nations High Commissioner for Refugees as *Amicus Curiae* in Support of Petitioner, 13 July 2010, No. 10/1724 (before the United States Court of Appeals for the Eighth Circuit).

30 G. S. Goodwin-Gill and J. McAdam, *The Refugee in International Law*, Oxford: Oxford University Press, 3rd edition, 2007, 355.

31 A. Edwards, 'Back to Basics: The Right to Liberty and Security of Person and "Alternatives to Detention" of Refugees, Asylum-Seekers, Stateless Persons and Other Migrants', UNHCR Division of International Protection, PPLA/2011/01.Rev.1, April 2011.

32 Human Rights First, 'US Detention of Asylum Seekers: Seeking Protection, Finding Prison', June 2009.

33 UNHCR, 'Global Roundtable on Alternatives to Detention of Refugees, Asylum-Seekers, Migrants and Stateless Persons: Summary Conclusions', Geneva, 11–12 May 2011.

34 M. D. Balde, J. Crisp, E. Macleod and V. Tennant, 'Shelter from the Storm: A Real-time Evaluation of UNHCR's Response to the Emergency in Côte d'Ivoire and Liberia', UNHCR, PDES/2011/07, June 2011.

35 Ibid.

36 A. Abou-El-Wafa, *The Right to Asylum between Islamic Shari'ah and International Refugee Law: A Comparative Study*, Riyadh: Naif Arab University for Security Studies, 2009.

37 UNHCR, 'Refugee Protection and Mixed Migration: A 10-Point Plan of Action', Geneva, 1 January 2007 (rev. 1).

38 Detailed information on the implementation of the 10-Point Plan in various regions of the world and the regional conferences is available on the UNHCR website.

39 UN General Assembly, United Nations Convention against Transnational Organized Crime, *UNTS*, Vol. 2225, I-39574.

40 See for example *SB (PSG - Protection Regulations – Reg. 6) Moldova v. Secretary of State for the Home Department*, CG [2008] UKAIT 00002, United Kingdom: Asylum and Immigration Tribunal.

41 UN High Commissioner for Refugees, Guidelines on International Protection No. 7: The Application of Article 1A(2) of the 1951 Convention and/or 1967 Protocol Relating to the Status of Refugees to Victims of Trafficking and Persons At Risk of Being Trafficked, 7 April 2006, HCR/GIP/06/07.

42 E. Feller, Address to the Counter-Terrorism Committee, United Nations, New York, 19 May 2011.

43 S. Kapferer, 'Article 14(2) of the Universal Declaration of Human Rights and Exclusion from International Refugee Protection', *Refugee Survey Quarterly*, 27/3, 2008, 53–75.

44 United Nations General Assembly Resolution 8 (I) 'Question of Refugees' 29 January 1946.

45 UNHCR Executive Committee Conclusion 92 (LIII) 2002 and United Nations General Assembly Resolution 57/187 of 9 February 2003.

46 The Council of Europe and its Human Rights Court, the European Union, and the Inter-American Commission on Human Rights are prime examples. There is also growing interest in asylum on the part of the African Human Rights Court, the various sub-regional courts in Africa, the Organization of Islamic Cooperation, and the ASEAN Human Rights Commission.

47 See the 'Summary Conclusions of the Expert Roundtable on Supervisory Responsibility'

organized in 2001 by the United Nations High Commissioner for Refugees and the Lauterpacht Research Centre for International Law, in the context of the Global Consultations on International Protection, in: E. Feller, V. Türk and F. Nicholson (eds), *Refugee Protection in International Law: UNHCR's Global Consultations on International Protection* Cambridge: Cambridge University Press, 2003, 667–671. See also V. Türk, 'UNHCR's Role in Supervising International Protection Standards in the Context of its Mandate,' Speech at York University, Toronto, Canada, May 2010.

48 The United Kingdom–UNHCR Quality Initiative ran from 2004 to 2009. As of 2010, it became known as the Quality Integration Project.

49 A. Guterres, 'Remarks at the Opening of the Judicial Year of the European Court of Human Rights', Strasbourg, 28 January 2011.

50 T. Hammarberg, 'Racism: Europeans ought to be more self-critical and remain open to thorough and frank UN discussions', 14 April 2010, in *Human Rights in Europe: Growing Gaps*, Council of Europe, Strasbourg, 12.

51 Human Rights Watch, 'World Report 2011', New York, 2011, 172–173.

52 There is little published data on the cost of maintaining asylum systems. For one source, see: E. Thielemann, R. Williams and C. Boswell, 'What System of Burden-sharing between Member States for the Reception of Asylum Seekers?' PE 419.620, European Parliament, Directorate-General for Internal Policies, Brussels, 2010.

53 UNHCR, Division of International Protection, 'Combating Racism, Racial Discrimination, Xenophobia and Related Intolerance through a Strategic Approach', Geneva, December 2009.

54 'Memorandum of Understanding between the OSCE Office for Democratic Institutions and Human Rights and the Office of the United Nations High Commissioner for Refugees', 22 June 2011.

CHAPTER 3

1 UNHCR's June 2004 paper on protracted refugee situations (EC/54/SC/CRP.14) defines a 'protracted' situation as one which involves more than 25,000 refugees who have been in exile for five years or more in a developing country. The number of refugees under UNHCR's mandate who are in protracted situations does not include the Palestinian refugees who fall under the responsibility of the United Nations Relief and Works Agency for Palestine Refugees in the Near East (UNRWA).

2 A. Guterres, 'Opening Statement to the 62nd Session of the Executive Committee', Geneva, 3 October 2011.

3 UNHCR, 'Protracted Refugee Situations: High Commissioner's Initiative', December 2008; information on the Protection Dialogue itself is available on the UNHCR website.

4 UN General Assembly Resolution 428 (V) of 14 December 1950, Statute of the Office of the United Nations High Commissioner for Refugees, paras. 8(d), (d), (e).

5 For a history of UNHCR's role in repatriation, see M. Zieck, *UNHCR and Voluntary Repatriation of Refugees*, Berlin: Springer, 1997.

6 D. Turton and P. Marsden, 'Taking Refugees for a Ride? The Politics of Refugee Return to Afghanistan', Afghan Research and Evaluation Unit Issues Papers series, Kabul, December 2002.

7 UNHCR Kabul, 'Initial Assessment of Reintegration of Afghan Refugee Returnees', Phase 1, Community-based Snapshot Survey, September 2011.

8 Data is based: a) for Pakistan, on the registration conducted by the Government of Pakistan's National Database and Registration Authority (NADRA) in 2011 and b) for Iran, on the Government of the Islamic Republic of Iran Amayesh 6 registration.

9 T. Kaiser, 'Dispersal, Division and Diversification: Durable Solutions and Sudanese Refugees in Uganda', *Journal of Eastern African Studies*, 4/1, March 2010, 50.

10 As follow-up to the Secretary-General's 2009 report on peacebuilding, the UN prepared a working document entitled 'Ending Displacement in the Aftermath of Conflict: a Preliminary Framework for supporting a more coherent, predictable and effective response to the durable solutions needs of refugee returnees and internally displaced persons'. The Secretary-General endorsed this framework in his Decision No. 2011/20 (October 2011).

11 H. Adelman and E. Barkan, *No Return, No Refuge: Rites and Rights in Minority Repatriation*, Ithaca: Columbia University Press, 2011.

12 Ibid.; see also e.g. R. Black, 'Return and Reconstruction in Bosnia-Herzegovina: Missing Link, or Mistaken Priority?', *SAIS Review of International Affairs*, 21/2, 2001, 177–199.

13 UNHCR (August 2009) 'Urban Reintegration: A Desk Review'; P. Weiss Fagen, 'Uprooted and Unrestored. A Comparative Review of Durable Solutions for People Uprooted by Conflict in Colombia and Liberia', UNHCR Policy Development and Evaluation Service, PDES/2011/09, August 2011, 59.

14 UNHCR Executive Committee Conclusion on Local Integration, No. 104 (LVI) 2005.

15 In particular, the US Committee for Refugees and Immigrants (USCRI) has spearheaded campaigns against refugee warehousing; see e.g. M. Smith, 'Warehousing Refugees, A Denial of Rights, A Waste of Humanity', *World Refugee Survey 2004*; see also A. Jamal, 'Minimum Standards and Essential Needs in a Protracted Refugee Situation: A Review of the UNHCR Programme in Kakuma, Kenya'. UNHCR Evaluation and Policy Analysis Unit, EPAU/2000/05, November 2000.

16 E. H. Campbell, 'Urban Refugees in Nairobi: Protection, Survival and Integration', Migration Studies Working Paper Series No 23, Forced Migration Studies Programme, University of the Witwatersrand, December 2005; V. Kalitanyi and K. Visser, 'African Immigrants in South Africa: Job Takers or Job Creators?', *South Africa Journal of Economic and Management Sciences*, 3/4, 2010.

17 A. Lindley and A. Haslie, 'Unlocking Protracted Displacement: Somali Case Study', Refugee Studies Centre, University of Oxford, Working Paper No.79, August 2011, 35.

18 See R. Allen, A. Li Rosi and M. Skei, 'Should I Stay or Should I Go? A Review of UNHCR's Response to the Protracted Refugee Situation in Serbia and Croatia', UNHCR Policy Development and Evaluation Service, PDES/2010/14,

December 2010; see also G. Ambroso, J. Crisp and N. Albert, 'No Turning Back: A review of UNHCR's Response to the Protracted Refugee Situation in Eastern Sudan', UNHCR Policy Development and Evaluation Service, PDES/2011/12, November 2011

19 Ambroso, Crisp and Albert, 'No Turning Back'.

20 Pledge made by Zambia in December 2011 at the Ministerial Meeting on the occasion of the 60th anniversary of the 1951 Refugee Convention.

21 The 15 countries which operated resettlement programmes in 2005 were: Argentina, Australia, Brazil, Canada, Chile, Denmark, Finland, Iceland, Ireland, the Netherlands, New Zealand, Norway, Sweden, the UK and the US. The seven countries added to this list in 2010 were the Czech Republic, France, Japan, Paraguay, Portugal, Romania and Uruguay—although some of these countries, notably France and Japan, had participated actively in resettlement in earlier years. New programmes announced by Bulgaria, Hungary, Spain and Germany are being launched in 2012 and 2013.

22 UNHCR, Working Group on Resettlement, 'The Strategic Use of Resettlement', 14 October 2009, 2.

23 'Report of the Secretary-General on peacebuilding in the immediate aftermath of conflict,' UN Doc. A/63/881-S/2009/304, 11 June 2009.

24 Statement by A. Guterres, to the United Nations Security Council, New York, 24 January 2006.

25 The UN International Strategy for Disaster Reduction (UNISDR) defines resilience as 'the ability of a system, community or society exposed to hazards to resist, absorb, accommodate to and recover from the effects of a hazard in a timely and efficient manner, including through the preservation and restoration of its essential basic structures and functions' in: UNISDR, 2009 *UNISDR Terminology on Disaster Risk Reduction*, United Nations, Geneva, May 2009.

26 Two early initiatives were the International Conference on Assistance to Refugees in Africa (ICARA) in 1981, and the International Conference on Assistance to Refugees in Central America (CIREFCA) process launched in 1987. For a review of these and subsequent initiatives, see A. Betts, *Protection by Persuasion: International Cooperation in the Refugee Regime*, Ithaca and London: Cornell University Press, 2009.

27 Conclusion No. 109 (LXI) 2009, 'Protracted Refugee Situations', para. (n).

28 Ibid., para. (j).

29 The World Bank, 'FY 2011 Annual Report, Global Program on Forced Displacement', 15 November 2011.

30 UNHCR, UNDP and the World Bank, 'Transitional Solutions Initiative: Concept Note', October 2010.

31 UNHCR Inspection and Evaluation Service, 'Review of UNHCR's Refugee Education Activities,' Geneva, 1997, 1.

32 UNHCR, Policy Development and Evaluation Service, S. Dryden-Peterson, 'Refugee Education: A Global Review', 2011, 6.

33 E. Feller, V. Türk and F. Nicholson (eds), *Refugee Protection in International Law: UNHCR's Global Consultations on International Protection*, Cambridge: Cambridge University Press, 2003, 493–499.

34 Fahamu Refugee Programme, 'Opposing Cessation of Protection for Rwandan Refugees', *Pambazuka News*, 22 September 2011.

35 UNHCR Executive Committee Conclusion on Cessation of Status, No. 69 (XLIII) 1992.

36 See e.g. N. Van Hear, R. Brubaker and T. Bessa, 'Managing Mobility for Human Development: the Growing Salience of Mixed Migration', UNDP Human Development Research Paper 2009/20, New York: UNDP.

37 O. Bakewell, 'Repatriation and Self-settled Refugees in Zambia: Bringing Solutions to the Wrong Problems', *Journal of Refugee Studies*, 13/4, 2000, 356–73; Ambroso, Crisp and Albert, 'No Turning Back'.

38 Allen, Li Rosi and Skei, 'Should I Stay or Should I go?', 17.

39 IRIN, UN Office for the Coordination of Humanitarian Affairs (OCHA), 'Ghana–Liberia: Refugees Protest Repatriation', 13 March 2008.

40 See e.g. Lindley and Haslie, 'Unlocking Protracted Displacement: Somali Case Study'.

41 A. Monsutti, 'Afghan Migratory Strategies and the Three Solutions to the Refugee Problem', *Refugee Survey Quarterly*, 27/1, 2008, 58–73; A. Monsutti,

'Afghan Transnational Networks: Looking Beyond Repatriation', Afghanistan Research and Evaluation Unit (AREU), Kabul, August 2006.

42 Joint Declaration of 7 November 2011 by Ministers of Foreign Affairs of Bosnia and Herzegovina, Montenegro, Croatia and Serbia on ending displacement and ensuring durable solutions for vulnerable refugees and internally displaced persons. See also Allen, Li Rosi and Skei, 'Should I Stay or Should I go?', which draws attention to the importance of mobility and dual citizenship as an alternative to the traditional paradigm of either integration or voluntary repatriation.

43 See O. Bakewell, 'Keeping Them in Their Place: The Ambivalent Relationship between Development and Migration in Africa, *Third World Quarterly*, 29/7, 2008, 1341–1358, for more discussion of 'sedentary bias'.

44 K. Long, 'Extending Protection? Labour Migration and Durable Solutions for Refugees', UNHCR New Issues in Refugee Research, Working Paper Series, No.176, October 2009; K. Long, 'Home Alone? A Review of the Relationship between Repatriation, Mobility and Durable Solutions for Refugees', UNHCR Policy Development and Evaluation Service, PDES 2010/2, March 2010.

45 Department for International Development (DIFID), 'Moving out of Poverty: Making Migration Work Better for Poor People', April 2007.

46 L. Hovil, 'Hoping for Peace, Afraid of War: the Dilemmas of Repatriation and Belonging on the Borders of Uganda and South Sudan', UNHCR New Issues in Refugee Research Working Paper Series, No.196, November 2010.

47 A. Adepoju, A. Boulton and M. Levin, 'Promoting Integration through Mobility: Free Movement and the ECOWAS Protocol', UNHCR New Issues in Refugee Research Working Paper Series, No.150, December 2007.

48 UNHCR, 'Updated Observations on the Proposal for a Directive of the European Parliament and of the Council amending Directive 2003/109/EC Establishing a Long-Term Residence Status to extend its Scope to Beneficiaries of International Protection', Brussels, August 2010.

49 K. Long, 'Protection-sensitive Migration as a Complement to Refugee Resettlement', Paper prepared for the Working Group on Resettlement Meeting, January 2011.

50 G.J. van Heuven Goedhart, 'Nobel Lecture: Refugee Problems and their Solutions', 12 December 1955.

CHAPTER 4

1 1954 Convention relating to the Status of Stateless Persons, 360 *UNTS* 117 and 1961 Convention on the Reduction of Statelessness, 989 *UNTS* 175.

2 UNGA Resolution 3274 (XXIX), 10 December 1974.

3 UNHCR Executive Committee Conclusion No. 78 (XLVI) 1995.

4 Ibid., paras (a) and (c).

5 UNGA Resolution 50/152 of 9 February 1996, para. 15.

6 Article 1(1) of the 1954 Convention.

7 UNHCR, 'The Concept of Stateless Persons under International Law (Summary Conclusions)', Expert Meeting, May 2010.

8 UNHCR, 'Statelessness Determination Procedures and the Status of Stateless Persons (Summary Conclusions)', Expert Meeting, December 2010.

9 UNHCR, 'Interpreting the 1961 Statelessness Convention and Preventing Statelessness among Children', Summary Conclusions of the Expert Meeting convened by UNHCR and the Open Society Justice Initiative in Dakar, Senegal on 23–24 May 2011, published in September 2011. Information on this and other expert meetings on statelessness can be found on the UNHCR website.

10 Inter-American Court of Human Rights, *Case of the Girls Yean and Bosico* v. *Dominican Republic*, Judgment of 8 September 2005, Series C, No. 130.

11 *Andrijeva* v. *Latvia*, Application No. 55707/00, Council of Europe: European Court of Human Rights, 18 February 2009.

12 *Kuric and Others* v. *Slovenia*, Application No. 26828/06, Council of Europe: European Court of Human Rights, 13 July 2010. At the time of writing, the Chamber's judgment had been referred to the Grand Chamber.

13 African Committee of Experts on the Rights and Welfare of the Child, Decision No. 002/Com/002/2009.

14 State succession is defined in the International Law Commission's Articles on the Nationality of Natural Persons in relation to the Succession of States, as 'the replacement of one State by another in the responsibility for the international relations of territory', see Annex to UN General Assembly Resolution A/RES/55/153 of 30 January 2001, Article 2(a).

15 UNHCR, 'Identifying Stateless Persons: Case Studies Serbia and Myanmar', *Statistical Yearbook* 2010, 30–32.

16 See: UNHCR, 'Background Note on Gender Equality, Nationality Laws and Statelessness,' Geneva, March 2012.

17 Recent studies commissioned by UNHCR include, 'Overview of Statelessness: International and Japanese Context', April 2010; 'The Situation of Stateless Persons in the Middle East and North Africa', October 2010; 'Statelessness in Central Asia', May 2011; 'Mapping Statelessness in the United Kingdom', 22 November 2011; and 'Mapping Statelessness in the Netherlands', November 2011.

18 UN Secretary-General, 'Guidance Note of the Secretary General: The United Nations and Statelessness', June 2011.

19 Council of Europe: Committee of Ministers, 'Recommendation of the Committee of Ministers to Member States on the Nationality of Children', 9 December 2009, CM/Rec (2009)13. The earlier recommendation was 'Recommendation R (1999) 18 of the Committee of Ministers to Member States on the Avoidance and Reduction of Statelessness', 15 September 1999.

20 UNHCR, 'Summary Overview: Regional Conference on Prevention and Reduction of Statelessness and Protection of Stateless Persons in Central Asia', Ashgabat, Turkmenistan, 9–10 December 2009.

21 See: 'Zagreb Declaration' of 27 October 2011.

CHAPTER 5

1 Internal Displacement Monitoring Centre (IDMC), 'Internal Displacement: Global Overview of Trends and Developments in 2010', Geneva, March 2011.

2 Article 1A(2) of the 1951 Refugee Convention stipulates that the inability or unwillingness of an individual to avail himself of the protection of his country of origin is one of the elements of the refugee definition.

3 An early attempt to define the term internally displaced person can be found in: 'Report of the Secretary-General, International Conference on the Plight of Refugees, Returnees and Displaced Persons in Southern Africa', UN Doc. A/44/520, 28 September 1989, para. 72.

4 F. Deng et al., *Sovereignty as Responsibility: Conflict Management in Africa*, Washington DC: Brookings Institution Press, 1996.

5 Guiding Principles on Internal Displacement, UN Doc. E/CN.4/1998/53/Add.2 of 11 February 1998.

6 Protocol on the Protection and Assistance to Internally Displaced Persons, adopted on 30 November 2006 by the Member States of the International Conference on the Great Lakes Region.

7 African Union Convention for the Protection and Assistance of Internally Displaced Persons in Africa (Kampala Convention), adopted in October 2009 by the AU Special Summit on Refugees, Returnees and IDPs in Kampala, Uganda.

8 Guiding Principles on Internal Displacement, Principle 15(d).

9 Brookings-Bern Project on Internal Displacement, *Addressing Internal Displacement: A Framework for National Responsibility*, Washington DC: Brookings Institution, 2005.

10 See e.g., 'The Well-Fed Dead in Bosnia', *New York Times*, 15 July 1992.

11 'Report of the Representative of the Secretary-General on the Human Rights of Internally Displaced Persons, Walter Kälin', UN Doc A/HRC/13/21, 5 January 2010, paras. 31, 62, 78 and 87.

12 G. McHugh, *Integrating Internal Displacement in*

Peace Processes and Agreements, Washington DC: US Institute of Peace; Brookings Institution, Brookings-Bern Project on Internal Displacement, 2010.

13 Report of the UN Secretary-General, 'In Larger Freedom: Towards Development, Security and Human Rights for All', UN Doc. A/59/2005, 21 March 2005, para. 210.

14 A. W. Bijleveld, 'Towards More Predictable Humanitarian Responses: Inter-Agency Cluster Approach to IDPs', *Refugee Survey Quarterly*, 25/4, 2006, 31.

15 In addition, UNHCR leads the emergency shelter and camp coordination clusters.

16 The ICRC definition of protection of civilians in armed conflict, originally adopted by a 1999 Workshop of the International Committee of the Red Cross (ICRC) on protection, encompasses 'all activities aimed at obtaining full respect for the rights of the individual in accordance with the letter and spirit of the relevant bodies of law, namely human rights law, international humanitarian law and refugee law.' See ICRC, 'Strengthening Protection in War: A Search for Professional Standards' (ICRC, 2001). The Inter-Agency Standing Committee (IASC) adopted the same definition in 1999; see Inter-Agency Standing Committee, XXIInd Meeting, New York, 6 December 1999, 'Protection of Internally Displaced Persons, Inter-Agency Standing Committee Policy Paper', 4.

17 E. G. Ferris, *The Politics of Protection: The Limits of Humanitarian Action*, Washington DC: Brookings Institution Press, 2011, 270–285.

18 World Summit Outcome Document, UN Doc. A/RES/60/1, 24 October 2005, para. 132; United Nations General Assembly Resolution UN Doc. A/RES/64/162, 2009, preambular para. 10.

19 Council of Europe, Committee of Ministers, 'Recommendation of the Committee of Ministers to Member States on Internally Displaced Persons'; CM/Rec (2006) 6; Council of Europe, Parliamentary Assembly Recommendation 1631 (2003), 'Internal Displacement in Europe'; Organization of American States, General Assembly Resolution AG/RES.2417 (XXXVIII-O/08), 2008.

20 For an overview of existing national instruments on internal displacement, see the 'National and Regional Laws and Policies on Internal Displacement Index' of the Brookings Institution, available at http://www.brookings.edu.

21 Law 387, 18 July 1997, *Diario Oficial* (Official Gazette) No. 43, 091 of 24 July 1997.

22 See M. J. Cepeda Espinosa, 'The Constitutional Protection of IDPs in Colombia', in: R. A. Rivadeneira (ed.), *Judicial Protection of Internally Displaced Persons: The Colombian Experience*, Washington DC: Brookings-Bern Project on Internal Displacement, 2009, 6–7.

23 Constitutional Court of Colombia, Third Chamber, Decision T-025/04 of 22 January 2004.

24 See Cepeda Espinosa, 'The Constitutional Protection of IDPs in Colombia', 19 and C. E. Reales, 'Design and Implementation of the Orders Issued in Decision T-025 of 2004: An Assessment of the Process', in: R. A. Rivadeneira (ed.), *Judicial Protection of Internally Displaced Persons*, 49ff.

25 Cepeda Espinosa, 'The Consitutional Protection of IDPs in Colombia', 32.

26 See for example: Inter-American Court of Human Rights, *Case of the Pueblo Bello Massacre* v. *Colombia*, Judgment of 31 January 2006 (Merits, Reparations, and Costs); *Case of the Ituango Massacres* v. *Colombia*, Judgment of 1 July 2006 (Preliminary Objections, Merits, Reparations, and Costs).

27 *Case of the Communities of the Jiguamiandó and of the Curbaradó* v. *Colombia*, Order of the Inter-American Court of Human Rights (IACrtHR), 6 March 2003, para. 10; Order of 5 February 2008, (IACrtHR), 'Provisional measures with regard to the Republic of Colombia: Matter of the Communities of Jiguamiandó and Curbaradó', para. 1.

28 See e.g. European Court of Human Rights, 11 May 2010, *Case of Jafarov* v. *Azerbaijan*, Judgment of 11 May 2010; *Case of Dogan and others* v. *Turkey*, Judgment of 29 June 2004; *Case of Aydin Içyer* v. *Turkey*, Judgment of 12 January 2006.

29 European Court of Human Rights, *Case of Dogan and others* v. *Turkey*, para. 153.

30 African Commission on Human and Peoples' Rights, application 276 / 2003–*Centre for Minority Rights Development (Kenya) and Minority Rights Group International on behalf of Endorois Welfare Council* v. *Kenya*, para. 298.

31 See e.g. ICTY, *The Prosecutor v. Vidoje Blagojevi and Dragan Jokic* (IT-02-60-T), Judgment of 17 January 2005, paras. 595 ff; ICTY, *The Prosecutor v. Milorad Krnjelac*, (IT-27-25-A), Judgment of 17 September 2003, paras. 217 ff.

32 Rome Statute, Articles 7(1)(d), 8(2)(b)(viii) and (e)(viii).

33 See ICC-02/04-01/05, *The Prosecutor v. Joseph Kony, Vincent Otti, Okot Odhiambo and Dominic Ongwen*, ICC-01/04-01/06, Trial, *The Prosecutor v. Thomas Lubanga Dyilo*, ICC-01/04-01/07, *The Prosecutor v. Callixte Mbarushimana*, ICC-02/05-01/09, Pre-trial, *The Prosecutor v. Omar Hassan Ahmad Al Bashir*.

34 See ICC-01/09-01/11, *The Prosecutor v. William Samoei Ruto, Henry Kiprono Kosgey and Joshua Arap Sang*.

35 See more generally, Ferris, *The Politics of Protection*.

36 Inter-Agency Standing Committee (IASC), 'Protection of Internally Displaced Persons', Policy Paper Series No. 2, 2000. See *supra* note 16, and *Strengthening Protection in War: A Search for Professional Standards*, Geneva: ICRC, 2001.

37 The Brookings-Bern Project on Internal Displacement (ed.), 'IASC Operational Guidelines on the Protection of Persons in Situations of Natural Disasters', Washington DC, January 2011, 6–7.

38 The Brookings-Bern Project on Internal Displacement (ed.), 'IASC Framework on Durable Solutions for Internally Displaced Persons', Washington DC, April 2010, 5–7.

39 Ibid., 15–19, 27–46.

40 Report of the Representative of the Secretary-General, Walter Kälin, para. 79.

41 IDMC, *Internal Displacement: Global Overview of Trends and Developments in 2010*, Geneva, March 2011. This figure relates to conflict-related displacement and does not include disaster and development-induced displacement.

42 Report of the Representative of the Secretary-General, Walter Kälin, 2010, para. 78.

43 See R. Cohen et al. (eds), *The Guiding Principles on Internal Displacement and the Law of the South Caucasus: Georgia, Armenia, Azerbaijan*, Washington DC: American Society of International Law, Studies in Transnational Legal Policy No. 34, 2003.

CHAPTER 6

1 'UNHCR Policy on Refugee Protection and Solutions in Urban Areas', Geneva, September 2009.

2 The first meeting of High Commissioner's Dialogue on Protection Challenges took place in 2007. Subsequent Dialogues were convened in 2008, 2009 and 2010. The Dialogue facilitates discussion of global protection issues by states, NGOs, academics and other stakeholders (*see chapter 2*).

3 The cities selected for 'real-time evaluations' were Dushanbe (Tajikistan), Kuala Lumpur (Malaysia), Nairobi (Kenya), San José (Costa Rica) and Sofia (Bulgaria).

4 UNHCR and Handicap International, 'Working with Persons with Disabilities in Forced Displacement', 2011, 9.

5 International Federation of Red Cross and Red Crescent Societies, 'World Disasters Report 2010: Focus on Urban Risk', 2010, 8.

6 T. Rosenberg, 'Beyond Refugee Camps, a Better Way', *New York Times*, 6 September 2011.

7 A. de Geoffroy, 'The Challenge of Protracted Displacement: The Case of Khartoum', Middle East Institute (United States) and Fondation pour la Recherche Stratégique (France), February 2011.

8 UNHCR Division of Operational Services, Operational Solutions and Transition Section, 'Desk Review on Urban Reintegration', August 2009.

9 A. de Waal, 'Do Darfur's IDPs Have an Urban Future?', *African Arguments*, 31 March 2009.

10 N. Obi and J. Crisp, 'Evaluation of UNHCR's Policy on Refugees in Urban Areas: A Case Study Review of New Delhi', UNHCR Evaluation and Policy Analysis Unit, EPAU/2000/04, November 2000; S. Sperl, 'Evaluation of UNHCR's Policy on Refugees in Urban Areas: A Case Study Review of Cairo', UNHCR Evaluation and Policy Analysis Unit, EPAU/2001/07, June 2001.

11 UNHCR Branch Office for Kenya, 'The Nairobi Refugee Program 2005–2007: Working with Partner Agencies and Refugee Communities to Strengthen Urban Refugee Protection', 2007.

12 A. Parker, 'Hidden in Plain View: Refugees Living Without Protection in Nairobi and Kampala', Human Rights Watch, November 2002; See also: E. Campbell, J. Crisp and E. Kiragu, 'Navigating Nairobi: A Review of the Implementation of UNHCR's Urban Refugee Policy in Kenya's Capital City', UNHCR Policy and Development Evaluation Service, PDES/2011/01, January 2011.

13 A. Li Rosi, M. Formisano and L. Jandrijasevic, 'Lives in Limbo: A Review of the Implementation of UNHCR's Urban Refugee Policy in Tajikistan', UNHCR Policy Development and Evaluation Service, PDES/2011/03, May 2011.

14 A. de Geoffroy, 'IDPs and Urban Planning in Khartoum', Forced Migration Review, 24, November 2005, 38; A. K. Tibaijuka, 'Report of the Fact-Finding Mission to Zimbabwe to assess the Scope and Impact of "Operation Murambatsvina" by the UN Special Envoy on Human Settlements Issues in Zimbabwe', July 2005.

15 With respect to IDPs in Kampala (Uganda), see e.g. P. Wyrzykowski and B. Kasozi, 'Violence, Exile and Transitional Justice: Perspectives of Urban IDPs in Kampala', Briefing Note No. 3, The 'Beyond Juba' Project, Faculty of Law, Makerere University, Uganda, August 2009.

16 A. Koscalova and E. Lucchi, 'Evaluation Report on the MSF Response to Displacement in Open Settings,' Médecins Sans Frontières, June 2010.

17 J. Krause-Vilmar, 'The Living Ain't Easy: Urban Refugees in Kampala', Women's Refugee Commission, March 2011, 15.

18 R. Delhaas, 'Forgotten and Marginalized: Displaced Persons in Khartoum: One Year after the Peace Agreement', Interchurch Organization for Development Co-operation (ICCO), 2006, 4.

19 R. Chambers and G. Conway, 'Sustainable rural livelihoods – practical concepts for the 21st century', IDS Discussion Paper 296, Brighton, 1991; DFID, 'The SL Distance Learning Guide', DFID Sustainable Livelihoods Guidance Sheets.

20 UNHCR, 'Refugee Livelihoods in Urban Settings', Discussion paper for the High Commissioner's Dialogue on Protection Challenges, December 2009, 2. See also: UNHCR, 'Promoting Livelihoods and Self-reliance: Operational Guidance on Refugee Protection and Solutions in Urban Areas', 2011.

21 D. Buscher, 'Bright Lights, Big City: Urban Refugees Struggle to Make a Living in New Delhi', Women's Refugee Commission, July 2011.

22 Refugee Consortium of Kenya, 'Self Settled Refugees in Nairobi: A Close Look at their Coping Strategies', 2005, 24. For example, nine per cent of respondents in focus groups convened by the Refugee Consortium of Kenya cited prostitution earnings as a means of livelihood.

23 E. Pittaway, 'Making Mainstreaming a Reality: Gender and the UNHCR Policy on Refugee Protection and Solutions in Urban Areas: A Refugee Perspective', Centre for Refugee Research, University of New South Wales (2010). Researchers consulted refugees in Nairobi (Kenya), Mae Sot (Thailand), New Delhi and Mizoram (India), Cairo (Egypt) and Kuala Lumpur (Malaysia).

24 UNHCR and the University of New South Wales, 'Survivors, Protectors, Providers: Refugee Women Speak Out', Summary Report, November 2011.

25 P. Wyrzykowski and B. Kasozi , 'Violence, Exile, and Transitional Justice: Perspectives of Urban IDPs in Kampala', 9.

26 J. Krause-Vilmar and J. Chaffin, 'No Place to Go But Up: Urban Refugees in Johannesburg, South Africa', Women's Refugee Commission, October 2011.

27 E. Campbell, J. D'Arc Kakusu and I. Musyemi, 'Congolese Refugee Livelihoods in Nairobi and the Prospects of Legal, Local Integration', Refugee Survey Quarterly, 25/2, 2006, 93–108.

28 J. Handmaker, L. de la Hunt and J. Klaaren (eds), Advancing Refugee Protection in South Africa, Oxford and New York: Berghahn Books, 2008, 38.

29 E. Ferris, 'Protecting the Displaced in Colombia: The Role of Municipal Authorities', Summary Report of a seminar held in Bogotá, Colombia, convened by the Brookings-Bern Project on Internal Displacement, Acción Social, UNHCR, and the Universidad de los Andes, 2008.

30 UNHCR, 'Displaced Colombians Turn an Unwanted Corner of a Major Coastal Port into a Decent Home', January 2010.

31 J. Charny, 'World Refugee Day: Where are the World's Hidden Refugees?' *Refugees International*, 2008.

32 Inter-Agency Standing Committee (IASC), 'Final Strategy for Meeting Humanitarian Challenges in Urban Areas', November 2010.

33 S. Corbett, 'One Mouth too Many', *New York Times*, 1 July 2011.

34 'UNHCR Policy on Refugee Protection and Solutions in Urban Areas', para. 12.

CHAPTER 7

1 A. Guterres, 'Statement to the Nansen Conference on Climate Change and Displacement', 6 June 2011.

2 UN Human Rights Council, Resolution 7/23, 'Human rights and climate change', 28 March 2008; UN Human Rights Council, 'Annual Report of the United Nations High Commissioner for Human Rights and Reports of the Office of the High Commissioner and the Secretary-General: Report of the Office of the United Nations High Commissioner for Human Rights on the relationship between climate change and human rights', Tenth Session, A/HRC/10/61, 15 January 2009. The World Bank has also started considering the human rights dimensions of climate change, see: E. Cameron, 'Development, Climate Change and Human Rights: From the Margins to the Mainstream?' The World Bank, Social Development Working Papers: Social Dimensions of Climate Change, Paper No. 123, 17 March 2011.

3 Foresight, 'Migration and Global Environmental Change', Final Project Report, The Government Office for Science, London, 2011.

4 UNHCR, 'Summary of Deliberations on Climate Change and Displacement', Report of an Expert Roundtable, Bellagio, Italy, 22–25 February 2011.

5 Nansen Conference on Climate Change and Displacement, Oslo, 5-7 June 2011.

6 V. Amos and W. Kälin, Foreword to the 'IASC Operational Guidelines on the Protection of Persons in Situations of Natural Disasters',

The Brookings-Bern Project on Internal Displacement (ed.), Washington, D.C., January 2011, v.

7 CARE International, Columbia University, UNHCR, UN University, World Bank, 'In Search of Shelter: Mapping the Effects of Climate Change on Human Migration and Displacement', 2009.

8 *Human Development Report 2007–2008. Fighting Climate Change: Human Solidarity in a Divided World*, Summary, published for the United Nations Development Programme (UNDP), 18. This is a worst-case scenario in as much as current discussions around the UN Framework Convention on Climate Change focus on limiting temperature rise to less than two degrees centigrade above pre-industrial levels.

9 Brookings–LSE Project on Internal Displacement, UN Office of the High Commissioner for Human Rights (OHCHR) and Office for the Coordination of Humanitarian Affairs (OCHA), 'Regional Workshop on Internal Displacement caused by Natural Disasters and Climate Change in the Pacific: Synthesis Report', Pacific Island Forum Secretariat, Suva, Fiji, 4–6 May 2011; M. Loughry, Jesuit Refugee Service and Boston College, 'Relocation, Adaptation, and Internal Displacement in Papua New Guinea', Paper presented at the Conference on Climate Change and Migration in the Asia-Pacific, University of New South Wales, 10–11 November 2011.

10 E. Correa (ed.), *Preventive Resettlement of Populations at Risk of Disaster: Experiences from Latin America*, World Bank, Global Facility for Disaster Reduction and Recovery (GFDRR), 2011; M. Stal, 'Flooding and Relocation: The Zambezi River Valley in Mozambique', *International Migration*, 49/Issue Supplement s1, 2011, 126–144.

11 'Climate Change, Migration and Displacement: Who will be Affected?', Working paper submitted by the informal group on Migration/Displacement and Climate Change of the IASC, 31 October 2008, in advance of the 2009 UN Conference on Climate Change in Copenhagen.

12 'The Climate Change–Displacement Nexus', Paper presented by W. Kälin, Representative of the Secretary-General on the Human Rights of Internally Displaced Persons, Panel on Disaster Risk Reduction and Preparedness: Addressing

the Humanitarian Consequences of Natural Disasters, ECOSOC Humanitarian Affairs Segment, 16 July 2008.

13 Guiding Principles on Internal Displacement, E/CN.4/1998/53/Add.2, 11 February 1998.

14 R. Zetter, *Protecting Environmentally Displaced People: Developing the Capacity of Legal and Normative Frameworks*, Oxford: Refugee Studies Centre, February 2011.

15 UNHCR, 'Climate Change, Natural Disasters and Human Displacement: a UNHCR Perspective', August, 2009.

16 Zetter, *Protecting Environmentally Displaced People*.

17 'IASC Operational Guidelines on the Protection of Persons in Situations of Natural Disasters', 55 and 58.

18 Intergovernmental Panel on Climate Change, 'Intergovernmental Panel on Climate Change Fourth Assessment Report: Climate Change 2007, Working Group I: The Physical Science Basis, Executive Summary, Direct Observations of Recent Climate Change', 2007.

19 S. Jennings, *Time's Bitter Flood: Trends in the Number of Reported Natural Disasters*, London: Oxfam GB, 27 May 2011, 4.

20 United Nations International Strategy for Disaster Reduction (UNISDR), '2009 UNISDR Terminology on Disaster Risk Reduction', Geneva, May 2009.

21 United Nations Office of the High Commissioner for Human Rights (OHCHR), Regional Office for the Pacific, 'Protecting the Human Rights of Internally Displaced Persons in Natural Disasters', 2011.

22 See e.g.: Internal Displacement Monitoring Centre (IDMC), UN Office for the Coordination of Humanitarian Affairs (OCHA), Norwegian Refugee Council (NRC), 'Monitoring Disaster Displacement in the Context of Climate Change', Geneva, September 2009; IDMC, 'Displacement due to Natural Hazard-induced Disasters: Global Estimates for 2009 and 2010', June 2011.

23 Office of the UN Special Envoy for Haiti, 'Press Conference by the Humanitarian Coordinator, Nigel Fisher, Port-au-Prince', Press Release, 11 January 2011.

24 B. Deschamp, M. Azorbo, and S. Lohse, 'Earth, Wind and Fire: A Review of UNHCR's Role in Recent Natural Disasters', UNHCR Policy Development and Evaluation Service, PDES/2010/06, June 2010, 3.

25 See 'UNHCR's Role in Support of an Enhanced Humanitarian Response for the Protection of Persons affected by Natural Disasters', Executive Committee of the High Commissioner's Programme (ExCom), Standing Committee, 51st meeting, 6 June 2011, EC/62/SC/CRP, 19; A. Guterres, 'Opening Statement to the 62nd Session of the Executive Committee', Geneva, 3 October 2011. Also see A. Guterres, 'Opening Statement to the 61st Session of the Executive Committee', Geneva, 4 October 2010.

26 R. Cohen, 'Human Rights at Home', Statement at the Harvard University Kennedy School of Government, 1 November 2006.

27 Amos and Kälin, 'IASC Operational Guidelines on the Protection of Persons in Situations of Natural Disasters'.

28 See e.g.: D. Mazurana et al., 'Sex and Age Matter: Improving Humanitarian Response in Emergencies', Feinstein International Center, Tufts University, August 2011.

29 UN Framework Convention on Climate Change, 'Outcome of the work of the Ad Hoc Working Group on long-term Cooperative Action under the Convention, Decision CP.16', 2010.

30 International Law Commission, 'Fourth Report on the Protection of Persons in the Event of Disasters,' by Eduardo Valencia-Ospina, Special Rapporteur, UN Doc. A/CN/4/643, 11 May 2011, 13.

31 See for example the IFRC's International Disaster Response Laws, Rules and Principles (IDRL) Programme.

32 'Joint UNHCR–OHCHR Return Advisory Update on Haiti', Geneva, January 2010.

33 *Applicant A. v. Minister for Immigration and Ethnic Affairs* [1997] HCA 4; (1997) 190 CLR 225, 248 (Dawson J).

34 See: K. Ester and R. Wasem, 'Temporary Protected Status: Current Immigration Policy and Issues', Congressional Research Service, 19 January 2010, 4. See also: V. Kolmannskog, 'To What Extent Can Existing Forms of Legal Protection Apply in Climate Change-related Cross-border Displacement?' Norwegian

Refugee Council, paper presented at the Oxford University Workshop on Environmental Change and Migration, 8–9 January 2009.

35 J. McAdam, 'Climate Change Displacement and International Law: Complementary Protection Standards', UNHCR, Legal and Protection Policy Research Series, May 2011, PPLA/2011/03, 39.

36 V. Türk, Remarks at the Nansen Conference on Climate Change and Displacement in the 21st Century, Oslo, 7 June 2011, 1.

37 A. Thomas and R. Rendón, 'Confronting Climate Displacement: Learning from Pakistan's Floods', Refugees International, November 2010.

38 UN Environment Programme, 'A Success in the Making: The Montreal Protocol on Substances that Deplete the Ozone Layer', Nairobi, 2007, 11.

39 A. Guterres, 'Maintenance of International Peace and Security: New Challenges to International Peace and Security and Conflict Prevention', United Nations Security Council Briefing, New York, 23 November 2011.

CHAPTER 8

1   UN General Assembly Resolution 59/193 of 18 March 2005.

2   Statement by A. Guterres, to the UNHCR Intergovernmental Meeting at Ministerial Level to mark the 60th anniversary of the 1951 Convention relating to the Status of Refugees and the 50th anniversary of the 1961 Convention on the Reduction of Statelessness, Geneva, 7 December 2011.

3   For a history of the post-war displaced population in Europe, see B. Shephard, *The Long Road Home: The Aftermath of the Second World War*, New York: Knopf, 2010.

4   United Nations, *Charter of the United Nations*, 24 October 1945, 1 UNTS XVI, Article 1(3).

5   Statute of the Office of the United Nations High Commissioner for Refugees, UN General Assembly Resolution 428 (V) of 14 December 1950, para. 2. The eight ways in which states can support the work of UNHCR are:

(a) Becoming parties to international conventions providing for the protection of refugees, and taking the necessary steps of implementation under such conventions;

(b) Entering into special agreements with the High Commissioner for the execution of measures calculated to improve the situation of refugees and to reduce the number requiring protection;

(c) Admitting refugees to their territories, not excluding those in the most destitute categories;

(d) Assisting the High Commissioner in his efforts to promote the voluntary repatriation of refugees;

(e) Promoting the assimilation of refugees, especially by facilitating their naturalization;

(f) Providing refugees with travel and other documents such as would normally be provided to other aliens by their national authorities, especially documents which would facilitate their resettlement;

(g) Permitting refugees to transfer their assets and especially those necessary for their resettlement; and

(h) Providing the High Commissioner with information concerning the number and condition of refugees, and laws and regulations concerning them.

6   1951 Convention relating to the Status of Refugees, 189 UNTS 150, Preamble.

7   1969 Convention on the Specific Aspects of Refugee Problems in Africa, 1000 UNTS 46, Article II(4).

8   Cartagena Declaration on Refugees, Colloquium on the International Protection of Refugees in Central America, Mexico and Panama, 22 November 1984, OAS/SER.L/V/II.66, Doc. 10, rev. 1, 190–193; Mexico Declaration and Plan of Action to Strengthen International Protection of Refugees in Latin America, 16 November 2004, available on UNHCR's Refworld website.

9   Guiding Principles on Internal Displacement, UN Doc. E/CN.4/1998/53/Add. 2, of 11 February 1998.

10 J.C. Hathaway and R.A. Neve, 'Making International Refugee Law Relevant Again: A Proposal for Collectivized and Solution-Oriented

Protection', *Harvard Human Rights Journal*, Volume Ten, Spring 1997, 119.

11 UNHCR, 'Agenda for Protection', 3rd edition, October 2003.

12 M. Zieck, 'Doomed to Fail from the Outset? UNHCR's Convention Plus Initiative Revisited,' *International Journal of Refugee Law*, 21/3, 2009, 387–420. Information on the Convention Plus process is available on the UNHCR website.

13 High Commissioner's Dialogue on Protection Challenges, 'Protection Gaps and Responses' (8–9 December 2010), Breakout Session 2: International Cooperation, Burden Sharing and Comprehensive Regional Approaches, Report by the Co-Chairs.

14 UNHCR, 'Summary Conclusions of the Expert Meeting on International Cooperation to Share Burdens and Responsibilities', Amman (Jordan), 27–28 June 2011.

15 For a critical examination see: M. Zieck, 'Snakes in Ireland: Questioning the Assumption of "Collective Responsibility" to Protect Refugees', Amsterdam Law School Legal Studies Research Paper No. 2011-12, 2011.

16 See e.g.: A. Slaughter and J. Crisp, 'A Surrogate State? The role of UNHCR in Protracted Refugee Situations', UNHCR New Issues in Refugee Research, Research Paper No. 168, January 2009; also, M. Kagan, 'We live in a Country of UNHCR: the UN Surrogate State and Refugee Policy in the Middle East', UNHCR New Issues in Refugee Research, Research Paper No. 201, February 2011.

17 In some cases these costs are subsidized by the international community through UNHCR. This can create vested interests which pose an impediment to durable solutions.

18 A thorough treatment of this issue is found in: G. Loescher and J. Milner, *Protracted Refugee Situations: Domestic and International Security Implications*, New York: Routledge: , 2005

19 A. Christensen and N. Harild, 'Forced Displacement: The Development Challenge', Conflict, Crime and Violence Issues Note, Social Development Department, The World Bank Group, December 2009.

20 J.C. Hathaway and R.A. Neve, 'Making International Refugee Law Relevant Again, 115–211; D. Vanheule, J. van Selm and C. Boswell, 'The Implementation of Article 80 TFEU on

the principle of solidarity and fair sharing of responsibility, including its financial implications, between the Member States in the field of border checks, asylum and immigration', European Parliament, Directorate-General for Internal Policies, 2011.

21 See the website of the Good Humanitarian Donorship Initiative at www.goodhumanitariandonorship.org

22 A. Betts, 'Development Assistance and Refugees: Towards a North-South grand bargain?' Refugee Studies Centre, University of Oxford, June 2009.

23 V. Türk, 'Capacity-Building', in Vincent Chetail (ed.), *Post-Conflict Peacebuilding: A Lexicon*, : Press, 2009, 34–47.

24 General Assembly Resolution 428 (V) of 14 December 1950, para. 2(c).

25 Ibid., para. 2(e).

26 C. Malmström, 'How Europe Failed', *Times of Malta*, 19 January 2012.

27 Agreement between the Government of Canada and the Government of the United States of America for cooperation in the examination of refugee status claims from nationals of third countries, 5 December 2002.

28 Council Regulation (EC) No. 343/2003 of 18 February 2003 establishing the criteria and mechanisms for determining the Member State responsible for examining an asylum application lodged in one of the Member States by a third-country national, Official Journal of the European Union L50/1, 25 February 2003.

29 The apprehension that collective action will result in convergence around the lowest common denominator is not limited to the context of the EU or the Dublin system. See for example, A. Suhrke, 'Burden-sharing during Refugee Emergencies: The Logic of Collective versus National Action', *Journal of Refugee Studies*, 11/4, 1998, 398–399.

30 Council Directive 2001/55/EC of 20 July 2011 on minimum standards for giving temporary protection in the event of a mass influx of displaced persons and on measures promoting a balance of efforts between Member States in receiving such persons and bearing the consequences thereof, Official Journal of the European Union L212/12, 7 August 2001.

31 Article 80 of the Treaty on the Functioning of the European Union stipulates that the policies of the Union in the area of asylum and migration, and their implementation, 'shall be governed by the principle of solidarity and fair sharing of responsibility (...) between the Member States.'

32 European Commission, 'Communication on enhanced intra-EU solidarity in the field of asylum: An EU agenda for better responsibility-sharing and more mutual trust', COM (2011) 835 final, 2.12.2011.

33 This referred to a pilot scheme set up in 2009 for the 'relocation' of beneficiaries of international protection from Malta, in view of the small size of that island state. Participation by other Member States (and by refugees) was strictly voluntary and the scale of the exercise remained modest. When the first phase ended in mid–2011, 227 refugees had been relocated to six other EU countries. Paradoxically, more asylum seekers and refugees were sent back to Malta under the terms of the 'Dublin II Regulation' and other arrangements than were relocated. A greater 'burden-sharing' impact was achieved through resettlement of refugees from Malta to the United States of America.

34 G. Noll, 'Seeking Asylum at Embassies: A Right to Entry under International law?' *International Journal of Refugee Law*, 17/3, 2005, 542–573.

35 UN High Commissioner for Refugees, Expert Meeting on International Cooperation to Share Burdens and Responsibilities: Summary Conclusions, Amman, Jordan, 27–28 June 2011.

36 Report of the High-level Panel on United Nations System-wide Coherence in the areas of development, humanitarian assistance, and the environment, UN Doc. A/61/583, 20 November 2006. See also: UNHCR, Policy Development and Evaluation Service, 'UNHCR's Engagement in the Delivering as One Pilots', PDES/2008/11, March 2008.

37 UNHCR, 'Advisory Opinion on *Non-refoulement* Obligations under the 1951 Convention relating to the Status of Refugees and its 1967 Protocol', January 2007.

38 UN High Commissioner for Refugees, 'Submission by the Office of the United Nations High Commissioner for Refugees in the Case of *Hirsi Jamaa and Others v. Italy*', 29 March 2011, European Court of Human Rights, Application No. 27765/09.

39 *Hirsi Jamaa and Others v. Italy*, Application No. 27765/09, Council of Europe: European Court of Human Rights, Judgment of 23 February 2012, para. 180.

ABBREVIATIONS

AGDM
Age, Gender and Diversity Mainstreaming

ASEAN
Association of Southeast Asian Nations

AU
African Union

BIA
Board of Immigration Appeals (USA)

CCCM
Camp coordination and camp management (cluster)

CEAS
Common European Asylum System

CEDAW
Convention on the Elimination of All Forms of Discrimination Against Women

CERF
Central Emergency Response Fund

CJEU
Court of Justice of the European Union

CPA
Comprehensive Peace Agreement

CRC
Convention on the Rights of the Child

DaO
Delivering as One

DRC
Democratic Republic of the Congo

EAC
East African Community

EASO
European Asylum Support Office

ECOWAS
Economic Community of West African States

ECtHR
European Court of Human Rights

EU
European Union

Excom
Executive Committee of the High Commissioner's Programme

Frontex
European Agency for the Management of Operational Coordination at the External Borders of the Member States of the European Union (known as Frontex)

GPS
Global Positioning System

IASC
Inter-Agency Standing Committee

ICAO
International Civil Aviation Organization

ICC
International Criminal Court

ICTY
International Criminal Tribunal for Former Yugoslavia

ICRC
International Committee of the Red Cross

IDMC
Internal Displacement Monitoring Centre

IDP
Internally Displaced Person

IFRC
International Federation of the Red Cross and Red Crescent Societies

IACHR
Inter-American Court of Human Rights

IOM
International Organization for Migration

IPCC
Intergovernmental Panel on Climate Change

LGBTI
Lesbian, gay, bisexual, transgender and intersex persons

LRA
Lord's Resistance Army

MINURCAT
United Nations Mission in the Central African Republic and Chad

MONUC
United Nations Organization Mission in the Democratic Republic of the Congo

MONUSCO
United Nations Stabilization Mission in the Democratic Republic of the Congo

OAS
Organization of American States

OCHA
Office for the Coordination of Humanitarian Affairs (UN)

OHCHR
Office of the High Commissioner for Human Rights (UN)

OSCE
Organization for Security and Cooperation in Europe

RSD
Refugee Status Determination

SADC
Southern African Development Community

SGBV
Sexual and gender-based violence

SPLM
Sudan People's Liberation Movement (SPLM)

TPS
Temporary Protected Status

TSI
Transitional Solutions Initiative

UNAMA
United Nations Assistance Mission in Afghanistan

UNDAC
United Nations Disaster Assessment and Coordination

UNDP
United Nations Development Programme

UNDSS
United Nations Department of Safety and Security

UNEP
United Nations Environment Programme

UNESCO
United Nations Educational, Scientific and Cultural Organization

UNFCCC
United Nations Framework Convention on Climate Change

UNFPA
United Nations Population Fund

UN-Habitat
United Nations Human Settlements Programme

UNICEF
United Nations Children's Fund

UNISDR
United Nations International Strategy for Disaster Reduction

UNMIS
United Nations Mission in Sudan

UNMISS
United Nations Mission in the Republic of South Sudan

UNOCI
United Nations Operation in Côte d'Ivoire

UNRWA
United Nations Relief and Works Agency for Palestine Refugees in the Near East

WHO
World Health Organization

STATES PARTY TO THE 1951 REFUGEE CONVENTION, THE 1967 PROTOCOL, THE 1969 OAU REFUGEE CONVENTION, THE 1954 AND 1961 STATELESSNESS CONVENTIONS AND MEMBERS OF UNHCR'S EXECUTIVE COMMITTEE (EXCOM), AS OF 31 DECEMBER 2011

United Nations member states	1951 Convention [a]	1967 Protocol [b]	1969 OAU Convention [c]	1954 Statelessness Convention [d]	1961 Statelessness Convention [e]	UNHCR ExCom members [f]
Afghanistan	2005	2005				
Albania	1992	1992		2003	2003	
Algeria	1963	1967	1974	1964		1963
Andorra						
Angola	1981	1981	1981			
Antigua and Barbuda	1995	1995		1988		
Argentina	1961	1967		1972		1979
Armenia	1993	1993		1994	1994	
Australia	1954	1973		1973	1973	1951
Austria	1954	1973		2008	1972	1951
Azerbaijan	1993	1993		1996	1996	
Bahamas	1993	1993				
Bahrain						
Bangladesh						1995
Barbados				1972		
Belarus	2001	2001				
Belgium	1953	1969		1960		1951
Belize	1990	1990		2006		
Benin	1962	1970	1973	2011	2011	2008
Bhutan						
Bolivia (Plurinational State of)	1982	1982		1983	1983	
Bosnia and Herzegovina	1993	1993		1983	1996	
Botswana	1969	1969	1995	1969		
Brazil	1960	1972		1996	2007	1951
Brunei Darussalam						
Bulgaria	1993	1993				2011
Burkina Faso	1980	1980	1974			
Burundi	1963	1971	1975			
Cambodia	1992	1992				
Cameroon	1961	1967	1985			2011
Canada	1969	1969			1978	1957
Cape Verde		1987	1989			
Central African Republic	1962	1967	1970			
Chad	1981	1981	1981	1999	1999	
Chile	1972	1972				2000
China	1982	1982				1958
Colombia	1961	1980				1955
Comoros						
Congo	1962	1970	1971			2011

STATES PARTY TO THE 1951 REFUGEE CONVENTION, THE 1967 PROTOCOL,
THE 1969 OAU REFUGEE CONVENTION, THE 1954 AND 1961 STATELESSNESS CONVENTIONS
AND MEMBERS OF UNHCR'S EXECUTIVE COMMITTEE (EXCOM), AS OF 31 DECEMBER 2011

United Nations member states	1951 Convention [a]	1967 Protocol [b]	1969 OAU Convention [c]	1954 Statelessness Convention [d]	1961 Statelessness Convention [e]	UNHCR ExCom members [f]
Costa Rica	1978	1978		1977	1977	2007
Côte d'Ivoire	1961	1970	1998			2000
Croatia	1992	1992		1992	2011	2011
Cuba						
Cyprus	1963	1968				2003
Czech Republic	1993	1993		2004	2001	
Dem. People's Republic of Korea						
Democratic Republic of the Congo	1965	1975	1973			1979
Denmark	1952	1968		1956	1977	1951
Djibouti	1977	1977				2009
Dominica	1994	1994				
Dominican Republic	1978	1978				
Ecuador	1955	1969		1970		2002
Egypt	1981	1981	1980			2004
El Salvador	1983	1983				
Equatorial Guinea	1986	1986	1980			
Eritrea						
Estonia	1997	1997				2007
Ethiopia	1969	1969	1973			1993
Fiji	1972	1972		1972		
Finland	1968	1968		1968	2008	1979
France	1954	1971		1960		1951
Gabon	1964	1973	1986			
Gambia	1966	1967	1980			
Georgia	1999	1999		2011		
Germany	1953	1969		1976	1977	1951
Ghana	1963	1968	1975			2005
Greece	1960	1968		1975		1955
Grenada						
Guatemala	1983	1983		2000	2001	
Guinea	1965	1968	1972	1962		2002
Guinea-Bissau	1976	1976	1989			
Guyana						
Haiti	1984	1984				
Holy See [g]	1956	1967				1951

STATES PARTY TO THE 1951 REFUGEE CONVENTION, THE 1967 PROTOCOL,
THE 1969 OAU REFUGEE CONVENTION, THE 1954 AND 1961 STATELESSNESS CONVENTIONS
AND MEMBERS OF UNHCR'S EXECUTIVE COMMITTEE (EXCOM), AS OF 31 DECEMBER 2011

United Nations member states	1951 Convention [a]	1967 Protocol [b]	1969 OAU Convention [c]	1954 Statelessness Convention [d]	1961 Statelessness Convention [e]	UNHCR'S ExCom members [f]
Honduras	1992	1992				
Hungary	1989	1989		2001	2009	1993
Iceland	1955	1968				
India						1995
Indonesia						
Iraq						
Ireland	1956	1968		1962	1973	1996
Iran (Islamic Republic of)	1976	1976				1955
Israel	1954	1968		1958		1951
Italy	1954	1972		1962		1951
Jamaica	1964	1980				
Japan	1981	1982				1979
Jordan						2006
Kazakhstan	1999	1999				
Kenya	1966	1981	1992			2003
Kiribati				1983	1983	
Kuwait						
Kyrgyzstan	1996	1996				
Lao People's Democratic Republic						
Latvia	1997	1997		1999	1992	
Lebanon						1963
Lesotho	1981	1981	1988	1974	2004	1979
Liberia	1964	1980	1971	1964	2004	
Libya			1981	1989	1989	
Liechtenstein	1957	1968		2009	2009	
Lithuania	1997	1997		2000		
Luxembourg	1953	1971		1960		2008
Madagascar	1967					1963
Malawi	1987	1987	1987	2009		
Malaysia						
Maldives						
Mali	1973	1973	1981			
Malta	1971	1971				
Marshall Islands						
Mauritania	1987	1987	1972			

STATES PARTY TO THE 1951 REFUGEE CONVENTION, THE 1967 PROTOCOL, THE 1969 OAU REFUGEE CONVENTION, THE 1954 AND 1961 STATELESSNESS CONVENTIONS AND MEMBERS OF UNHCR'S EXECUTIVE COMMITTEE (EXCOM), AS OF 31 DECEMBER 2011

United Nations member states	1951 Convention [a]	1967 Protocol [b]	1969 OAU Convention [c]	1954 Statelessness Convention [d]	1961 Statelessness Convention [e]	UNHCR'S ExCom members [f]
Mauritius						
Mexico	2000	2000		2000		2001
Micronesia (the Federated States of)						
Monaco	1954	2010				
Mongolia						
Montenegro	2006	2006		2006		2008
Morocco [h]	1956	1971				1979
Mozambique	1983	1989	1989			1999
Myanmar						
Namibia	1995	1995				1982
Nauru	2011	2011				
Nepal						
Netherlands	1956	1968		1962	1985	1955
New Zealand	1960	1973			2006	2002
Nicaragua	1980	1980				1979
Niger	1961	1970	1971		1985	
Nigeria	1967	1968	1986	2011	2011	1963
Norway	1953	1967		1956	1971	1955
Oman						
Pakistan						1988
Palau						
Panama	1978	1978		2011	2011	
Papua New Guinea	1986	1986				
Paraguay	1970	1970				
Peru	1964	1983				
Philippines	1981	1981		2011		1991
Poland	1991	1991				1997
Portugal	1960	1976				2006
Qatar						
Republic of Korea	1992	1992		1962		2000
Republic of Moldova	2002	2002				2009
Romania	1991	1991		2006	2006	2005
Russian Federation	1993	1993				1995
Rwanda	1980	1980	1979	2006	2006	
Saint Kitts and Nevis	2002					

STATES PARTY TO THE 1951 REFUGEE CONVENTION, THE 1967 PROTOCOL,
THE 1969 OAU REFUGEE CONVENTION, THE 1954 AND 1961 STATELESSNESS CONVENTIONS
AND MEMBERS OF UNHCR'S EXECUTIVE COMMITTEE (EXCOM), AS OF 31 DECEMBER 2011

United Nations member states	1951 Convention [a]	1967 Protocol [b]	1969 OAU Convention [c]	1954 Statelessness Convention [d]	1961 Statelessness Convention [e]	UNHCR'S ExCom members [f]
Saint Lucia						
Saint Vincent and the Grenadines	1993	2003		1999		
Samoa	1988	1994				
San Marino						
Sao Tome and Principe	1978	1978				
Saudi Arabia						
Senegal	1963	1967	1971	2005	2005	
Serbia	2001	2001		2001	2011	2002
Seychelles	1980	1980	1980			
Sierra Leone	1981	1981	1987			
Singapore						
Slovakia	1993	1993		2000	2000	
Slovenia	1992	1992		1992		2010
Solomon Islands	1995	1995				
Somalia	1978	1978				1988
South Africa	1996	1996	1995			1997
South Sudan						
Spain	1978	1978		1997		1994
Sri Lanka						
Sudan	1974	1974	1972			1979
Suriname	1978	1978				
Swaziland	2000	1969	1989	1999	1999	
Sweden	1954	1967		1965	1969	1958
Switzerland	1955	1968		1972		1951
Syrian Arab Republic						
Tajikistan	1993	1993				
The former Yugoslav Republic of Macedonia	1994	1994		1994		2008
Thailand						1979
Timor-Leste	2003	2003				
Togo	1962	1969	1970			2011
Tonga						
Trinidad and Tobago	2000	2000		1966		
Tunisia	1957	1968	1989	1969	2000	1958
Turkey	1962	1968				1951

STATES PARTY TO THE 1951 REFUGEE CONVENTION, THE 1967 PROTOCOL,
THE 1969 OAU REFUGEE CONVENTION, THE 1954 AND 1961 STATELESSNESS CONVENTIONS
AND MEMBERS OF UNHCR'S EXECUTIVE COMMITTEE (EXCOM), AS OF 31 DECEMBER 2011

United Nations member states	1951 Convention [a]	1967 Protocol [b]	1969 OAU Convention [c]	1954 Statelessness Convention [d]	1961 Statelessness Convention [e]	UNHCR'S ExCom members [f]
Turkmenistan	1998	1998		2011		2011
Tuvalu	1986	1986				
Uganda	1976	1976	1987	1965		1967
Ukraine	2002	2002				
United Arab Emirates						
United Kingdom of Great Britain and Northern Ireland	1954	1968		1959	1966	1951
United Republic of Tanzania	1964	1968	1975			1963
United States of America		1968				1951
Uruguay	1970	1970		2004	2001	
Uzbekistan						
Vanuatu						
Venezuela (Bolivarian Republic of)		1986				1951
Viet Nam						
Yemen	1980	1980				2003
Zambia	1969	1969	1973	1974		2004
Zimbabwe	1981	1981	1985	1998		
TOTAL	145	146	44	71	42	85

[a] Year of ratification, accession and/or succession to the 1951 UN Refugee Convention.

[b] Year of accession and/or succession to the 1967 Protocol.

[c] Year of ratification of the 1969 Refugee Convention of the Organization of African Unity (OAU).

[d] Year of ratification, accession and/or succession to the 1954 Convention relating to the Status of Stateless Persons.

[e] Year of ratification, accession and/or succession to the 1961 Convention on the Reduction of Statelessness.

[f] Refers to Executive Committee of the High Commissioner's Programme.

[g] Not member state of the United Nations.

[h] Morocco withdrew from the OAU and its obligations in 1984.

FURTHER READING

An attempt has been made to organize this list in accordance with the structure of the book, although many sources address topics discussed in more than one chapter. This list contains primarily works published over the past decade and only, works in the English language. During this period, an enormous volume of new materials related to forced displacement has been published. Obviously, it is not possible to mention them all. The inclusion of any item in this list does not imply its endorsement by UNHCR. This reading list includes only a limited number of UNHCR sources. However, much of the information in this book is drawn from UNHCR documents which are freely available on the UNHCR website. Additional sources are cited in the endnotes to each chapter.

CHAPTER 1

Barnett, M. and Weiss, T.G., *Humanitarianism in Question: Politics, Power, Ethics*, Ithaca: Cornell University Press, 2008.

Bassiouni, M. Cherif (ed.), *The Pursuit of International Criminal Justice: A World Study on Conflicts, Victimization, and Post-Conflict Justice*, Antwerpen: Intersentia, 2010.

Egeland, J., Harmer, A. and Stoddart, A., 'To Stay and Deliver: Good Practice for Humanitarians in Complex Security Environments', UNOCHA, February 2011.

Feller, E., UNHCR Assistant High Commissioner (Protection), Opening Address: 'Humanitarian Space, Protecting People in Conflict and Crisis: Responding to the Challenges of a Changing World', University of Oxford, Refugee Studies Centre, 22 September 2009.

Ferris, E., *The Politics of Protection: The Limits of Humanitarian Action*, Washington, DC: Brookings Institution, 2011.

Hodge, N., *Armed Humanitarians: The Rise of The Nation Builders*, New York: Bloomsbury, 2011.

Hubert, D. and Brassard-Boudreau, C., 'Shrinking Humanitarian Space? Trends and Prospects on Security and Access', *Journal of Humanitarian Assistance*, 24 November 2010.

Jessen-Petersen, S., 'Humanitarianism in Crisis', United States Institute of Peace Special Report 273, Washington, May 2011.

Lim, J., UNHCR Assistant High Commissioner (Operations), Keynote address: 'Contemporary Challenges for Humanitarian Engagement in Insecure and Complex Environments', Webster University 16th International Humanitarian Conference: Humanitarian Space, Geneva, 27 January 2011.

Lischer, S., *Dangerous Sanctuaries: Refugee Camps, Civil War, and the Dilemmas of Humanitarian Aid*, Ithaca: Cornell University Press, 2005.

Magone, C., Neuman, M. and Weissman, F. (eds), *Humanitarian Negotiations Revealed: The MSF Experience*, Médecins Sans Frontières, London: Hurst Publishers, 2011.

Melander, E., Öberg, M. and Hall, J., 'Are "New Wars" More Atrocious? Battle Severity, Civilians Killed and Forced Migration Before and After the End of the Cold War', *European Journal of International Relations*, 15/3, 2009.

Metcalfe, V., Giffen, A. and Elhawary, S., 'UN Integration and Humanitarian Space: An Independent Study Commissioned by the UN Integration Steering Group', Humanitarian Policy Group, Overseas Development Institute (London) and Stimson Center (Washington), December 2011.

Minear, L., *The Humanitarian Enterprise: Dilemmas and Discoveries*, Bloomfield, CT: Kumarian Press, 2002.

Morris, N. and Gaouette, M., 'Maintaining a UN Humanitarian Presence in Periods of High Insecurity: Learning from Others', United Nations

Office for the Coordination of Humanitarian Affairs (UNOCHA), January 2004.

Ogata, S., *The Turbulent Decade: Confronting the Refugee Crises of the 1990s*, New York: W.W. Norton & Company Inc., 2005.

Orbinski, J., *An Imperfect Offering: Humanitarian Action for the Twenty-first Century*, New York: Walker & Company, 2008.

Pantuliano, S., Mackintosh, K. and Elhawary, S., 'Counter-terrorism and Humanitarian Action: Tensions, Impact and Ways Forward', Humanitarian Policy Group Policy Brief 43, Overseas Development Institute, London, October 2011.

Roberts, A., 'Lives and Statistics: Are 90% of War Victims Civilians?', *Survival*, 52/3, June–July 2010.

Rimmer, S., 'Refugees, Internally Displaced Persons and the "Responsibility to Protect"', UNHCR New Issues in Refugee Research, Research Paper No. 185, 2010.

Smillie, I. and Minear, L., *The Charity of Nations: Humanitarian Action in a Calculating World*, Bloomfield, CT: Kumarian Press, 2004.

Tennant, V., Doyle, B. and Mazou, R., 'Safeguarding Humanitarian Space: A Review of Key Challenges for UNHCR', UNHCR Policy and Development Evaluation Service, PDES/2010/01, February 2010.

Walker, P. and Maxwell, D., *Shaping the Humanitarian World*, New York: Routledge (Global Institutions Series), 2009.

World Bank (The), 'World Development Report 2011: Conflict, Security, and Development', Washington, 2011.

CHAPTER 2

Abou-El-Wafa, A, *The Right to Asylum Between Islamic Shari'ah and International Refugee Law: A Comparative Study*, Riyadh: Naif Arab University for Security Sciences, 2009.

Abuya, E.O. and Mukundi, G.M., 'Assessing Asylum Claims in Africa: Missing or Meeting Standards?', *Netherlands International Law Review*, 53, 2006.

Agier, M., *Managing the Undesirables: Refugee Camps and Humanitarian Government*, Cambridge: Polity Press, 2011.

Alborzi, M.R., *Evaluating the Effectiveness of International Refugee Law: The Protection of Iraqi Refugees*, Leiden: Martinus Nijhoff Publishers, 2006.

Arimatsu, L. and Giles Samson, M., 'The UN Refugee Convention at 60: The Challenge for Europe,' Chatham House, International Law Briefing Paper IL BP 2011/01, March 2011.

Bhabha, J. and Crock, M., *Seeking Asylum Alone – a Comparative Study: Unaccompanied and Separated Children and Refugee Protection in Australia, the UK and the US*, Annandale: Themis Press, 2007.

Bohmer, C. and Shuman, A., *Rejecting Refugees: Political Asylum in the 21st Century*, New York: Routledge, 2007.

Elmadmad, K., 'Asylum in Islam and in Modern Refugee Law', *Refugee Survey Quarterly*, 27/2, 2008.

Feller, E., Türk, V. and Nicholson, F., *Refugee Protection in International Law: UNHCRs Global Consultations on International Protection*, Cambridge: Cambridge University Press, 2003.

Fiddian-Qasmiyeh, E. and Qasmiyeh, Y.M., 'Muslim Asylum-Seekers and Refugees: Negotiating Identity, Politics and Religion in the UK', *Journal of Refugee Studies*, 23/3, 2010.

Foster, M., *International Refugee Law and Socio-Economic Rights: Refuge from Deprivation*, Cambridge: Cambridge University Press, 2009.

Gammeltoft-Hansen, T., *Access to Asylum: International Refugee Law and the Globalisation of Migration Control*, Cambridge: Cambridge Studies in International and Comparative Law, 2011.

Gibney, M., *The Ethics and Politics of Asylum: Liberal Democracy and the Response to Refugees*, Cambridge: Cambridge University Press, 2004.

Gibson, J., 'The Removal of Failed Asylum Seekers: International Norms and Procedures', UNHCR New Issues in Refugee Research, Research Paper No. 145, 2007.

Goodwin-Gill, G.S. and McAdam, J., *The Refugee in International Law*, 3rd edition, Oxford: Oxford University Press, 2007.

Goodwin-Gill, G.S. and Lambert H. (eds), *The Limits of Transnational Law: Refugee Law, Policy*

Harmonization and Judicial Dialogue in the European Union, Cambridge: Cambridge University Press, 2010.

Handmaker, J., de la Hunt, L.A. and Klaaren, J., *Advancing Refugee Protection in South Africa*, Oxford and New York: Berghahn Books, 2010.

Hathaway, J., *The Rights of Refugees under International Law*, Cambridge: Cambridge University Press, 2005.

Hathaway, J., 'Why Refugee Law Still Matters', *The Melbourne Journal of International Law*, 8, 2007.

Hollenbach, D. (ed.), *Refugee Rights: Ethics, Advocacy, and Africa*, Georgetown University Press, 2008.

Jackson, I. C., *The Refugee Concept in Group Situations*, The Hague, London and Boston: Martinus Nijhoff Publishers, 1999.

Joly, D., *Global Changes in Asylum Regimes: Closing Doors*, Basingstoke and New York: Palgrave Macmillan, 2002.

Jubilut, L.L., 'Refugee Law and Protection in Brazil: A Model in South America?', *Journal of Refugee Studies*, 19/1, 2006.

Kagan, M., 'The Beleaguered Gatekeeper: Protection Challenges Posed by UNHCR Refugee Status Determination', *International Journal of Refugee Law*, 18/1, March 2006.

Lamey, A., *Frontier Justice: The Global Refugee Crisis and What to do About It*, Toronto: Doubleday, 2011.

Marfleet, P., 'Understanding "Sanctuary": Faith and Traditions of Asylum', *Journal of Refugee Studies*, 24/3, 2011.

McAdam, J., *Complementary Protection in International Refugee Law*, Oxford: Oxford University Press, 2007.

Milner, J., *Refugees, the State and the Politics of Asylum in Africa*, Basingstoke: Palgrave Macmillan, 2009.

Mole, N., *Asylum and the European Convention on Human Rights (Migration Collection)*, Strasbourg: Council of Europe Publishing, 2007.

Mountz, A., *Seeking Asylum: Human Smuggling and Bureaucracy at the Border*, Minneapolis: University of Minnesota Press, 2010.

Newman, E. and van Selm, J., *Refugees and Forced Displacement: International Security, Human Vulnerability and the State*, Tokyo: United Nations University Press, 2003.

Noll, G. (ed.), *Proof, Evidentiary Assessment and Credibility in Asylum Procedures*, Dordrecht: Martinus Nijhoff, 2005.

Oberoi, P., *Exile and Belonging: Refugees and State Policy in South Asia*, New Delhi, New York: Oxford University Press, 2006.

Paz, Y., 'Ordered Disorder: African Asylum Seekers in Israel and Discursive Challenges to an Emerging Refugee Regime', UNHCR New Issues in Refugee Research, Research Paper No. 205, 2011.

Perry, A., 'Solving Israel's Africa Refugee Crisis', *Virginia Journal of International Law*, 151/1, 2010.

Price, M.E., *Rethinking Asylum: History, Purpose, and Limits*, Cambridge: Cambridge University Press, 2009.

Ramji-Nogales, J., Schoenholtz, A. and Schrag, P., *Refugee Roulette: Disparities in Asylum Adjudication and Proposals for Reform*, New York: New York University Press, 2011.

Rutinwa, B., 'Prima Facie Status and Refugee Protection', UNHCR New Issues in Refugee Research, Working Paper No. 69, October 2002.

Shoukri, A.M., *Refugee Status in Islam: Concepts of Protection in Islamic Tradition and International Law*, London: I.B. Tauris, 2011.

Simeon, J.C. (ed.), *Critical Issues in International Refugee Law: Strategies Towards Interpretative Harmony*, Cambridge: Cambridge University Press, 2010.

Steiner, N., Gibney, M. and Loescher, G., *Problems of Protection: The UNHCR, Refugees and Human Rights*, New York: Routledge, 2003.

Türk, V., UNHCR Director of International Protection, 'Protection Gaps in Europe? Persons Fleeing the Indiscriminate Effects of Generalized Violence', Address, Brussels, 18 January 2011.

UNHCR, 'Safe at Last? Law and Practice in Selected EU Member States with Respect to Asylum-Seekers Fleeing Indiscriminate Violence', Brussels, July 2011.

Wouters, K., *International Legal Standards for the*

Protection from Refoulement, Antwerpen: Intersentia, 2009.

CHAPTER 3

Adelman, H. and Barkan, E., *No Return, No Refuge*, New York: Columbia University Press, 2011.

Adepoju, A., Boulton, A. and Levin, M., 'Promoting Integration through Mobility: Free Movement and the ECOWAS Protocol', UNHCR Policy Development and Evaluation Service, New Issues in Refugee Research Working Paper Series, No.150, 2007.

Ager, A. and Strang, A., 'Understanding Integration: A Conceptual Framework', *Journal of Refugee Studies*, 21/2, 2008.

Bakewell, O., 'Repatriation and Self-settled Refugees in Zambia: Bringing Solutions to the Wrong Problems', *Journal of Refugee Studies*, 13/4, 2000.

Black, R. and Koser, K. (eds), *The End of the Refugee Cycle? Refugee Repatriation and Reconstruction*, Oxford: Berghahn, 1999.

Black, R. and Gent, S., 'Defining, Measuring and Influencing Sustainable Return: The Case of the Balkans', Development Research Centre on Migration, Globalization and Poverty Working Paper No.7, 2004.

Bradley, M., 'Unlocking Protracted Displacement: Central America's "Success Story" Reconsidered', Refugee Studies Centre, University of Oxford, Working Paper No. 77, 2011.

Chatty, D. and Mansour, N., 'Unlocking Protracted Displacement: An Iraqi Case Study', Refugee Studies Centre, University of Oxford, Working Paper No. 78, 2011.

Chimni, B., 'From Resettlement to Involuntary Repatriation: Towards a Critical History of Durable Solutions to Refugee Problems', *Refugee Survey Quarterly*, 23/3, 2004.

Christensen, A. and Harild, N., 'Forced Displacement: The Development Challenge', Conflict, Crime and Violence Issues Note, Social Development Department, World Bank Group, December 2009.

Crisp, J., 'No Solutions in Sight: the Problem of Protracted Refugee Situations in Africa', UNHCR Evaluation and Policy Analysis Unit, New Issues in Refugee Research, Working Paper No. 75, January 2003.

Crisp, J., 'The Local Integration and Local Settlement of Refugees: A Conceptual and Historical Analysis', UNHCR New Issues in Refugee Research, Working Paper No. 102, April 2004.

Crisp, J., Riera, J. and Freitas, R., 'Evaluation of UNHCR's Returnee Reintegration Programme in Angola', UNHCR Policy and Development Evaluation Service, PDES/2008/04, August 2008.

Duffield, M., Diagne, K. and Tennant, V., 'Evaluation of UNHCR's Returnee Reintegration Programme in Southern Sudan', UNHCR Policy and Development Evaluation Service, PDES/2008/05, September 2008.

Fielden, A., 'Local Integration: An Under-reported Solution to Protracted Refugee Situations', UNHCR Policy Development and Evaluation Service, New Issues in Refugee Research, Research Paper No.158, June 2008.

Hammond, L.C., *This Place Will Become Home: Refugee Repatriation to Ethiopia*, Ithaca and London: Cornell University Press, 2004.

Hovil, L., 'Hoping for Peace, Afraid of War: The Dilemmas of Repatriation and Belonging on the Borders of Uganda and South Sudan', UNHCR Policy and Development and Evaluation Service, New Issues in Refugee Research, Research Paper No.196, November 2010.

Kaiser, T., 'Dispersal, Division and Diversification: Durable Solutions and Sudanese Refugees in Uganda', *Journal of Eastern African Studies*, 4/1, 2010.

Lindley, A. and Haslie, A., 'Unlocking Protracted Displacement: A Somali Case Study', Refugee Studies Centre, Working Paper No.79, August 2011.

Loescher, G., Milner, J., Newman, E. and Troeller, G. (eds), *Protracted Refugee Situations: Political, Human Rights and Security Implications*, Tokyo: United Nations University Press, 2008.

Long, K., 'Home Alone? A Review of the Relationship between Repatriation, Mobility and Durable Solutions for Refugees', UNHCR Policy Development and Evaluation Service, PDES/2010/02, March 2010.

Long, K., 'Extending Protection? Labour Migration and Durable Solutions for Refugees', UNHCR New Issues in Refugee Research, Working Paper Series, No.176, October 2009.

Milner, J., 'Refugees and the Regional Dynamics of Peacebuilding', *Refugee Survey Quarterly*, 28/1, 2009.

Monsutti, A., 'Afghan Migratory Strategies and the Three Solutions to the Refugee Problem', *Refugee Survey Quarterly*, 27/1, 2008.

Omata, N., '"Repatriation is not for Everyone": the Life and Livelihoods of Former Refugees in Liberia', UNHCR Policy Development and Evaluation Service, New Issues in Refugee Research, Research Paper No. 213, June 2011.

Ott, E., 'Get up and Go: Refugee Resettlement and Secondary Migration in the USA', UNHCR Policy Development and Evaluation Service, New Issues in Refugee Research, Research Paper No. 219, September 2011.

Pantuliano, S., Buchanan-Smith, M., Murphy, P. and Mosel, I., 'The Long Road Home: Opportunities and Obstacles to the Reintegration of IDPs and Refugees Returning to Southern Sudan and the Three Areas', Humanitarian Policy Group, Overseas Development Institute, Synthesis Paper, London, September 2008.

Strang, A. and Ager, A. 'Refugee Integration: Emerging Trends and Remaining Agendas'. *Journal of Refugee Studies*, 23/4, 2010.

Van Hear, N., 'From Durable Solutions to Transnational Relations: Home and Exile among Refugee Diasporas', UNHCR Policy Development and Evaluation Service, New Issues in Refugee Research, Working Paper No. 83, March 2003.

Veney, C., *Forced Migration in Eastern Africa: Democratization, Structural Adjustment, and Refugees*, New York: Palgrave Macmillan, 2007.

UNHCR, *Resettlement Handbook*, revised edition, Geneva, July 2011.

CHAPTER 4

Ali, P. and Lynch, M., 'Buried Alive: Stateless Kurds in Syria', Refugees International, 2006.

Batchelor, C., 'Transforming International Legal Principles into National Law: The Right to Nationality and the Avoidance of Statelessness', Refugee Survey Quarterly 25(3), 2006.

Bhabha, J. (ed.), Children without a State: A Global Human Rights Challenge, Cambridge MA: MIT Press, 2011.

Blitz, B.K., 'Statelessness and the Social (De)Construction of Citizenship: Political Restructuring and Ethnic Discrimination in Slovenia', Journal of Human Rights, 5/4, 2006.

Blitz, B.K. and Lynch, M. (eds.), Statelessness and Citizenship: A Comparative Study on the Benefits of Nationality, London: Edward Elgar Publishing, 2011.

Campbell, J.R., 'The Enduring Problem of Statelessness in the Horn of Africa: How Nation-States and Western Courts (Re)Define Nationality', International Journal of Refugee Law, 23/4, 2011.

Doek, J.E., 'The CRC and the Right to Preserve a Nationality', Refugee Survey Quarterly, 25/3, 2006.

Edwards, A. and Ferstman, C., Human Security and Non-Citizens: Law, Policy, and International Affairs, Cambridge: Cambridge University Press, 2010.

Equal Rights Trust, 'Unravelling Anomaly: Detention, Discrimination and the Protection Needs of Stateless Persons', London, 2010.

Forced Migration Review, Issue 32 (devoted to statelessness), April 2009.

Goldston, J., 'Holes in the Rights Framework: Racial Discrimination, Citizenship and the Rights of Non-citizens', Ethics and International Affairs, 20/3, September 2006.

Gyulai, G., 'Forgotten without Reason: Protection of Non-refugee Stateless Persons in Central Europe', Hungarian Helsinki Committee, 2007.

Gyulai, G., 'Statelessness in Hungary: The Protection of Stateless Persons and the Prevention and Reduction of Statelessness', Hungarian Helsinki Committee, 2011.

Human Rights Watch, 'Prisoners of the Past: Kuwaiti

Bidun and the Burden of Statelessness', June 2011.

Kanapathipillai, V., Citizenship and Statelessness in Sri Lanka: The Case of the Tamil Estate Workers, London: Anthem Press, 2009.

Kenya Human Rights Commission, 'Foreigners at Home: The Dilemma of Citizenship in Northern Kenya', 2009.

Lynch, M., 'Lives on Hold: The Human Cost of Statelessness', Refugees International, February 2005.

Lynch, M., 'Futures Denied: Statelessness among Infants, Children, and Youth', Refugees International, October 2008.

Manby, B., Struggles for Citizenship in Africa, London and New York: Zed Books, 2009.

Manby, B., Citizenship Law in Africa: A Comparative Study, New York: Open Society Foundations, October 2010.

Open Society Justice Initiative, 'Human Rights and Legal Identity: Approaches to Combating Statelessness and Arbitrary Deprivation of Nationality – Thematic Conference Paper,' May 2006.

Refugees International and Open Society Institute Equal Justice Initiative, 'Without Citizenship: Statelessness, Discrimination and Repression in Kuwait', May 2011.

Sawyer, C. and Blitz, B. (eds), Statelessness in the European Union: Displaced, Undocumented, Unwanted, Cambridge: Cambridge University Press, 2011.

Southwick, K. and Lynch, M., 'Nationality Rights for All: A Progress Report and Global Survey on Statelessness', Refugees International, March 2009.

UNHCR and the Inter-Parliamentary Union, Nationality and Statelessness: A Handbook for Parliamentarians, Geneva, 2005.

UNHCR, 'Overview of Statelessness: International and Japanese Context', prepared by Prof. A. Kohki, Yokahama, April 2010.

UNHCR, 'The Situation of Stateless Persons in the Middle East and North Africa', prepared by L. van Waas, Geneva, October 2010.

UNHCR, 'Statelessness in Central Asia,' prepared for UNHCR by M. Farquharson, Geneva, May 2011.

UNHCR, 'Mapping Statelessness in the United Kingdom', London, November 2011.

UNHCR, 'Mapping Statelessness in the Netherlands', The Hague, November 2011.

Van Waas, L., Nationality Matters: Statelessness under International Law, Antwerp: Intersentia, 2008.

CHAPTER 5

Abebe, A.M., 'Legal and Institutional Dimensions of Protecting and Assisting Internally Displaced Persons in Africa', Journal of Refugee Studies, 22/2, 2009.

Ali, G. and Gouda, B., Internal Displacement Law and Policy: Analysis of International Norms and Domestic Jurisprudence, Lake Mary, FLA.: Vandeplas Publishing, 2009.

Arango Rivadeneira, R., Judicial Protection of Internally Displaced Persons: The Colombian Experience, Washington, DC: Brookings-Bern Project on Internal Displacement, 2009.

Bagshaw, S., Developing a Normative Framework for the Protection of Internally Displaced Persons, Ardsley, NY: Transnational Publishers, 2005.

Birkeland, N.M., 'Internal Displacement: Global Trends in Conflict-induced Displacement', International Review of the Red Cross, 91/875, 2009.

Brookings-Bern Project on Internal Displacement (ed.), Protecting Internally Displaced Persons: A Manual for Law and Policymakers, 2008.

Brookings Institution (ed.), Addressing Internal Displacement: A Framework for National Responsibility, Brookings-Bern Project on Internal Displacement, 2005.

Brun, C., 'Hospitality: Becoming "IDPs" and "Hosts" in Protracted Displacement', Journal of Refugee Studies, 23/3, 2010.

Cohen, R., 'The Guiding Principles on Internal

Displacement: An Innovation in International Standard Setting', *Global Governance*, 10, 2004.

Cohen, R. and Deng, F.M., *Masses in Flight: The Global Crisis of Internal Displacement*, Washington, DC: Brookings Institution Press, 1998.

Couldrey, M. and Morris, T., *Putting IDPs on the Map: Achievements and Challenges: in Commemoration of the Work of Roberta Cohen*, Refugee Studies Centre, University of Oxford, Forced Migration Review, Special issue, December 2006.

Davies, S.E. and Glanville, L., *Protecting the Displaced: Deepening the Responsibility to Protect*, Leiden and Boston, MA: Martinus Nijhoff Publishers, 2010.

Diagne, K., 'UNHCR's Expanded Role in Support of the Inter-agency Response to Situations of Internal Displacement: Report of a Lessons Learned and Effective Practice Workshop', UNHCR Policy Development and Evaluation Service, PDES/2006/06, November 2006.

Fagen, P.W., 'Peace Processes and IDP Solutions', *Refugee Survey Quarterly*, 28/1, 2009.

Ferris, E., 'Internal Displacement and the Right to Seek Asylum', *Refugee Survey Quarterly*, 27/3, 2009.

Gilbert, G., 'Implementing Protection: What Refugee Law can Learn from IDP Law ... and Vice Versa', in Gilbert, G., Hampson, F. and Sandoval, C. (eds), *The Delivery of Human Rights*, London and New York: Routledge, 2011.

Global Protection Cluster Working Group, *Handbook for the Protection of Internally Displaced Persons*, Geneva: UNHCR, 2010.

Groth, L., 'Engendering Protection: An Analysis of the 2009 Kampala Convention and its Provisions for Internally Displaced Women', *International Journal of Refugee Law*, 23/2, 2011.

Ibáñez, A.M. and Velásquez, A., *Public Policies to Assist Internally Displaced Persons: The Role of Municipal Authorities*, Washington, DC: Brookings Institution – University of Bern Project on Internal Displacement, 2008.

Kälin, W., *Guiding Principles on Internal Displacement: Annotations*, Washington, DC: The American Society of International Law, 2nd revised edition, 2008.

Kälin, W., Williams, R.C., Koser, K. and Solomon, A., *Incorporating the Guiding Principles on Internal Displacement into Domestic Law*, Washington, DC: American Society of International Law, 2010.

Kellenberger, J., 'The ICRC's Response to Internal Displacement: Strengths, Challenges and Constraints', *International Review of the Red Cross*, 91/875, 2009.

Kumar Singh, V., 'A Critical Analysis of Normativity of the UN Guiding Principles on Internal Displacement', Indian Society of International Law (ISIL), *The ISIL Yearbook of International Humanitarian Law and Refugee Law*, 5, 2005.

Lanz, D., 'Subversion or Reinvention? Dilemmas and Debates in the Context of UNHCR's Increasing Involvement with IDPs', *Journal of Refugee Studies*, 21/2, 2008.

Lwabukuna, O., 'Internal Displacement in Africa: African Solutions to African Problems? Challenges and Prospects', *Journal of Internal Displacement*, 1/1, 2011.

Maru, M.T., 'The Kampala Convention and its Contribution in Filling the Protection Gap in International Law', *Journal of Internal Displacement*, 1/1, 2011.

McHugh, G., *Integrating Internal Displacement in Peace Processes and Agreements*, Washington, DC: US Institute of Peace; Brookings Institution, Brookings-Bern Project on Internal Displacement, 2010.

Mooney, E., 'Something Old, Something New, Something Borrowed ... Something Blue? The Protection Potential of a Marriage of Concepts between R2P and IDP Protection', *Global Responsibility to Protect*, 2/1–2, 2010.

Orchard, P., 'Protection of Internally Displaced Persons: Soft Law as a Norm-generating Mechanism', *Review of International Studies*, 36, 2010.

Phuong, C., *The International Protection of Internally Displaced Persons*, Cambridge and New York: Cambridge University Press, 2004.

Phuong, C., 'The Office of The United Nations High Commissioner for Refugees and Internally Displaced Persons', *Refugee Survey Quarterly*, 24/3, 2005.

Polzer, T. and Hammond, L., 'Invisible Displacement', *Journal of Refugee Studies*, 21/4, 2008.

Rabska, K. and Mehta, L., *Forced Displacement: Why Rights Matter*, Basingstoke and New York: Palgrave Macmillan, 2008.

UNHCR, 'UNHCR's Expanded Role in Support of the Inter-Agency Response to Internal Displacement Situations', *Refugee Survey Quarterly*, 26/1, 2007.

Weiss, T.G. and Korn, D.A., *Internal Displacement: Conceptualization and its Consequences*, London and New York: Routledge, 2006.

CHAPTER 6

Anderson, M., 'The Cost of Living: An Analysis of the Time and Money Spent by Refugees Accessing Services in Nairobi', UNHCR New Issues in Refugee Research, Research Paper No. 230, January 2012.

Bottinick, L. and Sianni, A., 'No Place to Stay: A Review of the Implementation of UNHCR's Urban Refugee Policy in Bulgaria', UNHCR Policy Development and Evaluation Service, PDES/2011/04, May 2011.

Buscher, D., 'Bright Lights, Big City: Urban Refugees Struggle to Make a Living in New Delhi', Women's Refugee Commission, July 2011.

Campbell, E., Crisp, J. and Kiragu, E., 'Navigating Nairobi: A Review of the Implementation of UNHCR's Urban Refugee Policy in Kenya's Capital City', UNHCR Policy and Development Evaluation Service, PDES/2011/01, January 2011.

de Geoffroy, A., 'The Challenge of Protracted Displacement: The Case of Khartoum', Middle East Institute (United States) and Fondation pour la Recherche Stratégique (France), February 2011.

Ferris, E., 'Protecting the Displaced in Colombia: The Role of Municipal Authorities', Summary Report of a seminar held in Bogotá, Colombia, and convened by the Brookings-Bern Project on Internal Displacement, Acción Social, UNHCR, and the Universidad de los Andes, 2008.

Fielden, A., 'Ignored Displaced Persons: The Plight of IDPs in Urban Areas', UNHCR New Issues in Refugee Research, Research Paper No. 161, July 2008.

International Federation of Red Cross and Red Crescent Societies, 'World Disasters Report 2010: Focus on Urban Risk', 2010.

Koscalova, A. and Lucchi, E., 'Evaluation Report on the MSF Response to Displacement in Open Settings', Médecins Sans Frontières, June 2010.

Krause-Vilmar, J., 'The Living Ain't Easy: Urban Refugees in Kampala', Women's Refugee Commission, March 2011.

Krause-Vilmar, J. and Chaffin, J., 'No Place to Go But Up: Urban Refugees in Johannesburg, South Africa', Women's Refugee Commission, October 2011.

Li Rosi, A., Formisano, M. and Jandrijasevic, L., 'Lives in Limbo: A Review of the Implementation of UNHCR's Urban Refugee Policy in Tajikistan', UNHCR Policy Development and Evaluation Service, PDES/2011/03, May 2011.

Metcalfe, V., Pavanello, S. and Mishra, P., 'Sanctuary in the City? Urban Displacement and Vulnerability in Nairobi', Humanitarian Policy Group Working Paper, Overseas Development Institute, London, September 2011.

Pavanello, S., Elhawary, S. and Pantuliano, S., 'Hidden and Exposed: Urban Refugees in Nairobi, Kenya', Humanitarian Policy Group Working Paper, Overseas Development Institute, London, March 2010.

Pittaway, E., 'Making Mainstreaming a Reality: Gender and the UNHCR Policy on Refugee Protection and Solutions in Urban Areas. A Refugee Perspective', Centre for Refugee Research, University of New South Wales, 2010.

Strandberg, A., 'Urban Refugees' Right to Work: Livelihood Options and Implications for Protection', UNHCR Operational Solutions and Transition Section (OSTS), January 2009.

UNHCR, 'UNHCR Policy on Refugee Protection and Solutions in Urban Areas', September 2009.

United Nations Inter-Agency Standing Committee, 'Final Strategy for Meeting

Humanitarian Challenges in Urban Areas', November 2010.

Wyrzykowski, P. and Kasozi, B., 'Violence, Exile and Transitional Justice: Perspectives of Urban IDPs in Kampala', Briefing Note No. 3, The 'Beyond Juba' Project, Faculty of Law, Makerere University, Uganda, August 2009.

CHAPTER 7

Beyani, C., 'Protection of and Assistance to Internally Displaced Persons, Section III Climate Change and Internal Displacement', Report of the Special Rapporteur on the Human Rights of Internally Displaced Persons to the General Assembly, UN General Assembly, A/66/285, 9 August 2011.

Brookings-Bern Project on Internal Displacement (ed.), 'Inter-Agency Standing Committee Operational Guidelines on the Protection of Persons in Situations of Natural Disasters', Washington, January 2011.

CARE International, Columbia University, UNHCR, UN University, World Bank (The), 'In Search of Shelter: Mapping the Effects of Climate Change on Human Migration and Displacement', May 2009.

Corlett, D., *Stormy Weather: The Challenge of Climate Change and Displacement (Briefings)*, Sydney: University of New South Wales Press, 2008.

Correa, E. (ed.), 'Preventive Resettlement of Populations at Risk of Disaster: Experiences from Latin America', The World Bank, Global Facility for Disaster Reduction and Recovery (GFDRR), 2011.

Deschamp, B., Azorbo, M. and Lohse, S., 'Earth, Wind and Fire: A Review of UNHCR's Role in Recent Natural Disasters', UNHCR Policy Development and Evaluation Service, PDES/2010/06, June 2010.

Ferris, E. and Petz, D., 'A Year of Living Dangerously: A Review of Natural Disasters in 2010', Washington: Brookings-LSE Project on Internal Displacement, 2011.

Foresight, 'Migration and Global Environmental Change: Future Challenges and Opportunities', Final Project Report, The Government Office for Science, London, 2011.

Internal Displacement Monitoring Centre (IDMC), 'Displacement due to Natural Hazard-induced Disasters: Global Estimates for 2009 and 2010', June 2011.

International Organization for Migration (IOM), 'Migration, Environment and Climate Change: Assessing the Evidence', 2009.

Jennings, S., 'Time's Bitter Flood: Trends in the Number of Reported Natural Disasters', Oxfam GB Research Report, 27 May 2011.

Laczko, F., 'Migration, the Environment and Climate Change: Assessing the Evidence', German Marshall Fund of the United States, Study Team on Climate-Induced Migration, June 2010.

McAdam, J., 'Swimming against the Tide: Why a Climate Change Displacement Treaty is Not the Answer', *International Journal of Refugee Law*, 23/1, 2011.

McAdam, J., 'Climate Change Displacement and International Law: Complementary Protection Standards', UNHCR, Legal and Protection Policy Research Series, PPLA/2011/03, May 2011.

McAdam, J. (ed.), *Climate Change and Displacement: Multidisciplinary Perspectives*, Oxford: Hart Publishing, 2010.

McInerney-Lankford, S., Darrow, M. and Rajamani, L., 'Human Rights and Climate Change: A Review of the International Legal Dimensions', The World Bank, Washington, 2011.

OHCHR, 'Report of the Office of the United Nations High Commissioner for Human Rights on the Relationship between Climate Change and Human Rights', UN General Assembly, A/HRC/10/61, January 2009.

Piguet, E., Pécoud, A. and de Guchteneire, A. (eds), *Migration and Climate Change*, Cambridge: Cambridge University Press, 2011.

Stern, N., *The Economics of Climate Change: The Stern Review*, Cambridge: Cambridge University Press, 2007.

UNHCR, 'Summary of Deliberations on Climate Change and Displacement', Report of an Expert Roundtable, Bellagio (Italy), 22–25 February 2011.

Zetter, R., 'Protecting Environmentally Displaced People: Developing the Capacity of Legal and Normative Frameworks', Research Report, Refugee Studies Centre, University of Oxford, February 2011.

CHAPTER 8

Bailliet, C., 'The Tampa Case and its Impact on Burden Sharing at Sea', *Human Rights Quarterly*, 25/3, 2003.

Barrett, S., *Why Cooperate? The Incentive to Supply Global Public Goods*, Oxford: Oxford University Press, 2007.

Barutciski, M., 'Observations on EXCOM's 60th session (2009): Does UNHCR Need (More) EXCOM Conclusions?', *Refuge*, 27/2, 2009.

Betts, A., *Protection by Persuasion: International Cooperation in the Refugee Regime*, Ithaca, NY: Cornell University Press, 2009.

Boswell, C., 'Burden-sharing in the New Age of Immigration', *Migration Information Source*, November 2003.

Byrne, R., 'Harmonization and Burden Relocation in the Two Europes', *Journal of Refugee Studies*, 16/3, 2003.

Chimni, B.S., 'Reforming the International Refugee Regime: A Dialogic Model', *Journal of Refugee Studies*, 14/2, 2001.

Fonteyne, J.-L., 'Burden-Sharing: An Analysis of the Nature and Function of International Solidarity in Cases of Mass Influx of Refugees', *Australian Yearbook of International Law*, 8, 1983.

Guterres, A., 'Millions Uprooted', *Foreign Affairs*, 87/5, 2008.

Haddad, E., *The Refugee in International Society: Between Sovereigns*, Cambridge Studies in International Relations, Cambridge University Press, 2008.

Hathaway, J. and Neve, R.A., 'Making International Refugee Law Relevant Again: A Proposal for Collectivized and Solutions-Oriented Protection', *Harvard Human Rights Journal*, 10, Spring 1997.

Helton, A., *The Price of Indifference: Refugees and Humanitarian Action in the New Century*, Oxford and New York: Oxford University Press, 2002.

Hurwitz, A., *The Collective Responsibility of States to Protect Refugees*, Oxford University Press, 2009.

Jubilut, L.L. and Carneiro, W.P., 'Resettlement in Solidarity: A New Regional Approach Towards a More Human Durable Solution', *Refugee Survey Quarterly*, 30/3, 2011.

Kritzman-Amir, T., 'Not in My Backyard: On the Morality of Responsibility Sharing in Refugee Law,' *Brooklyn Journal of International Law*, 34/2, 2009.

Loescher, G., *The UNHCR and World Politics: A Perilous Path*, London: Oxford University Press, 2001.

McDonough, P. and Tsourdi, E., 'Putting Solidarity to the Test: Assessing Europe's Response to the Asylum Crisis in Greece', UNHCR New Issues in Refugee Research, Research Paper No. 231, January 2012.

Miller, D. *National Responsibility and Global Justice*, Oxford: Oxford University Press, 2007.

Morel, M., 'The Lack of Refugee Burden-sharing in Tanzania: Tragic Effects', *Afrika Focus*, 22/1, 2009.

Schuck, P.H. 'Refugee Burden-Sharing: A Modest Proposal', *Yale Journal of International Law*, 22, 1997.

Slaughter, A. and Crisp, J., 'UNHCR, A Surrogate State? The Role of UNHCR in Protracted Refugee Situations,' New Issues in Refugee Research No. 168, 2008.

Suhrke, A., 'Burden-sharing during Refugee Emergencies: The Logic of Collective Action versus National Action,' *Journal of Refugee Studies*, 11/4, 1998.

Thielemann, E.R. and Dewan, T., 'The Myth of Free-Riding: Refugee Protection and Implicit Burden-Sharing', *West European Politics*, 29/2, 2006.

Thielemann, E., 'The Common European Asylum System: In Need of a More Comprehensive

Burden-sharing Approach', in Luedtke, A. (ed.), *Migrants and Minorities: the European Response*, Newcastle upon Tyne: Cambridge Scholars Publishing, 2010.

Ucarer, E., 'Burden-Shirking, Burden-Shifting, and Burden-Sharing in the Emergent European Asylum Regime', *International Politics*, 43/2, 2006.

UNHCR, High Commissioner's Dialogue on Protection Challenges, 'Protection Gaps and Responses' (8–9 December 2010), Breakout Session 2: International Cooperation, Burden Sharing and Comprehensive Regional Approaches, Report by the Co-Chairs: H.E. Mr. Fayssal Mekdad, Deputy Foreign Minister, Syrian Arab Republic, and Ms. Erika Feller, Assistant High Commissioner for Protection, 2010.

UNHCR, 'International Cooperation to Share Burdens and Responsibilities', Discussion Paper, Expert Meeting, Amman (Jordan), 27–28 June 2011

Wolfrum, R. and Kojima, C. (eds), *Solidarity: A Structural Principle of International Law*, Beiträge zum ausländischen öffentlichen Recht und Völkerrecht, 213, Berlin, Heidelberg: Springer, 2010.

SELECTED WEBSITES

UNHCR

United Nations High Commissioner for Refugees (UNHCR)
http://www.unhcr.org

UNHCR Refworld
http://www.refworld.org/

Refworld is a reference tool designed to meet the information needs of those interested in the problems of forced displacement: governments, judicial authorities, international organizations, voluntary agencies, academic institutions and legal counsels.

Refworld contains a vast collection of reports relating to situations in countries of origin; policy documents and positions; documents relating to international and national legal frameworks, national legislation; jurisprudence; international treaties and documents on human rights and refugee law; UN General Assembly and Security Council documents; thematic issues; and refugee statistics.

The information has been carefully selected and compiled from UNHCR's global network of field offices, governments, international, regional and non-governmental organizations, academic institutions and judicial bodies.

UN

Inter-Agency Standing Committee (IASC)
http://www.humanitarianinfo.org/iasc/

IRIN – Humanitarian news and analysis
http://www.irinnews.org/

United Nations
http://www.un.org

United Nations Development Programme
http://www.undp.org/

United Nations Framework Convention on Climate Change
http://www.unfccc.int/

UN-HABITAT
http://www.unhabitat.org/

UNICEF
http://www.unicef.org/

United Nations Office of the High Commissioner for Human Rights (OHCHR)
http://www.ohchr.org/

United Nations Office for the Coordination of Humanitarian Affairs (UNOCHA)
http://www.unocha.org/

United Nations Peacebuilding Fund
http://www.unpbf.org/

United Nations Peacebuilding Commission
http://www.un.org/en/peacebuilding/

United Nations Population Fund
http://www.unfpa.org/

World Food Programme (WFP)
http://www.wfp.org/

World Health Organization
http://www.who.int/

Other Websites

Amnesty International
http://www.amnesty.org

Brookings-LSE Project on Internal Displacement,
The Brookings Institution
www.brookings.edu/projects/idp.aspx

Centre for Refugee Research, University of New
South Wales, Australia
http://www.crr.unsw.edu.au

Centre for Refugee Studies, York University,
Toronto
http://crs.yorku.ca

European Council on Refugees and Exiles (ECRE)
http://www.ecre.org

Human Rights Watch
http://www.hrw.org

Humanitarian Policy Group, Overseas
Development Institute, UK

http://www.odi.org.uk/work/programmes/humanit
arian-policy-group

International Committee of the Red Cross (ICRC)
http://www.icrc.org/

International Council of Voluntary Agencies (ICVA)
http://www.icva.ch/

Internal Displacement Monitoring Centre (IDMC)
http://www.internal-displacement.org/

International Federation of Red Cross and Red
Crescent Societies (IFRC)
http://www.ifrc.org/

International Organization for Migration
http://www.iom.int/

Médecins Sans Frontières
http://www.msf.org/

Open Society Foundations
http://www.soros.org/

Refugee Studies Centre, University of Oxford
http://www.rsc.ox.ac.uk/

Refugees International
http://www.refugeesinternational.org/

Women's Refugee Commission
http://www.womensrefugeecommission.org/

The World Bank Group
http://www.worldbank.org/